Political Economy *of* International and Domestic Monetary Relations

EDITED BY

Raymond E. Lombra
Willard E. Witte

Political Economy of International and Domestic Monetary Relations

Political Economy of International and Domestic Monetary Relations

EDITED BY

Raymond E. Lombra
Willard E. Witte

IOWA STATE UNIVERSITY PRESS / *Ames*

© 1982 The Iowa State University Press. All rights reserved

Printed by The Iowa State University Press, Ames, IA 50010

No part of this book may be reproduced in any form, by photostat, microfilm, xerography, or any other means, or incorporated into any information retrieval system, electronic or mechanical, without the written permission of the copyright owner.

First printing, 1982

Library of Congress Cataloging in Publication Data
Main entry under title:

Political economy of international and domestic monetary relations.

    Revised papers presented at a conference, held June 12, 1980, at Pennsylvania State University.
    Bibliography: p.
    1. Currency question—Congresses. 2. Monetary policy—Congresses. 3. Monetary policy—United States—Congresses. I. Lombra, Raymond E. II. Witte, Willard E., 1944-   . III. Pennsylvania State University.
HG230.3.P64   332.4′973   82-15320
ISBN 0-8138-1372-7   AACR2

CONTENTS

PREFACE   vii

OVERVIEW   ix

SECTION I: INTERNATIONAL MONETARY RELATIONS AND POLITICAL ECONOMY

    Introduction   3

Paper 1. Inflation and the Decline of American Power, Robert O. Keohane   7
    Discussion, Michael R. Darby   24
    Discussion, Robert E. Harkavy   28
    Rejoinder   36
    General Discussion   38

Paper 2. Bretton Woods and International Political Disintegration: Implications for Monetary Diplomacy, John S. Odell   39
    Discussion, Henry N. Goldstein   58
    Discussion, Michael W. Doyle   63
    Rejoinder   68
    Comment, Will E. Mason   71
    General Discussion   72

Paper 3. Still an Extraordinary Power: America's Role in a Global Monetary System, Susan Strange   73
    Discussion, Robert Z. Aliber   94
    Discussion, Robert Solomon   98
    Rejoinder   101
    General Discussion   102

SECTION II: DOMESTIC POLITICS, OPENNESS, AND THE POLITICAL ECONOMY OF MONETARY POLICY

    Introduction   107

Paper 4. Strategic Aspects of the Political Assignment Problem in Open Economies, Stanley W. Black   111
    Discussion, Peter J. Katzenstein   130
    Discussion, Alan C. Stockman   134
    Rejoinder   140
    General Discussion   140

Paper 5. The Effects of Alternative International Monetary Systems on Macroeconomic Discipline and Inflationary Biases, Thomas D. Willett and John Mullen ... 143
    Discussion, J. David Richardson ... 156
    Discussion, Lucas Papademos ... 160
    General Discussion ... 171

SECTION III: MAKING MONETARY POLICY IN THE UNITED STATES
    Introduction ... 175
Paper 6. Politics, Economics, and Procedures of U.S. Money Growth Dynamics, Ira P. Kaminow ... 181
    Discussion, Thomas Mayer ... 196
    Discussion, John T. Woolley ... 199
    Comment, Thomas D. Willett and Leroy O. Laney ... 203
    Rejoinder ... 207
    General Discussion ... 209
Paper 7. External Pressure and the Operations of the Fed, Edward J. Kane ... 211
    Discussion, Allan H. Meltzer ... 233
    General Discussion ... 235
Paper 8. Policy Research, Policy Advice, and Policymaking, Henry C. Wallich ... 237
    Discussion, William G. Dewald ... 246
    Comment, Allan H. Meltzer ... 250
    General Discussion ... 253

SECTION IV: FINANCIAL INTEGRATION AND MONETARY CONTROL
    Introduction ... 257
Paper 9. The Role of Intervention Policy in Open Economy Financial Policy: A Macroeconomic Perspective, Dale W. Henderson ... 261
    Discussion, Herbert G. Grubel ... 290
    Discussion, John F. O. Bilson ... 293
    Rejoinder ... 297
    General Discussion ... 302
Paper 10. The Effects of Eurodollar and Domestic Money Market Innovations on the Interpretation and Control of Monetary Aggregates, Donald D. Hester ... 303
    Discussion, Thomas D. Simpson ... 324
    Discussion, Anthony M. Santomero ... 331
    Rejoinder ... 337
    General Discussion ... 338

BIBLIOGRAPHY ... 339

CONTRIBUTORS ... 357

PREFACE

In recent years it has been increasingly obvious that our understanding of the economic and political forces determining domestic and international monetary policy is seriously incomplete. It is our belief that to a considerable degree this void is a reflection of two factors: first, the tendency for economists and political scientists to abstract from even the most salient features of the others' discipline; and second, the continuing tendency to analyze U.S. economic problems within a purely domestic, as opposed to an international, framework. These themes, developed more fully in the overview that follows, guided our selection of topics, authors, discussants, and other participants for a conference convened on June 12, 1980, at The Pennsylvania State University. Participants included economists and political scientists from the United States, other countries, academia, and government.

The volume that follows begins with an overview by the editors. The proceedings are then organized into four sets of papers, each of which is preceded by a brief introduction and summary. Each paper is followed by the discussants' comments, in some cases an author's rejoinder, and a synopsis of the general discussion at the conference. The published papers are revised versions of those presented at the conference.

We recognize that no single volume or conference can deal completely with the myriad of issues affecting domestic and international monetary relations. As a result, there are undoubtedly important issues underrepresented in the volume. Nonetheless, we believed from the outset that the ultimate success of any undertaking of this type depends to a great degree on the precision with which central issues can be specified, the depth and breadth of the analysis, and the resulting guidance provided to future researchers and policymakers. Measured against these criteria, the assembled contributions, reflecting the diverse background and viewpoints of the conference participants, as well as their hardwork and thoughtfulness, should have a noticeable impact on future thinking in this area.

No undertaking of this scope would be possible without the cooperation and support of many people. The initial impetus was provided by thoughtful suggestions from Robert Schultz, acquisitions editor of the Iowa State Press. We also would like to thank Merritt Bailey, director of book publishing, the Iowa State Press, for his continuing assistance, support, and enthusiasm for the project. The financial support that made the whole project possible was graciously provided by a grant from the Ford Foundation; special thanks go to Peter Ruof and Allan Pulsipher of the Foundation's staff for their guidance, assistance, and confidence in the project. The Pennsylvania State University and in particular Monroe Newman, head of the Economics Department, also deserve our gratitude; considerable financial support was provided, including release time for the editors, and administrative and secretarial services. Finally, we would like to thank a group of dedicated people from the Economics Department: Anna McMullin, Judy Byron, Yvonne Stover, and Debbie Hoy; they helped coordinate and administer the conference, and prepared this manuscript for final publication. We are in your debt.

OVERVIEW

Over the decade of the 1970s the world economy experienced a series of severe economic dislocations. Early in the decade the international monetary regime established at Bretton Woods after World War II disintegrated and was replaced by an ad hoc "system" of flexible, but managed, exchange rates. The subsequent volatility of exchange rates has proven to be far greater than proponents of flexible rates had predicted. In 1973 and again in 1979 the Organization of Petroleum Exporting Countries (OPEC), exerting the leverage associated with its control over a large portion of the world's oil supply, engineered two quantum increases in petroleum prices. These oil price "shocks" gave rise to major shifts in international trade patterns and capital flows and had profound effects on the economic performance of most oil importing countries. Domestically, the United States experienced the worst recession since World War II in 1974-1975, and subsequently the rate of inflation more than doubled.

Given these events, it is not surprising that confidence in, as well as the confidence of, economic policymakers (and their advisors) have been greatly reduced. Public dissatisfaction with economic developments has been reflected in political outcomes in many countries, most notably in the United Kingdom with the election of the Thatcher-led Conservative government and in the United States with the election of Ronald Reagan. With inflation emerging as a chronic, secular problem, and monetarism apparently gaining converts around the world, monetary policymakers in particular have been severely criticized. Reflecting on the rising trend of world inflation during his tenure as Federal Reserve Board chairman (1970-1978), Arthur Burns has admitted that "despite their antipathy to inflation and the powerful weapons they could wield against it, central bankers have failed" (Burns 1979b, p. 7). Interestingly, both Thatcher and Reagan have made control of the money supply a central feature of their economic policy strategies.

By now it is well understood by both model builders and policymakers that inflation cannot persist without a concomitant expansion of the money supply. This virtual tautology has been invoked by many researchers as the central tenet of a proof that the inflation of the 1970s was an avoidable outcome, reflecting errors in policymakers' judgment and fatal flaws in the techniques used to implement policy. This approach and the obvious policy prescription to which it leads is aptly summarized by Hirsch and Goldthorpe (1978, p. 2):

> Confronted by political and social disturbances, economists ... have slid easily and often unthinkingly into the assumption-cum-

conclusion that the non-economic factors are the extraneous variables that can be expected in the end to adapt to an overriding and objective economic reality. Technical remedies are available and adequate; all that is necessary is for them to be accepted at the political and popular levels.

The analysis of international developments has often followed similar lines. "Misbehavior" of the money supply is viewed as the cause of periodic crises during the fixed exchange rate period and of exchange rate instability during the post-1973, flexible rate period. Thus, it is argued that the collapse of the so-called Bretton Woods system and the subsequent volatility of exchange rates are the legacies of unstable monetary policies pursued by the United States, in particular, and central bankers around the world, generally.

The genesis of this conference was our belief that such explanations beg several fundamental questions. If everyone understands that money supply expansion causes or permits inflation, then why do monetary authorities accept such expansion? What are we to make of Burns's contention that the Federal Reserve did not slow monetary growth in the United States because it "was itself caught up in the philosophic and political currents that were transforming American life and culture" (Burns 1979b, p. 15)? If United States monetary authorities wanted to maintain the Bretton Woods system, why did they pursue policies that doomed it? Why was the transition to the new "system" so traumatic and haphazard? If exchange rate stability is a concern in a flexible rate regime, why do policymakers pursue policies inconsistent with such stability? Unfortunately, the answers to such important questions are not readily obtainable within the confines of standard economic analysis where "policy" is usually treated as an "exogenous" adjustment of a policy instrument. The need to broaden and deepen the scope and method of economic analysis to include domestic and international political considerations is, we feel, compelling.

In organizing the conference we sought to bring together people working on political, economic, domestic, and international aspects of monetary analysis. While we recognized that abstraction from complexity is a necessary part of developing hypotheses and theories, it was our judgment that the connections between these various aspects of the monetary policy process have rendered research which abstracts entirely from these interrelationships, an increasingly empty exercise. At the same time we felt that the paucity of work on the relevant linkages ruled out survey-type papers designed to integrate existing work. As Thomas Willett has noted, "All too often the political assumptions of economists and economic assumptions of political scientists reflect more wishful thinking than they do careful analysis" (Willett 1979b, p. 377).

The result is that the papers that comprise this volume represent ongoing research on key aspects of the political economy of domestic and international monetary relations. This approach has its own problems, of course. Papers reflecting current research by scholars in different disciplines and in different subfields within these disciplines cannot be constrained to a common analytic framework. This makes the task of the reader more difficult, but he will find that these papers do contain a great many common themes.

In editing the volume we have attempted to aid the integration process in two ways. First, we have encouraged revisions to emphasize recurrent themes. We have also reordered the papers into groupings that, after the fact, seem more coherent than the order of presentation at the conference. Second, in the next several pages we will suggest some of the interrelationships that we discerned from the papers and the discussion at the conference. It is, we think, revealing that the result is considerably different from what we might have supposed without the experience of the conference.

Ignoring politics is a widespread, but not universal, characteristic of economic analysis. For example, public choice theory and work on the political business cycle represent a merging of political analysis and economic theory. However, political scientists at the conference forcefully argued that there is more to political economy than this. They particularly objected to the failure to integrate the concept of "power" into economic analysis. Power viewed as the currency of politics is not just a cliche; "The notion of power," Elster affirms," would seem to be the most important single idea in political theory, comparable perhaps to utility in economics" (Elster 1976, p. 249). In general, economists studiously avoid the concept of power because it is incompatible with the competitive market paradigm. Even on those rare occasions when "market power" is introduced, its role is constrained by the voluntary exchange that underlies nearly all economic models.

Political scientists argued that power is in fact an integrative element in that it cuts across the dividing lines often found convenient in model building. Both economists and political scientists at the conference argued that to understand the policymaking process it is important to recognize that power can be both an input and an output. Put another way, changes in power, political and economic, can be the cause or the effect of particular policies. This perspective may help to explain why some policy actions can be viewed as "errors" based on economic criteria, but as "successes" based on political criteria.

The relationship between power and policy is a recurrent theme. It appears prominently in a number of papers where it is argued that the political disintegration accompanying the breakdown of Bretton Woods and the dislocations associated with the rise of OPEC were not inevitable, but in part the result of policies, particularly those of the United States.

The status of power as both an input and an output in the policy process is in some ways similar to the role of the capital stock in the production process. Just as the production process uses the capital stock (without necessarily using it up), the policy process draws on the power resources of decision makers. Furthermore, just as the production process can be used to produce more capital goods, thus enhancing future production, the policy process can be used to enlarge power resources.

Before we push the power-capital stock analogy too far, it should be recognized that a decline in power is more likely to become part of a self-perpetuating process than is a depreciation of the capital stock. Policy decisions that turn out badly and reduce the economic or political power of governments are likely to engender an erosion of confidence in the will or leadership of decision makers. This perception may, in turn, reduce the power of decision makers beyond that which more objective measures of power might suggest. Of course, secular declines or accumulations of power are not irreversible. It may be that Europeans see this more clearly than Americans. They, after all, have had considerably more experience with the dissipation and reaccumulation of power.

In sum, power is both a means and an end of the policy process. Understanding the dynamics of this relationship is an essential aspect of political economy.

Another dominant theme that surfaced repeatedly at the conference is that political analysis of economic policy almost inevitably raises serious questions about the insights and guidance provided by conventional economic analysis of economic policy. As Willett argues, "Frequently, proposals by economists receive little sympathy from people of practical affairs because they abstract from crucial political considerations" (Willett 1979b, p. 375). A specific illustration is provided by Maier: "Monetarism focuses on keepers of the printing press and summons them to abstinence, but rarely explains what pressures sustain or overcome their resolution" (Maier 1978, p. 38).

The apparent vacuousness of popular, existing explanations of inflation offered by economists or political scientists has contributed to an encouraging broadening of the relevant scope of inquiry. Work presented at the conference and emerging in the literature (e.g., Havrilesky 1979) is focusing increasingly on distributional issues. Goldthorpe (1978, p. 195) summarizes this approach this way:

> Inflation, understood as the monetary expression of distributional conflict, is ultimately grounded not in error, ignorance, or unreason on the part of actors involved, in the way that economic analyses are constrained to suggest, but rather in on-going changes in social structures and processes.

The implications of this view are, of course, startling for practitioners of conventional economic analysis; inflation is in effect the solution (at least in the short run), not the problem!

A third major focus of the conference was on the implications of openness, that is, the fact that a country is not "closed" but is part of the world economy. Virtually all agree that ignoring the inevitable complexities introduced by openness cannot be justified. Regarding the implications for economic analysis, for example, Frenkel and Mussa (1981, p. 253) have recently argued that "international linkages between national economies influence, in fundamentally important ways, the effectiveness and proper conduct of national macroeconomic policies." On the political side, it is clear that political pressures emanate from the international environment and that central bankers, in particular, are often more sensitive to these pressures than are other economic policymakers. In particular, such pressures can alter policy actions that might seem desirable on strictly domestic grounds. For example, many times in recent years United States policymakers have been summoned "to defend the dollar." Frederick Schultz, vice-chairman of the Federal Reserve Board, gives us at least one reason why monetary policymakers often respond to such calls: "I think it is because large and rapid changes in the foreign exchange value of a currency are often an indication of changes in public confidence in the government's economic policies" (Schultz 1980, p. 1).

Potential conflicts between defending a currency's international value and domestic economic considerations, especially over the short-run horizons that often seem to dominate policymaker consciousness, are in many ways simply a reflection of the conflicts between internal and external stability associated with the inevitable political, economic, and social disparities that will always exist within and among sovereign nations. Recognizing these conditions has not resulted in the adoption of a common line of inquiry.

Those economists and political scientists who view domestic and international politics as constraints governing economic policy, call for increased cooperation and coordination among nations. The benefits thought to be associated with such political integration are in fact the motivation for the various postmortems on the factors contributing to the collapse of the Bretton Woods agreement. Other scholars (mostly economists) believe that calls for international monetary diplomacy cannot possibly succeed and should be abandoned, especially if any agreement that could be reached is viewed as a substitute for "appropriate" domestic monetary and fiscal policies. Karl Brunner, a leading monetarist, has provided a hard-hitting critique of international monetary diplomacy in a recent review of the collapse of the Bretton Woods agreement (Brunner 1978, p. 390):

> The first rupture [1971] was followed by various attempts of the bureaus [treasuries and central banks] to restore "international order" and reinstitute a system of fixed exchange rates. The Smithsonian agreement reflected this phase, and a variety of committees associated with appropriate international agencies drew plans, met and discussed with little effect on crucial underlying circumstances [i.e., domestic policies]. The ultimate break occurred in February 1973 and finally destroyed the old system. Bureaus continued to plan and propose, and committees continued to meet and talk. But these activities were essentially bureaucratic expressions of piety and homage to the dead.

Those who doubt that various national goals and policies can be harmonized believe that viable international monetary relations require sufficient flexibility of exchange rates to reflect the relevant disparities across nations.

The effects of openness on policymakers' perceptions, procedures, and performance are, of course, not limited to the economic and political complications reviewed above. Various other technical and analytical difficulties must be handled. For example, no open economy is immune from foreign disturbances, many of which may be inherently unpredictable and unfamiliar in their effect. Domestically, the effectiveness of certain policy instruments (e.g., interest rates ceilings and reserve requirements) may be eroded by trading opportunities in foreign financial markets. More generally, the widening of the opportunity set available to borrowers and lenders may change the balance of power between the state and the market in a way that weakens the ability of policymakers to measure, monitor, and react to emerging developments. To illustrate, most observers agree that private sector innovations to avoid various financial regulations have been facilitated by the increasing integration of world financial markets. At the same time, such innovations have contributed to increased integration. The continuing sequence of action (regulation) and reaction (innovation), by which government authorities seek to maintain or increase their control and the private sector seeks to evade such control, has, among other results, made the monetary aggregates used by policymakers in the formulation and implementation of policy harder to measure and control.

Openness, the absence of a formal agreement among nations pegging exchange rates, and the short-run political and economic consequences associated with movements in exchange rates, have also made official intervention in foreign exchange markets less mechanical than in the fixed rate era. As a result, there is considerable scope for central bank intervention policy. As in the past, such policy is predicated on the twin premises that such intervention is effective and that fluctuations in exchange rates often reflect undesirable speculation, which in the absence of intervention, would generate "disorderly markets." Frederick Schultz puts it this way: "If there are short-run periods when the dollar moves so far as to be clearly out of line with economic fundamentals, we will deal with this by intervening in the exchange markets to the appropriate extent" (Schultz 1980, p. 8). The problem with this position is summarized succinctly by Michael Dooley, a senior staffer at the Fed. "In reality, the government will never know with certainty if a given exchange rate change is justified by changes in fundamental factors or if the change is due to a miscalculation by private speculators" (Dooley 1979, p. 228). Beyond these considerations it should be obvious that intervention cannot be viewed in isolation from other countries or other policies. Foreign nations will by definition be affected by intervention. In addition, intervention may interfere with domestic policy actions, such as the attempt to control monetary growth. Causation could also run the other way; changes in monetary growth may cause changes in exchange rates, which policymakers try to forestall or moderate by intervening. As Dooley has argued: "The temptation to pursue inconsistent monetary and exchange rate policies is likely to be very strong" (Dooley 1979, p. 229).

These conference proceedings leave little doubt that monetary analysis must address the confluence of short-run and long-run, micro and macro, political and economic, and domestic and international considerations. The development of workable solutions to pressing problems depends on our collective willingness and ability to produce analyses that abstract less and integrate more.

Our goal has been to reverse an apparent widening of the gap between theory and policy. Unless the interdependencies highlighted in the volume become a more systematic part of economic and political analyses, Robert Keohane is probably right: "Inflation in the 1990s will probably be high. But it will also be among the least of our problems" (Keohane, Paper 1).

I

International Monetary Relations and Political Economy

INTRODUCTION

The three papers in this section, all authored by political scientists, examine from different perspectives the relationship between U.S. monetary actions and the international economic system. Central to each paper is the role of power in the international system. Collectively, they suggest that U.S. use of its power in this area has been deficient during the past decade.

The first paper, by Robert Keohane, professor of political science at Stanford University, argues that erosion of U.S. power during the late 1960s and early 1970s contributed significantly to both the breakdown of the Bretton Woods monetary regime and the OPEC oil price increases in 1973 and again in 1979. In turn, these events are, in Keohane's view, part of the explanation of the world wide inflation of the 1970s. Thus, as he puts it, "International political changes contributed to inflation in the 1970s: a causal chain leads from the decline of American power, through the collapse of international stabilizing arrangements, to the acceleration of world inflation." Keohane views this causal chain as a partial explanation of the inflation of the 1970s. It is a complement, not a substitute, for analyses that emphasize other underlying causes of inflation, such as domestic political pressures (see the papers in Section II) and monetary policymaking procedures (see the papers in Section III).

Power in Keohane's analysis reflects the ability of a government to use resources to influence the behavior of others relative to its own dependence on the actions of others. In the case of the Bretton Woods regime, U.S. power had declined as the United States shifted from a creditor to a debtor position. In 1971 the United States was able to break the link between the dollar and gold. This exercise of power, however, was not a substantial American victory. Quoting Keohane, "The United States did not have sufficient power resources to reestablish a viable system that would be consistent with its own inclinations in monetary policy." Instead the outcome was the Smithsonian agreement and a period of uncertainty surrounding the international regime during which the international constraints on inflationary domestic policies were particularly weak.

Keohane suggests that the best single indicator of U.S. power in the oil price area is the relative balance between U.S. capacity to produce petroleum and its consumption. By 1973, U.S. excess capacity was smaller than imports by a sizable margin. In addition, the political and military dominance of the United States in the Middle East had been eroded by Arab nationalism and by increased Soviet involvement. Other factors played a role, but "the decline in U.S. power was a necessary condition for the drastic nature of the oil price increases."

Keohane concludes his paper with a discussion of the role of U.S. policies in bringing about the dissipation of U.S. power both in the monetary and energy areas. He concludes, "The United States was not merely a victim of events, but played an active role in its own undoing."

The discussants of the Keohane paper are Michael Darby, professor of economics at UCLA, and Robert Harkavy, associate professor of political science at The Pennsylvania State University. Darby is skeptical that a significant part of the inflation of the 1970s can be traced to either the breakdown of Bretton Woods or the OPEC oil price increases. He finds the first linkage implausible, seeing no mechanism by which the breakdown induced increased growth rates of national money supplies and price levels compared to what would have taken place had the 1971 Bretton Woods exchange rates been maintained. With respect to oil prices, Darby contends that their impact on the inflation rate, while positive, is trivial--perhaps a one-time, 2 percent rise in the price level.

Harkavy, in his discussion, focuses on the political link in Keohane's causal chain (between the decline in U.S. power and the Bretton Woods collapse and the emergence of OPEC), rather than on the political economy link (relating the latter two to inflation). Keohane, he suggests, tends to view the decline of U.S. power in primarily economic terms. But Harkavy contends that "high" politics--the geopolitical strategic situation--was an important factor. He also observes that Keohane's analysis may be overly unidirectional. Inflation in the United States after 1965 may be a cause of the U.S. decline as well as one of its consequences.

The second paper in this section, authored by John Odell, assistant professor of government at Harvard University, analyzes the international monetary diplomacy that surrounded the collapse of the Bretton Woods system. The Bretton Woods regime was characterized, Odell argues, by a fairly high degree of international political integration and policy coordination. It embodied a relatively strong set of explicit rules and procedures and implicit patterns of expected state behavior in the monetary area. "During the 1970s," he concludes, "this regime disintegrated to a substantial degree, and was replaced by much weaker rules and procedures accompanied by selective, informal, intergovernmental coordination. With the benefit of hindsight we may conclude that substantial modification of the Bretton Woods rules was highly likely, but that political disintegration was hardly inevitable."

A modification of the system was made necessary by the increasing integration and growth of international capital markets, by the overvaluation of the dollar, and by the long-term diffusion of economic power among the major states. While some of the blame for political disintegration rests with the policies followed by key surplus countries, especially Japan and France, the most important cause of disintegration, Odell suggests, was the failure of senior American leaders to lead a negotiated transition to a new politically integrated regime. Rather, "The U.S. strategy for responding to the fundamental challenges to Bretton Woods relied on market forces to bring about separate appreciations by surplus countries."

Odell's paper is discussed by Henry Goldstein, professor of economics at the University of Oregon, and Michael Doyle, of the Woodrow Wilson School at Princeton University. Goldstein rejects Odell's contention that the situation that emerged from the Bretton Woods breakdown is inferior to possible alternatives that would incorporate greater mutual commitment among participating nations. To the contrary, Goldstein sees alternatives to the current situation, for instance, a crawling peg or a reference rate system,

Introduction

as seriously flawed. Fixed rates, on the other hand, are disintegrative given the unwillingness of governments to subordinate monetary and fiscal policies to balance of payments considerations. Goldstein goes on to suggest that the U.S. strategy in 1971 and earlier was necessary to force foreign acceptance of exchange rate adjustment and (with hindsight) a right decision, which led to a desirable modification of the Bretton Woods regime.

Doyle examines Odell's paper in the context of the evolution of the political science of international political economy. In Doyle's view, Odell examines the Bretton Woods collapse mainly in terms of the domestic sources of foreign economic behavior. In particular, Odell focuses on the range of choices available to national governments and on the consequences of choices poorly made. Doyle sees this focus as rounding out analyses that concentrate on the structure of specific economic issues involved in the collapse or on the general structure of declining American hegemony. Doyle suggests, however, that Odell may go too far in his separation of economic and diplomatic leadership and hegemony. Furthermore, the interrelationships between these elements depend on the structure of the issue in question. The decline of American monetary reserves was far more marked than its loss of predominance in GNP, trade, or nuclear security, notes Doyle, and the decline in cooperation and U.S. leadership dominance in the monetary area was also greater than in other areas such as trade and military affairs.

The third paper, by Susan Strange of the London School of Economics and Political Science, examines the current state of power relationships in the international monetary system as seen from an European perspective. Her central theme is that the United States remains the dominant power in the international monetary system. However, she does argue that events of the past decade have affected this U.S. dominance in two ways. First, the power of the private sector, through financial markets in particular, has grown relative to the controls on private action exercised by national governments and international agencies. This loss of authority does not, however, diminish the U.S. position relative to that of other states. Furthermore, Strange contends it is reversible "since market operators still depend for their security on the state . . . and can in the last resort be obliged to accept whatever restrictions powerful states may choose to put on them." Second, increasing economic integration between the United States, Europe, and Japan has lessened the ability of the United States to independently carry out smooth and effective changes in the system. But even so, the United States retains preeminence in three fundamental ways: strategically, due to its nuclear capability; economically, due to its control of the largest single market in the world economy; and financially, due to its position as issuer of the still preferred medium of international exchange. "The three together," she concludes, "make sure that it will retain its monopoly of power to initiate and the power to veto change in the international monetary system."

Strange focuses in particular on the third area of U.S. preeminence, in financial matters. She examines a variety of evidence relating to the role of the dollar as a reserve currency, the use of the dollar as a vehicle currency in international financial transactions, the United States as a preferred location for international investment, and the position of United States-based financial institutions in the international system.

The first discussant of Susan Strange's paper is Robert Aliber of the University of Chicago's Graduate School of Business. He asserts that economic power may be defined as the ability or capacity to induce other countries to follow certain actions or to refrain from following others. It might be thought of as a stock of accumulated favors, which may be depleted by the demand for favors from others. Aliber suggests that the measures of monetary power discussed by Strange are not unique to the United States and are not unambiguously related to the degree of U.S. economic power. He goes on to sketch out the "pothole theory of power," which contends that U.S. international economic power has declined in significance due to a reduction in the ability of the U.S. authorities to generate a domestic surplus that could be allocated (in favors) to foreign governments. During World War II and in the Marshall Plan era, the United States transferred substantial resources to other countries, enhancing its own standing and its capacity to induce them to follow its lead. More recently, as domestic demands for expenditures have risen, there has been a decline in the surplus available to the U.S. government for international activities. The United States is consequently no longer able to maintain the infrastructure of its international power.

Robert Solomon of the Brookings Institution, the second discussant, feels that while Strange gives a catalogue of the attributes of monetary power, she fails to give a clear statement of the uses of power. Like Aliber he feels that several of the measures of U.S. power are ambiguous and might be interpreted in other ways. The extent to which foreigners acquire U.S. government debt, for instance, is one indicator of U.S. monetary power used by Strange. Solomon suggests such accumulations can also be seen as a result of U.S. balance of payments deficits, which are not necessarily indicative of strength. Solomon does, however, agree with the main thesis of the paper, that the United States is not a pitiful and weak monetary giant. This recognition should be helpful in understanding the dimensions of U.S. power and in analyzing how it can be applied to problems in the international economy.

PAPER 1 • *Robert O. Keohane*

Inflation and the Decline of American Power

I. INTRODUCTION
 This paper examines the contention that the decline of U.S. dominance in the international political economy contributed significantly to world inflation during the 1970s. According to this argument, the erosion of American power during the late 1960s and early 1970s contributed to the collapse of the postwar arrangements that had provided the capitalist world system with relatively stable exchange rates and cheap oil in the years between 1947 and 1971. Expansionary domestic monetary policies were encouraged by the collapse of the Bretton Woods international monetary regime and their effects were reinforced by the demise of Anglo-American control of world oil production and world oil markets. Thus, according to this thesis, international political changes contributed to inflation in the 1970s; a causal chain leads from the decline of American power, through the collapse of international stabilizing arrangements, to the acceleration of world inflation.
 This analysis is suggested by a more general "theory of hegemonic stability" (Keohane 1980a), derived from theories of collective action (Olson 1965) as applied to questions of international political economy (Kindleberger 1973; Krasner 1976). According to this theory, hegemonic powers are more likely than middle-sized powers to provide collective goods, such as international monetary order, for the international system as a whole. Order is maintained not by consensus, negotiation, or beneficence, but by the dominant state, whose interest in order is sufficient to induce it to pay for it. As the power of the dominant state erodes, to the benefit of second-rank states, the ability and willingness of the leading state to provide order are likely to decline at the same time that the second-rank states demand more autonomy for themselves (Keohane and Nye 1977, pp. 42-46).
 This theory abstracts from particular state policies, foreign or domestic. It focuses, as does microeconomic theory, on the constraints and incentives facing actors within a given system. Since it does not pay attention to decision making within the units of action, it cannot provide a full explanation of behavior. In particular, such a theory cannot explain the failure of actors to respond effectively to systemic incentives and constraints; it cannot account for the overexpansionary, regime-destroying American monetary policy of the decade after 1965 any more than an analysis of the U.S. automobile market could account for Chrysler's near bankruptcy in 1980 (for a discussion of the limits of systemic theory, see Simon 1976). Thus no pretense is made here of offering a complete political account of inflation. Such an account would have to analyze domestic politics--in

particular, factors affecting decisions about the growth rate of the money supply--in a number of different countries. Only through a systemic comparative analysis of national political economies will we be able to understand, for example, why Italy's inflation rate has been much higher than that of France, or Britain's than that of Japan. Only by taking into account both the effects of national policies and those of the international system, could a complete political-economic account of inflation be provided. This paper does not attempt such a task.[1]

Instead, we focus on the impact of changes in the structure of the international political system--in particular, changes in the distribution of power internationally--on national policies and national capabilities (for a theoretical analysis along these structural lines, see Waltz 1979). Most accounts of inflation, by contrast, emphasize the domestic context of decision making. Yet if the theory of hegemonic stability is correct, and applicable to the contemporary world economy, this focus on domestic sources of policy is inadequate. It needs to be complemented (not replaced) by the international systemic orientation adopted here.

Behavior that affects the world economy is not necessarily determined by the dictates of a competitive market inhabited by utility maximizing actors. On the contrary, it often reflects attempts by states and nonstate actors such as banks (Aronson 1979) to influence one another, for purposes that include maintenance of national autonomy and enhancement of state power, as well as increases in income or welfare. Actors' power resources and political interests are as important as their wealth positions and economic interests in affecting both what they want to do and what they can achieve in the world economy. The international economy is therefore a political economy and requires political as well as economic analysis (Polanyi 1944; Gilpin 1975; Strange 1975).

One can think of a political economy as an economic system that is affected at many points by political action; i.e., by attempts of actors to influence one another to achieve their purposes. To understand international political sources of inflation, we need to begin with a conception of the economic system, and in particular, of the economic factors that affect international price levels and their rates of change. The sources of inflation identified by economists--their independent variables--become the dependent variables for this analysis. In analyzing a political economy, the political scientist must work his or her way back through the chain of causation, in order to analyze the noneconomic factors that ultimately determine, or at least affect, economic outcomes. The political scientist attempts to explain behavior that would be regarded as exogenous in a purely economic analysis. Within a domestic political-economy context, for instance, political analysis may be required to understand central bank decisions on monetary policy, or legislative enactment of tariff measures (for an interesting political-economic analysis of tariffs by an economist, see Pincus 1977; on political parties and macroeconomic policy, see Hibbs 1977). For the international political economy, political analysis may be necessary to account for the liberality or tightfistedness of creditor policies; the success or failure of international negotiations, and the reactions of governments to changes in other states' foreign economic policies (see Block 1977; Hirsch and Doyle 1977; Gardner 1980). Both economics and political science contribute to unraveling part of the tangled skein of the international political economy; neither is sufficient by itself.

There is a price to be paid for this broadening of analytical horizons. Taking into account international politics means incorporating strategic interaction into our analysis; and it is well known that where strategic interaction is involved--in oligopoly behavior as well as world politics--theory does not yield stable, determinate equilibria. (Fellner 1949; Shubik 1970; Simon 1976). Thus it is impossible on a theoretical basis to generate precise and accurate predictions about particular state actions, or even about the direction of change in the system insofar as it depends on particular state actions. Political-economic theories based on systemic factors--such as the "theory of hegemonic stability"--can only be expected to account successfully for general trends and tendencies rather than specific developments.

The problem of scientific explanation at the international level is compounded by the limited number of observations available to the student of the international system. Comparative analysis at the level of the state is facilitated by the fact that data are available on many countries; hypotheses about tendencies can be tested statistically (Hibbs 1977; Cameron 1978). Since there is only one international system, this cannot be done at the international level over a short period of time; hypotheses about tendencies can only be assessed systematically if one has diachronic data covering at least several decades.

To explore the international political sources of inflation in the 1970s is therefore to engage more in an interpretive than a theory-testing enterprise. The purpose is to use the theory of hegemonic stability to raise questions about international political sources of inflation, rather than to provide definitive answers. We know so little about the political sources of inflation at the international level that it seems useful, even if precision eludes us, to explore some plausible propositions linking world politics--in particular, the decline of American power--to contemporary inflationary trends.

II. THE ARGUMENT IN BRIEF

It is well known that inflation has accelerated in the 1970s in the advanced industrialized countries of the Organization of Economic Cooperation and Development (OECD). The rate of increase in consumer prices for the OECD countries as a whole rose from an annual average of under 4 percent for 1962-1972 to 13.2 percent in 1974; after a decline by 1978 to under 8 percent, the rate of price increase rose again in 1979 to over 10 percent (OECD 1975, Table 19; 1977a, Table 24; 1979a, Table 23). The question addressed by this paper is whether international political conditions--and in particular, a decline in American power--had anything to do with these patterns of inflation.

We will assess two different lines of argument that can be traced backwards, causally, from inflation to the decline of American power. The first line of argument concentrates on monetary issues. Inflation, in this argument, is largely accounted for by rates of national money supply growth relative to the demand for money. Those rates of money supply growth were affected, it is contended, by the breakdown of the Bretton Woods regime and that breakdown can itself be traced in significant part to a decline in American power capabilities in the monetary area previous to that time. The hypothesized causal linkages are therefore as indicated in Figure 1.1:

As the diagram indicates, this line of argument only identifies <u>one</u>

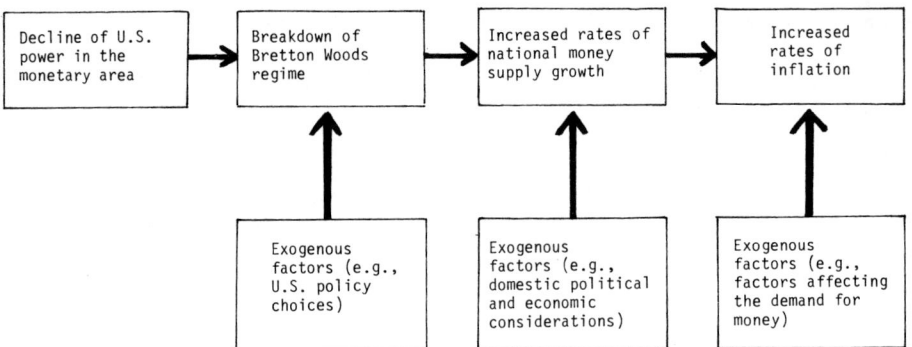

Fig. 1.1. The monetary line of argument.

factor influencing inflation; it is not an attempt at complete explanation. Many factors exogenous to the model may exert effects at each point in the chain. The question addressed in this paper is whether the linkages addressed by horizontal arrows are plausible and non-trivial, not the precise magnitude of their effects as compared to other factors.

The second line of argument addresses the issue of oil price rises and inflation. It can be diagrammed as in Figure 1.2.

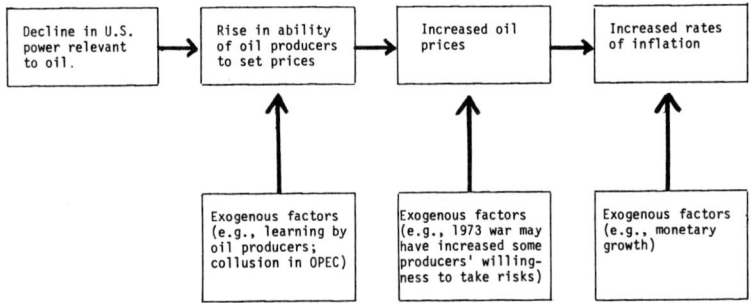

Fig. 1.2. The oil price line of argument.

As in the monetary argument, the question is whether the links indicated by the horizontal arrows are plausible, not whether this comprises a complete explanation (which it does not).

As indicated earlier in this paper, our method will be to work our way backward through the hypothesized causal chain, from inflation to decline in American power. The third section will discuss the monetary line of argument as sketched in Figure 1.1. Since inflation is a monetary phenomenon, affected most strongly by monetary forces, this line of argument is the central one of this paper. If the thesis is correct that the decline of American power is linked to world inflation, our monetary line of argument must be sustainable.

The fourth section considers the causal chain from decline of American power to increased oil prices to inflation in the industrialized countries. This is a secondary argument. If it is correct, it reinforces our thesis about the effects of hegemonic decline on inflation. Yet due to the relatively small effect of increased oil prices on inflation, compared to the effects of monetary policy, this line of argument could not constitute, by itself, a major explanation of world inflation.

In the fifth section both lines of argument are critiqued, by focusing on American policy rather than American power as the source of inflationary pressure. The collapse of international stabilizing arrangements, and international inflation, were not results of a natural decline of American power so much as consequences of American policies that rapidly and unnecessarily reduced American power. Focusing on the decline of American power is important, but it does not provide a sufficient answer to our questions; and it could even be misleading if taken to imply that the process we have observed was somehow inevitable.

The paper's conclusion raises issues of policy. In light of the analysis, what are the prospects for stabilization of world inflation rates? In particular, what American policies might begin to construct the conditions under which inflation could be brought under control?

III. INTERNATIONAL INFLATION, THE BREAKDOWN OF THE BRETTON WOODS REGIME, AND THE DECLINE OF AMERICAN POWER

Working from right to left in Figure 1.1, the first link in our monetary line of argument ties increased rates of inflation to increased rates of money supply growth within major OECD countries. This follows the contentions of monetarist economists, who explain inflation by comparing the rate of growth of nominal money supplies with the growth rate of the demand for money. Thus defined, "monetary expansion becomes the main determinant (or concomitant) of the rate of inflation, however complicated the dynamics of interaction may be in the short run" (Swoboda 1977, p. 12; see also Laidler 1975, 1977).[2]

The Breakdown of the Bretton Woods System and National Monetary Expansion

The second link in our monetary line of argument is more controversial: that the breakdown of the Bretton Woods international monetary regime contributed to increased rates of national money supply growth in major OECD countries. This international political argument is meant to be complementary to, rather than competitive with, analyses of national political sources of inflation, such as those represented by political business cycle arguments (see Willett and Mullen, Paper 5, and references cited therein), or by other attempts to explain macroeconomic policy decisions with reference to political factors (Alt 1979; Hibbs 1977, 1978, 1980a, 1980b). Both sets of arguments use monetarist analysis as a starting point for political analysis. Rather than asking the vague question, why do governments permit inflation to occur, we are now led to ask, why do monetary authorities permit the money supply to increase so rapidly that inflation ensues? As Bert G. Hickman (1977, p. iii) has pointed out, this leads us immediately to political analysis:

> Saying that an excess supply of money is the cause of inflation may be instrumentally true but may not get one very far toward controlling inflation. The underlying problem is the political one of mediating among various interest groups in the struggle for real income shares and equitably distributing the incidence of inflation control.

From the perspective of the internationally oriented analysis in this paper, the key political question has to do with the constraints imposed by an international monetary regime on national monetary policies.[3] The pegged rate regime of Bretton Woods failed to impose effective restraints on the United States. Until 1968, the Johnson administration financed the Vietnam war without a tax increase, and monetary policy was expansive from the fourth quarter of 1966 through 1968. The Nixon administration turned to monetary expansion in 1970. Indeed the crucial defect of the Bretton Woods regime was its inability to restrain the United States, as the key reserve currency country, from following overexpansionary monetary policies (for an account of U.S. policy, see Shapiro 1977).

After August 1971, the constraints on U.S. policy were even further reduced. The United States was no longer committed to a fixed gold value of the dollar; furthermore, its policymakers were on record as desiring a greater devaluation of the dollar than was eventually agreed to by America's partners at the Smithsonian Institution in December. In this context, an argument for tight monetary policy "to defend the dollar" was unlikely to be even as persuasive in 1972 as it would have been a year or two earlier. Huge American balance of payments deficits thus persisted after the Smithsonian agreements; the U.S. official settlements deficit for 1970-1973 totaled over $50 billion (OECD 1977b, p. 54).

As the McCracken report indicates (OECD 1977b, p. 56), the huge American deficits reduced constraints on other countries' monetary growth policies:

> The size of United States payment deficits over the period effectively removed balance-of-payments constraints in other OECD countries, and facilitated a massive expansion of money supplies. Although it is not argued simplistically that such expansion is a mechanical consequence of an automatic link from international reserves to money supply, it is reasonable to assume that the scale of reserve creation contributed to the synchronized boom of 1972-73 and was therefore inflationary.

Although the effects were broadly similar, the paths to monetary expansion were different. Some governments (the United Kingdom, Italy, and initially France) sought expansion; others (including Japan and the Netherlands) accepted it; and still others (especially Germany) had monetary expansion thrust upon them through the effects of capital inflows. Great Britain was perhaps the most expansionist. The Conservative government of Edward Heath felt released, finally, from the shackles of defending the pound, and able to make a "dash toward growth." When expansionary British monetary policy precipitated a sterling crisis in June 1972, Britain quickly unpegged the pound and let it depreciate. Although British and American actions were rather extreme, especially for countries previously seen as responsible leaders of the system, other governments happily or unhappily followed suit. The conditions of 1972 reduced incentives for tight monetary policies throughout the industrialized world. As a result of the breakdown of the Bretton Woods regime, "more expansionary action was taken than would otherwise have been the case and, especially, more of this action took the form of _monetary_ expansion" (OECD 1977b, p. 56; italics in original).

The short-lived Smithsonian arrangements achieved the worst of both worlds: they did not constrain the United States or other inflation prone countries such as Britain from following expansionary monetary policies, but they did prevent strong currency countries, such as Germany, from reacting to those policies by letting their currencies appreciate. Despite increasingly strict controls imposed by German monetary authorities, the Bundesbank had to take in $4.5 billion worth of foreign currencies during June and July alone; and for the entire year, the German money supply grew by about 15 percent (Yeager 1976, pp. 514-15; OECD 1977b, pp. 85-87). The combination of a pegged rate exchange regime with an irresponsible reserve currency country was predictably disastrous, both for the regime itself and for world price stability.

Evidence for the inflation proneness of the Smithsonian arrangements is provided by examining actual monetary policies of the seven major OECD countries between 1965 and the end of 1978. This period includes three subperiods, delineated according to exchange rate regime: (1) a period of relatively fixed exchange rates under the Bretton Woods regime (first quarter of 1965 through the second quarter of 1971); (2) a period of uncertainty, with the short-lived pegged rates established at the Smithsonian Institution in force throughout much of the period and with substantial official intervention taking place (1971 III-1973 I); and (3) a third period of floating rates (1973 II-1978 IV). Table 1.1 indicates, for each period, the number of quarters in which the seven governments engaged in monetary restraint as defined by the OECD.

TABLE 1.1. Quarters of monetary restraint in seven major OECD countries, 1965-1978

Periods	U.S.	Japan	Ger.	France	U.K.	Italy	Canada
1. 1965I-1971III (26 quarters)	7	7	19	8	17½	5	2
2. 1971III-1973I (7 quarters)	2	½	2½	2½	0	0	0
3. 1973II-1978IV (23 quarters)	10½	8	6	7	10	6	13½

Percentage of time restraint was exercised (unweighted average)

    Period 1): 36%
    Period 2): 15%
    Period 3): 38%

Source: Calculated from OECD 1977b, Charts 14B, pp. 83-95; OECD 1979b, Charts B1-B7.

It is readily apparent that the <u>least</u> restraint was exercised during the period between the middle of 1971 and the spring of 1973, the period of "Smithsonian uncertainty." Restraint was much greater both under the pegged rates prior to August 1971, and the flexible rate arrangements after March 1973.

The argument here suggests that static "pegged vs. flexible" exchange rate arguments are not as important as arguments that focus on change--in particular, the impact of periods of uncertainty. Although discussions of international sources of inflation often focus on the contention that flexible exchange rates contribute to inflation, economic analysis lends little definitive support to this argument. Theory strongly suggests that under flexible exchange rates, countries will be able to choose their own rates of inflation more easily than under fixed rates--under which national inflation rates will tend to converge toward the world rate. But economic theory provides little guidance on the question of whether flexible rates will increase the <u>average</u> world inflation rate. Salant (1977) and Corden (1977) both conclude that the answer on theoretical grounds is indeterminate, since to reach a conclusion one would need additional information about national policies under fixed and flexible exchange rate systems.

Taking politics into account does not produce a more definitive conclusion. In a fiat (paper) money system, even with pegged exchange rates, the reserve currency country is not constrained by short-term liquidity concerns. It can always print more "international currency." Under the Bretton Woods regime, deficit countries other than the reserve currency center also had a good deal of leeway, since international credit arrangements were often made to meet a foreign exchange crisis. As Fred Hirsch (1978, pp. 278-79) commented:

> Critics who see these international monetary arrangements as embodying a ratchet effect for world inflation are probably right. But the relevant question is whether a liberal international economy could have been purchased at any more acceptable price. This international influence is essentially accommodative, opening the way to monetary accommodation domestically. It responds to the domestic tensions that produce inflation as the insurance against a still worse outcome.

As Willett and Mullen point out in Paper 5, pegged exchange rates create a long-term constraint on inflationary policies if equilibrium in external accounts is to be maintained without devaluation. Yet Willett and Mullen also argue that this constraint will not, in general, be sufficient to eliminate the inflationary bias in Western political economies; and that in the short run, the pegging of exchange rates increases incentives to manipulate the economy in an inflationary way for political purposes. Thus pegged exchange rates do not effectively deter political leaders from following inflationary policies. Yet neither are flexible rates sufficient to bring inflation under control. The key issue from the perspective of monetary theory is not pegged versus flexible exchange rates per se, but rather how international arrangements, and changes in them, affect the rates of national money supply growth in the major economies.[4] In the 1970s, it was the breakdown of any coherent regime, rather than the existence of one regime or another, that lifted the international constraints on money supply growth and therefore contributed to inflation. Between 1971 and 1973, those constraints were probably less severe than under either the previous Bretton Woods pegged rate regime or the subsequent flexible rate system to which monetary authorities have now become accustomed.

The Decline of U.S. Power and the Collapse of the Bretton Woods Regime

We have now reached the last link in our monetary chain: the proposition that the decline of U.S. power in the international monetary arena before 1971 contributed to the collapse of the Bretton Woods regime. Since "power" is such an ambiguous word, it is necessary, before pursuing this line of argument further, to specify what is meant by power in this paper and to indicate the sort of power analysis being attempted.

The thesis that this paper examines is an implication of the theory of hegemonic stability, which uses a conception of power as tangible resources at the disposal of actors. This sort of power theory attempts to explain behavior by reference to state capabilities; power as used in this paper therefore refers to "tangible resources that can be employed to affect the behavior of others in desired directions." The thesis examined here is therefore an example of what James G. March calls a "basic force model," in which outcomes reflect the tangible and known capabilities of actors. Basic force models typically fail to accurately predict particular political outcomes, in part because differential opportunity costs often lead competing actors to use different proportions of their potential power resources (Harsanyi 1971). Yet they offer clearer and more easily interpretable explanations than "force activation models," which incorporate assumptions about the differential willingness of actors to exercise power. The problem with "force activation models," as with discussions of "will" in politics, is that they are essentially post hoc and ad hoc rather than a priori models. One cannot specify "will" in advance, but one can always think of reasons, after the fact, why an actor may not have used all available potential power (March 1966, pp. 54-61).

To undertake a basic force analysis, one must specify the appropriate indices of power resources, in view of the purposes being sought by the power wielder. For our monetary line of argument, the most appropriate conceptualization of power resources, as Robert Aliber pointed out at the conference, is in terms of the ability of a government to use financial resources to influence the behavior of others, relative to its own dependence on the financial actions of others. Power, in this conception, is the converse of dependence: asymmetrical dependence confers power on the less dependent actor in a relationship (Keohane and Nye 1977; Baldwin 1979).

In world politics, power as defined above depends not merely on one's underlying resources but on the international context within which their use is facilitated or constrained. Under the Bretton Woods regime, the United States was in a relatively weak bargaining position. Other countries and their citizens held large quantities of dollars, which the United States was required to redeem for gold at the fixed price of $35 an ounce. In order to preserve the regime, the United States would have had to follow policies that would convince those holders of dollars (and after the changes in the rules of 1968, the central banks holding dollars) not to present them for redemption into gold. This meant that United States macroeconomic policy would have been dependent on the financial decisions of foreign central banks. Since most of these central banks (the Bank of England excepted) held abundant quantities of dollars, they were not sensitive, within the confines of the Bretton Woods regime, to reciprocal American financial pressure. Thus from a political point of view, by the late 1960s the Bretton Woods regime had become a liability for the United States, since its rules (as written largely by Americans in a bygone era) favored creditor over debtor countries.

Yet on an underlying basis, the United States was still by far the most important of the advanced capitalist countries. It had a vastly larger economy than any of its partners. It had much greater political and military resources than its allies. Thus the United States, far from having a political incentive to support the Bretton Woods regime at 1970 exchange rates, had every incentive, on the political side, to force major changes in the rules. As Henry Aubrey had pointed out in 1969: "Surely a creditor's influence over the United States rests on American willingness to play the game according to the old concepts and rules. If the United States ever seriously decided to challenge them, the game would take a very different course" (Aubrey 1969, p. 9). Only by breaking the rules could the United States regain the freedom of action that it demanded.

The breakdown of the Bretton Woods regime was therefore affected by the discrepancy between the power position of the United States within the context of the regime, and its stronger underlying position. Yet the collapse of Bretton Woods alone does not fully explain the uncertainty and chaos that reduced international constraints on overexpansionary monetary policies in the early 1970s. We also have to account for the inability of the major powers quickly to reconstruct a viable international monetary regime that would restrain governments from engaging in such excesses.

Here it is once again important to analyze the United States power position as of 1970. As Susan Strange emphasizes in Paper 3, the United States was neither a pygmy nor a helpless giant. But neither was it the overwhelming hegemon it had been at the Bretton Woods conference, in 1944, or during the subsequent decade. In those years, its partners included a debt-ridden Britain in need of dollar loans, and a set of weak continental European countries engaging in postwar reconstruction (Block 1977; Gardner 1980). The United States in those years could determine the general outlines of the international monetary system, if not every detail of practice or timing (Hirsch and Doyle 1977). The United States was genuinely hegemonic: "powerful enough to maintain the essential rules governing interstate relations, and willing to do so" (Keohane and Nye 1977, p. 44).

Had the United States been so dominant in 1971, it could have forced other countries to revalue their currencies; it had attempted to achieve this objective in the years preceding its decision in August 1971, to cut the formal links between the dollar and gold and to impose an import surcharge. But by 1971 the United States was no longer strong enough to do this, even after destroying the old Bretton Woods rules. The best it could secure was an agreement that partially met its demands, but that did not provide the basis for a viable system, given the continuing inclination of the U.S. government to follow expansionary monetary policies for domestic reasons. The United States had been able to destroy the old exchange rate system, but was unable--given its unwillingness to tighten monetary policy--quickly to reconstruct a new, stable set of arrangements.

Tactically, the American actions of 1971 were successful in forcing the major European countries and Japan to agree on a devaluation of the dollar, both in terms of gold and other currencies (see Odell's essay, Paper 2; also Odell 1979 and Mayer 1980). The United States forced a new pattern of exchange rates and demonstrated that its compliance with the wishes of others could not be taken for granted. From a longer-term standpoint, however, the American victory appears rather illusory. The United States did not have sufficient power resources to reestablish a viable international system that would be consistent with its own domestic monetary policy. Thus the Smithsonian arrangements began to collapse almost as soon as the documents had been signed; and inflationary pressures were accentuated rather than contained.

This section has argued that the decline of American power between the late 1940s and 1971 contributed to the breakdown of the Bretton Woods regime, which in turn removed constraints on monetary expansionism, leading to higher rates of inflation in industrialized countries. In this argument, the decline of American power is not regarded as a sufficient condition for the collapse of the regime, since that regime could have lasted much longer if U.S. monetary policy had been more restrained. The decline of American power is a necessary condition, however, for the collapse of the regime, since if the United States had remained as dominant as it was in the late 1940s, it could have forced its partners to revalue periodically while keeping gold at $35 an ounce. Under these hypothetical arrangements, the form of the Bretton Woods regime could have been preserved, although the actual operation of the regime could (if revaluations were frequent enough) have resembled more closely a floating rate than a fixed rate exchange rate arrangement. With frequent enough revaluations, other governments could have resisted the transmission of American inflation to themselves, and a smooth transition to an effective, floating rate system (under the guise of a continuation of the Bretton Woods regime) could have been imagined. Under this scenario--in which U.S. power and leadership would have been crucial ingredients--the inflationary period of the Smithsonian arrangements could have been avoided.

IV. THE DECLINE OF AMERICAN POWER, THE OIL PRICE INCREASE, AND INFLATION

One of the links in the oil price argument diagrammed in Figure 1.2 seems to require little explanation: the producing countries, given the opportunity, would raise prices substantially from the levels of 1970 or 1973. After all, those price levels were well below either the short-run or the long-run opportunity costs of substitutes. Two of the links in the argument require more sustained discussion. First, we must establish that increased oil prices in 1973-1974 and 1979 affected general price levels, at least in the short term. If this is the case, then an explanation of oil price increases will help to explain the periodicity of inflation rates--rising in 1974-1975, falling until 1979, then rising again--in the 1970s. The second step is to show that a decline in American power resources, relevant to oil pricing, contributed to the rise in oil prices by making it possible for the producing country governments to take greater control of oil pricing practices.

Oil Price Increases and Inflation

In a true but ultimately trivial sense, inflation is a monetary phenomenon. Even supply shocks of the magnitude of the oil price rises of 1973-1974 and 1979 would have only negligible inflationary effects if monetary policy were strict enough to reduce other prices (including wages) sufficiently, and sufficiently rapidly, to compensate for higher oil prices. The inflationary effects of a supply shock can therefore only be established if one takes into account the monetary postures of the authorities. Any "inflationary effect of supply shocks" argument is only valid with that caveat.

Yet the real economic world is not frictionless, either economically or politically. Very large supply shocks cause economic disruption, and can lead to unemployment since "during the period following an energy price increase but before the accommodating change in the wage, labor is priced too high for full employment" (Mork and Hall 1979, p. 3). Yet in the short run, indexation provisions in wage contracts often mean that higher oil prices increase nominal wages, taking them even farther from their equilibrium levels. If nominal wage rates are sticky downward, inflation will be required to restore equilibrium. In such a situation, monetary policies sufficient to restore ex ante price levels would be likely to entail widespread unemployment and loss of output, if not serious financial and political crisis. Where the supply shock is external to the economy, this problem is compounded by the fact that the price increase will have reduced real incomes, and consumption levels, within the oil importing country, contributing to declines in demand and output, and therefore in the demand for money, at least in the short run. After the oil price rises of 1973-1974 and 1979, monetary authorities therefore faced at least a short-term tradeoff between maintaining the level of economic activity on the one hand, and combatting the inflationary effects of oil price increases, on the other. Insofar as political pressures are brought to bear on the monetary authorities, these are likely to accentuate the tendency to weigh heavily the short-term costs, in terms of unemployment and foregone output, of a strict monetary policy. This does not mean that governments will necessarily accommodate the effects of oil price increases--indeed, the tendency in the wake of the 1973-1974 price rises was rather to reduce rates of growth of money supplies (OECD 1979a, p. 33)--but it does suggest that they will not restrict the money supply sufficiently to counteract entirely the effects of exogenous price shocks in the short term.

Various estimates have been made of the effect of the 1973-1974 oil price increases on the price level in OECD countries. The McCracken report estimates that the oil price rise had a 2 percent direct price effect in the OECD countries, with almost another 2 percent rise as a result of corresponding price increases for domestically produced energy (OECD 1977b, p. 17). Using an aggregate model of the U.S. economy, Mork and Hall (1979) find that the oil shock led to an increase in the U.S. price level, in 1974 and 1975, of about 6 percent; five other models also find price effects, although estimates of magnitude vary widely. For most major OECD economies, rates of price increase were higher in 1974 and 1980, <u>relative to monetary growth rates two years earlier</u>, than in 1972 and 1978--again, relative to monetary growth rates two years previously. This finding is consistent with the argument that oil price increases had a significant impact on price levels in the short term.[5] With respect to the 1979 oil price increases, the OECD estimated that the direct effects on OECD price levels would reach almost 2 percentage points by the end of 1980, and that the total effect, including indirect impacts, would be on the order of 3 percent (OECD 1979a, pp. 41-43).

All of this, of course, begs the question of the long-term impact of increased oil prices on inflation. Monetarists would expect that, if the long-term growth rate of the monetary aggregates is not affected, the inflation rate will return to the level determined by the growth rate. Yet other factors such as indexation of wage rates, trade union ability to resist nominal wage decreases, expectations about underlying inflation rates, and political resistance to the adverse short-term effects on unemployment and output of low monetary growth rates may under some circumstances make consistent, long-term monetary policy difficult to sustain. This paper makes no attempt to resolve the dispute about the long-run effect of oil price increases on inflation--a dispute that would require detailed political-economic analysis, taking into account the institutional characteristics and experiences of particular countries, as well as monetary theory. The relevant point for our analysis is that in the short run oil price increases have effects on changes in the price level--the "inflation rate" as generally reported. Thus any effective political-economic explanation of the pattern of inflation in 1970 should account for the sharp rises in oil prices experienced in 1973-1974 and 1979 as well as for growth rates of the monetary aggregates during the 1970s.

The Decline of American Power and Oil Price Increases

To measure changes in the power position of the United States in the energy area, the best single indicator is the relative balance between U.S. capacity to produce petroleum and its consumption. A surplus of production capacity over consumption--which prevailed until the late 1960s--gave the United States the ability to influence the price of oil, as well as to provide oil supplies to its allies in the event of supply disruptions such as took place in 1956-1957. With the Suez Canal closed after the Suez War of 1956, Europe was threatened with a severe oil shortage, which the United

States met by increasing its own production and allowing the major oil companies to reorganize tanker routes collectively (Keohane 1982). In 1967, after the June War, Saudi Arabia threatened an oil embargo against the West, but found itself disregarded by the United States and its allies. In both years, the excess domestic oil capacity of the United States was greater than the volume of its imports; indeed, prior to each crisis production capacity comparable to about 25 percent of its consumption was not being used (Darmstadter and Landsberg 1976, pp. 30-31).

By 1973, however, U.S. excess capacity was down to 10 percent of its oil consumption, but imports amounted to over 35 percent, a substantial proportion of which came from the Middle East. Between 1956 and 1973, proved American reserves grew only slowly in absolute terms and fell in relative terms, from 18.2 percent to 6.4 percent of total world reserves (Darmstadter and Landsberg 1976, pp. 30-32). In the earlier crises the United States could (from the Western perspective) be "part of the solution"; in 1973 it was "part of the problem." Its fundamental petroleum resource base had been greatly weakened.

During the same period of time, U.S. political and military dominance in the Middle East had also eroded, under the dual challenges of Arab nationalism and increased Soviet involvement in the area. In the 1950s the United States, along with Britain, had a virtual monopoly of great power influence in the area. The United States had been able in 1953 to engineer the overthrow of a nationalistic Iranian premier and reinstall the Shah on his throne; and in 1958 to land marines in Lebanon in the wake of a revolution in Iraq. In 1973, by contrast, Iraq, Egypt, and Syria were all rather closely linked to the Soviet Union.

The erosion of American power, both within the energy area per se and in related political-military resources, took place in the context of other developments that strengthened the hands of the oil producers. Strong increases in demand for petroleum during the early 1970s tightened the oil market, putting producers in a better position. Furthermore, the relationships of producing country governments to the oil companies had changed in important ways between the 1950s and 1970s. In the earlier period, a small number of multinational oil firms, mostly based in the United States, had controlled oil production worldwide. These firms had complex cooperative arrangements with each other, and collectively dominated relations with the governments of oil exporting countries, particularly in the Middle East. They possessed greater financial resources, more technological knowledge, and greater sophistication about the complexities of the industry than the host governments; furthermore, in extreme situations they could call on the economic or even the military power of the United States and Britain. The interests of U.S. corporate and government officials were usually complementary: "Both were interested in seeing plentiful and secure supplies of oil flowing within the noncommunist world and both preferred to deal with stable, pro-western governments" (Turner 1978).

As the structure of power in petroleum changed, so did the interests and inclinations of the companies. Aramco, for instance, was highly responsive to the demands made upon it by Saudi Arabia during the 1973-1974 embargo. Morris Adelman had earlier described the companies as "tax collecting agents" of OPEC; Anthony Sampson later asserted that they were "closer in their interests to the producing countries than to the Western consumers"; and Louis Turner admitted that "there now [1978] is a community of interests between companies and host producer governments which did not exist before the 1970s," although he warned against exaggerating this harmony (Adelman

1972-1973, p. 88; Turner 1978, pp. 139, 147). For the U.S. government and its allies, weakness bred weakness; the shift in companies' allegiance itself contributed to an erosion of the Western governments' position.

The decline in U.S. power was a necessary condition for the drastic nature of oil price increases. Only in this context could the political catalysts of those years have led to such vast shifts in relative prices. OPEC remained only a pale shadow of a true cartel; it was weakly institutionalized and had no agreed upon scheme for prorating production cutbacks. The United States was not skillful in its bargaining with OPEC states, or in its coordination with its own allies, at the Teheran meetings in February 1971 (Schuler 1976; U.S. Senate 1974). The subsequent decline in the value of the dollar--in which the prices agreed upon at Teheran were denominated--reduced the real value of oil exporting countries' earnings, and in conjunction with rising product prices sharply reduced the share of profits being received by the countries, as opposed to the international oil companies, giving oil producing governments an additional incentive to renegotiate the Teheran agreement (Penrose 1976). And the Yom Kippur war made Arab members of OPEC willing to assume greater risks and bear greater costs (in the form of the embargo), with dramatic effects on prices. Nevertheless, had these events taken place in the context of Western strength and OPEC weakness, their impact would have been much less important. It is crucial not to become so mesmerized by policy errors and accidents that we fail to see the changes in international political structure underlying oil price increases.

A causal chain can thus be traced between the decline of American power and inflation in the industrialized countries to the oil price argument as well as to the monetary argument. In the oil price argument, the connection between the decline of U.S. power and oil price increases is relatively clear: the former was a necessary condition for the magnitude of the latter. By all estimates, however, the impact of oil price rises on inflation was substantially less than the effect of domestic monetary policies in the major countries; so as an explanation of inflation, this line of argument remains subordinate to the monetary argument discussed above.

V. AMERICAN POLICY, POWER, AND INFLATION

The erosion of American power seems to have contributed to the breakdown of established international economic arrangements and, indirectly therefore, to inflation. Yet to end the analysis here would be to obscure the crucial role played by U.S. policy, in two senses. First, American policies contributed directly to the decline of American power: the United States was not merely a victim of events, but played an active role in its own undoing. Secondly, American policies in the monetary area--quite apart from their effects on U.S. power--independently fostered inflation. Without an examination of U.S. actions, therefore, an explanation of inflation on the basis of changes in international power distributions (adverse to the United States) is too neat, and too empty.

Both in money and oil, the United States followed policies of resource dissipation for significant periods of time during the 1960s and 1970s. American oil policy was one of "draining America first": oil import quotas, in force throughout the 1960s, ensured that higher cost domestic reserves would be used in preference to lower cost foreign supplies, even during a period in which the latter supplies were secure. This policy, sought by domestic oil and coal interests, was followed despite the prescient forebodings of State Department officials who had, in 1945, tried to use a proposed Anglo-American oil agreement to increase imports of Eastern Hemisphere petroleum, thus reducing in relative terms the rate of exploitation in the New World.[6]

In the monetary field, substantial U.S. current account deficits in the 1970s--reaching a combined deficit of $28 billion for 1977-1978--entailed an increase in American liabilities abroad. The dissipation of political resources, however, was as serious as the increase in economic liabilities. Confidence in the United States was reduced, and respect for American policy declined. During the 1950s the United States had invested in power resources--building its alliances, supporting international organizations, and acquiring great prestige in the process--at the expense of some short-term costs. During the 1970s, the pattern was reversed; the United States sought to avoid having to bear the costs of adjustment to change in the short term, at the expense of its long-term position and of the stabilizing arrangements that it had laboriously helped to construct in the past (Keohane 1979; Mayer 1980).

In addition to accelerating the decline of American power, U.S. policy has directly increased the rate of world inflation at critical points during the last fifteen years. We have already noted the impact of American fiscal and monetary policy during the late 1960s and early 1970s on the collapse of the Bretton Woods regime and the rapid rates of monetary growth in the OECD countries associated with that set of events. Despite the relative decline of American power resources during the 1960s, the United States could have exercised a much more constructive influence on the international monetary system (not to speak of Southeast Asia) by abandoning its involvement in Vietnam and concentrating its attention on building a dynamic, productive economy, with a relatively stable price level, at home.

Control of U.S. oil prices at levels below those on world markets encouraged greater American consumption, which was in any case higher on a per capita basis than that in most other advanced industrialized countries. Robert Stobaugh and Daniel Yergin point out: "Low prices encourage consumers to use more oil than they otherwise would do. This increased consumption, in turn, makes the world oil market tighter than it otherwise would be. A tighter world oil market, even without a major accident such as Iran, can result in disastrously higher oil prices" (Stobaugh and Yergin 1979, p. 588). The failure of the United States in the 1970s to implement an effective policy to conserve energy--an essential element of which would have been the decontrol of oil prices--contributed directly to world inflation as well as to the undermining of American power. American energy policy was thus doubly inflationary--through the effects of its imports on the world oil market, encouraging price rises, and through depletion of U.S. power resources (as the United States became more vulnerable to oil supply disruptions), reducing American ability to counteract price rises effectively when they did take place.

U.S. policy failures thus bear a substantial share of the blame for world inflation. They have operated in two ways: first, by weakening the <u>ability</u> of the United States to prevent or combat inflationary actions by others, or to maintain stabilizing arrangements in monetary and petroleum affairs; second, by <u>directly accelerating</u> inflation through actions that raised rates of U.S. monetary growth or encouraged U.S. consumption of oil. The natural decline of American economic power as a result of European and Japanese growth might well have made it more difficult to maintain a stable world monetary system in any event, and could therefore have contributed to inflationary pressures. But farsighted U.S. policies would surely have made the problem less severe and more manageable.

The thesis explored in this paper--that a decline in American power contributed to world inflation--contains an important kernel of truth. Alone, however, it is one-sided, since it obscures the role played by inadequate American policies both in dissipating U.S. sources of power (political as well as economic) and in directly accelerating inflation. The theory of hegemonic stability from which it is derived was appropriately labeled a "thin theory" by Professor Michael Doyle at the conference where an earlier version of this paper was given. It provides a necessary but not sufficient basis for the understanding of international political-economic change in general, and inflation in particular.

VI. CONCLUSION

The chief implication of this analysis for American policy is that the control of world inflation requires more responsible national policies for monetary stability and greater energy self-reliance. The United States no longer has the capability of controlling or subsidizing others to maintain stable arrangements such as those in force during the 1950s. Ignoring the problems will hardly make them disappear. Better international coordination of policy is always desirable, but this is not the root of the problem. U.S. monetary and energy policies have been distinctly more inflationary than those of Germany and Japan. More effective international cooperation will be elusive as long as American policies are destabilizing. Coherent and effective American policies would not be a sufficient condition for international policy coordination--careful diplomacy, thoughtful institution building, and a willingness to make concessions on short-run issues will also be important--but they are necessary conditions for long-term cooperation.

In my view the United States needs to adopt a set of policies that emphasize long-term investment in resources that will contribute to power as well as to wealth--resources such as efficient industrial technology, new energy sources, and energy conservation. A cluster of Schumpeterian innovations is needed, but these innovations will require government policies that exact short-term sacrifices. The problem is one that Charles P. Kindleberger has discussed in terms of "static" and "dynamic" models of response to adversity (Kindleberger 1973, p. 239). As Kindleberger puts it:

> A static society folds under handicaps; a dynamic one overcomes at least some of them, if the challenge is not too great. The social scientist on the whole is not in a position to indicate when a static and when a dynamic response will be forthcoming, nor is the historian in such a position before the event.

Without a dynamic response by the United States in the 1980s, the political-economic future looks bleak for this country, and probably for the other economically advanced, capitalist democracies as well. If the U.S. response is static--forcing adjustment costs onto others, protecting inefficient sectors, consuming much and investing little--inflation in the 1990s will probably be high. But it will also be among the least of our problems.

NOTES
 An earlier version of this paper, "The International Politics of Inflation," was written for the Brookings Institution project, "The Politics and Sociology of Global Inflation." Some of the material in this paper will probably be incorporated also into the final version of that paper, which will include a number of other arguments as well. I am grateful to the Brookings Institution and to the leaders of the project, Leon Lindberg and Charles Maier, for permission to publish this paper first. I am also indebted to a number of people for comments on earlier versions of this paper, particularly to Tom Borcherding, Peter F. Cowhey, Peter Gourevitch, Ernst B. Haas, Robert E. Hall, Albert O. Hirschman, Peter J. Katzenstein, Peter Kenen, Charles Maier, and Marina v. N. Whitman, as well as to participants at the conference at The Pennsylvania State University.

1. Accounts of the politics of inflation that attempt to be comprehensive usually become simply descriptive. Attempts to specify some specific political sources of inflation--such as the "political business cycle"--have developed more coherent arguments, but do not always fare well when confronted with extensive cross-national evidence (Tufte 1978; Hibbs and Fassbinder, 1981).

2. I accept the general argument of monetarist economists here, while leaving the exact form of the money-price relationship for economists to dispute. I note only this cautionary work from a recent OECD report: "The complexity and occasional instability of the estimated functions (of the demand for money), notably the importance of interest rates, inflation, and institutional changes in influencing the underlying money/income relationships, suggests that the causal linkages between the rate of monetary expansion and the rate of inflation are less direct and more complicated than is often claimed by 'monetarist' economists" (OECD 1979b, p. 66).

3. This argument does not rest on the "global monetarist" proposition that a direct link exists between world liquidity, however defined, and international inflation. As Salant has pointed out (Salant 1977, pp. 186-87), there is not a one to one relationship between inflows of international reserves and increases in domestic money supplies. World liquidity as defined by OECD economists increased dramatically between 1969 and 1973, reflecting the expansionary national monetary policies of the time; but it would be too much to assert a direct causal relationship between world liquidity and inflation. At any rate, the argument of this paper does not rely on such a link, since it focuses on the impact of international conditions on _national_ monetary policies.

4. Economic arguments can be constructed that relate exchange rate systems to inflation without focusing on changes in the money supply. See, for instance, Scitovsky (1978). Scitovsky's argument rests on microeconomic theory, particularly oligopoly theory; but it is not precisely specified and must be regarded only as suggestive. In this paper I limit myself to the more common contentions linking exchange rate systems to monetary policies and therefore to inflation.

5. If monetary policy were the only relevant factor determining inflation rates, one should expect that the ratios of price increases to earlier money supply growth (two years in advance, to allow for lags) would be roughly the same, for a given country, before and after the oil price rises of 1973-1974 and 1979. If oil price increases had a positive impact on inflation, one would expect the ratios immediately after 1973-74 and after

1979 to be higher, reflecting a higher inflation rate associated with a given level of earlier money supply growth. Examining data for the seven major OECD countries, it appears that for five of them (all except Germany and Britain), the latter is the case [calculated by the author from M2 data for 1970, 1972, 1976, and 1978 (OECD 1979a) and from GNP deflator data for 1972, 1974, 1978, and estimates for 1980 (OECD 1973, 1976; IMF 1980)].

6. Internal memo of John A. Loftus, acting chief of the Oil Division of the State Department, May 31, 1945. National Archives of the United States, decimal file 1945-49, box no. 5849, file no. 841-6363/5-3145. Loftus acknowledges that increasing Eastern Hemisphere production relative to that in the Western Hemisphere "is an objective which probably cannot be stated in precise or quantitative terms without provoking acute internal political controversy here." Loftus and other State Department officials went to great pains to conceal that this was a chief purpose of the proposed Anglo-American oil agreement (which later died in the U.S. Senate).

DISCUSSION • *Michael R. Darby*

The Political Basis of International Inflation

> Pay no attention to what the critics say;
> no statue has ever been put up to a critic.
> **Jean Sibelius**

I. INTRODUCTION

If the critic's lot is a thankless one, doubly thankless is the lot of a scholar from one discipline called upon to criticize the work of a scholar from another discipline. As an economist, I must doubly emphasize my agreement with Keohane that political scientists can make a valuable contribution to our understanding of world wide inflation by explaining the existence of certain policy strategies and institutions that lead to the proximate economic causes of inflation. I recall that George Stigler used to tease Milton Friedman, saying, "Milton, if you tell me that excessive money growth causes inflation, I presume that you just don't want to discuss the subject."

Of course economists have dabbled in political science for some time by supposing that central bankers and other policymakers react to political pressures with respect to inflation, unemployment, the balance of payments, interest rates, and changes in taxes. This reaction function explains money growth in a dynamic setting in response to movements in endogenous variables such as inflation and unemployment and to exogenous shocks such as the Vietnamese war, which caused rapid changes in government expenditures relative to taxes.[1] This approach, however, cannot explain relatively unique events such as a change from a pegged to a floating exchange-rate system, the creation of OPEC, which made Saudi Arabia aware of its dominant-firm role, and the Iranian revolution. Further it simply estimates rather than explains the parameters that represent the responsiveness of policymakers to variables.

Thus political scientists, on the economic principal of comparative advantage, should be able to make significant contributions to our understanding of inflation by improving on the schoolboy's political science practiced by economists. Unfortunately, Keohane's schoolboy's economics misdirects his efforts so that little is learned about world inflation despite some interesting political observations.

Keohane argues, in brief, that a decline in American power contributed to international inflation via two channels: (1) via the breakdown of the Bretton Woods regime to increased growth rates of national money supplies, to increased inflation rates; and (2) via increased ability of oil producers to cartelize to increased oil prices, to increased inflation rates.[2] Keohane does not claim that these channels explain everything, but does suggest as a minimal standard that the "linkages. . . are plausible and nontrivial." My judgment is that each channel fails to meet this dual test. Specifically, I will argue that it is implausible that the breakdown of the Bretton Woods regime caused increased growth rates of national money supplies and that the effect of increased oil prices on inflation rates is close to trivial. Keohane comes close to admitting that the oil price argument is trivial as an explanation of inflation,[3] so the main difference between us appears to concern the Bretton Woods argument.

It will be useful to organize my discussion around a tautology: the rate of inflation equals the growth rate of the nominal quantity of money minus the growth rate of the real quantity of money. Economic theory tells us that the nominal quantity of money is determined ultimately by the supply decisions of the monetary authorities. The real quantity of money on the other hand is determined by the demand decisions of the public. The price level--and other variables in the short run--adjusts to equate the quantity of money demanded to the quantity supplied when both are measured in nominal (e.g. dollar) units. Thus there are only two ways in which a given factor can increase the inflation rate: by increasing the growth rate of nominal money supply or by decreasing the growth rate of real money demand.

II. THE BRETTON WOODS ARGUMENT

On the perfectly appropriate assumption that increased growth rates of national money supplies cause no offsetting increase in the long-run growth rates of real money demand, the last step in Keohane's Bretton Woods argument is perfectly correct. It is the first two steps that appear implausible. Keohane's argument is far from clear, but it seems to have two key elements: the Bretton Woods system was stabilizing in a way in which the Smithsonian system was not, and the decline of American power explains the difference between the two systems.

The first question is, In what way was the Bretton Woods system an "international stabilizing arrangement," whereas the Smithsonian system was not? In particular, by what mechanism did the breakdown of the Bretton Woods system induce increased growth rates of national money supplies? Keohane gives no clear answer to this question. The nearest thing to an answer is found in the discussion surrounding Table 1.1. But I see no evidence of any shift in U.S. monetary policy following the official acceptance of nonconvertibility of the dollar for gold at a fixed exchange rate.[4] Nor is there any evidence that the nonreserve countries were inflating faster than would be expected given U.S. monetary policy. Keohane himself noted that with few observations, statistical tests are impossible. This requires that careful, rigorous analysis be presented to convert a coincidence into a causal relationship. The reader is offered instead sweeping generalities.[5] If American monetary policy was indeed unaffected, it would take a great deal of careful argument to convince this reader that the general <u>appreciation</u> of foreign currencies relative to the dollar from 1971 to 1973 did not <u>reduce</u> growth in their money supplies and price levels compared with maintenance of the 1971 Bretton Woods exchange rates.

Without such a repeal of purchasing power parity, the Smithsonian system could have been relatively destabilizing only if it had relaxed previously binding constraints on U.S. monetary policy. Perhaps the gold constraint is a candidate, although there is no evidence of its having been a constraint. But how can we attribute the acquisition of <u>greater</u> U.S. monetary freedom to <u>declining</u> U.S. power?

In summary, the appreciation of other countries' currencies relative to the dollar during the Smithsonian period is prima facie evidence that their national money supply growth rates slowed relative to U.S. money supply growth as compared to what would have occurred with continuation of the Bretton Woods system. No real case was made for relaxation of a significant constraint on U.S. money supply growth and it would be hard to explain greater U.S. monetary freedom as due to decreased U.S. power. I conclude that Keohane's Bretton Woods argument is completely lacking in plausibility.

III. THE OIL PRICE ARGUMENT

Keohane's oil price argument meets his first criterion of plausibility but may fail on his second criterion of nontriviality. Since his published paper incorporates my comments from the earlier conference,[6] it is not surprising that Keohane and I are in general agreement on the effects of oil price changes, and only differ in judgment of their importance.

Keohane is correct that in a general equilibrium framework the oil price increase tends to reduce the real quantity of money demanded. While central banks have also tended to reduce the nominal quantity of money supplied, they have not done so--at least in the short-run--by as much as the decrease in real money demand.[7]

As Keohane indicates, there is much uncertainty as to the effect of the 1973-1974 oil price increase on real money demand, with estimates ranging all the way from 0.5 to 2, or perhaps even 5, percent. This is a once and for all shift, however, which may be partially offset by a once and for all decrease in nominal money supply. A 2 percent shift in the price level will add 2 percent to the inflation rate if it occurs during one year or an average of 1 percent per year if it occurs over two years. When we look at inflationary trends over four years, we are talking about an increase of only 0.5 percent per annum in the average inflation rate. Thus the influence of oil price changes on inflationary trends is negligible, although they may have played an important role in influencing money supply growth in the period 1973-1974. Whether this is judged as having "contributed significantly to world inflation during the 1970s" is largely a matter of opinion, best left to the reader.

IV. CONCLUSIONS

Keohane has essayed a difficult task--relating world inflation to the decline in American power--and come up largely empty-handed. Inept American monetary policy rather than the breakdown of the Bretton Woods system seems to have been the dominant force. While declining American power may have led to the 1973-1974 oil price increases, this played only a brief and supporting role to the leading one of monetary factors. As it happens, I think that the decline of American power is most unfortunate, but not because it has had any significant effect on inflation at home or abroad.

NOTES

1. An example of this approach near to my heart is embodied in Darby and Stockman (1980). Similar modeling efforts are under way at the Board of Governors of the Federal Reserve System and at the International Monetary Fund.

2. These arguments are summarized in Keohane's Figures 1.1 and 1.2.

3. On page 10, only the "plausible" criterion is specifically suggested for the oil argument with "nontrivial" conspicuous by its absence. Two paragraphs later, Keohane flatly states: "Yet due to the relatively small effect of increased oil prices on inflation, compared to the effects of monetary policy, this line of argument could not constitute, by itself, a major explanation of world inflation."

4. In Keohane's Table 1.1, "monetary restraint" is unchanged for the United States. In an earlier work (Darby 1980b), I could find no evidence of an effect of the balance of payments or gold flows on the U.S. money supply reaction function. This is perfectly appropriate for a fiat reserve country; see Darby (1980a). Keohane seems aware that gold convertibility was mere window dressing that was promptly abandoned as soon as it might be a constraint on U.S. policy.

5. For example: "In the 1970s, it was the breakdown of any coherent regime, rather than the existence of one regime or another, that lifted the international constraints on money supply growth and therefore contributed to inflation. Between 1971 and 1973, those constraints were probably less severe than under either the previous Bretton Woods pegged rate regime or the subsequent flexible rate system to which monetary authorities have now become accustomed."

6. Those comments were based in turn on Darby (1980b).

7. This simply implies that short-run unemployment effects carry some weight in the central bank reaction functions.

DISCUSSION • *Robert E. Harkavy*

Politics High and Low

Robert Keohane, in his excellent and stimulating essay, posits a two-step causal chain in which the altogether evident recent decline in American power--its extent and desirability are much disputed--is said to have resulted in loss of control over two crucial international economic regimes or "stabilizing arrangements" (the international monetary and world oil market regimes), which in turn contributed mightily to global inflation. The overall analysis is derived from the more general "theory of hegemonic stability," which numerous recent commentators have used to portray some analogies between the seemingly ongoing American "climacteric" and the claimed similar unravelings of some predecessors' power, for example, that of Britain (Gilpin 1975; Silk 1976; Modelski 1980).

This brief critique will not quarrel with Keohane's main lines of argument; basically, it is in agreement with them. Rather it will attempt to extend some of them, to probe even further into their wide peripheries, and to raise some further questions that are suggested, particularly those dealing with the relationship of military to economic power. And, as Michael Darby has concentrated almost entirely on the second link in Keohane's chain--that dealing with the relationship between the balance of payments, liquidity and inflation--murky, arcane regions more the bailiwick of economists than political scientists, I will focus more on the first, that involving the link between hegemonic power and the hegemon's control over various regimes.[1] More than a little bemused and bewildered by the contrasting (?) arguments put forth by Keohane and Darby (the former apparently considers pure monetarist explanations trivial, even if technically correct), I was relieved to unearth the following quote from Edward Morse (1976, p. 181):

> Yet the causes of global inflation remain the subject of a serious theoretical debate. <u>Europeans</u> have a tendency to see its basic origins in the breakdown of the international monetary system. Others focus on both real and artificial shortages in raw materials, which have resulted in the manipulation of supplies. Still others argue that intransigent labor demands in the absence of collective social compacts between labor and government are its source.

Just why Europeans might be more inclined to attribute inflation to international monetary matters is a fascinating problem for the sociologist of knowledge. So too, one wonders what relative weight the third area noted by Morse--that dealing with <u>internal</u> "beggar thy neighbor" policies by contending groups in an era characterized by rising expectations--might play in Keohane's complex causal schemas, though such matters are indeed bruited in his discussion of the manner in which governments handle the oil supply shock by allowing inflation rather than reducing wages as a concession to altered terms of overseas trade (we also try to pass the inflation on via higher priced industrial and agricultural exports). But, will later historians also dwell on the "psychological," and somewhat "nonrational" component of contemporary inflation, that is, on the role of <u>expectations</u> of further inflation as causative (Kraft 1980)? Could we be witnessing, as some journalistic pundits profess, a "final fling" of orgy spending, after which comes a different type of deluge? And, what about productivity, and the relationship between savings and investment, matters often mentioned in popular discussions of inflation? I'll leave such issues to Keohane and Darby.

One might, of course, at the risk of seeming a bit unfair, wax a bit curious about why Keohane has chosen inflation as his bottom line item in a discussion that investigates broadly the impact of the erosion of American power on the international economy--not that inflation is unimportant! But, one senses rather that he really wants to investigate the more general problem of economic instability, in a way subsuming inflation (maybe ironically, he makes a cogent case for uncertainty and instability as the <u>cause</u> of monetary growth and hence inflation in the early 1970s). Nowadays, many seemingly serious analysts are predicting a great depression and the collapse of the Western world's economies; the scenarios usually begin with a collapse of the Third World's OPEC-induced debt structure translating to New York bank failures, and in turn to panic in the financial markets (alternative scenarios are triggered by the exhaustion of the American middle class's capacity to spend out of savings and attendant massive personal bankruptcies) (Davis 1980; Gall 1980). If such things should occur, one can easily imagine Keohane's causal sequence being used to explain depression as easily as it is now used to explain inflation; with diffusion of power, erosion of hegemonic regime control, and unpredictability and instability-- also inflation--as intervening variables. That would not, of course, be anything new.

And, speaking of bottom line dependent variables to supplement that of inflation in connection with the aforementioned causal chain, what about current congressional findings about massive, growing foreign ownership (presumably mostly OPEC) of American domestic assets, now apparently at $350 billion, with no end in sight? May that not one day dwarf in significance the data for inflationary epidemics as a bottom line result of the waning of American power, particularly when the interest and dividend remittances really begin to flow out? Does that not speak to a complete reversal of center and periphery?

Then too, Keohane's theoretical analysis appears to raise some interesting questions of comparative history; he himself notes that "scientific" explanations concerning the international system are here thwarted by the lack of "diachronic data covering at least several decades." But, Keohane himself rightly argues elsewhere the value of discussion of "tendencies" even where rigor is not possible, so why the shyness about at least inquiring as to whether global inflation has or has not been associated with the declines of earlier hegemonic powers, and whether or not it was translated through the loss of control over key monetary regimes or commodity markets? George Modelski's recent work on the "long cycles" of international relations, which deals with the serial hegemonic reigns of "oceanic powers," may provide some basis for comparative analysis using the successive cases of Venice, Portugal, the Netherlands, Britain, and (in a fifth cycle) the United States (Modelski 1978). Historian C. R. Boxer, sociologist I. Wallerstein, and others have dealt extensively with the rises and falls of the Portuguese and Dutch seaborne empires in ways that provide grist for such a mill (Boxer 1965; Boxer 1969; Wallerstein 1974). Finally, Keohane, though he refers repeatedly to "world" or "global" inflation in his discussion, does not venture beyond an intra-Atlantic discussion of it, leaving one to wonder whether the relationship between it (inflation) and the international monetary regime is truly one of global applicability (quite probably it is).

For the political scientist, at any rate, the aforementioned first link in the chain is the most intriguing, all the more so as it is so difficult to pinpoint just what we are talking about when we speak of a decline of American power. Even though it is the principal coin of politics (as money is of economics), power has never been easy to define or measure. In the first draft of his paper, delivered at the Penn State conference, Keohane spoke of power almost as an undefined "first cause." In the foregoing chapter, he chooses to define it specifically as the "converse of dependence," with a seemingly very predominant economic cast. Here he perhaps subjects himself to the criticisms elsewhere directed at the joint works of Nye and Keohane for prematurely trumpeting the decline of the central role of military force in arbiting world affairs (Keohane and Nye 1970; Keohane and Nye 1977). Elsewhere in this volume, Susan Strange chooses to split the subject into two altogether separate tracks. In so doing, she makes a case for the essential retention of U.S. international economic power, but leaves the (less significant?) "military-security regime" to others even while herself recognizing its inseparability from the monetary regime.

As Stanley Hoffman has noted, everyone has come to agree that power is not quantifiable, nor can it play in international politics the role of the single yardstick that money plays in economics (political scientists may here, however, overestimate the degree of consensus among economists on definitions and measurements of central concepts). Confounding the matter still further, he argues that there has been a recent and significant transformation in the elements, the uses, and achievements of power; it has become increasingly elusive, considering

> The increasingly varied and rapidly shifting nature of its most salient ingredients or, if one prefers, the temporary and dubious character of whatever advantages a momentary superiority in one of those components provides, the bewildering uncertainties and complications that affect the exercise of power, the disproportion between ingredients and uses on the one hand, and outcomes on the other. It is therefore not surprising to find that, at any given moment, perceptions of power turn out to be both misleading and fleeting; and that calculations of power are even more delicate and deceptive than in previous ages. If power was once a promise, as well as a burden, today the burdens keep growing, but the promises turn into illusions or frustrations, or, at best, into the kinds of gains that condemn the winner to permanent anxiety (Hoffman 1975, pp. 183-84).

In that vein, Hoffman proceeds to discuss the traditional definitions of power related to military force levels versus those defined by levels of dependence. He also argues the fluidity and fragility of "reputations" for power, the variety of current international chessboards on which power games are played, and even the uses of weakness as a form of blackmail power. It is a set of arguments (and perhaps a studied relativeness) common to a new (pre-1981) U.S. foreign policy elite, and one found questionable by traditionalists not yet convinced that something new under the sun has emerged since Vietnam, nor also that strategic superiority is useless.[2] Actually, the traditional textbook coverages of power measurements--Morgenthau, Organski, et al.--had always insisted upon its subjective and unmeasurable nature; Morgenthau had stressed the efficacy of a nation's diplomacy as perhaps the <u>key</u> element determining its power (Morgenthau 1968; Organski 1968).

There does appear growing agreement, however, that the most common, standard, traditional, aggregate measure of <u>potential</u> power--GNP--is not terribly useful for explaining real world events. Many analysts resort rather to some variant of defining power as "A's ability to make B do something he would have preferred not to do or stop him from doing something he otherwise would have done," respectively capturing the compellent and deterrent aspects of it (Hoffmann 1975, p. 188). Keohane's stress on dependence is actually quite close to such definitions, again, with a seemingly strong tilt toward an economic interpretation or focus, regarding diminished U.S. power over various regimes.

One additional conceptual or theoretical point bears mention here concerning the relationship of political to economic power, which is emphasized in a recent work by Robert Gilpin. In contrasting the concepts of power and wealth as respectively the "stuff" of politics and economics, he points out that the former is meaningful <u>only</u> in a relative sense, that is, involving essentially zero-sum relations, whereas the latter can or at least <u>ought</u> to be important in an absolute sense, hence, the traditional liberal dream of Pareto optimization where one person's gain is no one else's loss.[3] The U.S. in recent years has still experienced some small growth in per capita wealth, even as some West European (not to mention the smaller OPEC) nations have surpassed it by that measure. What that means in relation to Susan Strange's insistence upon America's retention of economic power may be subject to debate.

Virtually no one, however, argues with the proposition that the U.S. has undergone a <u>loss of relative military</u> power over the past fifteen years; in that sense, <u>power diffusion</u> is an accurate characterization (Thompson 1980). The parameters of that are familiar enough, though the degree of change and more so, its implications, are much argued over. On the whole, simply stated, it is commonly assumed: (1) the USSR has, at minimum, achieved nuclear strategic parity, if not a degree of superiority or "sufficiency-plus," albeit with mutual second-strike deterrence firmly maintained; (2) the Soviets have widened their edge in conventional military force applicable to Central Europe and perhaps now also the Middle East; and (3) the USSR has achieved--or is en route to achieving--at least a balance with the U.S. in long-range intervention and power projection capability, hinged on naval power, long-range air transport, and an expanded, overseas basing access network. Further, the spread of conventional weapons technology, nowadays also involving various PGMs--precision-guided munitions--is claimed to have caused a significant diffusion of conventional military power to many middle and small powers, a trend reinforced by rapidly rising Third World military expenditures, not to mention, in some cases, nuclear weapons proliferation (Kemp 1977; Rosen 1979). All of these trends have resulted, in combination, in restricting the application of U.S.

military power overseas, if not quite in rendering America merely an "ordinary nation" (Rosecrance 1976). Again, whether these trends have been ineluctable (aside from their pace), that is, merely one more historical "rise and fall" case, or whether they have unnecessarily been caused in major part by U.S. actions, is much debated.

Keohane, reflecting some ancient arguments about policy versus "process" (free will versus determinism) reminiscent also of the Lenin versus Kautsky debates over the nature of imperialism, asserts that American power has waned more rapidly and unnecessarily than it should have; because of the idiotic draining of America's domestic oil reserves, the casualness with which our current accounts deficits were earlier handled, and the decision(s) to control domestic oil prices below world levels. Others such as Gilpin might be more inclined to stress the "natural," cyclical side of decline, as all "peripheries" become new "cores" and vice versa in a timeless game. American "hawks," more inclined to see a failure of will and elan from different causes than those perceived by Keohane, point to the present 5 percent ratio of defense expenditures to GNP (the lowest since before the Korean War), compare it to the near trebled such ratio sustained of late by the USSR, and nervously await the fading of the counterculture and its post-Vietnam induced "malaise" to allow for a new reversal. Such a reversal is clearly aspired to by the new Reagan administration.

Throughout his essay, Keohane appears primarily to be writing about the decline of U.S. economic power as measured by the rise in its dependence (or vulnerability, as once defined by his long-time collaborator, Joseph Nye) (Nye 1976). Yet, toward its close, he acknowledges the importance of "related political-military resources," recalling the earlier U.S. (and British) monopoly of influence in the Middle East, which allowed reinstalling the Shah on his throne in 1953 and the bolstering of Lebanon in 1958 with U.S. marines after the Iraqi revolution. In "extreme" situations, he notes, the oil multinationals might also earlier have had recourse to the marines; now, they are said to have interests closer to the oil producer countries than to the United States. As Keohane says, "weakness bred weakness," and he elliptically implies, perhaps not able to bring himself to state outright, that everyone concerned knows the marines are no longer there. Most importantly, of course, this discussion hints at, but does not meet head-on, the hypothetical question of whether OPEC would have or could have risen to its present pinnacle of economic might had its key Middle Eastern members more greatly feared U.S. military action, a situation clearly rendered improbable toward the close and in the wake of Vietnam. At the close of the 1973 war, it was widely noted that the United States could in no way match the seven or eight Soviet airborne divisions mobilized and on alert status, one of the reasons the United States placed such heavy pressure on Israel to abort its near victory.

The linkage between high and low politics is less clear in Keohane's discussion of America's loss of control over the "Bretton Woods system"; there he focused entirely on economics, noting how the United States lost leverage as Europe piled up dollars supposedly convertible into gold. In his rejoinder to discussions of Paper 2, however, Odell stresses the linkage between the economic and political-military chessboards within the Atlantic Alliance in the 1960s and 1970s, the reinforcing nature of political and economic trends culminating in a vastly altered if not reversed set of relationships.[4]

Standard analysis would have it that the Bretton Woods system was embedded in a larger set of arrangements, a bargain of sorts, particularly after the Europeans' dollar shortage had turned into a dollar glut. One side of the bargain was U.S. military protection of Europe along with American responsibility for protecting Western interests (i.e., investments and raw materials sources) elsewhere in the world via "extended deterrence." As the hegemonic alliance leader, the United States has long carried a disproportionate share of the Western defense effort, even as measured relatively by the MILEX/GNP ratio.[5]

So long as the United States maintained a favorable trade balance, the financing of its overseas security commitments (forward troop deployments, bases, and associated military and economic aid--in Europe and in other "forward countries") was not a major problem; rather, it was merely one reflection of its "surplus security." Indeed, during the 1950s such expenditures were explicitly justified as, in part, assisting others' balance of payments deficits so long as they could not yet compete in export trade with the United States. When the trade balance changed, those overseas commitments were, to a degree, then effectively financed by the dividend remittances of by then well-established overseas American corporate subsidiaries (Gilpin 1975, pp. 138-62).

The United States was long able to persuade its allies to absorb massive dollar accumulations in exchange for the provision of military security. As the problem worsened, however, Germany was asked to help out with offset payments, including apparently some for U.S. weapons it might not otherwise have acquired (Katzenstein 1976b; Johnson 1979). Generally, however, dollar accumulations and offset payments were accepted as a fair trade-off for the security provided. And, above all, there was the unchallenged prestige and reputation of American military might and also its successful political system, in the former case achieving a zenith in the Cuban missile crisis in 1962. Europe's awe and respect was, of course, admixed with some envy, so well expressed by J. J. Servan-Schreiber at a time some Europeans actually feared the emergence of a unipolar global system headed by the United States; after would come an ambivalent mix of contempt, Schadenfreude, and fear, when America's fortunes waned (Servan-Schreiber 1968).

Still, during the 1960s there were some incipient signs of the problems that would later plague the Atlantic Alliance and that would curtail the American leadership role that fed automatically into hegemony within the monetary regime. France under de Gaulle revolted, withdrawing effectively from NATO and even flaunting a "tous azimuths" nuclear doctrine for its force de frappe, which paradoxically was also justified as a hedge against the waning credibility of the U.S. nuclear deterrent shielding Europe. France also revolted against the role of the dollar as a reserve currency, and its inflated value, claiming that it greased increasing takeovers by U.S. firms in Europe and financed U.S. military adventures abroad, for instance, in Vietnam. Later, Germany under Chancellor Brandt, in pursuing its Ostpolitik, also rebelled against U.S. alliance leadership, though not nearly to the lengths pursued by France.

In short, the period preceding the collapse of Bretton Woods in the early 1970s, pertaining to the respective roles of high and low politics, appeared to evidence two conflicting, almost paradoxical, trends in explaining the European reaction to U.S. hegemony. On the one hand, Europe appeared to revolt against a resented, looming power; on the other, there was a questioning of the security actually provided by that now waning power. In the period preceeding 1971, after all, Europe had the Vietnam debacle in full view, not to mention the internal disarray of American politics and the advent of the vaunted "counterculture," all of which was critical in altering external perceptions of America's strength and its continuance as a successful society. Not incidentally, too, only seven years after the Cuban missile crisis, the USSR in 1969 surpassed the United States in total strategic launchers, in turn engendering U.S. efforts to achieve a SALT I agreement. The same period saw the beginnings of a massive Soviet naval buildup, the importance of which is only now looming into view.

The United States responded to the unfavorable trends of that period, variously, with detente, SALT, and the "China card," the latter a classic example of a balance of power ploy offsetting the strength of a nascent hegemonic power. Some or all of these events and efforts are presumably important in explanations of American inability to reconstruct the international monetary system in the early 1970s, in ways interwoven and not easily discerned. As well, the frustrations involved, signaling decline of power, apparently made it politically difficult for the United States to accept a currency devaluation, perceived within the United States as too overtly symbolic of national decline. As Odell notes, however, President Nixon became so sensitive to the disarray within the alliance on the eve of negotiations with Peking and Moscow, that he was impelled to lower his demands from them and to pledge dollar devaluation after all. In short, the U.S. failure to put together a new international monetary regime in the early 1970s appears to have had far-ranging, complex causes, involving politics high and low.

One other aspect of Keohane's causal construct bears commenting upon, and that concerns its perhaps overly unidirectional nature, where a more complex feedback mechanism might be appropriate. After all, the decline of U.S. power has _its_ prior causes too (be they policies or "processes"), one of which may be _inflation_ acting here as an independent variable.

As Odell points out in his Paper 2, inflation accelerated in the United States after 1965 relative to other developed countries (no doubt, as Keohane discusses, in great measure a result of the Johnson administration's attempt to finance the Vietnam war without increased taxation), and in turn the American current account further deteriorated. The eventual result, of course, was devaluation.

According to Susan Strange's Paper 3, the relative value of the currency should not be read as a measure of a nation's economic power; rather, again, the latter has to do with whether a nation can work its will in a variety of decisional contexts. But, if it is not a _measure_ of economic power per se, surely it would appear to be at least one element _determining_ military power and national security, as the recent history of U.S. overseas force deployments and facilities would suggest.

In the early postwar period, the United States was easily able to finance a massive "forward" overseas presence, involving large troop deployments in Europe and the Far East, and an elaborate chain of air and naval basing facilities around the southern rim of Eurasia. Since then, many of these facilities have been lost due to decolonization and/or the radicalization of numerous former western possessions or client states. These adverse trends--coming at a time when the USSR had achieved a significantly enhanced overseas basing network--have been only somewhat mitigated by ongoing technological developments, i.e., longer-range aircraft, aerial refueling, and nuclear-powered ships, which in combination have lessened the quantitative requirements for overseas facilities (Cottrell and Moorer 1977; Hagerty 1977; U.S. Senate, Committee on Foreign Relations 1979).

In recent years, the remnants of a once much more elaborate U.S. overseas basing structure have come under considerable economic as well as political strain. At a time of tight budgets, a falling dollar, and an unfavorable balance of payments, erstwhile U.S. clients such as the Philippines, Spain, Portugal, Turkey, Greece, and others have been demanding increasingly high rents for use of facilities, often in the indirect form of economic and military aid. And recent U.S. attempts to beef up its naval and air presence in the Middle East-Indian Ocean arena have also run into imposing financial demands from Somalia, Kenya, Egypt, and Oman, occasioning some sharp and not yet conclusive bargaining. A $400 million military aid package offered to Pakistan--in the past a not altogether derisory sum--was dismissed as "peanuts," almost an affront; and it was indeed peanuts relative to the kinds of largesse being scattered about the area by Saudi Arabia and some of the other oil producers (New York Times 1980), the former having assumed the earlier U.S. role as provider of economic and military aid to "moderate" regimes such as those in Morocco, Tunisia, Jordan, Somalia, and Sudan.

This nexus of the fall of the dollar and relative inflation to overseas U.S. military power (and more is involved than bases--note the growing problem of military aircraft fuel costs) brings us full circle to the traditional, hoary, geopolitical frameworks of Mackinder, Mahan, Spykman, et al., with their concerns regarding the spatial relationship between the Eurasian heartland and its rimland peripheries (Walters 1974; Gray 1977). That is, the recent, relative, U.S. economic decline--featuring until recently the fall of the value of the dollar--has affected its military position all the more because of the disadvantages labored under by the United States in light of its geographical distance from the primary points of superpower competition, such as the Persian Gulf. While the impact of the "power over distance gradient" may vary according to situation and the state of technology, its basic validity appears rather unarguable.

Professor Keohane comes to an intriguing and certainly alarming conclusion, which also spans the economic and security domains discussed above. Clearly pessimistic about the future of the U.S. economy, he asserts that a dynamic response, some "Schumpeterian innovations" (others refer to "Kondratieff waves"), i.e., the reindustrialization of America and the development of new energy sources, are necessary to halt and reverse these trends (Gilpin 1975, pp. 68-70).

Interestingly, Keohane--in contrast to some "no-growth" proponents, or those resigned to such a fate--implies nonacceptance of redistribution of wealth to less developed countries in consonance with a global "steady state" economy. He looks to a still expanding global pie. If that cannot be brought about, he says, inflation will be very high by the 1990s, but may also "be one of the least of our problems." I take that as a prediction that zero-sum economic conflict between North and South (perhaps also in the intra-North or even intra-OECD cases) will inevitably produce serious international violence, as the West eventually reacts to the economic warfare of the less developed countries. With that merely hinted conclusion, Keohane appears to reveal that he doesn't entirely identify with the recent vogue of "the irrelevance of force," and as such, the number of links in his causal chain appears supplemented by at least one more. The point, indeed, is that "hegemonic stability" unavoidably encompasses and interweaves both economic and military elements.

NOTES

1. If space permitted, one might have probed further into Keohane's analysis of the relationship between regime control and international inflation, particularly regarding the expansion of global liquidity via the Eurodollar market and the "recycling" of OPEC bank investments as loans to the less developed countries. For some relevant analyses, see (Gall 1980) and (Whalen 1980).

2. Gershman (1980) offers a rather acid commentary on the "belief-system" of the then (preelection) "new" U.S. foreign policy elite, which came to power with the Carter administration. That elite is discussed, for better or worse, virtually in the past tense, and the article reflects the view of the "neo-conservative" foreign policy network, which, in large numbers, was to populate foreign policy positions within the Reagan administration.

3. Gilpin (1975), in a chapter entitled "The Nature of Political Economy," offers a detailed analysis of these relationships. Historical perspective on them can be gleaned from Viner (1948) and Viner (1951), specifically, concerning the manner in which the respective values of power and wealth are reciprocally utilized to achieve the other.

4. In the Chace and Ravenal volume (1976), there are various elaborations upon this point, particularly in the chapters by Ronald Steel, Seyom Brown, David Calleo, Andrew Pierre, and Nicholas Wahl. A more recent analysis of the impact of the U.S. power decline on the Western alliance is in Laqueur (1980).

5. For recent data in graphic form, see <u>U.S. News and World Report</u> (1980, pp. 21-23). For a more theoretical treatment of the claimed tendency of alliance leaders to bear disproportionate shares of common defense burdens, see Olson and Zeckhauser (1966).

REJOINDER ● *Robert O. Keohane*

My paper argues, as Professor Darby notes, that plausible and nontrivial causal linkages can be identified between the decline of U.S. power in the issue areas of oil and monetary affairs, on the one hand, and inflation in the advanced industrialized countries, on the other. I also argue, as Professor Darby fails to note, that such an explanation is, by itself, "too neat, and too empty". We must also take into account the direct impact of American policies, particularly American monetary policies, during the late 1960s and 1970s. With this point, Professor Darby seems to be in implicit agreement.

On the second page of his commentary, Professor Darby argues that both my monetary and oil price arguments fail to meet the dual test of plausibility and nontriviality. When he comes to the oil price argument, however, he seems to concur with it--indeed, making the immodest (and exaggerated) claim that my views now "incorporate" his own. He agrees with the plausibility of my argument and says only that it "may fail" on the grounds of triviality, or that whether oil price changes significantly contributed to world inflation "is largely a matter of opinion."

This leaves as Professor Darby's only real objection his critique of my "Bretton Woods argument." Despite his condescending reference to my "schoolboy economics," Professor Darby does not take issue with my economics but rather with my political analysis. He asks whether national monetary growth rates for countries other than the United States would have been lower under the continuation of a Bretton Woods regime than they were under the Smithsonian accords--and concludes that they would not. Unfortunately, Professor Darby chooses the wrong point of comparison with the Smithsonian arrangements. I do not claim that mere continuance of the Bretton Woods regime, in view of the weakness of the United States and the propensities of American monetary policies, would have produced superior results. What I seek to demonstrate, on the contrary, is the importance of the power factor. My argument is that if the United States had been dominant in 1971, as it was in 1944-1949, it could have forced changes in the regime that would have been significantly less inflationary than the Smithsonian arrangements. For example, it could have insisted on greater appreciation of others' currencies, which would have further restrained money supply growth in those countries. As I stated, "The United States had been able to destroy the old exchange rate system, but was unable--given its unwillingness to tighten monetary policy--to quickly reconstruct a new, stable set of arrangements."

Professor Darby and I agree that American monetary policies directly fostered inflation, quite apart from their effects on U.S. power. In my paper, I contend that the decline of U.S. power contributed further to inflation through its impact on oil price rises and on increased rates of money supply growth in the advanced industrialized countries. Professor Darby does not dispute the former argument, although he attempts to minimize its importance. He attacks the latter argument, but erroneously compares the results of the Smithsonian accords with a hypothetical continuation of the Bretton Woods regime, in which U.S. power would have been weak and declining, rather than with the hypothetical alternative that I posed of a more U.S.-dominated set of arrangements. In sum, Professor Darby's critique fails to undermine the plausibility of my argument.

GENERAL DISCUSSION

In the general discussion of Keohane's paper, Susan Strange suggested that Keohane was talking about "will" rather than "power." What Americans perceive as a loss of power is really disillusionment and despair. From a European perspective the United States was under a delusion to begin with concerning its ability to reshape the world. In many ways (both official and through business, finance, etc.) U.S. influence is greater than earlier. The ability to shift adjustment to OPEC onto other countries demonstrates U.S. power, in her view. Keohane responded that Strange is concerned with power consumption, while his analysis examines the longer-run consequences of power accumulation and use.

Much of the rest of the discussion concentrated on the degree to which the OPEC price shock could be a cause of inflation. In particular, did it lead the Federal Reserve to pursue a policy of more rapid money supply growth than would have been the case? Darby commented that estimated Federal Reserve reaction functions show a negative reaction of money supply growth to higher prices and a positive reaction to higher unemployment. He saw no reason to believe the latter would dominate following an oil price shock. Others noted that wage adjustments to such a shock (both nominal and real) complicate the story. It was also pointed out that econometric estimates of reaction functions tend to be quite unstable, making their application to specific incidents questionable. Evidence of a different sort can be found in the testimony of Arthur Burns, at the time, before Congress. He stated that the OPEC action had indeed influenced the Federal Reserve. There was some skepticism among conference participants of the significance of such statements.

PAPER 2 • *John S. Odell*

Bretton Woods and International Political Disintegration: Implications for Monetary Diplomacy

I. INTRODUCTION

The Bretton Woods international monetary regime was, among other things, an example of a fairly high degree of international political integration.[1] Between 1970 and 1973 this regime disintegrated as the result of a spasmodic series of actions by national governments and private actors. The international monetary system went through a conflictual monetary transition to a much weaker set of rules and procedures for interstate policy coordination. Granting that basic changes in the effective rules of the monetary game were unavoidable, it was nonetheless possible to move the system through a smoother transition to a new regime embodying a higher level of mutual commitment among states. My purpose here will be to analyze why the major states failed to realize their common interest in such a transition. A look back at this major transformation may yield valuable conclusions about the effectiveness of alternative strategies of monetary diplomacy.

The saga is now fairly familiar. In 1970 Canada abandoned its obligation to maintain its currency at parity. In May 1971 West Germany also began a temporary unilateral upward float, provoking conflict with its European Community (EC) partners. In August 1971 the U.S. government dramatically reversed its domestic and international policies, suspending dollar-gold convertibility, slapping a surcharge on imports, and demanding a substantial depreciation of the system's key currency. Negotiations, culminating in the Smithsonian conference in December 1971, partially restored the Bretton Woods foundation with a return to pegged exchange rates. The U.S. dollar was devalued by approximately 8 percent against OECD currencies, but Washington declined to resume dollar defense.

In the fall of 1972 the United States laid on the table a blue print for new adjustment rules, and international discussion got under way in earnest. Meanwhile, the pound sterling had already been floated again under pressure. In late January 1973 a capital flight from Italy to Switzerland touched off another dollar crisis. This crisis was met first by central bank intervention, and then by a second devaluation of the dollar plus a floating of the yen in February. At that point officials and market operators were in widespread agreement that the U.S. dollar was no longer overvalued, and was possibly even undervalued. Nevertheless the markets were almost immediately swamped by another huge wave of net dollar selling. In March, fourteen major financial powers met in Paris and certified what German Finance Minister Helmut Schmidt termed "the end of Bretton Woods." The only agreement, apart from the European snake, was a minimal one of all to consult in order to prevent exchange markets from becoming "disorderly." They later continued their discussions aimed at a revised set of monetary rules for the long term.

Most expected the collapse to be temporary. Accelerated and uneven worldwide inflation was becoming visible, however, and later in 1973 OPEC suddenly quadrupled world oil prices. In fact the new mixed international monetary regime, elaborated in the second amendment to the International Monetary Fund (IMF) Articles of Agreement, was more than temporary. Its basic patterns, already in practice in 1973, have continued with only marginal changes.

Some elements of this "collapse" were improvements and were probably inevitable. This transition made the international monetary regime more flexible, relying more on frequent exchange rate change as a means of adjusting payments imbalances. Pressures to initiate adjustment measures are now more symmetrical between deficit and surplus states. Evidence to date strongly suggests that major exchange rate changes since 1970 have made important contributions to current account adjustment, though adjustment has tended to lag substantially.[2]

Under flexible rates, governments have resorted less to direct trade and exchange restrictions than they would have if they had been attempting to maintain fixed rates. Despite relatively hard times, governments have generally avoided the competitive depreciations and other forms of intense conflict that accompanied floating during the 1930s depression. Surely the monetary instabilities and disputes of the 1970s have been due less to the international monetary regime per se than to other causes--domestic policies, sharply changing real oil prices, internationally diverging inflation rates, and differing cyclical positions. Thus at least given this highly uncertain environment, the new regime must be considered an improvement over the old one in some respects.

But the new regime is less than optimal, from the standpoint of each member state, including the United States. Each of the IMF states would have gained from a smoother transition and a stronger international monetary organization. The new regime is probably economically wasteful. Under haphazard floating, exchange rate movements seem to overshoot and to oscillate wastefully during short periods. The real adjustment effects of depreciation seem to be offset to some extent by resulting price inflation in the home country. Furthermore, the transition by collapse rather than by negotiated agreement was probably inflationary, as Keohane suggests in Paper 1.

The actual transition also unnecessarily wounded attitudes of mutual trust among the major Organization of Economic Cooperation and Development (OECD) governments, attitudes that are decisive for realizing wide common interests in international economic relations, as well as in military-political affairs. Partly as a result, these governments were unable to agree during the 1970s on an equally strong new international monetary regime. Indeed the new regime is close to a free-for-all. Under the new Article IV and IMF guidelines for floating, no exchange rate practice whatever is prohibited specifically (except denominating a par value in gold). States have bound themselves only to collaborate with the IMF, to aim for "orderly economic growth with reasonable price stability," to "intervene in the exchange market if necessary to counter disorderly conditions," and to "avoid manipulating exchange rates or the international monetary system in order to prevent effective balance of payments adjustment or to gain an unfair competitive advantage over other members."[3] All the key terms were left vague. The IMF was given authority to exercise "firm surveillance" over exchange rate practices, but in fact is left without precise standards for judging behavior and without sanctions for violators. In general, countries' relative obligations to initiate adjustment remain unclear and thus remain grounds for repeated conflict.

The period since "the end of Bretton Woods" has seen several conflicts over exchange rates, even if none so far has exceeded moderate intensity. As the dollar sank through its "third devaluation" during March-July 1973, there were heated criticisms in Europe and talk in France of slapping a surcharge on American exports. The British government was accused of competitive objectives during the mid-1970s decline of the pound. Americans complained to Japan for resisting appreciation, amid continuing general criticism of Japan in the United States. The Carter administration was attacked for "talking down the dollar" during 1977 and 1978. Monetary disputes were reportedly among the issues causing a decline in European willingness to follow U.S. policies generally, including military-political ones. The European Community redoubled its efforts to form its own monetary zone, and there was even discussion in West Germany of neutralism.

The present monetary regime relies heavily on ad hoc, informal understandings among groups of countries. The danger of informal restraints is that they might break under pressure in the future. In general, without a more precise framework of rules, states are less likely to realize the collective good of avoiding mutually harmful conflict. Each is more likely to yield to the temptation to beggar its neighbors when it and its neighbors have refused to join in renouncing such measures specifically in advance. Each separate state is then rational to ask, Why should we restrain our quest for gain at the expense of other states, if no one else is prepared to assure comparable restraint? The weaker the regime, the more it permits day to day outcomes to depend on the exercise of power, and hence the less legitimate the regime will appear to the weaker parties. The less their attachment to it, the more they in turn will be willing to politicize day to day transactions when they see an opportunity. Selective cooperative arrangements also risk alienating excluded third parties. For all these reasons the present weak regime also may not be politically stable.[4]

Might it have happened otherwise? Consider the following imaginary history, sketched with shameless reliance on the benefits of hindsight. A counterfactual scenario may prove a useful device against which to analyze the actual regime change. Suppose that in 1969 at the conclusion of the negotiations to create and distribute the first Special Drawing Rights (SDRs), the United States proposes to institutionalize a high level effort to reform the international monetary regime, perhaps through something like the proposed IMF Interim Council. The United States decides to continue its international monetary strategy of seeking multilateral agreement at the political level, moving from the liquidity problem to the adjustment problem. The strategy is to propose a grand package deal, entailing U.S. concessions to its major partners in Western Europe, Japan, and Canada, in order to secure from them its primary demand. The United States will accept some new constraint substantially limiting its freedom to finance its deficits with liabilities, if the other powers will agree to a new mechanism obliging surplus countries to take prompter adjustment measures. In effect, if newer surplus states are willing to commit themselves to additional obligations for maintaining a cooperative system, by adjusting more promptly, then the United States would give up some of the privilege of sole leader on the liquidity side.

The negotiations are lengthy. Discussions of exchange rate change make currency markets nervous (though no more disorderly than they in fact were.) At some point either a discrete devaluation of the dollar or a period of floating is necessary, and perhaps a suspension of dollar-gold convertibility as well until some agreement to deal with the "overhang" is reached. The interstate bargaining is necessarily tough, since it involves trade shares as well as disagreements about the relative dangers of inflation and unemployment. But this struggle among allies transpires in the context of a joint ministerial-level effort to remold the monetary system to fit new long-term realities. A clear signal that the United States itself is prepared to make concessions makes it highly uncomfortable for Japan and Western allies to refuse to compromise.

    A package deal along these lines is therefore accepted. The new regime includes, for example, some obligation for each state to redeem its currency with reserves and some accepted scheme for optimum exchange rate flexibility. The salient features of the exchange rate scheme are that it is more flexible than rates had been in recent years, and that through it governments nevertheless remain wedded to the principle that exchange rates are a matter for joint decision. Thus, concretely, if an adjustable peg regime were preferred, it might operate according to reserve indicators or a crawling peg rule. If a managed floating basis were preferred, something like the "reference rate"[5] proposal might provide a minimal constraint of joint decision making. After the new regime is in place, it is perhaps subjected to shocks or strains. Whatever adjustments are necessary, the existence of an established procedure for joint decision making provides protection against an unraveling of conflict.

    Why, then, did the Bretton Woods regime collapse as it did? Why did the major states fail to realize their common interest in a cooperative transition to a new system stronger than the actual one of the 1970s? This essay will first point briefly to three fundamental causes, now fairly widely acknowledged. But these fundamental factors are not sufficient to explain the actual outcome. One must then examine the proximate causes, which were largely intellectual and subject to some policy control: the preferences of national leaders, miscalculations about official and market reactions, and the revolving interaction of policies and expectations. Attention will be directed especially to U.S. policy during the early Nixon administration.[6]

II. FUNDAMENTAL CAUSES OF REGIME CHANGE

Opening and Integration of International Capital Markets

    One background reason for some regime change was the reopening, integration, and growth of international capital markets. With the relaxation of wartime controls in the late 1950s and the spread of multinational industries and Eurobanking, private financial actors controlled increasing capabilities to shift funds quickly between countries when they came to expect exchange rate changes. It is now widely recognized, as it was not at the time, that these private market capabilities were by the early 1970s sufficient to overwhelm exchange controls and central bank intervention in cases where markets no longer had confidence that an exchange rate peg would hold. Thus, given that fundamental price indicators in different countries diverged during the 1970s, it is difficult to imagine how a par value regime could have been kept orderly without at least provision for more frequent exchange rate changes and wider bands to increase speculative risk.

Deficit in the Reserve Center

Another of the fundamental causes of regime change, given the system's reliance in practice upon the U.S. dollar as reserve currency, was the development of a persistent large deficit in the U.S. payments position. Robert Triffin pointed out the inherent dilemma of a reserve currency system, and in response governments created the SDR in the 1960s to deal, at least in principle, with half of that dilemma--the liquidity shortage that might result if the United States failed to run a substantial deficit. The opposite risk of running a large deficit, the United States maintained at the time, would have to be avoided by determined U.S. and allied action to defend the dollar.

Nevertheless, after 1965 inflation in the center country accelerated relative to other major countries. The U.S. current account, already insufficient for overall balance, deteriorated. U.S. costs and prices gradually moved out of line at existing exchange rates,[7] and by the summer of 1971 it was apparent that the United States would have in that year its first yearly trade deficit since 1893. Thus the Bretton Woods rules were presented with a serious challenge--a fundamental disequilibrium in the center country. Not only was the American dollar overvalued vis-a-vis a number of currencies, but several of the others were also out of line with each other. These payments trends gave rise to periodic and increasing disorders in the currency and gold markets, making it increasingly costly for governments to avoid a major exchange rate realignment, whether by negotiation or separate action. Such a dollar realignment would in itself constitute a regime change.

Diffusion of Economic Power

A third fundamental cause of regime change--though not necessarily of a spasmodic collapse--was the long-term shift in the underlying structure of economic power capabilities among states. The Bretton Woods system had been established under conditions of extraordinary centralization of economic and military power resources in the United States. The increasing diffusion in this power structure undermined certain aspects of the Bretton Woods arrangements, and also made certain alternative regimes unlikely.

By the early 1960s, a diffusion of economic capabilities among the industrial capitalist states was becoming evident, and by 1970 the trend was even clearer with Japan's rapid growth. Over this period the earlier large asymmetry favoring the United States eroded, though to a lesser degree than is sometimes suggested in the United States.

Increasingly the structure was becoming one of recovered great powers and rising peripheral states, yet all still linked to a relatively self-sufficient superpower at the center. From 1950 to 1970 the six members of the European Community increased their share of world gross product from 11 percent to 15 percent; Japan raised her share of output from 1.5 percent to 6 percent. Even so, in 1970 the United States alone still produced 30 percent of the total, down from 39 percent in 1950. The U.S. share of world exports hardly declined at all, from 16 percent in 1950 to 15 percent in 1960, and to 14 percent in 1970.[8] Many foreign governments also remained very much aware of the importance of the U.S. market for their own exports. Actually, the American share of the rest of the world's exports was higher in 1970 (17 percent) than in 1960 (14 percent).[9] The U.S. dollar had no significant rivals as a usable international currency, commercially or officially. Perhaps most important, because the U.S. economy was much less penetrated by international transactions than those of most of its partners, each of their economies remained far more vulnerable to American decisions than vice versa.

Parallel changes were evolving in the global military structure. The U.S. relative power base was reduced as the Soviet Union gradually improved its strategic forces, and as imperial domination of less developed countries became more difficult. Here too, however, the diffusion was limited. Each of America's major power allies still had little realistic alternative except dependence on the United States for protection from attack. This dependence was especially sharp for that country with which much of the monetary maladjustment was concentrated--Japan. The security arena and continued Japanese belief in their U.S. connection gave Washington additional structural leverage.

One implication of this power diffusion was to make it somewhat more likely that the United States would insist that its recovered allies with payments surpluses accept a new regime assigning them more of the political costs of adjusting the common open system. When the Bretton Woods arrangements were created, the superpower was a surplus country, and under those arrangements pressures to take official action to promote or permit international adjustment fell more heavily on deficit countries than on surplus countries. Now that the superpower was a deficit country, and might continue to be, this earlier regime was no longer quite in accord with power realities.

One might also have expected that the erosion of American relative strength would make the U.S. government slightly less likely to lead the way to an equally strong new regime, in the sense of initiating high-level negotiations by offering the first potential concession. The "hegemony theory of stability" argues that generally states are more likely to realize their common interests in a hegemonic structure dominated by a single state than in a more diffused or balanced structure (Kindleberger 1973; Krasner 1976).

The data just presented show, however, that in this case the erosion had been limited and the United States retained a substantial stake in a stable world monetary order. As far as the international power structure is concerned, such an American reform initiative would still not have been surprising. The United States retained impressive sources of international influence for protecting its interests in bargaining over a new monetary regime. And the United States remained the only state likely to succeed as initiator of a negotiated regime adaptation. The decline in U.S. relative power was too small to account for the regime's disintegration.[10]

The power diffusion implied, on the other side, that Japan and continental Europe were now more able to resist American policies and to extract concessions before agreeing to compromise arrangements. America's relative invulnerability and influence nevertheless continued to present these allies with strong incentives to bargain cooperatively in response to a U.S. initiative.

The effects of this power structure manifested themselves in the allies' behavior during two phases of recent experience, the first being the international liquidity negotiations of the 1960s. Continental European governments vetoed Robert Roosa's early ideas for harnessing the strength of their currencies to the dollar.[11] Most were also cool to the American proposal beginning in 1965 to generate additional liquidity through a new synthetic reserve asset. Nevertheless, in response to a sustained campaign by the U.S. Treasury Secretary, the Group of Ten countries were persuaded during 1967 and 1968 to accept a contingency SDR plan, even though the U.S. balance of payments was deteriorating sharply during 1967. America's partners insisted upon American concessions, and the United States eventually agreed.

America's allies further demonstrated their incentives to abide by U.S. leadership in the March 1968 agreement not to buy more gold from private markets, and their restraint in converting dollars to gold thereafter. After 1969 the U.S. deficit plunged, yet surplus governments deluged with dollars were unwilling on the whole to use their formal authority to pressure the United States by converting dollars. During the first eight months of 1971, U.S. liquid liabilities to foreign governments swelled by no less than $21 billion, while gold sales to foreign governments came to only $843 million, half of which was to France for repayment to the IMF.[12] In contrast to 1931, it was not a heavy exercise of a gold weapon that caused the regime to collapse.[13]

This international power analysis recalls the truism that the interstate system itself, so long as it consists of sovereign states without higher authority to protect them, brings the units inherently into conflict with each other. The system gives the rational statesman incentives to enhance his state's influence relative to other states, and also its reputation for influence (often misleadingly called "prestige"). Interstate relations necessarily have their zero-sum arenas as well as areas for joint gain. The zero-sum arenas always make policy coordination chancy and invite escalating, mutually harmful conflict. In the present case the major surplus and deficit governments also found themselves with a direct conflict of interest concerning domestic politics. Each chief executive stood to generate some domestic opposition in the short run if he acted to initiate international adjustment. Waiting for a foreign government to take the action was a way to push this short-run political headache abroad, even if his own economy would feel some of the real effects of adjustment regardless.

These conflicts of interest were not insurmountable, however. There are ways to offset domestic political criticism. And these states also shared notable common interests, including reducing immediate instability in currency markets, and preserving a framework of policy integration for the long term. No government preferred that Bretton Woods disintegrate in disorder--least of all those of Europe, the developing countries, or Japan. Even in the United States, as we will see in a moment, the preponderant school of informed opinion actually opposed a floating rate regime and preferred preserving most of the essence of Bretton Woods. Moreover, almost all the major financial powers were military allies as well. As usual, the structure of power and "interests," short-term and long-term, was sufficiently complex and ambiguous to permit genuine differences of diagnosis and to leave scope for policy choices.

III. PROXIMATE CAUSES OF POLITICAL DISINTEGRATION

Benign Neglect

The increasing economic integration of international capital markets, the overvaluation of the dollar, and the diffusion in the international economic power structure were fundamental causes for at least major modifications in the Bretton Woods regime. But these factors did not make political disintegration inevitable. More proximate reasons for the actual collapse, as opposed to the hypothetical history, are found in the ideas that defined the U.S. national interest during the Nixon administration, and the policy choices made in Washington. The international system did not travel a smoother negotiated transition largely because the United States did not lead in that direction. U.S. policy was in part the result of explicit miscalculation, some of the effects of which have been felt by the United States itself.

The early Nixon administration, to summarize, allowed the previous high-level monetary reform effort to lapse. From abroad the United States increasingly seemed to be sending conflicting signals in its international monetary diplomacy. Washington eschewed both high-level promises and high-level threats, and implicitly relied most on the operation of international market forces to bring about a major adaptation in the international monetary system. This depoliticized policy, like Robert Roosa's early ideas, ran aground on the changed power structure, producing instead an interstate stalemate.

To point to ideas reigning in Washington is not necessarily to argue that the United States sought and expected floating exchange rates. During the late 1960s and early 1970s most informed Americans shared the transnational belief that floating rates might well be accompanied by commercial and financial disruptions like those of the 1920s and 1930s, or that at best they would not be optimal. Floating rates were also seen by many as "isolationist," a retrogression from a generation's promising efforts to nurture a fragile world order. Never before generalized floating became a reality in March 1973 did the U.S. government reach a decision to advocate such a regime. At the outset of the Nixon administration, most U.S. officials publicly favored the preservation of the par value framework.[14]

At least one American official preferred renewing the high-level reform campaign. C. Fred Bergsten, economics deputy to National Security Adviser Henry Kissinger, campaigned vigorously within the administration in 1969 and 1970 for a reform aimed at more flexible exchange rates and substitution of the SDR for the dollar as reserve currency. Bergsten was convinced that maintaining the dollar's reserve role was contrary to the purely American interest as well as the world's interest (Bergsten 1975). Later, in late July 1971 Federal Reserve adviser Robert Solomon also sent a memorandum to Fed Chairman Arthur Burns and Treasury Under Secretary Paul Volcker with a proposed American initiative to be made at the 1971 IMF annual meeting. With the purpose of engineering a concerted revaluation by other industrial countries, this plan would have had the United States offering to negotiate a reform in which it would give up the reserve role of the dollar (Solomon 1977, pp. 183-84). A different bold departure was also recommended to President Nixon by one of his closest advisers. This adviser told Nixon in late 1968 that he ought to devalue the dollar against gold upon taking office.[15]

Several economic advisers counseled that bold high-level initiatives could be and should be avoided in favor of reliance on market forces. Hendrik Houthakker, member of the President's Council of Economic Advisers, was one of the most active internal advocates of the idea of "benign neglect." In this view the United States would make its greatest contribution to the world economy by operating its domestic policies so as to stabilize the home economy, removing capital controls, and remaining passive with regard to its payments deficit. Then if surplus countries chose to maintain undervalued exchange rates and accumulate dollars, this was considered acceptable to the United States. But Houthakker and others were convinced that the dollar was fundamentally overvalued and would have to be depreciated. He expected that the pressure of market forces under American "benign neglect" would force surplus countries to appreciate against the dollar within perhaps a year, without high-level negotiations or concessions by the United States. If so, a major regime adjustment--dollar depreciation--could be brought about while preserving the par value framework with the dollar at its center.[16]

America's senior diplomatic strategists, President Nixon and Henry Kissinger, presented with a range of options, assigned international monetary reform a very low priority. They neither accepted the more active options, nor did they ever make a high-level decision to implement "benign neglect" as a coherent strategy intended to depreciate the dollar, according to available evidence. Rather the President evidently relegated the issue to middle-level officials in a manner that permitted different official schools of thought each to believe that its diagnosis was operative.

Kissinger and Nixon devoted themselves to their global strategy for basing a "stable structure of peace" on the U.S.-Soviet-Chinese relationship. The two regarded international economic problems as "Quartermaster Corps stuff," as one observer puts it, and they largely neglected these until 1973.[17] In addition, they kept close personal control over high priority issues. As far as dollar devaluation was concerned, Nixon no doubt shared the common Washington fear that any president and treasury secretary who devalued the dollar "would be tarred and feathered," in the words of a former high treasury official. Domestic political fears delayed that action.[18]

In practice, U.S. external monetary policy became bifurcated into two conflicting lines. On the whole the Treasury continued to send orthodox signals to other states. Initial domestic economic policy produced a budget surplus and then record high interest rates. In their public statements the Treasury leadership reiterated American adherence to the Bretton Woods regime and support for the dollar, and cast doubts on schemes for greater exchange rate flexibility. Asked about wider bands for currency fluctuation, Under Secretary for Monetary Affairs Paul Volcker replied that there had been "a lot of discussion (of these ideas) in academic circles, and that's where they can stay."[19] Far from demanding that foreign governments give serious thought to fundamental monetary system changes, before August 15, 1971, even Treasury Secretary John Connally consistently denied that "our international financial problems can be taken care of by some sort of monetary magic."[20] In a speech in Munich in May 1971, three weeks after West Germany floated the deutsche mark, Connally warned: "The danger is plain. To revert to the use of exchange rates as a supplementary tool of domestic policy is fraught with danger to the essential stability and sustainability of the system as a whole."[21]

Meanwhile, though, "benign neglect" pulled other aspects of American policy in a second direction. The Nixon administration began to relax controls on capital outflows. In 1970 the Federal Reserve allowed monetary growth to accelerate and interest rates to begin declining. When a huge overall external deficit reemerged, the administration refrained from introducing new balance of payments programs. While Volcker was raising doubts, Houthakker was traveling through Europe gathering support for discussions of greater but limited flexibility.

Middle-level U.S. and other officials led such a discussion within the IMF Executive Board in 1969 and 1970. It might be argued that this constituted an attempt by Washington to lead toward a new regime. But the content of American flexibility proposals, as seen by foreign political leaders, amounted to an invitation for others to make political concessions while the United States made none. Despite the long-term erosion of U.S. relative size and influence, the proposals would have preserved the unique status of the United States and the dollar. The U.S. dollar would remain immovable while the others did the flexing. In the presence of an American deficit, Washington would remain passive while the political onus of exchange rate change fell more frequently on other governments. U.S. officials sought this agreement from foreign governments without showing any interest in discussing new constraints on their own unique freedom to run deficits and increase the world's supply of dollars. And this was during a time when the United States was not seen as succeeding in stabilizing the domestic value of the dollar, one of the key premises in the rationale for a passive U.S. role in the world.

Above all, the American President sent no signals to his counterparts abroad indicating that this technical-level debate involved a matter on which the United States was eager to bargain seriously. Nor did the top U.S. leadership invest any political resources in achieving a major one-time realignment before August 15. Instead they threw most of their foreign economic policy effort into a long campaign to extract from Japan restraints on exports of manmade textiles. The United States never attempted to negotiate a yen revaluation/dollar devaluation with Japan before resorting to an import surcharge.[22]

The result of the bifurcated, early Nixon administration external monetary policy was an interstate stalemate. Major foreign governments were no longer so weak and dependent on the United States as they had once been, and they politely brushed aside American schemes without American concessions. They called on Washington to deal with its own payments problem.[23] No reform was adopted in the IMF. By July 1971, despite the floating of the Canadian dollar, the German mark, and the Dutch guilder, the U.S. dollar had depreciated less than 3 percent.[24] A depoliticized strategy of relying on market forces to accomplish a major adaptation within the par value framework had produced only meager results. Meanwhile, a period favorable for negotiation--while the dollar was temporarily buoyed by tight money in the United States--had elapsed. By mid-1971 the deterioration of the U.S. trade balance was becoming pronounced, and accompanying capital outflows produced an extreme overall deficit.

In the midst of this stalemate, the United States reversed course dramatically. On August 15 President Nixon attacked the inflation problem with a wage-price freeze, and the unemployment problem with tax cuts. Dollar-gold convertibility was suspended. Washington might have used these measures as part of a bargaining strategy seeking currency realignment. The incomes policy could have been described in private negotiations as a response to foreign government pleas for the United States to initiate adjustment, perhaps accompanied by a hint of willingness to devalue the dollar as part of a satisfactory realignment package. If necessary, Nixon and Connally could have added an explicit threat to impose an import surcharge otherwise. In short, one could imagine an attempt at traditional carrot-stick diplomacy. In any case, Nixon and Connally refused to negotiate immediately or to suggest an acceptable package, and they flatly refused to devalue the dollar "one iota." The United States demanded large revaluations from foreign governments, and slapped a surcharge on exports to the United States until they complied. U.S. international monetary diplomacy suddenly switched from no-carrots and no-sticks to fait accompli and a big stick. And having jarred one of the pillars of the Bretton Woods framework, the United States declined to suggest any new long-term framework of mutual obligations.

The top leadership of the United States chose a unilateral demarche now rather than a multilateral bargaining initiative for two main reasons. John Connally, the new Treasury Secretary, believed that foreign countries were hurting American business and taking unfair commercial advantage. At a time when few were saying so, Connally perceived a fundamental international shift of economic strength. He argued that shock treatment would be necessary in order to extract the necessary exchange rate concessions abroad, as well as to change attitudes in Washington itself. He reasoned that to present an American initiative toward a compromise would encourage the other governments to combine against the United States and shave the potential American short-run gain. In Connally the President had selected a person unrepresentative of the relevant informed public, in that Connally came to office without a strong predisposition to preserve the Bretton Woods monetary system.[25] Several other participating American officials opposed using the import surcharge. Arthur Burns, chairman of the Federal Reserve, opposed closing the gold window and spoke up tenaciously for a less unilateral diplomatic strategy based on greater trust in allied willingness to bargain. The President, again presented with conflicting views, approved Connally's entire package. A second reason for unilateralism involved domestic political expectations. As explained by a Connally associate, Connally and Nixon were also concerned about possible domestic criticism for abandoning defense of the dollar. A high visibility campaign casting blame on foreigners could blunt these attacks.

The response for four months was continued stalemate. The other financial great powers--especially Japan and France--refused to accept sweeping American demands, now accompanied by the sudden public resort to economic coercion, as long as the United States refused to take the lead by offering equally visible concessions to them. They did feel compelled by the pressure of imbalanced markets and the American jolt to permit their currencies to rise grudgingly during the deadlock. In time President Nixon decided that the political costs of continuing the monetary stalemate would exceed the economic gains for the United States. Nixon was sensitive to the marked disarray in the alliances and the prospect of further fragmentation and retaliation, on the eve of his negotiations in Peking and Moscow.[26] The United States lowered its demands and pledged to devalue the dollar after all and to withdraw the import surcharge. When the United States decided to make explicit concessions, the other major governments agreed to revaluations that gave the United States a dollar depreciation of approximately 8 to 9 percent against OECD currencies.[27] Pegged exchange rates were restored with slightly wider bands, but the United States did not resume convertibility or any obligation to defend the new rates. The Smithsonian conference left long-range questions unanswered--namely, how future international imbalances were to be adjusted, and what was to be the future role of the dollar.

Allied Calculations and Miscalculations

The United States was the only single state with the power to bring the major financial powers together in a compromise adaptation of the monetary regime that would have preserved the prevailing degree of political integration. Germany, France, or Japan, for example, had less capacity to shape Washington's policies than vice versa. Moreover, the accepted international rules legitimated a presumption that adjustment would be initiated by the deficit, rather than the surplus, country.

Still, an American initiative was not a sufficient condition for such a coordinated transition. The official beliefs and behavior of major U.S.

allies and their interaction with American policy became a final proximate reason for the collapse. For present purposes I will concentrate on Japan and France. Japan had a large and rapidly growing payments surplus, and her bilateral surplus with the United States accounted for the single largest share by far of the dollar's global deficit. France was and is able to play a prominent role diplomatically, especially because of her ability to shape EC policies.

U.S. allies' governments sat on the opposite side of this complex, mixed motive game, having some interests in conflict with those of Washington, but others in common. For example, Japan as a whole stood to reap the familiar real consumption gains from revaluation. Many IMF countries would suffer from the potential international economic disorder and foreign policy friction generated by the failure of adjustment. All shared an interest in avoiding a collapse of the par value regime itself, or so most certainly thought. The policies of Japan, France, and others reflected two miscalculations perhaps as great as those of Washington.

First, while many allies had earlier shown willingness to bargain in response to American high-level initiatives, and to refrain from triggering a collapse, in the early 1970s several of them did little to encourage a Washington initiative toward reform of the adjustment process that might have preserved a coordinated exchange rate regime. Allied power was rising, and in retrospect their governments might have done more to ease the stalemate that provided grounds for American unilateralism. In 1969 Hendrik Houthakker asked the EC director of international monetary affairs what the European response would be if the United States followed the rules and devalued the dollar. "He stated flatly that all European currencies would be devalued by the same percentage on the same day" (Houthakker 1978, p. 54). In response to the admittedly partial, technical-level, U.S. initiatives on behalf of limited flexibility, Japan and France consistently and firmly resisted such ideas for encouraging strong currencies to appreciate. The Japanese even refused to discuss the issue bilaterally at the technical level.[28] Japan was slow to relax import barriers despite its strong current account. Thus before August 15 U.S. allies not only responded to but also influenced U.S. behavior, and helped to undermine those in Washington who argued for negotiated adaptation.

Second, once Washington shifted to an active policy of adjustment and showed willingness to bargain, Japan and Western Europe fought hard for every percentage point. Canada had been floating since 1970 and was joined in May 1971 by West Germany and the Netherlands. But France adopted a two-tier market and prevented the commercial franc from appreciating much, putting a drag on the adjustment of the deutsche mark vis-a-vis the dollar. In November 1971 Japan's Finance Minister Mikio Mizuta was still insisting that the yen could not be revalued more than 5 percent, while Secretary Connally was demanding 25 percent. In retrospect this bargaining appears shortsighted. Fourteen months after the Smithsonian meeting European and Japanese officials found themselves approving a further 10 percent dollar devaluation and a further yen float. Japan, France, and others used their power in a way that made the dollar's adjustment a prolonged, piecemeal affair. If the U.S. position had prevailed in 1971, a one-time depreciation of 12 to 15 percent would have taken place. It is conceivable that Washington might then have been persuaded to support the new rates. In any case currency market expectations might then have been favorable and stable long enough to permit the negotiation of a regime providing greater flexibility under an agreed-upon framework. As it was, market operators saw parities declared, challenged, and abandoned repeatedly. Spasmodic adjustment destabilized currency markets. In the end the allies got not only revaluation but collapse.

Several factors, some already suggested, help explain the allies' policies. One was the traditional attitude among financial officials of many countries, and the IMF, that exchange rate change should be discouraged in general. According to this predisposition, if countries avoid improvident domestic policies there will be less need for exchange rate change; reforms that encourage exchange flexibility would enlarge the temptation to "sin." Another factor was the belief that in this case the imbalance was due to American errors, along with the U.S. refusal to acknowledge responsibility to act before August 1971.[29] The public, unilateral character of Nixon-Connally diplomacy then probably stiffened resistance for a time.

Governments of France and Japan may have deliberately preferred maintaining an external surplus and an undervalued currency, together with capital controls and other tools of their more statist systems.[30] In Japan the view was widespread that the country remained less than fully developed and was of course critically dependent upon imports, and hence exports. Memories of the struggle to overcome payments deficits were still fresh (little attention was given to the fact that yen appreciation would also aid exports to the extent that they were composed of imported inputs).[31] The government insisted that it intended to reduce the surplus that swelled in 1970, but preferred to do so by relaxing controls on imports and capital exports, and reducing export subsidies. In June 1971 a new "Eight Point Program for Avoiding Yen Revaluation" was announced. The government and private economists also maintained that the surplus would be reduced as Japan moved from recession to recovery in 1971 and 1972.[32] Japan's exchange controls were still formidable, but Japanese officials reportedly underestimated the difficulties of insulating against speculative inflows, for example, through leads and lags, in an integrated and nervous international capital market.[33]

Finally, relations <u>among</u> these countries impeded a multilateral settlement, particularly one relying on separate moves without a joint negotiation. Surplus countries like Germany and Japan were reluctant to yield much to Washington without some assurance that other surplus countries would also appreciate against the dollar to some extent. Also the European Community countries had launched their plan for economic and monetary union in 1969. Their representatives cited this internal effort to stabilize exchange rates as a reason why they opposed efforts toward greater flexibility in the IMF.

U.S. Reform Initiative

A year after the August bombshell the United States came forward with a comprehensive plan for renovating the battered monetary regime, a plan that would have entailed fairly precise mutual obligations.[34] It presupposed a par value framework, but one in which reserve changes would trigger obligations of surplus as well as deficit states to take adjustment measures. A state could choose to float, but it would then have to meet "more stringent standards of behavior in other respects." As to reserves, "the SDR would increase in importance." The United States did not encourage the prohibition of the dollar's reserve role, but did indicate a willingness to resume on-demand convertibility as part of the deal, and perhaps to arrange for existing dollar reserve holdings to be converted into SDRs. These were signs of a serious intention to bargain about long-term arrangements. The U.S.

proposal would also have changed international institutions so that they would bring high-level officials from national capitals together on a regular basis to keep the new system working.

But when the short-term crisis came in January-February 1973, and U.S. allies quickly agreed to a further dollar devaluation, the United States did not then act in accordance with the notion of a modified pegged rate system. After achieving the symmetrical sort of adjustment they sought, and a dollar exchange rate they believed was sustainable, the U.S. officials nonetheless made a point of announcing that the government had undertaken no obligations to support the new rate by foreign exchange market intervention. In fact, in the same statement the Treasury Secretary also announced the decision to phase out capital export restrictions. Furthermore, these moves were taken against the background of a domestic economic policy that raised questions about future price stability in America. On January 11, 1973, the new Nixon administration had unexpectedly relaxed price controls. Before lifting the lid, the government had also accelerated monetary growth.[35] Once again the United States seemed to be sending conflicting signals.

The interstate bargaining process was again part of the reason. For the United States to intervene heavily during this crisis would imply temporary restoration of convertibility. American negotiators regarded convertibility as their major bargaining chip in the reform talks, but these talks were not yet to the point of agreement. Perhaps more important, by 1972 President Nixon had given the monetary reins to a senior decision group dominated by "ideological floaters," in the words of one of them. Their personal ideological predispositions inclined them away from central bank intervention or pledges to defend rates.

After the second dollar devaluation it would have been difficult to sustain a stable pegged system much longer with any policies. Much time had been lost without the creation of a legitimate international regime for greater but coordinated flexibility. Parities had been challenged and abandoned spasmodically too many times. Thus, major governments, through their collective action, helped bring about an outcome desired by few of them.

Soon, furthermore, came the oil price explosion, adding to the greater uncertainty of accelerating worldwide inflation. It is possible that any pegged system would have given way to a managed floating system of some variety, if other things had remained equal. That is, to repeat the earlier qualification, policies other than external monetary ones to deal more successfully with inflation and energy may have also been necessary to avoid a weakening of the world monetary regime.

IV. CONCLUSION

The Bretton Woods international monetary regime was one of history's examples of a fairly high degree of international political integration or policy coordination. During the early 1970s this regime disintegrated to a substantial degree, and was replaced by much weaker rules and procedures accompanied by selective, informal intergovernmental coordination.

With the benefit of hindsight we may conclude that substantial modification of the Bretton Woods rules was highly likely, but that political disintegration was hardly inevitable. The reopening, integration, and growth of international capital markets made greater flexibility difficult to avoid. The overvaluation of the world's key currency posed a unique challenge. A third fundamental cause of some regime change, though not necessarily of a spasmodic collapse, was the long-term diffusion of economic power among the major states. Bretton Woods did not collapse because U.S. "interests" clearly called for smashing it. But the power diffusion did modify "interests" and it did increase the capacity of Japan and continental Europe to influence American policy. And the very nature of the interstate system gave all these governments certain conflicts of interest.

A more proximate cause of the actual political disintegration is found in the policies followed by key surplus countries. Failing to foresee the actual alternative, Japan's leadership held firmly to existing exchange rate policy. France and other states were cool to American suggestions for reform of the international adjustment process, thus helping to undermine those in Washington inclined to interpret America's interest as requiring multilateral compromise negotiations. These countries also limited the size of the first dollar depreciation.

But U.S. allies remained far more dependent on the superpower than the United States was on them. The most potent proximate cause of the disintegration was that American senior leaders did not attempt to lead a negotiated transition to a new strong regime. Early in the Nixon administration senior officials with the authority to make significant concessions and threats turned away from international monetary issues, and the United States began to send conflicting signals. On the whole, the U.S. strategy for responding to the fundamental challenges to Bretton Woods relied on market forces to bring about separate appreciations by surplus countries (but not generalized floating).

Obstacles to a depoliticized strategy of reliance on market processes to change international arrangements had long been identified by theorists of political integration at the regional level. While the experience of Western Europe was obviously not fully comparable with that of the larger domain of the Group of Ten or the IMF, some parallels are striking. According to early functionalist and neofunctionalist theories of European political integration, once states begin lowering barriers and freeing market forces across borders in certain sectors, they begin to perceive more clearly distortions caused by barriers in other sectors. The logic of policy integration is then expected to "spill over" into other sectors and issues. A project begun by technocrats could then spread. States would experience crises arising from partial economic and political integration and would see and act upon their shared interests in preventing breakdown by elevating their mutual commitments.

The actual European experiment departed from this theory at an early stage. Senior political leaders like Schuman, De Gaspari, and Adenauer certainly played active roles in the initiation of political integration. Theories expecting increased integration stumbled most spectacularly, however, when they came upon President de Gaulle. Particularly following the EC constitutional crisis of 1965-1966, theorists devoted attention to processes of "spill back" and outcomes of political disintegration as well as integration.

Thus more complex regional theory was developed, arguing that as economic integration increases the process becomes more controversial and draws in a wider set of political actors. Consequently, "except for the early stages of integration in certain settings, important decisions affecting the integration process must be channeled through the political legitimizing leadership. This enriches the model by allowing the possibility of negative as well as positive syndromes of responses."[36] "Politicization" was seen as making international decisions more complicated but not necessarily impossible, and conceivably more stable when reached. Actual outcomes were seen to depend more on whether actual top leaders bring to office strong preferences on the question of political integration.

Another element of this revised theory has particular relevance here. It is the proposition that as economic integration progresses, it is likely to change the interstate distribution of wealth and power. If governments then attempt to tackle the difficult task of forging agreements to strengthen common political institutions in time, the redistributive process can benefit the region as a whole and can be kept under control. But "to the extent that governments take the apparently easy way and rely almost solely on market forces, redistribution may generate resistances that become a brake on the integration process" (Nye 1971, pp. 89-91). Presumably it could also lead to disintegration.

These elements of the theory of regional political integration, stretched a bit to apply to monetary relations among all the largest industrial capitalist countries, can explain consequences of the early Nixon policy surprisingly well. The earlier lowering of barriers and increase in international transactions had facilitated a redistribution in favor of U.S. allies. Few governments were prepared to give authority over exchange rates to technical-level officials or market forces. The redistributive process gave rise to some feelings of exploitation on both sides. A few Americans began to resent allies' policies. Surplus countries felt that the United States was living beyond its means and exporting inflation to them. They were not assured that the Americans could be trusted to operate a dollar standard without new constraints on their freedom. In this case however, the relative "loser" from redistribution was still the superpower, in contrast to the case, say, of the East African Common Market. Nevertheless, the American "political legitimizing leadership" did not bring to office in 1969 a strong preference to advance this type of political-economic integration. Rather than tackling the more difficult project, they relied on market forces to adapt the regime. Surplus countries applied the brakes. (For these reasons it seems unlikely that waiting longer without offering concessions could have elicited sufficient compliance to permit a stable realignment.) The "benign neglect" policy seems to reconfirm the proposition that when economic power shifts among a set of partially integrated countries, a depoliticized strategy of adaptation is likely to fail to preserve or enhance the level of integration.

It might be objected that high-level international meetings between politicians tend to be even worse. The contentious, November 1968, monetary negotiations in Bonn were a prominent object lesson in the ability of ministerial-level encounters to enhance as well as reduce tensions. This instance may in fact have weighed heavily on the incoming Nixon strategists. In the other column, however, we have a long list of cases in which high-level negotiations enhanced policy integration or helped resolve conflicts: the formation of the European Communities at various stages, including the European Monetary System (EMS); the creation of the SDR; General Agreement on Tariffs and Trade (GATT) rounds of trade liberalization; the formation of the International Energy Agency; and summit meetings as in the Azores in December 1971. High-level meetings are no more a panacea than reliance on markets. If politicians go to a particular meeting mainly to criticize their counterparts through the press, or to refuse to make any concessions, then that meeting will of course fail to achieve agreement.

But there are conditions under which it is a fallacy to believe that there is a realistic alternative--conditions such as 1969 and 1970. Attempts to preserve exchange stability and the par value regime by suppressing negotiation of exchange rates were not a success. Exchange rates were and remain a salient concern for high officials of most states. In such conditions--partially integrated states that have experienced a power shift or other major challenge to the existing regime, and that seek to preserve or heighten their policy coordination--true political-level bargaining to create new rules is the worst alternative, excepting all the others.

NOTES

1. By "international regime" is meant a set of explicit rules and procedures and implicit patterns of state behavior that "govern" international relations on a particular subject or subjects. Regimes can be compared as to their weakness or strength, that is, the degree to which member states observe specific obligations limiting their exercise of autonomy, sometimes including obligations to enforce decisions of international or supranational institutions. A regime committing states only to consult and jointly study a problem is relatively weak; a stronger, more precise rule committed IMF members to defend specific parities within a 2 percent band. A still stronger regime might include, for instance, a rule whereby states commit themselves to set their national rates of monetary growth through joint decision. To take another hypothetical example, an equally severe limitation on state authority would be represented by a rule whereby states bind themselves never to interfere in market adjustment processes. Deliberate joint acceptance of a rigorous regime of floating or a classical gold standard would represent a high level of international political integration. I use this concept of international political integration/disintegration to refer to changes along this dimension, rather than to refer only to the extreme, the creation of a new larger state or a supranational body like a world central bank. Intermediate degrees of political integration may be called policy coordination or "policy integration". For a convenient conceptual review, see Keohane and Nye (1975).

2. See, e.g., IMF Annual Reports 1977, 1978, and 1979; International Linkages under Flexible Exchange Rates, a tripartite report by seventeen economists from Japan, the European Community and North America (Washington, D.C.: The Brookings Institution, 1979). Note that there is no inconsistency in saying both that the Bretton Woods regime was relatively strong as international organizations go, and also that payments imbalances were still not adjusted promptly enough under that regime. Also note that, while the period after 1973 has seen lower political integration and more flexible adjustment simultaneously, there is no inherent conflict such that the former is necessary for the latter. Stronger regimes, such as those exemplified in footnote 1, are also consistent with more flexible adjustment.

3. IMF Survey, January 19, 1976 and May 2, 1977.

4. See Cohen (1977, Chapters 4,5,8); Hirsch and Doyle (1977); and Williamson (1977). For a different view see Willett (1977).

5. The reference rate proposal "turns the basic idea of a par value inside out: it gives a point of reference away from which the market exchange rate must not be deliberately forced by official intervention, as opposed to a pegged rate that the authorities must defend. It is important to emphasize that [this rule] never requires any specific kind of market intervention" (Ethier and Bloomfield 1975, p. 10). It requires each state to accept an internationally negotiated "reference rate" for its currency, and

the rule constrains the government from keeping or pushing its rate outside its band.

6. One qualification should be noted. The emphasis here is placed on explicitly external monetary policies and states' interactions. External policies are of course intertwined with domestic policies and domestic objectives; I have no wish to deny the significance of, perhaps even the preeminence of, domestic policies in the origins of recent experience or as solutions for current problems. Evidence about actual domestic policies will be mentioned as part of the empirical analysis. But an analytical distinction between domestic and foreign policies is still preserved. The paper mainly argues that external policies also can matter greatly.

7. Unit labor cost trends are compared in U.S., <u>International Economic Report of the President</u> 1973, p.39. Also see U.S. <u>Economic Report of the President 1972</u>, putting most of the blame on relative costs and prices. The international secretariats of the IMF and the OECD also came to the conclusion during 1971 that exchange rate realignment was called for. See de Vries (1976, vol.I, pp.537-38) and <u>New York Times</u>, July 2, 1971, p.45. For other evidence of this spreading experts' diagnosis, see <u>New York Times</u>, July 25, 1971, p.III-15, and <u>Financial Times</u>, editorial, August 14, 1971.

8. U.S., President, <u>The United States in the Changing World Economy</u>, Report by Peter G. Peterson, 1971, vol. II, charts 1 and 12.

9. Computed from IMF, <u>Direction of Trade</u> 1950 and 1970, and UN, <u>Statistical Yearbook</u> 1960. On these points, see also paper 3, by Susan Strange.

10. Real U.S. capability to influence monetary policies and rules declined by much less than the decline in the United States share of world reserves. This would have been clearer if Washington had mounted a serious, high-level, coherent attempt to use its power resources for monetary reform. As argued below, the president did not do this.

11. Roosa initially hoped the United States could meet future world liquidity needs by issuing more dollars against a "bouquet" of strong foreign currencies acquired by the United States (Roosa 1967, pp.108, 229).

12. U.S., <u>Treasury Bulletin</u>, February 1972, Tables IFS-1, IFS-2, and IFS-6.

13. There was a request for cover. But before then, by July 1971, President Nixon, Treasury Secretary Connally, and top Treasury staff were already seriously discussing their "New Economic Policy." In July Connally's top advisers concluded from current account data that time had run out. The advisers recommended that they should close the gold window now as a means of achieving a dollar depreciation (whether or not there were further gold outflows). The combined events of August may, however, have helped convince Connally and Nixon to bite the bullet. In early August another reserve loss was announced and another flight from the dollar began. The expectation or fear of further gold losses probably accelerated the decision. Nixon and Connally scheduled a secret meeting of a few advisers for August 13. That morning they received the celebrated request from the Bank of England for cover for British dollar reserves; cover, not gold itself, was provided (interviews with participants; Thomas A. Forbord, "The Abandonment of Bretton Woods: The Political Economy of U.S. International Monetary Policy," Ph.D. dissertation, Harvard University, 1980.) The U.S. policies discussed in this paper are analyzed more fully in John Odell, <u>Markets, Power, and Ideas: Sources of Change in U.S. International Monetary Policy During the 1960s and 1970s</u>, Princeton: Princeton University Press, forthcoming.

14. Evidence for this study includes interviews with most of the

participating U.S. officials. The major exceptions are President Nixon, John Connally, and Henry Kissinger. Most requested anonymity.

15. Interview with a U.S. official.

16. Interview with an American official. See also Houthakker (1978). The "benign neglect" strategy was devised by a preinauguration task force chaired by Professor Gottfried Haberler. Some members of the task force may have questioned whether the dollar was overvalued, judging from Haberler and Willett (1971).

17. Kissinger acknowledges this neglect in his memoirs (1979, pp.950-51). Nixon's account of his "New Economic Policy" dwells mostly on domestic wage-price controls (1978, pp.515-22).

18. Nixon remained worried about the domestic political risks of tampering with the dollar as late as the August 1971 Camp David meeting. See his questions and comments transcribed and published by Safire (1975, pp.512-18).

19. New York Times, February 13, 1969, p.63. Volcker hoped U.S. domestic measures would be sufficient to put the dollar right (Business Week, September 11, 1971, p.120).

20. U.S., Congress, Senate, Committee on Finance, Foreign Trade: Hearings, 92d Cong., 1st sess., May 17, 1971, p.21. Connally dwelled on trade policies and military cost sharing.

21. U.S., Department of State Bulletin 65 (July 12, 1971): 42-46.

22. See Coombs (1976, pp.210-11). On one occasion in late May 1971, Assistant Secretary of State Philip Trezise was reported to have raised the matter of yen revaluation in Tokyo. The Japanese finance minister and the U.S. State Department denied press reports that the United States had asked for revaluation. The U.S. Treasury called the idea "preposterous" and reprimanded Trezise. (Japan Times, May 25, 1971, p.1; May 26, 1971, p.1; May 28, 1971, p.12; Journal of Commerce, May 25, 1971, p.1; interviews with U.S. officials.)

23. See remarks by IMF governors at the annual meetings of 1969 and 1970 (IMF, Summary Proceedings 1969 and Summary Proceedings 1970).

24. U.S., Economic Report of the President 1974, pp.222. This U.S. Treasury index computes a weighted average exchange value of the dollar against 22 OECD currencies, with weights derived from each country's share of U.S. trade.

25. Connally's views have been described by official associates; Kissinger (1979, pp.956-57) and Brandon (1972, chap. 14), Safire (1975, pp.513-18), and congressional documents. See U.S., Congress, Senate, Committee on Finance, Hearings: Nomination of John B. Connally of Texas to be Secretary of the Treasury, 92d Cong., 1st sess., 28 January 1971, and idem, Foreign Trade: Hearings, 17 May 1971.

26. Interviews with associates of Nixon, Kissinger, and Connally; Kissinger (1979, pp.956-62); see also New York Times, December 27, 1971; Brandon (1972, pp.235-36).

27. U.S., Congress, House, Committee on Banking and Currency, To Amend the Par Value Modification Act of 1972: Hearings, 93d Cong., 1st sess., March 1973, p.74.

28. Interview with an American official.

29. U.S. responsibility is emphasized by Komiya (1975).

30. On France, see Schmiegelow and Schmiegelow (1975).

31. Far Eastern Economic Review, May 22, 1971, pp.77-78; Japan Times, May 27, 1971, p.1; and August 29, 1971, p.1.

32. Saxonhouse (1972); Krause and Sekiguchi (1976).

33. Interview with a Japanese official.
34. "Reforming the International Monetary System," U.S., Depártment State Bulletin 67 (October 23, 1972): 460-66.
35. The rate of growth of M1 from December to December was 3 percent in 1969, 5 percent in 1970, 7 percent in 1971, and 9 percent in 1972. (U.S., Economic Report of the President 1980, Table B-58.)
36. Nye (1971, p.63). Nye's comprehensive model is used here to represent this second or third generation of integration theorizing.

DISCUSSION • *Henry N. Goldstein*

In Defense of "Benign Neglect"

Professor Odell's paper makes two claims: that changes in the rules of the international monetary game introduced during 1970-1973 could have been achieved in a smoother, less confrontational fashion than actually occurred; and that the new rules are inferior to alternatives that could have been devised which would have incorporated "a higher level of mutual commitment" among the participating nations.

Both claims strike me as dubious.

The New System Versus Alternatives

Let me begin with the pros and cons of the system that emerged--managed or dirty floating with almost no constraints on official intervention other than those imposed by the market. In this system, the dollar prices of other currencies are set mainly by private demand and supply, which, of course, incorporates effects of, and expectations about, policy actions by relevant governments and central banks. Although the monetary authorities frequently intervene to influence the rate, and often counter significant and sustained market pressure through substantial intervention, market pressure nonetheless plays the dominant role in determining the exchange rate. And with the United States abstaining from intervention at cross purposes with other authorities, no official intervention war, so to speak, has erupted in the seven years since May 1973.

Noting that "major exchange rate changes since 1970 have made important contributions to current account adjustment," Odell agrees that this loosely knit floating rate regime has served the world better over these past seven years than any fixed parity arrangement would have done. (An equally important contribution of floating, not mentioned by Odell, is that it has enabled nations to regain control over their national money supplies; recall that Germany floated in May 1971, again in March 1973, and earlier in mid-1969, mainly because speculative capital inflows, stimulated by an undervalued pegged rate, forced it to expand its money supply at a much

John S. Odell

faster rate than it desired, not because it wanted, per se, to cut its trade surplus.)

But if loosely constrained floating is superior to fixed or jumping parities, it is also, argues Odell, inferior to an adjustment rate regime having "a more precise framework of rules." What rules? Those, he suggests, that would impose "some obligation to convert currencies into reserves" and would provide "optimum exchange rate flexibility."

The first objective presumably refers to all those unwanted dollars held by foreign central banks. But, in fact, I don't see that these dollars have been unwanted. After all, over time they yield a decent return in the Eurodollar market or elsewhere, and can be converted into monetary assets denominated in other currencies, or into nonmonetary assets, or into incremental imports of real goods and services. (Odell speaks of their being convertible into reserves; in fact they are reserves.)

Few would argue with the second objective, "optimum exchange rate flexibility." But the question is, How is it achieved? Odell's prescription--without any supporting argument--is to adopt either the crawling peg arrangement or the reference rate proposal. In my view, however, both of these alternative are inferior to the present arrangement and hence both are distinctly suboptimal. A similar view is expressed by McKinnon (1978) and Emminger (1980).

Consider, first, the crawling peg. Even if the scheme started with a configuration of equilibrium rates, before long significant payments imbalances would surely materialize, best coped with by a prompt and substantial appreciation or depreciation of one or more currencies. But this would be ruled out by the crawling peg constraint. The result would be massive speculative or interest-arbitrage capital flows and the usual sort of problems associated with one-way uncertainty with an overvalued or undervalued rate. For an elaboration see Goldstein (1966).

Nor is it clear, at least to me, that the reference rate proposal would prove superior to the present system. Here the question is, Can technicians design a set of indicators that will on the average do a better job than the market of revealing changing equilibrium exchange rates? (If they can, the central banks can make a tidy profit on their intervention efforts!) I do not believe they can and I await evidence to the contrary.

"Without a more precise framework of rules" Odell claims, "states are less likely to realize the collective good of avoiding mutually harmful conflict. Each is more likely to yield to the temptation to beggar its neighbors when its neighbors have refused to join in renouncing such measures specifically in advance."

But consider recent history. The present system has experienced some huge shocks, including OPEC's imposition of a collective current account deficit of some $70 billion on the oil importing countries in 1974. Yet, despite the lack of precise rules, can anyone point to a single significant instance of any country beggaring its neighbors since the advent of unconstrained floating? Note that such a policy would presumably require the "aggressor country's" central bank to make massive purchases of foreign exchange in order to keep its own currency at an undervalued level. But there is a powerful constraint limiting any such policy--namely, the rapid and undesired expansion of its domestic money supply. Thus, the current British Chancellor of the Exchequer, Sir Geoffrey Howe, in recently rejecting appeals for direct intervention to cut the external value of sterling in order to fight recession in England, noted, "An intervention on the exchange

rate stokes up inflation at a faster pace" (Revzin 1980).
So much for the alleged defects of the post-1973 arrangements as compared with the alternatives suggested by Odell.

How the New System Was Negotiated
Let me turn now to the contention that the Nixon-Connally actions of August 1971 were overly rude and crude--i.e., that the United States could have obtained the substantial currency realignment that it sought in a way that would have been less disagreeable to our major trading partners and rivals.

What the United States should have done, Odell contends, is to have pursued traditional "carrot and stick" diplomacy in order to persuade foreign leaders that existing parities needed revamping and that some process for ensuring that any additional necessary exchange rate changes would take place. Instead, the Nixon administration initially chose "benign neglect"--a "no-carrot and no-stick" approach. Then, with the disequilibrium in payments positions becoming increasingly apparent to one and all, with the deutsche mark forced to float in May 1971, and with the announcements of an official reserve transactions deficit at an annual rate of $23 billion during the first quarter of 1971, the Nixon administration unilaterally slammed shut the gold window and imposed a 10 percent import surcharge--thus switching, as Odell nicely puts it, "to fait accompli and a big stick."

All this Odell deplores. But why?

There is ample evidence that the Japanese, the French, and others were obdurately unreceptive to overtures that they appreciate their currencies. Indeed, Odell himself observes, "In response to the admittedly partial, technical-level, U.S. initiatives on behalf of limited flexibility, Japan and France consistently and firmly resisted such ideas for encouraging strong currencies to appreciate. <u>The Japanese refused to discuss the issue bilaterally at the technical level</u>" (emphasis mine).

Moreover, he also observes:

> Once Washington shifted to an active policy of adjustment and showed willingness to bargain [after August 1971], Japan and Western Europe fought hard for every percentage point . . . France adopted a two-tier market and prevented the commercial franc from appreciating much, putting a drag on the adjustment of the deutsche mark vis-a-vis the dollar. In November 1971 Japan's Finance Minister Mikio Mizuta was still insisting that the yen could not be revalued more than 5 percent, while Secretary Connally was demanding 25 percent.

In the light of this behavior, why should we believe that a different, more conciliatory strategy, would have worked?

I believe that the evidence, both from foresight <u>and</u> hindsight, suggests that the U.S. decision to play hardball in August <u>1971</u> was the right decision. It was necessary to make foreign governments accept exchange rate adjustments that would restore U.S. competitiveness at the expense of their own current account surpluses. The U.S. actions of August 1971 stimulated their rethinking on this question in a most effective way. Here is how the London <u>Economist</u> viewed the situation in its issue of August 21, 1971:

> Only harm can come from early meetings at which befuddled or advantage-seeking ministers try to guess what their new fixed of semi-fixed exchange rates should be. Not even the best-informed

computer could say at the present time what the best fixed exchange rate for any currency would be; and, even if one could, the finance ministers with undervalued currencies would not agree with it. The object of guardians of undervalued currencies (like the yen) at any international conference will be to limit the extent of their up-valuations to rates below those that a free market would decide, and to bully guardians of relatively undervalued currencies (like the British and Americans) to mortgage their reserves by staying near to them.

That is why America . . . really wanted to avoid any special financial conferences like the plague that they could conceivably become. . .

[The Americans] think that there must now be a period during which countries decide what the future exchange parities, if any, should be.

After the Smithsonian agreement in mid-1972, the United States advanced a comprehensive plan for, in Odell's words, "renovating the battered monetary regime." Odell praises this action, but deplores the subsequent U.S. refusal to commit itself to exchange rate intervention in February 1973, following the further devaluation of the dollar.

But surely the U.S. refusal to enter into widespread pegging commitments was right. For such commitments, as history abundantly documents, lead to growing competitive imbalances, to multifarious government controls and restrictions, to massive hot money flows that severely hamper sensible monetary policies, and to wealth transfers from unknowing taxpayers to alert and informed speculators (such as you and me). Contrary to what Odell suggests, fixed or even heavily managed exchange rates are not integrative. Instead, they are disintegrative because governments will--rightly or wrongly--refuse to subordinate monetary and fiscal policies to balance of payments considerations on the scale required to validate those rates; instead, they will resort to controls and eventually and belatedly to discrete exchange rate adjustments (see Willett and Mullen, paper 5). During the 1960s, for example, there were seven discrete realignments of leading industrial country parities against the U.S. dollar. Almost all of these involved painful struggles against the inevitable, including macropolicy distortions and direct restrictions on current and capital transactions, a pattern predicted by Milton Friedman in his famous paper, "The Case for Flexible Exchange Rates," originally written in 1949 (Friedman 1953).

Further evidence is provided by Canadian-United States economic relations since 1950. For twenty of the past thirty years the Canadian dollar has fluctuated against the U.S. dollar in a managed float without a priori restrictions. What evidence suggests that this arrangement has been "less integrative" than either a fixed rate arrangement or an adjustable rate arrangement with preagreed "rules" for management?

Odell concludes that during 1970-1973, "major governments, through their collective action, helped bring about an outcome desired by few of them". True enough, if we are talking about the governments of the 1960s. But that simply means that the individuals in charge at the time simply lacked a suitable education in economics as provided by the University of Chicago. (Leading sinners in this regard included such members of the U.S. establishment as Charles Coombs, Robert Roosa, and John F. Kennedy--all Harvard men!) "Defending the dollar" was a mischievous and misguided enterprise; once it was abandoned, both the United State and its trading partners were better able to confront the ever-changing fundamentals that impinged on their economies.

Make-believe Realpolitik

Finally, a few words on the "imaginary history scenario" sketched by Odell. Here he has the United States proposing "a grand package deal"--accepting some new constraint on its freedom to finance its deficits in exchange for an undertaking by surplus countries to take prompter adjustment measures.

But what sort of novel arrangements does he have in mind? After all, it was the foreign central banks in surplus countries who were absorbing dollars from the exchange market and who, thereby, were simultaneously forcing the imbalance to continue (instead of letting the rate adjust to eliminate it) and enabling the United States to finance the deficit with its liabilities. If they stopped absorbing the dollars, then, by definition, the payments imbalance would necessarily cease as would its financing through the issuance of additional U.S. liabilities. Of course they had the right, de jure, to use their dollars to buy gold from the U.S. Treasury. But, de facto, that right ceased long before August 1971 with modest exceptions for France and a few other boat rockers.

The only alternatives to continued financing of the deficit at unchanged parities or to an elimination of the deficit through exchange rate adjustments were controls and deflation by the United States or controls and inflation abroad. These options, quite properly, were anathema to statesmen in quest of a liberal international order and to politicians seeking reelection. So what really was there to bargain about, other than whether the currency realignments should or should not involve a change in the nominal official dollar price of gold? But whether the official price was set at $35 an ounce, or $50 an ounce, or $70 an ounce seems largely inconsequential since it should have been apparent that the U.S. Treasury was not about to buy or sell the stuff on any significant scale at any of those prices.

In sum, the specifics of the "grand package deal" that Odell refers to seem--to me at least--either trivial or mysterious.

A Postscript

In responding to the above comments at the conference, Professor Odell indicated that I had failed to perceive the main point of his paper--namely, that the U.S. policy of "benign neglect" prior to the August 1971 actions was a mistaken policy. Instead of using neither carrots nor sticks, Odell argues, we should have used both in order to induce our major trading partners to accept a more viable and coherent set of international monetary arrangements than those that eventually emerged.

With the advantage of hindsight, and the conviction that floating exchange rates (without preagreed rules) are the most effective mode of maximizing worldwide economic gains from more liberal trade and capital flows, I disagree with this assessment. In retrospect, it seems to me that "benign neglect" was a masterful policy to have pursued because it enabled the underlying and growing fundamental disequilibrium in the U.S. payments position to become increasingly (and painfully) clear to the surplus countries of Europe and Japan as well as to currency speculators all over the world. It thus set the stage for the August 1971 actions and justified their apparent severity.

DISCUSSION • *Michael W. Doyle*

International Political Economy and Hegemonic Stability

I would like to make three comments on Professor Odell's paper. One concerns what I think is the place of the arguments he makes within the evolution of the political science of international political economy--its intellectual history. A second concerns the importance of a criticism of structural models from the perspective of the politics of policymaking. And a third set of comments seek to qualify his criticism of the role "declining hegemony" played in the collapse of Bretton Woods.

INTELLECTUAL HISTORY
This paper represents a further step, a most useful step, in the incorporation by political scientists of international relations theory into the theory of international political economy. The past fifteen years have witnessed both the rediscovery of international political economy by non-Marxist political scientists and the recapitulation of the body of classical international relations theory into the debate on the nature of international political economy. This paper together with other recent works by political scientists and economists adds to that debate a striking emphasis on the effects of the politics of domestic policy choices on international political economy. With those other works, it begins to round out the incorporation of a substantial heritage of international relations theory (Hirsch and Goldthorpe, 1978; Destler, 1980; Keohane, paper 1; Black, paper 4; Willett and Mullen, paper 5).
    A thumbnail sketch of the evolution of international relations theory in the modern age can, I would suggest, reveal a substantial shift in the leading levels and sectors of analysis that have engaged the minds of scholars developing original insights. Machiavelli can be taken as a starting point. By reevaluating, indeed transvaluating, the traditional literature of the "mirror of princes" school, he placed a fundamental emphasis on policy advice and the domestic determinants of foreign policy behavior. Writing in <u>The Prince</u> for new princes as opposed to hereditary princes, he advised his audience how to win and secure power, how to gain glory and expand the state, how to take into account necessity, and how to take advantage of fortune. His insights rested on important distinctions between new and old regimes, between domestic structures characterized by princes and ministers (centralized states, weak societies) and princes and barons (decentralized states, strong societies). Despite efforts to reintroduce transcendental visions or models of foreign policy, such as those of Bodin and of Protestant and Catholic theorists, the next telling step in

the evolution of international relations theory rested on the elaboration of an international, systemic, structural perception of international relations. This was Hobbes's metaphor of the state of nature in which the anarchy of the interstate system renders competition for relative security a necessity, and thus conflict inevitable. Lacking a global sovereign who could maintain interstate law and order, attempts by each individual state to enhance its security by expanding its armed forces creates additional insecurity for all the other states. As each responds in kind, a vicious circle of insecurity comes to characterize interstate relations.

The eighteenth century developed the themes of the sixteenth and seventeenth centuries. Montesquieu, in his <u>Considerations on the Causes of the Greatness of the Romans</u>, . . . elaborated on Machiavelli's model of the domestic sources of international relations. Rousseau, in his <u>Judgement on the Abbe' de St. Pierre</u>, achieved a grand restatement of the structuralist thesis of the international state of war, of anarchy, that made pressures for competition and conflict override mutual interests in peace and prosperity. New themes that were critical of Hobbes's and Rousseau's general, structural theory of international relations entered with a concern for differentiating the various issues that comprised the relations between states and societies. Hume elucidated the special operation of a gold standard in the international economy; Smith did the same for trade.

In the nineteenth century, international relations differentiated into separate models for separate issues and competing models for each of these issues. Drawing first on the American and later on the German responses of developing countries to the world economy, List challenged Smith's defense of free trade. Marx challenged the foundations of both on a domestic plane. Hobson challenged them internationally. Clausewitz redefined the military dimension; Brougham and Gentz focused on the balance of power and Wakefield and Sir George Cornewall Lewis on the economics of colonial development and on the politics of imperial development. Each issue was judged to have special features that made a general structural model inappropriate.

To the extent a rough summary of the evolution of international relations theory reveals a pattern, it grows from policy and domestic political sources in Machiavelli; to international structure in Hobbes and Rousseau; to issue structures in Smith, Clausewitz, and others. By 1900 these foundations, though rudimentary, were largely complete for political scientists concerned with international relations. The international economy had devolved to economists. <u>International</u> political economy later became a field relegated largely to Marxists (Magdoff, Mandel, A. Gunder Frank, Amin), to historians (Condliffe, Lewis, Shonfield, Strange), to certain economists (Viner, Hirschman, Kindleberger, Knorr, and others) attuned to political determinants, and to public officials (Monnet, Wallich, Solomon) concerned with the theoretical foundations of their policies.

The revival of international political economy among liberal and statist political scientists in the past 15 or 20 years seems to have recapitulated the development path of international relations theory. But an evolution comprising 400 years has been telescoped into a twentieth of that time, and this evolution has been conducted in reverse. From the issue structuralists examining regional integration theory in the 1950s and 1960s (Haas 1964, Nye 1971), we stepped to the structuralists stressing hegemonic stability and power of the early 1970s (Krasner, 1976; Gilpin, 1975; Hirsch and Doyle, 1977). From the lively debate between general structuralists and issue structuralists in "complex interdependence" (Keohane and Nye, 1977), we have seen a revival of a concern with the domestic determinants of foreign economic behavior that again focuses on the different outcomes within the same international economic regime of strong versus weak states and societies (Katzenstein 1976a; Krasner 1978b). Now we see a return to policy--to a concern with the process and politics of choice, where necessity leaves room, if not for Machiavellian fortune, at least for alternatives not completely preconstrained.

This, in short, is where I think the contribution of this paper lies. Focusing on the two-step disintegration of Bretton Woods (1971, 1973), Professor Odell has sought to shift our attention both from the issue of international monetary flows and from the general structure of the rise and decline of American hegemony. Neither the integration of capital markets, nor the overvaluation of the dollar, nor the decline of relative American influence and predominance fully accounts for the fall of Bretton Woods. Instead, he would have us direct our attention to choices and mistakes made in Washington, Paris, and Tokyo. He would have us look at the domestic sources of foreign economic behavior and particularly at the range of choices available to national governments and the consequences of choices poorly made.

THE LIMITS AND VALUE OF INTERNATIONAL STRUCTURE

The emphasis he gives to domestic sources and policy choices is, in my view, an important addition and as I mentioned an important step in the catching up--maturing, if you will--of the political science of international political economy. For there are good reasons to be wary of a complete reliance on international--general or issue specific--models of international political-economic outcomes. In examining transnational trends such as capital market integration, it is difficult to attach specific outcomes in the stability of international economic regimes to these flows of finance. Massive flows of capital could be a sign either of arbitrage within a very effective regime or of a regime in the throes of collapse with money fleeing from temporary haven to temporary haven. Moreover, capital integration as well as overvaluation of the reserve currency of the predominant state can easily be seen as consequences of the effective operation of a general structural hegemony rather than as independent causes of its demise. An American deficit in an ultrastable regime could be the equivalent of reserve requirements imposed by an international equivalent of a central bank.

On the other hand, the structural model of hegemonic stability in the provision of collective international goods (such as a common alliance defense, lowered tariff barriers, international liquidity, exchange rate stability, and lending at last resort by a single "large provider" state) introduces a range of analytical resources to international political economy. Drawing on Olson (1965) and other public choice economists, Kindleberger (1973), Gilpin (1975), Krasner (1976, 1978a) and Hirsch (1978) stimulated new interest in cycles of leadership and hegemony in the field of international political economy. But as a sole model its difficulties are apparent. Neither periods of provision of collective goods via predominance nor periods of nonprovision (attributed to symmetrical competition of states nearer to equality) are recognizably equivalent. Monetary instability in the 1970s bears only a slight relationship to the competitive devaluations of the 1930s. Moreover, for those who note Dutch seventeenth century, British nineteenth century, and American postwar predominancies, the provisions of these providers were radically different. The Dutch helped integrate finance, but closed trade and neglected defense. (See Wight 1979, chapter 2, for a discussion of "dominant powers".) The British helped open trade and offered services in finance, but left the holding of reserves to France. Following 1815, they policed the oceans but abdicated a role in providing strategic stability for the continent of Europe. The United States, uniquely, was capable of and did undertake the provision as well as reaping the benefits of all three--defense, trade, and finance.

These substantial differences suggest that hegemonic stability at best is what philosophers might call a "thin" theory of international cooperation. It accounts for incentives to cooperate that would not be expected in a competitive, "oligopolistic" international system--the fundamental theoretical foundations of the international anarchy and power. But it neither explains the degree nor the specific content of cooperative regimes; nor does it predict which specific state will become a hegemonic provider.

However, I would like to emphasize that, in my view, it is also at least an adequate, thin theory of international cooperation among effectively sovereign states and that no other explanation can fully substitute for it in this role. A theory resting on purely coercive hegemony or imperialism can account for policy and international outcome integration but would neglect the ability of independent states in Western Europe and Japan in the postwar period to successfully resist a general imposition of an entirely coercive economic regime (Hirsch and Doyle 1977). Marxist, Kautskyite theories of "ultraimperialism" fail to take into account the force of uneven development that Lenin argued would overwhelm an attempt at a stable division of the world among monopolies. Nor does liberal economic exchange fully account for international cooperation. The mutual advantages of unrestricted trade in goods and factors are discounted by the pressures present in an anarchic international system of states pursuing relative security. The distribution of gains becomes as important as their absolute level. States restrict exchanges to prevent rivals from acquiring a relative increase in resources even if the restricting state would itself achieve a welfare gain from the exchange (such is known as "economic warfare"). Alternatively, states subsidize exchanges, provide exports at less than market value, or purchase imports at greater than market value (Soviet oil exports to Eastern Europe 1975-1976; the U.S. sugar quota system, and others; see Hirschman, 1945) in order to employ trade as a source of influence. Both--two forms of power--reflect a primacy of politics, of relative power, over purely economic calculation, of the pursuit of particular advantages over international cooperation. The relations of amity among states such as those characterizing the OECD that allow for a flowering of relatively unfettered exchange themselves have to be explained. When incentives for cooperation are always present and yet when the international political economic system reveals periods and areas of restriction as well as cooperation, we should not neglect explanations that attempt to account for variation between cooperation and conflict.

The theory of hegemonic cooperation does offer an account for periods and areas of cooperation in an otherwise rivalry prone international system. The existence of a predominant "large provider" state that itself benefits from a cooperative regime--an international "collective good"--to such a degree that it can afford to bear the costs such a regime entails helps to explain international cooperation. Side payments, the benefits of free riding, and fear of coercion can account for the acquiescence of lesser states (Olson 1965; Olson and Zeckhauser 1966; also in Russett 1965). Despite the important limits of a collective goods explanation (Haas 1980;

above citations), hegemonic cooperation remains, in my view, an important foundation for international political economy.

CRITICISMS OF PROFESSOR ODELL'S ANALYSIS OF DECLINING HEGEMONY

My criticisms of Professor Odell's paper touch on this last point--his analysis of the role played by hegemony in the decline of Bretton Woods:

1. I think that on the most general level of international structure it is misleading to separate to the extent that he does economic, diplomatic, and strategic leadership. While far from identical, they are exchangeable and in much of the postwar system mutually compatible and self-reinforcing under U.S. hegemony.

Currency and exchange rates are particularly likely to be influenced by political factors. Reflecting the "full faith and credit" of the state as a store of value, currency and exchange rates can become subject to political panic (Strange, Paper 3). The flight from sterling in 1931 was accelerated by a false report of a naval mutiny (Kindleberger 1973, p. 60). In the postwar period the predominance of the dollar rested not only on the U.S. trade position but also on U.S. protection of the OECD states. The strategic security that American, nuclear and conventional weapons provided for Western Europe and Japan helps us to understand the willingness of some of America's allies to provide accommodation for excess dollars and to regulate their trade in the interests of American producers. Furthermore, strategic considerations offer an additional perspective on French reluctance to accommodate American desires with respect to restraining the "cashing in" of dollars for gold.

The United States shifted in the early 1960s from a strategy of "massive retaliation" wherein the United States would retaliate with its strategic nuclear forces against a Soviet attack on American allies, to a strategy of "graduated response" wherein NATO would meet a Soviet attack first with conventional forces, second with theater nuclear weapons in Europe, and only third with American strategic nuclear forces. This strategy formed a more credible response under the circumstances of the new Soviet retaliatory capability, but it also shifted the battlefield from the superpowers to Western Europe. Germany, totally dependent on U.S. military forces, had little alternative but to accept the new doctrine. Britain, hundreds of miles behind NATO's front line, may have found the new doctrine acceptable because it seemed more credible. While France faced the threat that a tactical nuclear war would commence quite near its own borders, it knew that it would also automatically be protected if Germany were protected. This combination of strategic free riding, with the prospect of destruction helps account for France's special reluctance to follow the U.S. lead either in NATO or in other policies, including money. More broadly, America's industrial allies found themselves in a less secure relationship with the United States. Dependence on the American nuclear deterrent remained, yet the deterrent was much less reliable. This strategic condition added to the economic tensions that found their expression in economic challenges to U.S. leadership.

2. Even though questions of hegemony need to be approached on a wide basis there are also good reasons to focus special attention on the structure of the issue in question. In a study of the decline of Bretton Woods, the decline in American monetary reserves relative to other members of the OECD merits specific attention. The declines in American predominance in GNP,

trade, and nuclear security were not nearly as marked as the decline in reserves. Monetary reserves are in many respects a special form of international influence, an issue structure with a characteristic not matched by other issues. Odell has suggested, correctly in my judgment, that it is a composite measure, one readily subject to adjustment by policy choices, such as alterations in interest rates. But, while different in degree, other issues, including military power, are also subject to such adjustment. These adjustments are not costless. And the influence monetary reserves hold operates in a distinct regime of financial flows, the IMF and foreign exchange markets. Sources of influence are not completely fungible; particular attention should focus on the particular resource sustaining each regime.

3. Lastly, the fact that both the U.S. and its industrial allies had a substantial, continuing stake in a cooperative international regime does not discredit the theory of hegemonic stability. This is consistent with hegemonic structure as an interpretation of regime decline. Under circumstances of the relative decline of a single provider, the absolute value of potential international cooperation does not necessarily fall; only the net benefit to the single provider of providing the cooperation falls. Continuing stakes, yet no attempt to preserve the regime, are thus fully consistent with the theory.

CONCLUSION

These criticisms do not challenge the merit of Professor Odell's overall contention concerning the importance of analyzing policy choices made by the political leaders of differing political systems. Hegemonic stability is much too thin a theory to be our steady diet. But I do think that hegemonic structure remains an important "first cut" in explaining the stability and decline of international regimes.

REJOINDER • *John S. Odell*

I have profited much from comments made on my paper. I might explain briefly why I am not persuaded by Michael Doyle's suggestion that the special power structure of the monetary system is important for explaining the collapse of the Bretton Woods regime. This argument holds that a state's (share of) international reserves is significant in determining its influence over monetary rules and policies, and hence its "interest" in a given regime. Thus it was because the U.S. share of world reserves fell so sharply that the United States jettisoned its obligations unilaterally in 1971.

I would argue, in the first place, that the monetary issue area is by definition one of macropolicy. It involves exchange rates, which deeply cut across all other issues involving international transactions, in contrast to the issues of trade in textiles, regulation of civil aviation, use of the oceans, and others. Thus on theoretical grounds international monetary policies and regimes should reflect general capabilities, as opposed to special ones, more than most issues. In this light, I have shown that because of its general capabilities, the United States was able to achieve compliance from its major power allies on monetary issues (through bargaining) prior to 1971. They enjoyed increasing "reserve power," but they failed to exercise it by demanding gold, because of their general dependence on U.S. military protection and the U.S. market. U.S. real capabilities for influencing monetary rules and policies (and hence its "interest" in avoiding unilateralism) fell by much less than its decline in reserves.

There are other difficulties with the hypothesis that relative reserve positions determine monetary interests and influence. Briefly, during the time when Britain was at the peak of her influence in the international monetary system, it was not her reserves that were responsible. During the early 1970s when West Germany's reserves were rising rapidly, these increases were unwelcome to the German government; hence they are an odd measure of power capabilities. In general, reserves tend to be highly sensitive to policy choices and market conditions, and otherwise seem to reflect more lasting, nonmonetary sources of influence.

Much of Henry Goldstein's comment leaves untouched the main causal analysis of my paper, namely the argument that the superpower's failure to initiate a negotiated regime change during 1969 and 1970--its reliance instead on market forces to achieve change--was the chief proximate cause of the international political disintegration. In this regard his contention is not that reliance on market forces can preserve political integration, but rather that in this case it was the surplus states that caused the disintegration. All they had to do was to appreciate separately. If the United States had made a high-level, bargaining initiative, the surplus states would have been just as obdurate as they in fact were. Therefore a big stick was the ideal policy.

Goldstein and I agree up to the point that a U.S. initiative would not have been sufficient to preserve political integration. But our disagreement beyond that point is significant. I believe it reflects the scant attention Goldstein and many others give to power consequences, both domestic and interstate, when analyzing international economic relations. A major reason Japan, for example, did not simply appreciate was that such a move was bound to generate domestic attack on the incumbent political leaders. Not surprisingly, given that the imbalance was caused partly on the U.S. side, Japanese politicians were unwilling to absorb these domestic political consequences without having any American compromise to show their constituents. If instead U.S. political leaders had offered a promise to accept a share of the domestic heat, together with a threat of sanctions if there were no adjustment, allied politicians would have been less "obdurate." Many American economists continue to think that a mere "change in the nominal official dollar price of gold" could not have had any importance since it had little economic importance, once the gold window was closed. Foreign economic policies and agreements require domestic political calculations as well as economic calculations. They also depend on international power relations. The only way to expect middle powers to have taken the lead toward negotiated adjustment is through a puzzling disregard of the dominant position of the United States.

But of course Goldstein's heart is not in it. He really thinks that political disintegration is better. Most of this comment is an attack on the contrary premise of my paper. He mainly wants to press the elemental argument that floating rates are better than fixed rates, on economic grounds. Not intending to settle that debate here, I cited in note 4 some of the considerable literature that has detailed the problems, particularly the political risks, of the post-1973 regime. I will only add a few brief comments about this premise.

There may be some misunderstanding. Goldstein thinks that any stronger regime would be inferior to the present mixture of weak rules and varying practices. He fails to realize, first, that to move from the present to his ideal world of free floating would itself entail a much stronger regime than exists today. Modern governments would have to surrender much autonomy for such a world to operate. But if somehow they were to agree to such a global rule prohibiting all intervention, they would have found one way to dampen potential interstate conflicts. Political integration does not equal fixed rates.

I mentioned other examples of rules somewhat stronger than actual ones, yet also compatible with exchange rate flexibility. The "reference rate" proposal would not oblige any government to fix its exchange rate or to intervene under any circumstances. But it would prohibit certain antisocial practices.

In some circumstances, however, official management of exchange rates may bring gains--among them, efficiency. Unlike Goldstein, many analysts recognize the possibility of market failure, as for example in the oscillation of the dollar during the year following February 1973. Even George Shultz admitted that something was wrong with the market then.

Another familiar reason for departing from laissez faire, even at some cost in efficiency, is that unregulated markets may cause more foreign policy damage than alternative arrangements. Goldstein shows relatively little interest in such objectives or how to reach them, and I believe this neglect helps him reach his conclusion. He does mention the argument that the free market is always best because governments, if they manage rates, will always ensure lasting disequilibria, which will lead to even worse conflict, fought by means of controls. This may be a case against a stronger regime requiring or permitting lasting disequilibria, but it is hardly a persuasive case against all stronger rules. He also cites the absence of an "official intervention war" between 1973 and 1980. My paper too avoids hysterical doomsaying, but the evidence cited at the outset leads me to a less rosy description. Behavior until now may have been constrained by attitudes molded by the 1930s, a legacy that is receding as memory fades and the waters get choppy.

In general Goldstein seems to represent those who have faith that the attractions of the market are so compelling as to provide all the restraint the world political economy needs to protect it from destructive conflict. For me this is a strangely ahistorical outlook, almost reminiscent of Mill's faith that free trade in the midnineteenth century was making war obsolete. We know from experience in international economic affairs that such confidence is itself obsolete, unless markets are supplemented with an adequate framework of agreed upon rules among states.

COMMENT • *Will E. Mason*

Internal and External Stabilization

The papers were insightful, and the discussants were perceptive. The combination provoked candid exchanges that were occasionally sharp, often entertaining, and always edifying. However, no one and one half day conference on the Political Economy of Domestic and International Monetary Relations can exhaust the subject. Consequently, a few gaps remained.

Some of the issues might have been sharpened, if not resolved, by sufficient attention to the concept of money needed to permit distinction of money from other "monetary aggregates" that substitute for money as stores of value of more or less liquidity. This would reduce the current confusion of the supply and demand for money and permit separation of substance from semantics in discussions of alternatives facing theorists and policymakers.

The issue of internal versus external stabilization was never directly confronted; hence the question as to whether the ultimate failure of the International Monetary Fund (IMF) is explained by unresolved contradictions in the "system" or by faulty diplomacy could not be answered. The IMF foundered on the same issue that this conference failed to highlight. Although domestic and international stability are not incompatible--and achievement of stability in one area will contribute to stability in the other--both are not simultaneously attainable (Mason 1963, pp. 110-13, 118). One or the other must be given priority as a monetary goal, and nonmonetary means must be used to moderate the destabilizing effects in the other area (Mason 1963, pp. 113-15).

Stabilization (internal or external) may be real or monetary. The IMF implied the priority of real external stabilization by specifying "fundamental disequilibrium" (equilibrium) of the balance of payments as the criterion for changing (maintaining) parity rates of exchange (Mason 1963, pp. 106-7, 118). Adjustments to structural changes were to be effected by altering exchange rates instead of the levels of prices, incomes, and employment. It was thought that this external monetary (exchange rate) adjustment would permit implementation of the national preferences for internal stabilization that had caused the collapse of the gold standard. Thus, the regime was conceived as a workable compromise between the internal stability preferred by the people in each country and the external stability preferred by the international financial bureaucrats.

Editors' note: Although Mason's comment is directed at a number of papers and discussions, its central message is most closely related to Odell's paper and exchanges surrounding it.

The IMF was to be used to cover only temporary deficits in the balance of payments. Chronic deficits were to be corrected by appropriate modification of exchange rates. In the immediate postwar period ascertaining equilibrium exchange rates was impossible. By the time it was tried in 1958, the adjustable pegged exchange rates had become more pegged than adjustable, and member nations had grown accustomed to chronic balance of payments deficits covered by loans from the Fund made possible by its periodic enlargement and by other devices including the ultimate paradox, "paper gold." The IMF Agreement, which related to <u>policies</u> on the prices of gold and foreign exchange, came to be thought of as establishing a "gold exchange <u>standard</u>."

Inadvertently, the IMF adjustment mechanism was rendered inoperative. Thus, the international financial community imposed the priority of external stability upon the peoples of the world, who preferred internal stability. International and domestic policies were contradictory. Neither mechanical gimmicks, enlargement of the Fund, nor improvement of diplomatic skills could preserve such an inconsistent "system."

Throughout the meetings of the Committees of Five, Ten, and Twenty, I contended that the best we could hope for was failure to agree until the financial bureaucrats became accustomed to exchange rate flexibility compatible with the disparity of national institutions and goals. This appears to be happening. There is, therefore, hope that a future conference will focus on the fundamental issue that conditions and constrains national monetary policies and international monetary relations--the compatibility and priority of internal and external stabilization.

GENERAL DISCUSSION

In the general discussion several people suggested that Odell tended to idealize the Bretton Woods System. Meltzer contended that U.S. policy leading to the collapse reflected not failure, but rather wisdom resulting from education of policy makers (by economists) during the 1960s concerning the defects of the fixed rate system and the advantages of flexible rates. Others saw the switch to flexible rates as reflecting the overvaluation of the dollar manifest in current account deficits (as opposed to capital account deficits earlier). It was also suggested that the sharpness of U.S. actions in 1971 may have been motivated partly by a desire to clear the matter away in order to give full attention to other international issues (for instance, relations with China).

PAPER 3 • *Susan Strange*

Still an Extraordinary Power: America's Role in a Global Monetary System

CONTEXTS AND CAVEATS

Not perhaps since the 1930s have American and European perceptions of the world differed quite so sharply as they have in the early 1980s. Americans have been audibly dismayed at their apparent lack of power, at all the things their government could not do. Unable to stop the Soviet Union marching into Afghanistan, unable to secure the early release of the diplomats in Tehran, the sense of lost power was compounded by a sense of damaged dignity. Meanwhile, for Europeans, the fall of the shah in Iran reminded them more forcibly than any event since the Cuban missile crisis in 1962 that their lives and security lay almost entirely in American hands. Yet it seemed that American ears were deaf to European voices--indeed, to any voices but their own. Through 1979 and 1980, European spines were chilled by the shortsightedness of President Carter's sanctions policy against Iran, and by the insouciance (even more than the ineptitude) of the abortive helicopter raid to rescue the hostages. In Europe--and indeed in Japan, the Middle East, and elsewhere--the attention given by the American media to the fate of the hostages seemed disproportionate to attention given to the fate of the world and the superpower balance. Had the raid succeeded but started widespread fighting and civil disturbance, the door would have opened wide to a Soviet expeditionary force. The scenario of an escalating world crisis was only too easily imagined. And what worried Europeans was the demonstration that a few American lives mattered so much more to Washington than many millions of non-American lives. The promise implicit in Kennedy's "Ich bin ein Berliner" speech, it seemed, no longer held good. American diplomacy was apparently no longer inspired by a long-term vision of the future for the world, or even of a future role for America in the world. Foreign as well as domestic policy in 1980, far more than in most American election years, so it seemed to Europeans, was being shaped and trimmed only in response to the latest opinion poll.

As the only non-American present at the conference, it seemed to me necessary at the very outset of our apparently technical and even academic discussions to remind ourselves of the broad political and emotional context in which they took place. For social scientists, including economists, can no more claim to be immune to emotional responses to momentous outside events than other people, and if people's perceptions about change in the distribution of power in the world's military and security system were coming to differ so much, it was more than likely that perceptions would differ just as sharply about the distribution of power in the monetary system, and about its consequences. In monetary as in security matters, Americans seemed acutely conscious of a loss of power, a loss of control over events, at the same time that Europeans were experiencing a heightened sense of vulnerability to apparently arbitrary American policy decisions made in response to primarily domestic pressures and needs, political as well as economic. Better then, that these diverging perceptions should not be fudged, but made clear and explicit.

No doubt, in monetary as in military matters, there was on both sides a strong tendency to exaggerate and to rationalize. Subconsciously, American perceptions might be biased by the successive disillusionments of Vietnam, Watergate, and OPEC. Each in a different way had undermined confidence in the validity of American goals, in the virtue of American political processes, and in the prestige of the United States in the world at large. But if Americans were inclined to overreact by understating their power, so were Europeans inclined to overreact by overstating their dependence. They too have a strong need to rationalize the causes of their current predicament, and to shift responsibility for it from their own to other shoulders. It is easier for Americans than for Europeans to see that a part, at least, of the explanation of Europe's vulnerability to decisions made in Washington lies in the wrangling and indecision of the European Community. Just as the Third World finds it easier to put the entire blame for poverty and underdevelopment on Western capitalism and/or imperialism, so Europeans find it much easier to put the whole blame for their monetary difficulties, as well as for their military insecurity, on the United States.

Nonetheless, despite the elements of exaggeration and rationalization, I argue that there is a core of truth in European perceptions of the global monetary system, which American economists, in and out of government, would do well to recognize. The purpose of this paper, therefore, is to attempt in a rather elementary and necessarily brief way an analysis of the nature of power in the contemporary global monetary system, and to draw from it some thoughts about how one might test the European hypothesis of an acute asymmetry in the distribution and exercise of monetary power in the international political economy.

I finish the paper with some tentative conclusions about the relations of domestic monetary measures to the global system and to other participants in it, to which I suggest the available evidence leads.

Note that the question at issue relates to the power of the United States in the monetary system, not to the value of the dollar. To the man in the street, the distinction may be obvious. But it is surprising how often the experts and the politicians have confused the two. One need only recall the importance British economists, bankers, and politicians attached in the 1920s to restoring the pound to its prewar gold value and the $4.86 dollar parity. Or the conviction that persisted well into the 1960s that Britain's international status and influence could be preserved only if sterling held its value and its reserve asset role.

Simple as the point may be, it must be reiterated that monetary virtue is not the same as monetary power, any more than commercial virtue or sexual virtue necessarily confers power on the possessor. If it did, Switzerland, which has virtuously held the real value of its currency longer and better than any other country would be calling the shots, persuading others to adopt Swiss principles of banking secrecy and security.

Indeed, it is more than possible for a decline in the value of a currency in terms of goods or in terms of other currencies to coincide with an increase in the monetary power of the issuing authority. Robert Keohane has pointed out that the relation of power to wealth is such that wealth can be accumulated as a stock and later "spent" (as in a defense budget) in order to exert power in achieving political or military goals (Keohane 1978; see also Baldwin 1979). But the "spending" of wealth seen in this way does not cause it to vanish so much as to be converted into a political asset. The period in which power is exercised is more likely therefore to follow, than to coincide with, the period in which the wealth is accumulated by exercising the protestant virtues of self-denial and saving.

For example, it could be argued that the period when British monetary power was most visibly expanding was between 1890 and 1914. This was when colonial currency systems were being imposed on various parts of Africa and when the incorporation of India into a British-dominated world monetary system was completed and made virtually irreversible, short of political independence. Yet in this period the competitiveness of the British economy was rapidly weakening as Germany and the United States, and even Japan, began exporting their manufactures in earnest. The value of sterling was only maintained through the capital account and the return flow of unearned income from past foreign investments (Imlah, 1958). For the moment, though, the point I feel necessary to stress is simply that it is power we are concerned with, not value--however that may be defined.

There is another basic presumption of the whole analysis that also should be made explicit before we go any further. Though it seems no more than the most obvious common sense to operators in world finance, it has not as yet penetrated all the corners of economic theory and model-making. It is simply this. The international monetary system which we have to analyze is neither a single fully integrated global system in the sense that, say, Bagehot's British monetary system of the nineteenth century was one coherent system, nor is it just a collection of such single coherent national systems linked together by trade but each having its own currency and system of monetary government. It is rather a halfway house between the two. The billiard ball model beloved of the old-fashioned realist school of international relations, in which each state is an entity and the international relations between one billiard ball and the rest are carried on quite separately from the domestic politics within each ball, no longer fully represents reality, even in matters of national security and defense for which it was conceived and still less in economic matters. Even if one acknowledges that the balls are of different size and weight and can be classified as superpowers or great powers, middle powers and small powers, the model is still a false one. It is so for two reasons. One is that it is essentially a static model. In a dynamic world economy growing at the pace of the last thirty years, the individual states are not balls of a determined given size but could be better represented as mushrooms, growing unevenly and thus differentially able to translate internal economic development (wealth) into external political influence (power). The other is that the entities, whether static balls or dynamic mushrooms, are not in fact impermeable, separate, social and economic systems, but are each increasingly susceptible to what goes on in the global system (see Keohane and Nye 1975). For the integration of national financial and other key markets (insurance, banking and management services, commodities, and construction and technology, to name only the most important) has proceeded so far by 1980 that we can no longer conceive of the world (outside of China and the Soviet bloc, perhaps) as consisting simply of separate national monetary systems, linked together only by trade and intercurrency exchange rates. More and more we have to try to think of it <u>both</u> as a collection of national systems <u>and</u>, at the same time, as a <u>single</u> global monetary system, unevenly and incompletely integrated perhaps, but basically functioning as a single interacting system offering global opportunities and incurring global risks.

When we do so, another pictorial metaphor may be helpful--that of the seesaw, where, as in balance scales, a plank rests on a central fulcrum and tilts one way or the other according to the relative weight on the end. In any modern market economy, this metaphor fairly represents the relationship of state or political authority to market operators. The symbiotic system works best if neither side too heavily outweighs the other. For example, if market operators increase the scale or extent of their operations and the political authority fails to maintain the balance of increasing the scale and extent of its controlling managing power, then the political economy is apt to become unstable and insecure. Conversely, if the state becomes too powerful and interventionist so that the market operators cannot function properly, then the political economy is apt to stagnate and become less productive. And in our halfway house, mixed national-global monetary system, the problem of maintaining this productive balance is complicated by the fact that while the market end of the seesaw operates as an integrated whole, the authority on the state end of the seesaw is not a single state but a multiplicity of authorities, national and international, who can act effectively to increase their power only when they are able to agree.

The point of the three pictorial metaphors will be more apparent when we come to the analysis of power in the system. For they serve to remind us that the power of the state has to be concurrently exercised in three directions or dimensions. In one dimension, represented by the billiard ball model, the state has to preserve the security of society and economy and to that end has to engage in a power game with other states, exerting pressure and resisting pressure. In a second direction or dimension--which may also be seen as the necessary economic foundation of the political power exercised in the first dimension--states are engaged in a development competition, a race for wealth and security, each seeking to grow into a bigger mushroom better able to sustain an effective foreign and defense policy to secure the national interest, however that may be perceived.

And in the third dimension, represented by the seesaw, states are exercising power in relation to markets and their operators. They can be characterized as weak states (Krasner 1978a) or as strong states. Loss of power by one state in this authority/market dimension does not necessarily result in the acquisition of more power by another state, but possibly in the loss of power by all. For as markets expand beyond the confines of the national economy it is very likely that all states must find a way to adapt and develop the processes by which they exercise authority or else be prepared to suffer a collective decline in their ability to control the operators. Yet because the purposes for which they want to control, manage, or supplement market forces will be different, agreement on the adaptive path will not be easy.

POWER AND MONEY

Let us start with some simple, general propositions about the nature of power. We can see how these might be applied in relation to the exercise of power within and upon monetary systems. This preliminary exercise is the more necessary because power is a topic so studiously avoided by many liberal economists--but not by economic historians, however--and carefully excluded in consequence from much contemporary economic analysis and theorizing (Rothschild 1971).

We need first to make the following important distinctions concerning the nature of power, whether used within or between states and by whatever means or instruments--military, diplomatic, commercial, or financial.

1. Power can be exercised deliberately and intentionally; and it can be exerted involuntarily and unintentionally. That is, the individual, group, or institution exercising power does not necessarily wish or intend the consequences. When Otmar Emminger said it was uncomfortable being in bed with an elephant, he did not impute to the elephant any wish to trample or overlay its bedmates (Emminger 1977).

2. Power can be exercised positively to achieve an objective; and it can be exercised negatively to frustrate or prevent the achievement of an objective--to change the status quo or to maintain it. Power consists both of the ability to realize aims and of the ability to stop or block any development one considers inimical to one's interests.

3. Power can be exercised relationally and structurally. That is to say, in the billiard ball model power has been defined as the ability of A to get B to do something B would not otherwise do (or, conversely as the power of B to frustrate A's wish). That is relational power, but it may also be conceived of as the ability of A to change (or preserve) a common structure or environment within which relational power is exercised. Such common structures, which Wolfers long ago christened 'milieu goals' (Wolfers 1962) can be as broadly defined as the capitalist mode of production or as narrowly as the Law of the Sea or the IMF's Articles of Agreement. Structural power implies the ability in contemporary parlance to create or destroy international regimes, to frame and enforce or to change the rules of the game in international affairs.

Therefore, in any analysis of power in international monetary relations, we must look for evidence of the exercise of power, whether it is intentional or unintentional; whether it is positive and creative, or negative and conservative; and finally, whether it is relational or structural.

But before proceeding to consider the application of these simple classifications of the nature of power to monetary matters, there are two parenthetical observations to be made. One is that although power is usually and mostly exercised by states and political groups within states, this is an artificial limitation of the analysis created by political scientists for their own convenience. Sociologists need not be confined by such a limited application of power analysis, nor need economists. For states and political parties are by no means the only entities to exercise power, whether intentional or unintentional, positive or negative, or relational or structural in a political economy. All these forms of power can also be exercised (though perhaps to a lesser extent) by, for instance, dominant firms in a market or sector, or dominant labor unions in an industry.

The second observation is more directly relevant to the purposes of this paper. It concerns the imputation of greater morality to certain forms of power as compared with others. Some writers with an emotional or professional commitment to the expansion of international organization have sometimes been inclined to jump to the conclusion that the use of structural power to create regimes is necessarily "a good thing," and whenever it is exercised it must be pro bono publico, for the general welfare of mankind--whereas relational power is evidently self-interested. But it must be stressed that this is not necessarily so. Relational power can be used for the good of the weaker entity; and structural power is just as likely to be self-serving when used at the global level as it is when used within states and national political systems. There we can recognize easily enough that classes or races or interest groups of all kinds seek to frame the constitution of the state and its laws in such a way as to favor their own interests and concerns (moral as well as material) over those of others. Similarly in international trade regimes, it is fairly widely recognized that strong traders tend to favor free trade regimes, and not solely because of the ideological conviction that the efficient allocation of resources is the sole criterion of good economic management. We must therefore be ready to concede the possibility that in international monetary arrangements those with structural power may use it in their own interests as well as in those of the international community.

When we talk of "interest," moreover, we must not think only about the maximization of benefits and the minimization of costs, as economists are sometimes inclined to do. Politics and the exercise of power are concerned as much or even more with the management of risks and opportunities as they are with the management and distribution of costs and benefits. Political power in any system, whether it is democratic, socialist, or despotic is used to avoid costs and obtain benefits. But it will also be used to avoid or restrict risks, or to shift them elsewhere, and to extend opportunities.

The study of liberal or market economics has always tried to depoliticize the question of risk by supposing a strict separation between entrepreneurial risk and actuarial risk. In a perfect market, since no one buyer or seller can influence price, entrepreneurial risks are equally distributed among all, and the rewards of risk taking can be defended as both equitable and systemic. Actuarial risks are risks of conditions, external to the system, and can properly be converted through insurance into costs and spread widely through it. Economists have also tended to ignore, overlook, and otherwise exclude from their calculations both these actuarial risks and all others connected with the political system, notably the risks of war but also risks of nonelection, of inflation, of revolution or rioting, and so forth. (Only recently and under pressure from the business schools has political risk management become a respectable subject for economic analysis.)

So, if we are to try to analyze rationally (even if, of necessity, somewhat imprecisely) the functioning of the international monetary system, we cannot very well rule out the question, Who takes the risks and who is given the opportunities? For when they have observed the international political system, students of international relations have habitually asked this question regarding the military and strategic security of the state: How have states acted to avoid all unnecessary or avoidable risks of attack or invasion of their territory, destruction of their property, or violence to their people? They explore, too, how state power has been used to obtain and to exploit as many opportunities as possible: to make and break alliances, to adopt or abandon neutrality, to retreat into or break out of isolationism. The more powerful state was always the one able to enjoy such options. As just one instance, consider the familiar concept of "Fortress America." This concept predicates that the United States has a choice in its defense strategies of abandoning its allies and its world role, battening down the hatches, and retreating to the last redoubt of the North American continent. Such a choice is not open to others. They lack any conceivable opportunity to choose isolationism and must perforce cope in some other way with the risks of an insecure world. In itself, the option of Fortress America is an attribute of power (and in a sense a source of power) no less than the convention in feudal society that the option of taking to the ultimate security of the keep of the castle belonged to the lord and his soldiers, but not to serfs and peasants.

Now, with the extended concern of governments with questions of economic growth and economic security, we must expect that political power will increasingly be used by those who have it to secure for themselves the maximum possible immunity from avoidable risks and the maximum possibility of exploiting every available opportunity for profit, growth, and development. For example, when world markets for ships, steel, and textiles shrink or stagnate, those with the power conferred by a large home market immediately insist that the foreign exporters rather than the domestic producers should be the ones to accept "voluntary" export restrictions on their market share. In this way the burden of unemployment is shifted from those with developed welfare and social security systems onto those without—just as the Overseas Private Investment Corporation offers more security and less risk to U.S. foreign investors, even when they may be far better able to bear the risks than their local competitors. And when OPEC oil prices rise, it is those with the power conferred by owned or controlled energy resources who are able to insulate themselves from the shock, and shift to others the uncomfortable dependence on a volatile spot market to make good their supplies. So if we can show, however roughly, how risk and opportunities are distributed throughout a system, we shall have found out something important about the distribution of power within it.

POWER IN MONETARY SYSTEMS

A monetary system, whether national, global or regional can be defined as a set of customs or rules concerning the use of money in economic transactions of production and exchange and additionally (but not necessarily) as a store of value and a unit of account. It is a means to economic growth and development; the alternative to the development of a monetary system is the extensive use of coercive political authority to direct and manage factors of production and to extract surplus value from current production for investment in future production. The price of economic growth in monetary systems is their tendency to increase material inequality by allowing the rich to get richer. The price of growth in centrally planned systems is to limit individual freedom of choice, because the state and not the market decides what is to be produced, where, how, and by whom. Consequently, in a monetary system, the material inequality tends to be reflected in some inequality of political power, but also in a generally greater limitation of the power of central authority (the state) over individuals. (In a monetary system, to take a simple example, an individual can store wealth and opt out, temporarily or permanently, from the production system, a freedom not available to people in a planned system.) Money in other words confers some negative power on individuals, groups, and enterprises, and some positive power on the very rich.

Monetary systems can be primitive and limited (using shells or copper bars, for example, and serving only limited exchange needs), or they can be highly developed and extensive (using credit and thus incorporating time as well as current transactions). They can be anarchical (in which operators mutually agree on the form of money to be used, which can be cigarettes or gin or Maria Theresa dollars), or governed (in which a political authority determines what shall be legal tender, and enforces the collection of debts and the validity of monetary contracts). And if governed, they may be governed by a single political authority (the state) or by multiple authorities who will agree on the division and demarcation of their authority and on the rules concerning the exchange of different monetary media and the management of monetary markets and institutions.

The global monetary system that we have to analyze is clearly highly developed and extensive. And though areas of anarchy remain, on the whole the use of money is governed not by a world central bank or by the IMF but by the multiple authority of recognized sovereign states.

Indeed, the element of government is almost a sine qua non of monetary development. If operators have to reach agreement on the rules every time they make a transaction, this inevitably slows everything down and limits the extent of the money economy. The intervention of authority to sustain and manage money has, throughout economic history, been a necessary condition for the wider use of money and, thus, for the opportunity to achieve economic growth without loss of liberty. The defense of the realm and the security of the currency have for centuries been recognized as the basic attributes of national state power operating in a market economy. Both have strings attached. The state (whether it be Machiavelli's prince or the U.S. federal government) exacts a price for both the military and the monetary security it provides. And this price is commonly much greater and more subtle than the forms of seigniorage familiar to economists.

The state does not simply make a profit out of minting coins or printing paper money. It demands a privileged right, shared with no others, to exploit and tax the whole system and to demand at the same time the loyalty and cooperation of those it is exploiting and taxing. This demand exactly parallels the price that states exact for providing security and defense. Whether godfathers or Borgias, absolutist monarchs, republics, or, indeed, superpowers, those providing the military force necessary to achieve security have claimed in return a loyalty overriding other loyalties. On the basis of this loyalty they have demanded, and been accorded, the right to tax in payment for their services as well as the security. And when those providing the security have also been those managing the currency, they have almost always used the monetary system as an additional source of finance for the security, whether by debasing the currency (i.e., adding lead), by diminishing it size but not face value, or by substituting something less valuable (paper) but proclaiming it of equal value.

With modern developed monetary systems the means of monetary exploitation--not necessarily a pejorative term if value is given in return--become far more subtle, numerous, and sophisticated. For example, in almost every developed economy the state claims, and normally succeeds in enjoying, a privileged position as borrower and debtor, as well as the right to monopolize taxation of capital, income, or transactions by whatever means it sees fit. Using a variety of means, governments make sure that, no matter who wants to raise money in the market, government demands are met first and others afterwards. And, if as often happens in an international political system depending on various balance of power systems, the state itself disappears, or its successor repudiates its debts, then the creditors who have borrowed on the security of the state are just unlucky. In the last resort they are powerless to get their money back, and they cannot distrain on the property of the state as they might hope to do with private defaulters.

One of the most blatant instances of a state's taking advantage of its creditors and using political authority to save itself money was the War Loan conversion operation by which the British government in 1935 decided forcibly to exchange the 5 percent bonds that it had sold to innocent patriots during World War I for 3 percent bonds that would save it the expense of borrowing to meet the difference between wartime and depression interest rates. In short, there are very few states in the world that at some point or other have not repaid their debts in part only or repaid them in full but in depreciated money.

In international monetary relations one might add the example of the United States, when President Nixon and Treasury Secretary Connally decided unilaterally to "close the gold window" and make the dollar holdings of foreign governments inconvertible into gold. By this act, it changed the terms on which it had borrowed from foreigners without renegotiating the contract and transformed, as Triffin has put it, a gold dollar exchange standard into a paper dollar standard (Triffin 1978-79).

In short, standards of financial probity and integrity observed by governments (including the American and Russian governments) are substantially lower than those they themselves demand of private borrowers. So a possible hypothesis would be that the more powerful and/or invulnerable a state in the international monetary system, the more likely it is to be tempted to exploit its privileged position first by borrowing more freely and second by depreciating the currency in which it borrows. This may well be the most significant attribute of power in the international monetary system--a measure both of its distribution between states and its variation over time for particular states.

For example, the United States under President Carter decided to guarantee the value of U.S. treasury bonds not in dollars but in deutsche marks or Swiss francs. By this step the dollar became in effect a negotiated currency while still retaining its place, *faute de mieux*, as the world economy's top currency (Strange 1975). The need to do so might be interpreted as a sign of some loss of power by the United States--but in the authority/market seesaw dimension, rather than the state/state billiard ball dimension. Neither Switzerland nor West Germany gained additional power in the system from the change--at least in the short run before economic strength (as in a mushroom metaphor) could be translated into political power. And given their continued military dependence on the United States for security this could not happen quickly.

For the other attributes of power we have only to look at the kinds of power that governments have managed to exercise within their own national monetary systems and to ask whether any asymmetries exist in the exercise of similar powers transnationally in the integrated financial and banking system.

The first attribute of power, as the monetarists at least would surely agree, is the ability to control the money supply, and thus to determine for the economy and for society this important variable affecting the rate of economic growth and the rate of decline in the value of money--in short, of inflation. Without dwelling at this point on the very considerable difficulties of defining and counting up the world money supply, one need only note that there are two main and distinct sources feeding it. There is the creation of credit by governments for themselves, for each other, or for third parties; and there is the credit creation practiced (usually under limits and restrictions) by banks and other financial institutions. Which governments, we must therefore ask, have created most credit or allowed the banks and others to do so?

A second and related attribute of monetary power common to all monetary systems is the ability to control access to credit. (In developed monetary systems most money is credit in one form or another, so access to the sources of credit is an important political issue.) At times, states have denied credit facilities to almost all but themselves. (The Christian church in the Middle Ages, having great authority to tax, had little need to borrow and preserved its power therefore by condemning usury and therefore restricting the supply of credit to laymen.) At other times, states or banks or both together have denied credit to black Africans, to Caribbeans, or to women, excriminals, infants, lunatics, bankrupts, or debtors. Perhaps this power may not seem important to those who enjoy access to credit. But it is a big issue to those at the margin, whose prospects--in every sense--depend on the opportunity to borrow today and repay later.

Today that power lies with the U.S. government through its controlling voice in the decisions of the IMF and the World Bank, and to a lesser extent with the big U.S. banks. An authoritative recent survey of international capital markets observed an important change in the structure of Eurocredit banking in the 1970s: "The management of most credits has passed to the world's biggest commercial banks by the early 1970s" (Mendelsohn 1979). And by 1976-1977 over half of $63 billion worth of publicized Eurocredits lent to governments and private borrowers had been arranged by just ten very large banks, two of them consortium (i.e., joint multinational) banks, and the other eight American. Just five big banks, four of them American and one German, arranged as much as 40 percent of these credits (Mendelsohn 1979, Table 7, adapted from material published by Euromoney).

The converse, in developed monetary systems, is also an important attribute of power: that is, the power to license credit-creating institutions and, indeed, all other operators in the market--in short, to give or withhold access to the financial markets and even to decide which markets are legitimate and which are not. The choice of policies regarding the conduct of secondary markets and of futures markets, for example, substantially affects the "who gets what" of the system. On the whole, decisions in favor of freedom for market operations increase the opportunities for gain but also those for loss. The chance of gain may be the incentive for enterprising responses to the needs of the economy but may also carry risks for the system--as, for instance, the operations of the Hunt brothers in the silver market. If, in the international monetary and financial system, the decisions of one or some governments regarding the markets or their operators have much more effect on what goes on than those of others, then this too is a test of power in the system.

EVIDENCE--INCOMPLETE BUT SUGGESTIVE

Some of the evidence suggests that, though the value of the dollar may have declined, American power in the international monetary system is still rather formidable--and likely to remain so. And if any loss has been sustained it has been in the second dimension--from authority to market--and not in the first dimension, to any other state or political authority. It is therefore much more easily reversible since the market operators still depend for their security on the state (or, if you wish, on the balance of power) and can in the last resort be obliged to accept whatever restrictions powerful states may choose to put on them. For example, U.S. monetary authorities have demonstrated by their increased control of the surveillance over the lending operations of U.S. banks to less developed countries that they can (when they want to) exercise very substantial extraterritorial control. As with antitrust regulations, even transnational companies have vulnerable, home-based operations and offices, and their executives carry U.S. passports and, however footloose, are bound to obey the injunctions of U.S. courts.

One attribute of power, it may be recalled, was the capacity to borrow from others, to preempt lending capacity and to repay in depreciated

TABLE 3.1. Foreign holdings of U.S. government debt (in U.S. $ billion)

Year	Total U.S. Gov. Debt	Foreign and International Holdings
1972	332.4	55.3
1973	340.2	55.5
1974	351.5	58.8
1975	437.3	66.5
1976	506.5	78.1
1977	563.8	109.6
1978	618.2	137.8
1979 (Oct.)	638.8	124.4

Source: International Financial Statistics, January 1980.

currency. Tables 3.1 and 3.2 certainly seem to show that the United States has not lost the capacity to get foreign governments and citizens to assist substantially in the financing of U.S. government spending. Table 3.1 shows that the total of U.S. government borrowing almost doubled in the last eight years of the 1970s--but the amount of foreign-held U.S. government debt more than doubled in the same period. In Table 3.2 the foreign contribution to the central consolidated account is seen to be substantial if rather variable from year to year. For instance, in 1974 foreign government conversions out of dollars produced a net negative figure, although in 1973 foreign financing had actually been larger than domestic. Over the five years 1973-1977, over 20 percent of U.S. federal spending was financed by foreign borrowing. It is also notable that the proportion of foreign financing through the sale of U.S. long-term bonds--before the Carter Swiss franc and deutsche mark bonds were introduced--increased rather markedly in 1977, though subsequent dollar depreciations have drastically reduced their real or converted value. In this connection, Robert Triffin has remarked:

> Our government indebtedness (mostly Treasury securities) and banks' (including their branches abroad) liabilities to foreigners nearly doubled in the years 1970-1972 (rising from $78 billion at the end of 1969 to $146 billion at the end of 1972) and increased further 2½ billion times in the following five years (to $363 billion at the end of 1977). Their total increase of $285 billion over these eight years is exactly equal to the total increase of our Federal debt over this period, from $279 billion at the end of 1969 to $564 billion at the end of 1977: a bizarre coincidence undoubtedly, but arguably not entirely fortuitous (Triffin 1978-79).

TABLE 3.2. U.S. consolidated central government account (in U.S. $ billion)

Types of Financing	1973	1974	1975	1976	1977
Total financing	16.46	4.53	54.33	75.78	52.49
Domestic financing	6.19	7.47	45.88	70.96	31.27
Financing abroad, total	10.27	-2.94	8.45	4.82	21.22
Foreign governments	10.37	-2.98	7.29	2.71	20.44
International organizations	-0.10	-0.06	0.81	1.77	-0.09
Other foreign borrowing	0.0	0.10	0.35	0.34	0.87
Financing abroad, total					
Long-term bonds	3.59	-1.93	1.31	3.76	17.60
Short-term bonds, bills	-2.86	2.50	8.94	2.74	3.43
Long-term loans	3.60	-0.06	3.04	1.08	0.53
Short-term loans, advances	5.94	-3.45	-4.84	-2.08	-0.34

Source: IMF, Government Finance Statistics Yearbook, vol. III, August 1979.

By comparison with the United States no other country is able to borrow abroad for official financing on this scale. Neither of the two "locomotive economies" as they were once called do so. Only Britain, with an abnormally large national debt by European standards (and the inescapable need therefore to roll over the public sector borrowing) and with the aid of very high interest rates, has continued to maintain foreign holdings of sterling debt. And the wisdom of doing so in view of the continued weakness of the British economy when North Sea oil acts as breakwater for the balance of payments has been seriously questioned (Forsyth 1980).

The total contribution of U.S. policy decisions to the expansion of the world money supply is too vast a subject to go into proper detail in this paper. (Indeed, it would seem to me a rather large area for economic research.) I only offer two rather substantial pieces of evidence that suggest it has not been by any means negligible, one in respect to government to government, or public, credit creation and the other concerning credit creation in the private sector.

There have been two major ways in which credit has been created by governments for governments: the swap network and the accumulation of foreign exchange reserves chiefly in dollars. Table 3.3 shows the expansion of the swap network initiated by the U.S. in 1962 by which short-term credit is extended to countries needing to intervene in foreign exchange markets to defend exchange rates. Totaling less than $1 billion in 1962, it had been extended to a total of over $30 billion by the end of the 1970s. Half of this was in arrangements with the three strong currency countries--West Germany, Japan, and Switzerland. Between them they accounted for half the network in 1979, up from a sixth in 1962. The point here is that whether the swap is made by the U.S. exchanging dollars for deutsche marks or by the Bundesbank exchanging deutsche marks for dollars, the consequent intervention on foreign exchange markets must add to the combined totals of U.S. and German money supplies. For the global money supply consists of the sum of national money supplies plus any credit available internationally not included in national totals. During the 1960s the network had been used by the United States mainly for the defense of sterling--from 1966 to 1968 especially. In the 1970s, it was pressure on the dollar after the oil price rise and after the elimination of U.S. capital controls and before the announcement of the November 1, 1978 measures that led to the biggest increases.

The most important form of longer-term, intergovernment credit creation is, of course, the accumulation of reserve assets by one country denominated in the currency of another. Table 3.4 shows the increase in world reserves of foreign exchange and of dollars through the 1970s--when according to most popular accounts, the dollar really began to go downhill, the Bretton Woods regime to collapse, and U.S. monetary power to be eclipsed (Bergsten 1975; and Mayer 1980).

Tables 3.4 and 3.5, however, show first a really phenomenal and quite unprecedented increase in world reserves of foreign exchange during the 1970s, and second, a fairly steady proportion of the increase in the form of dollars and Eurodollars. Indeed, the climb back to 76 percent of the total from under 72.6 percent in 1973 actually accompanied the declining real and exchange value of the same dollar assets.

The evidence for the contribution of U.S. policy decisions (or nondecisions or indecisions) in the expansion of private credit creation in the international monetary system is to be found in the continued and even accelerating expansion in Eurocurrency lending and Eurobank operations over

TABLE 3.3. Federal reserve swap network (in U.S. $ million)

Institution	1962	1963	1964	1965	1966	1967	1968	1969	1970	1971	1972	1973	1974	1975	1976	1977	1978	1979
Austrian Nat. Bank	50	50	50	50	100	100	100	200	200	200	200	250	250	250	250	250	250	250
Nat. Bank of Belgium	50	50	100	100	150	225	225	500	500	600	600	1000	1000	1000	1000	1000	1000	1000
Bank of Canada	250	250	250	250	500	750	1000	1000	1000	1000	1000	2000	2000	2000	2000	2000	2000	2000
Bank of Denmark	...	...	...	...	...	100	100	200	200	200	200	250	250	250	250	250	250	250
Bank of England	50	500	750	750	1350	1500	2000	2000	2000	2000	2000	2000	3000	3000	3000	3000	3000	3000
Bank of France	50	100	100	100	100	100	1000	1000	1000	1000	1000	2000	2000	2000	2000	2000	2000	2000
German Fed. Bank	50	250	250	250	400	750	1000	1000	1000	1000	1000	2000	2000	2000	2000	2000	6000	6000
Bank of Italy	150	250	250	450	600	750	1000	1000	1250	1250	1250	2000	3000	3000	3000	3000	3000	3000
Bank of Japan	...	150	150	250	450	750	1000	1000	1000	1000	1000	2000	2000	2000	2000	2000	5000	5000
Bank of Mexico	...	...	...	...	...	130	130	130	130	130	130	180	180	360	360	360	360	700
Netherlands Bank	50	100	100	100	150	225	400	300	300	300	300	500	500	500	500	500	500	500
Bank of Norway	...	...	...	...	...	100	100	200	200	200	200	250	250	250	250	250	250	250
Bank of Sweden	...	50	50	50	100	200	250	250	250	250	250	300	300	300	300	300	300	300
Swiss Nat. Bank	100	150	150	150	200	400	600	600	600	1000	1000	1000	1400	1400	1400	1400	4000	4000
Bank for International Settlements																		
Swiss franc (in $)	100	150	150	150	200	400	600	600	600	600	600	600	600	600	600	600	600	600
Other authorized European currencies (in $)	...	...	...	...	...	600	1000	1000	1000	1000	1000	1250	1250	1250	1250	1250	1250	1250
Total	900	2050	2350	2800	4500	7080	10,505	10,980	11,230	11,730	11,730	17,980	19,980	20,160	20,160	20,160	29,760	30,100

Source: Federal Reserve Bank of New York, Quarterly Review, Winter 1976, updated in subsequent issues.

Table 3.4. Official holdings of foreign exchange (in SDR billions)

Year	Official claims on U.S.	Eurodollar holdings	Other Euro-currency holdings	Total official foreign exchange holdings
1970	23.8	10.5	0.4	45.4
1971	46.7	10.4	1.1	75.0
1972	56.7	16.8	3.2	95.9
1973	55.4	18.5	5.3	101.8
1974	62.7	31.8	5.8	126.3
1975	68.9	38.0	7.2	136.9
1976	79.2	45.6	7.6	159.8
1977	103.8	53.6	12.2	200.1
1978	120.2	47.7	14.7	220.8

Table 3.5. Percent dollar share of official foreign exchange reserves

Reserves	1970	1971	1972	1973	1974	1975	1976	1977	1978
Official claims on U.S.	52.4	62.3	59.1	54.4	49.6	50.3	49.6	51.9	54.4
Eurodollars	23.1	13.9	17.5	18.2	25.2	27.8	28.5	26.8	21.6
Official $ holdings plus Eurodollars	75.5	76.2	76.6	72.6	74.8	78.1	78.1	78.7	76.0

Source: IMF Annual Report, p. 59.

the past decade, and, more particularly in the late 1970s, as shown in Tables 3.6 and 3.7. Without going into detail here, most monetary historians would, I believe, agree first that U.S. banking regulations and the freedom given to banks to hold dollars in their foreign branches free of the interest rate restrictions applying at home and to relend them without reserve requirements substantially encouraged the early growth of the Eurodollar and other Eurocurrency markets; and second that United States policies did nothing to restrain and much to encourage the expansion of Euromarkets, first to

TABLE 3.6. Sources of Euromarket funds (in billions of U.S. $)

Areas	1977	1978	1979	1980
European area	117.3	144.5	181.0	235.0
OPEC	54.5	54.7	68.6	98.6
Nonoil LDCs	29.6	39.8	46.0	38.0
Offshore centers	33.4	45.4	56.9	64.0
E. Europe	7.0	8.8	8.2	7.0
Other LDCs	18.8	26.2	31.1	34.0
Canada & Japan	8.4	13.0	14.2	14.0
United States	25.4	37.0	46.5	56.0
Unallocated	...	...	7.0	7.3
Total	300.0	377.0	459.5	555.6

Source: Bank for International Settlements and Amex bank estimates (December 1979).

TABLE 3.7. Uses of Euromarket funds (in billions of U.S. $ at year end)

Areas	1977	1978	1979	1980
European area	110.4	139.5	155.6	185.0
OPEC	15.7	24.3	28.0	33.0
Nonoil LDCs	30.3	40.1	66.0	86.0
Offshore centers	43.9	55.0	70.0	90.0
E. Europe	25.7	31.4	34.5	37.5
Other LDCs	30.8	34.7	39.1	46.5
Canada & Japan	18.7	24.6	28.5	36.5
United States	21.3	24.6	32.8	34.1
Unallocated	...	3.0	5.0	7.0
Total	300.0	377.0	459.5	555.6

Source: Bank for International Settlements and Amex bank estimates (December 1979).

accommodate the needs of corporations and developed economy governments and then to take care of recycling "petrodollars" in order to finance the oil deficits of developing countries in the mid-1970s. It would have been hard and costly, if not impossible, for European states to restrict this expansion without the leadership or against the will of the United States.

Thus despite the fall in its value (whether in real terms or in terms of Swiss francs), the dollar remained the key currency of the international monetary system and the main reserve asset for the settlement of international payments accounts. This expansion of credit was not necessarily bad. Far from it. If world reserves had remained the same as in 1965, or even 1970, balance of payments constraints would have made necessary restrictive, deflationary policies in many countries with a consequent slowdown in world trade and production. The point made here is simply that in this key area of credit creation the United States took the lead and with the "consent of the governed" carried out a policy of reserve creation. What this may have done to national money supply totals is still unclear even to economists, for it depends on variables including the ability of national monetary authorities to insulate their monetary base from the effect of swelling reserves of foreign exchange, especially dollars. For example, from 1971 to 1979 the foreign exchange component of German reserves changed by more than the monetary base in six of nine years. Judging by German inflation rates, new methods of insulating the latter from the former must have intervened.

Tables 3.6 and 3.7 highlight the continued importance of Euromarkets in this financing role for subsequent oil price rises, the importance of flows in and out of banks in the European area compared to the United States, and growth of offshore bank centers (again reflecting the extraterritorial permissiveness of U.S. banking rules). Mendelsohn is emphatic that this expanded market filled a gap left by governments and international agencies (Mendelsohn 1979, p. 61).

The dominating influence of United States domestic monetary policies on international markets and currency exchange rates will be more fully explored in other papers. It must already be clear that the precise relation of cause and effect is by no means certain. It requires much further detailed investigation and even then can never be entirely conclusive.

But pending such investigation and research, two European perceptions of the impact of the United States on international monetary regimes and of the latter on national economic management are worth noting.

First, the Europeans are much more disillusioned, not to say disappointed, with the flexible exchange rate regime than are Americans. Floating was earnestly advocated in Washington and by the entire American economic establishment as the ideal escape from the dilemma of the overvalued dollar (Bergsten 1975) and as the magic solution to recurrent international tension and crisis. But in this life no solution is costless--and to some Europeans at least the costs seem to have landed unequally on their side of the Atlantic (and the Japanese side of the Pacific) and the opportunities on the American side. As perceived in Europe, the resort to floating rates did not work exactly as it was supposed to in economic theory. Its effect was rather to bring about a polarization of weak and strong currencies, between which the United States was able more or less to balance. The United States avoided both the weak countries' Scylla of payments deficits, high inflation rates, and high interest rates and the strong countries' Charybdis of payments surpluses and low inflation and interest rates with poor employment rates and flagging production. Swiss employment rates in 1977--more indicative than the unemployments rates of a slowdown in the economy because of the gastarbeiters (guest workers)--were 15 percent below 1973; German rates were 11.2 percent below; and Dutch and Japanese both around 10 percent below, compared with the U.S. rate of 2 percent lower than 1973 (OECD statistics). Paul Fabra wrote of the post-OPEC appreciation of the Swiss franc, the deutsche mark, and the yen(Fabra 1978):

> None failed to have powerful deflationary effects on the Swiss, German and Japanese economies. Obliged to respond to the ever stronger competition of imported products on their own internal markets, German producers were obliged to slash their profit margins. . . . At the same time and for converse reasons American producers were profiting from the fall of the dollar and from the inflationary boom which soon followed the end of the 1974-75 recession. Just as the rise on foreign exchange markets of the strong currencies was a consequence of the dollar's fall, so the relative deflation suffered by the strong currency countries was the converse of American inflation. What introducing floating rates allowed was a geographic share-out of these contrary evils.

This relative invulnerability of the United States in the 1970s to either of Fabra's twin evils is something we shall return to in a moment. The second point I think worth making is that the United States has seemed--to Europeans at least--to have been on successive occasions the leader in the upward trend of interest rates, which, unevenly but universally, has marked the decade of the 1970s and the start of the 1980s (see Chalmers 1972). For example, in the spring and early summer of 1974 the Fed "led the rest of the world in raising interest rates". Later, at the turn of the year, it led other central banks in a round of discount rate cuts (Bank for International Settlements, Annual Report, 1975, pp.16, 19). More recently, after the interest rate rises that accompanied the November 1,1978 measures, interest rates were raised within two weeks in Canada, Britain, Singapore, and Hong Kong (Economist, November 11, 1978, p.10). And again in late 1979 and early 1980 there seems little doubt that the U.S. authorities led the way in raising rates to heights unprecedented in a world of peace (Economist, October 13, 1979; February 23, 1980; and March 22, 1980).

Another indication of American power in these recent years of alleged "decline," of which Europeans (and I suspect Japanese) are acutely aware but Americans less so, has been the extent to which U.S. monetary authorities have been able to get others, as it were, to help out, massively, in the business of intervening in foreign exchange markets to hold a supposedly floating rate. This applies particularly to the Germans and recently the Japanese. Not only has the Federal Reserve come on numerous occasions since the summer of 1978 to intervene strongly--to the tune of over $9, $6, and $5 billion respectively, in each of the three quarters up to January 1, 1979--but these amounts have been matched by nearly equivalent sums in deutsche marks. In addition, the Bundesbank and the Bank of Japan have been reported by the Federal Reserve itself in its semiannual reports as lending added weight to these market operations. It seems paradoxical--yet understandable with the deterioration of world security--that the Germans should so readily come to the aid of the dollar yet should be rather more reluctant to support the weaker currencies in the European Monetary System.

What cannot, I feel, be too strongly stressed is the fundamental difference between the position of sterling in the middle and late 1960s and that of the dollar in the late 1970s. The pressure of foreign exchange

TABLE 3.8. International issues of bonds by currency of issue (in U.S. $millions)

Currency of Issue	1971	1972	1973	1974	1975	1976	1977	1978	1979[a]
Deutsche mark	859.8[b]	1,237.7	1,077.9	638.5	3,099.3	2,821.4	5,215.2	6,531.2	3,813.7[c]
Japanese yen	–	–	–	–	–	–	111.3	78.9	115.1
Pound sterling	61.0	160.0	29.5	23.9	–	–	220.9	287.1	291.3
SDR	–	–	–	–	172.9	–	–	32.1	106.7
United States dollar (X)	2,694.8	4,302.2	2,891.8	3,082.9	4,922.1	9,999.2	12,336.4	7,693.4	8,886.5
Total (including all other currencies) (Y)	4,245.9	6,927.6	4,701.9	4,511.7	10,519.5	15,367.8	19,484.1	15,939.8	14,900.6
X as percent of Y	63.5	62.1	61.5	68.3	46.8	65.1	63.3	46.4	59.6

[a] Provisional three quarters.
[b] Nil or no transaction over the period.
[c] Only for second and third quarters.

TABLE 3.9. Traditional foreign issues of bonds by market countries (in millions of U.S. $)

Market Countries	1971	1972	1973	1974	1975	1976	1977	1978	1979[a]
Germany	391.7	575.6	626.9	260.5	604.9	1,309.3	1,511.1	1,676.8	1,113.9
Japan	334.3	635.8	782.4	196.2	341.5	287.3	1,393.5	4,686.0	1,785.9
Switzerland	867.1	1,014.5	1,535.3	972.4	3,529.0	5,443.6	4,959.3	7,608.9	7,472.7
United Kingdom	141.9	-	8.7	-	32.8	-	-	-	-
United States	1,342.7	1,575.1	1,487.5	3,546.8	6,854.6	10,631.6	7,668.2	6,358.6	3,676.3
Total (for all countries)	3,490.8	4,384.6	5,349.8	7,722.8	12,300.8	18,943.3	16,610.2	21,542.1	14,738.7

Source: OECD Financial Statistics 1979, no. 13/1.
[a] First three quarters.

markets on the sterling exchange rate was bound, sooner or later, to lead official and other holders of sterling to diversify into dollars; whereas, despite all the pressures of the market on dollar exchange rates, there is no comparable risk of very large shifts out of dollars into anything else. There is nowhere else to go without upsetting the whole applecart and damaging the system. The gold price rise last autumn (1979) was perhaps a sign of strong discontent with dollar depreciation, but once the gold price has risen, its subsequent volatility is likely to limit the importance of gold reserves as a practical large-scale alternative. And neither the deutsche mark nor the yen are likely in the foreseeable future to be realistic alternatives to the dollar. Most estimates of deutsche mark reserve holdings vary around 9 or 10 percent of the total, with a possible high including Euromarks of 15 percent; yen holdings are estimated at around 4 or 5 percent. Nor does the idea of an IMF substitution account (now effectively shelved) offer a realistic alternative. Until the United States is prepared to accept the same rules and submit to the same constraints as other countries--surely a rather improbable eventuality judging by the whole of international monetary history since Bretton Woods--a substitution account through which surpluses and deficits could be settled could only be a supplement to, and never a substitute for, the use of the dollar in international trade and finance.

To European eyes, one possibly significant indicator of continued U.S. dominance in the system is to be found in international capital markets and the flow of investment funds. Tables 3.8 and 3.9 show clearly the continued popularity of internationally issued bonds denominated in dollars despite the dispersion of actual marketing to centers outside the United States. The value of dollar-denominated bonds is still twice that of deutsche mark bonds and still nearly 60 percent of the total international bond market. The success of the Swiss in providing a marketplace is a reflection of demand and of the efficiency of the market operators.

The unabated popularity of investments in the United States--both direct investment and portfolio investment--is also worth remembering. Tables 3.10,

TABLE 3.10. Foreign direct investment in three countries (in millions of SDRs)

Country	1971	1972	1973	1974	1975	1976	1977	1978	1979
U.S.	360	880	2,350	3,970	2,150	3,750	3,170	5,040	2,310[a]
Japan	210*	150*	-30*	170*	190	100	20		n.a.
Germany	1,130	1,780	1,700	2,120	1,050	1,310	1,220	1,320	n.a.

Source: IMF Balance of Payments Yearbook, vol. 30 (December 1979), and supplement to vol. 30 (December 1979).
[a] First two quarters only.
*Denotes figures not comparable. Up to 1974 Japanese direct and indirect private investments were not differentiated.

TABLE 3.11. Foreign portfolio investment (in millions of SDRs)

Country	1971	1972	1973	1974	1975	1976	1977	1978
U.S.	9,940	12,960	4,190	1,420	9,140	11,130	25,390	8,910
Japan	950*	550*	-660*	-660*	2,180	2,510	1,910	2,060
Germany	n.a.	3,490	2,240	-350	-420	1,900	1,040	1,500

Source: IMF Balance of Payments Yearbook, vol. 30 (December 1979), and supplement to vol. 30 (December 1979).
*Denotes figures are not comparable. Up to 1974 Japanese direct and indirect private investments were not differentiated.

3.11, and 3.12 give some of the relevant figures and show that foreign direct investment into the United States is nearly four times as large as investment in West Germany and that portfolio investments, though predictably volatile from year to year, only in 1974 showed a small negative net total. In any monetary system, the control of others' deposited wealth confers possibilities of leverage and influence--as shown by the U.S. action on Iranian assets.

The reasons for this popularity, it is clear to the corporations and the investors making these decisions, are by no means exclusively monetary. The simple fact is that in sector after sector of the international economy, the U.S. market is the largest single outlet under one government--if you exclude China and the Soviet Union as being still so closed off by autarkic planning and restrictions on foreign investment as to exist in a somewhat different world. Take, as just one example, the world market for machine tools. The United States may not be the major producer, nor yet the major exporter. But any large machine tool producer whatever the nationality has to break into or operate inside the U.S. market to achieve the scale of sales necessary for profitable operation. Not only is it the largest, it is still the last bastion of the world market economy, the keep of the castle. Anything else will go first--a truth very clearly reflected in the strengthening of the dollar in relation to European currencies in the immediate aftermath of the invasion of Afghanistan.

This strongly suggests the difficulty of isolating our discussions of the interaction of domestic and international monetary affairs from their economic and political contexts, both domestic and global.

It also suggests that any attempt that United States policymakers make to secure or maintain relative invulnerability for the U.S. economy has a far better chance of success than similar attempts by the Europeans, the Japanese, or the OPEC countries. To that extent, the United States still enjoys relative superpower status in the state/state power game. A quick check over the major decisions taken in the international monetary system during the 1970s surely shows that always the options preferred by the United States were the ones adopted. In 1973/1974, in the face of the OPEC demand for redistribution of the benefits of oil production, the United States was the hard-liner. The result was that the industrialized world opted (as ruling elites within national societies have often done before), for

TABLE 3.12. Portfolio investment, net balance of payments (in millions of SDRs)

Country	1972	1973	1974	1975	1976	1977	1978	Total 1972-1978
U.S.	+12,380	+3,640	-100	+3,980	+3,450	+20,720	+6,120	+50,190
Japan	+90[a]	-1,470[a]	-710	+2,140	+2,400	+770	-990	+2,230
Germany	+4,250	+2,170	-1,170	-1,410	+1,330	-1,170	-220	+3,780

Source: IMF Balance of Payments Yearbook, vol. 30 (December 1979), and supplement to vol. 30 (December 1979).
[a] Denotes figures not comparable. Up to 1974 Japanese direct and indirect private investments were not differentiated.

inflation as an easier option than making room for increased consumption by the dissidents. Similarly, there was a choice of ways of meeting the NOPEC payments deficits after the oil price rise: either a large official borrowing facility could have been created along lines suggested in the Brandt Commission Report, or the immediate problem could be solved by allowing the privatization of LDC debt by resorting to Eurocurrency borrowing. Incidentally, one consequence of this privatization of debt has been the shifting of risk for changing interest rates in response to the London inter-bank overnight rate from the investor (as in long-term bonds) to the borrower. The floating interest rate imposed by the need to roll over less developed countries Eurocurrency borrowings relieves the lenders and the banks of this risk.

CONCLUSION

The implication in terms of power analysis seems clear enough. The strategic preeminence of the United State among all other states outside China and the Soviet Union is assured by its nuclear capabilities. Its economic preeminence is similarly assured by the fact that its government controls the largest, richest, single market in the world market economy, as its financial preeminence is assured by its unassailed position as the issuer of the world's still preferred medium of international exchange and transactions. The three factors together make sure that it will retain its monopoly of the power to initiate and the power to veto change in the international monetary system.

The only thing that has changed (and that for two coincident reasons) is that the United States in now more dependent on European, Japanese, and OPEC--and even, on some issues, Third World--cooperation to carry out such changes smoothly and effectively. One reason for this is the intensification of economic integration and the consequent involvement with the rest of the world not only through trade and oil imports but through extensive foreign investment, and the need of American banks and corporations to recoup the costs of technological development from profits derived from a worldwide market. The other reason is the relatively rapid growth of these companion "mushrooms", together constituting a much larger share of world production and of the world market. American dependence on European and Japanese cooperation in managing interdependence (Camps 1980) is disguised in monetary matters by the readiness with which all rally round whenever crisis threatens the fragile, precarious balance between authorities and markets. No one is anxious to experience the sudden bump when the seesaw tilts too suddenly. All authorities share a heightened consciousness of the potentially disruptive forces of the markets, especially financial markets. But none of them have the same power of initiative and veto that the United States still has, as attempted initiatives by Giscard d'Estaing or Helmut Schmidt repeatedly demonstrated.

What this adds up to is a sharpening of the familiar dilemma of all those in positions of power, whether fathers of families, or heads of departments, of companies, of political parties, or of states or the elites of world empires. To each of these, power offers privilege and opportunity. There are extra benefits to be reaped, extra opportunities and the extra freedom of a wider choice of options, besides the greater security of a special immunity from threat or risk. Enjoyment of these privileges brings immediate short-run satisfaction. But sharing them or forgoing them may increase the opportunity to build for a long-run future for the whole group. The United States, in short, faces a difficult choice as the going gets rougher—to use the very substantial residue of power to enjoy the privilges of its position and its strategic, economic, and financial preeminence, or to take the chances inherent in a more farsighted and disinterested strategy.

One particularly clear example of this choice or dilemma, with large, direct effects upon the international monetary system, has been seen in the choice between energy consumption and energy conservation. The United States issued the clarion call for conservation in 1974 by setting up the International Energy Agency. But as with the International Trade Organization in 1948, it was the United States itself that lagged behind in responding to that call by increasing prices of gasoline and heating fuel. The policy (or nonpolicy) in energy opted for taking the strain on the dollar rather than on the voter; and the long-run costs of this policy were obscured as the resulting weakness of the dollar was mitigated by monetary inflows, by collective market intervention, by higher interest rates, and by the deterioration in world security. The industrialized countries have been kept quiet, as it were, by making it easy for them to finance deficits and to resort, as the United States did, to protection of domestic markets by the use of reference prices and "voluntary" export restrictions. The costs of taking these options rather than the harder ones are not to be found in redistribution of economic power to other countries in the sort of multipolar system imagined by Kindleberger and others. They are to be found in a substantial (and many would say dangerous) shift in the balance between public and private, between authority and market, a shift most clearly reflected in the volatility of exchange rates and monetary movements against which the United States, as well as other states, has been powerless to defend itself.

They are powerless, it is important to add, only if you assume that the political preferences for taking the easier rather than the harder way out are never reversed. As Paul Fabra recalled in his analysis of the current predicament, there have been times in the past when political resolution has snatched monetary stability and renewed confidence in the system out of the jaws of worsening disaster. The arrest of the German hyperinflation in 1923, the currency reform of Germany in 1948, and the liberalization and reform of French policy in 1958 perhaps give hope that the international system, too, is not beyond redemption.

NOTE

In revising the first draft of this paper, I have had the benefits of valuable comments and counsel from the editors and my two discussants. I am also indebted to Professor Kagami and his associates, John Lepper and Sheilagh Vasiliou, of the Nomura Research Institute's London branch for their helpful suggestions.

DISCUSSION • *Robert Z. Aliber*

The paper by Susan Strange, like that by Robert Keohane (Paper 1), raises the central issue of power in international political economy--what power is, how power is measured, and how the power of the United States may have changed in the last decade. Strange differs from Keohane in believing that U.S. power is still substantial, indeed, extraordinary. Some of her measures imply a significant increase in U.S. international economic power, while Keohane asserts that U.S. power has declined significantly; his story is that the increased U.S. dependence on imported petroleum meant that OPEC was able to sustain a fourfold price increase, which in turn led to a surge in U.S. inflation and a weak U.S. dollar. The differences between Strange and Keohane reflect both what international economic power is, and how international economic power should be measured.

The next section of this comment summarizes Susan Strange's paper. Then a personal view of power in the international economy is developed; this view is used to appraise both Susan Strange's assessment and measure of international economic power.

A SUMMARY OF SUSAN STRANGE'S PAPER

The first half of Susan Strange's paper deals with the conceptual issues involved in analysis of national power in the international economy, and the second half presents a set of empirical measures of changes in U.S. international economic power in the last several decades. The first question raised by Strange is whether the current American or the current European perception of U.S. power is more nearly correct. The Americans remain frustrated by their inability to do much about the hostages in Iran and the Russians in Afghanistan. In contrast, the Europeans are worried that they have no significant impact on the major life and death security decisions that are determined in Washington and in Moscow.

Strange asserts that international economic power is not identical with the foreign exchange value of the dollar. Thus international economic power might be increasing even though the foreign exchange value of the dollar is declining.

There are two major themes in the Strange paper. One is that the United States is still a "Giant Among Nations." The second is that there has been a decline in the power and effectiveness of the U.S. government relative to the scope of the market. Most of the empirical measures noted by Strange involve financial market phenomena.

Power can be analyzed in the context of the theory of exchange. Power is the ability of one government to affect the actions of another government, perhaps because the first government can bestow favors and inflict injury. Governments exchange favors: the recipient of a favor is better able to enhance its standing with its constituents. Governments build up credits and debits in the exchange of favors; a government with a credit balance can draw down its credits, and a government with a debit balance must be prepared to reciprocate, lest it find itself unable to attract favors from others. At one stage, the United States was in a central position to provide various types of favors; the dollar was strong, and U.S. financial markets were open.

So the term economic power requires qualification. Economic power is the ability or capacity to induce other countries to follow certain actions or policies and to refrain from following others. Thus the United States may have economic power. U.S. economic power may at any moment be increasing with respect to some countries and declining relative to others. Moreover, for any given country, the U.S. ability to induce a country to follow certain monetary policies may be increasing even as the U.S. ability to affect the country through trade or aid measures may be declining. Hence the critical question involves the ability or capacity of the United States to induce other countries to take particular types of measures at specified times.

Economic power might be thought of as the stock of accumulated favors. During the Marshall Plan era and in the 1950s the United States added to this stock by grant, loan, and military assistance. In the early 1960s, however, the United States began to draw on this stock of favors as it sought the assistance of other countries in measures to limit U.S. gold sales and then, in the late 1960s, in measures that would maintain the dollar price of gold. Efforts by U.S. authorities to induce other countries to revalue their currencies were in general not successful.

Strange discusses four measures of monetary power. The first is that ability to manage the rate of money supply growth. The second is the ability to regulate access to credit. The third is the ability to control entry of banks and their branches. The fourth involves the distribution among countries of risks and opportunities in the international economy; these are the opportunities to control or affect the national choices.

Consider the view that the ability to control the money supply is a demonstration of economic power. Two points might be noted. The first is that every country with a central bank has this power; indeed, it is hard to see how this power differs among countries or changes over time. More importantly, however, the statement fails to make an adequate distinction between monetary variables and real variables, and whether there is any change in the ability to deal with real variables. Consider the view that regulation of access to credit is measure of economic power. Most countries have this power through their willingness to use exchange controls. And many countries have been much more reluctant to open their markets for bank deposits and loans than have others; U.S. banks, for example, can't conduct a banking business in Mexico or Denmark.

The second half of the paper involves a set of tables designed to illustrate changes in U.S. international economic power. One shows foreign financing of U.S. government deficits, that is, the acquisition of U.S. government debt by foreign official institutions. Other measures include the share of dollar assets in total international reserves, the share of dollar assets in the Eurobond market, and the growth of foreign investment in the United States. The implication is that U.S. economic power cannot have declined because these measures show an increase in foreign involvement in the United States. Hence, the foreign financing of the U.S. government reflects the economic power of the United States, a form of tribute to the United States. And the foreign ownership of the U.S. dollar reflects the attractiveness of the U.S. dollar.

The shortcoming of the Strange Paper is that the evidence presented doesn't answer the question posed.

THE POTHOLE THEORY OF POWER

The pothole theory of power was developed several years ago when driving on Second Avenue in New York City immediately after a return from Great Britain. The roughness of the roadway, which might have paralyzed a World War I tank, seemed symbolic of the decline of the public infrastructure in many American cities. What needed to be explained is why public infrastructure declines while the public sector grows and per capita incomes increase. One answer is that the combination of the bill for wages and transfer payments has increased, depleting the ability of the city or the government to maintain the public infrastructure. The city may be becoming richer, in the sense that the per capita income of its residents is higher, but the government's ability to use revenues to prevent the quality of its public capital stock from declining has eroded because of other demands on its services.

The international counterpart of the pothole theory is that the ability of the U.S. government to generate financial resources to enhance its power and standing with various foreign governments has declined because of the increase in private domestic demand and government expenditures. For example, during the Marshall Plan era, the U.S. current account surplus was $2\frac{1}{2}$ percent of U.S. national income and foreign grants and loans were 2 percent of national income. Moreover, during the war, under a variety of programs, the United States had transferred substantial resources to other countries, and enhanced its own standing and its capacity to induce them to follow the U.S. lead. However, over the years, the surplus the U.S. government could command for international activities has declined and U.S. foreign aid has declined.

In addition, the U.S. government facilitated strengthening U.S. relationships by permitting foreign firms ready access to both the U.S. capital market and the U.S. commodity markets. Such access was increasingly constrained, and the U.S. authorities leaned on foreign authorities not to buy gold and to reduce their payments surpluses; such requests incurred "costs" to the United States. These costs were a charge on the stock of favors the United States had build up; unlike the earlier period, the United States was using its power, although observers may have felt that the use of U.S. power was for issues of second-order importance. Then access to the U.S. capital market was constrained by the Interest Equalization Act of 1963. Access to the U.S. product markets was constrained by a variety of "voluntary" export quotas.

The implication of the pothole theory is that the U.S. government's ability to obtain agreement of others has declined because of the increased pressure of domestic demands on U.S. revenues. Hence the thesis of the pothole theory is that the reduced ability of the U.S. authorities to generate a domestic surplus that could be allocated to foreign governments was a major factor behind the decline of U.S. power; the supply of carrots declined, and there were more immediate U.S. demands on foreign governments to make adjustments that would ease the problems encountered by the U.S. authorities. There were, however, several other factors that meant that the effectiveness of the supply of U.S. carrots had declined. One was the more rapid growth of other industrial countries relative to the United States, which was virtually inevitable given the differential growth rates in the 1940s, which meant the demand for carrots might have been decreasing relative to the U.S. supply of carrots. The second was that the need for carrots on the part of other industrial countries declined, partly because so many of them were in payments surpluses. The third was that those countries with payments deficits could readily adjust by permitting their currencies to depreciate; the demise of the Bretton Woods system meant the demand for carrots was somewhat attenuated.

International, political-economic power appears largely concerned with how countries adjust to each other--and two sorts of issues are involved. One concerns the size of the current account balance, and whether the surplus countries are willing to lend to the deficit countries. A second concerns the policy adjustments, and where the initiatives for such adjustments should be taken to correct imbalances. In part, international economic power consists of providing real resources to ease the policy burden if not the real burden.

Hence, while the economic power of the United States is distinct from the foreign exchange value of the U.S. dollar, the several devaluations of the dollar and then the subsequent depreciation have reduced U.S. economic power because they are almost certainly associated with a decline in the ability of the United States to supply favors for other countries.

A COMPARISON OF THE STRANGE MEASURES OF ECONOMIC POWER WITH THE MEASURES SUGGESTED BY THE POTHOLE THEORY

The empirical data noted by Susan Strange provide insights about various dimensions of the importance of the U.S. economy in the world, but little insight into whether U.S. economic power is increasing or declining, and of the importance of the dollar as a currency. The problem is that there is no theory that relates the data measures of economic power. Consider, for example, the increase in foreign official holdings of dollar assets; Strange suggests this increase is a measure of the increase in U.S. economic power. A competing story, however, is that this increase might reflect the weakness of the dollar and the inability of the United States to induce other countries to revalue their currencies. To some extent, the surge in foreign dollar holdings reflects the ability of OPEC to sustain the fourfold increase in the price of crude petroleum and the resulting OPEC payments surpluses. The growth in foreign, official holdings of dollars reflects that private parties, American as well as non-American, have been sellers of dollar assets, and that foreign central banks have acquired dollars to limit the rate of appreciation of their currencies. The reports of the growth of foreign dollar holdings would generally suggest a decline in U.S. international economic power rather than an increase.

Or consider the growth of direct foreign investment in the United States, which surged in 1977 and 1978, presented to show the increase in U.S. economic power. An alternative interpretation, however, is that the surge reflects the excessive weakness of the dollar, and the combination of an undervalued currency and a depressed stock market. The U.S. economy was for sale--and at a very low price. Indeed, casual observation suggests that countries that have substantial international economic power are likely to be engaging in direct foreign investment. And the switch from the 1960s, the decade of <u>Le Defi American</u>, to the 1970s, a decade of the dollar glut, reflects the decline in U.S. international economic power.

Strange's observation that the power of the state has declined relative to that of the market is plausible for the United States; the power of Washington has declined relative to that of New York, Chicago, and other financial and industrial centers. Whether the reverse has happened abroad is less clear. An alternative version of the same statement is that the system more nearly resembles a perfectly competitive model; there are fewer monopoly centers of power. Small countries have limited, if not trivial, power; they have no significant surplus which can be used to win friends and influence people. In a perfectly competitive model, no one has power; any seller who charges above the market price goes bankrupt because there are no sales, and anyone who charges below the market price goes bankrupt because his profits are inadequate. The monopolist must strive to maintain his monopoly, even though he is continually undertaking actions that erode his position. So his power may involve foreign aid, or capital market access, or landing rights; power arises from being able to distribute something scarce. Size is important, as with most monopolies, because the rents to share have larger values.

One reason that the Strange analysis does not enable her to answer her question is that the popular concern in the United States and Europe with measures of power involves military and security issues, while her paper deals more narrowly with economic measures. While changes in economic power and in military power are likely to be in the same direction, the relations between them are complex. Moreover, even military or security power is multidimensional; the United States may lack the power to fight conventional war even if it has the power to fight nuclear war. Even if it has conventional power in Western Europe, the United States may lack the ability to undertake certain amphibious operations. But even if it had this ability, the United States might lack the ability to conduct these operations at some distance. Even in economic terms alone, the lack of a model or theory means that there is no ability to determine which financial variables are relevant to the assessment of changes in U.S. international economic power.

DISCUSSION • *Robert Solomon*

Power to What End?

Discussants usually come to bury rather than to praise, sometimes even to inflate their own egos while deflating the ego of the author of the paper they are discussing.

I have no such motivations. My ego is in good shape and I am pleased to have this opportunity to make the acquaintance of Susan Strange, whose name and work I have long been aware of.

My intention is to be constructive. I offer two classes of comment. First, I pose some questions--questions to which I, perhaps because I am not well read in political science, feel answers should be given in the paper.

Second, though I have no quarrel with the main message of the paper, I find myself uncomfortable with the facts and the economic analysis that are marshalled to support the thesis that the United States is still an extraordinary power in the monetary field.

Susan Strange begins her paper by pointing to a difference in perceptions, between Americans and Europeans, of American power in the area of security. Americans, she says, feel helpless while Europeans feel vulnerable to American whims. Though she suggests that both perceptions may be exaggerated, when she comes to examine monetary power she pushes hard on the hypothesis that the European perception is correct--that the United States continues to have a considerable degree of power.

I should like to begin by expressing some puzzlement concerning the initial discussion of monetary power. What I failed to find in the paper was a clear statement of the ultimate uses of power. Benefits and costs, as well as opportunities and risks, are referred to; but how, if at all, American power enhances its benefits or opportunities and reduces its costs or risks is unclear to me.

What is presented to us in detail is a catalogue of the attributes of power--for example, the ability to control the money supply or to control access to credit. But these attributes are, if I understand the paper, instruments of power. They are means, not ends. What I am unclear about is what are the ends to which power is directed.

I turn now to some of the economic analysis in the paper.

One of the attributes of power, we are told, is the "capacity to borrow from others, to preempt lending capacity and to repay in depreciated currency." We are then presented with two tables that are said to show that the United States "has not lost the capacity to get foreign governments and citizens to assist substantially the financing of U.S. government spending." What the tables show is the extent to which budget deficits were "financed by foreigners." The proportion was as high as 62 percent in 1973 and as low as 40 percent in 1977.

Now, it is a fact of life that the dollar serves as a reserve currency and that foreign central banks, when they acquire dollars, often invest them in U.S. government securities, regardless of the financing needs of the Treasury. Moreover, financing government spending is not a particularly onerous task requiring the assistance of foreigners.

Thus the suggestion that the U.S. Treasury was dependent on foreign financing or that foreign financing of the budget deficit was of substantial benefit to the United States is rather misleading. The cumulative total of foreign financing shown in the table is a drop in the bucket relative to the size of flows through U.S. financial markets or relative to total U.S. savings flows. During the five years covered by Table 3.2, foreign financing amounted to $41.82 billion. During the same period, gross saving in the U.S. economy was $1,129 billion. Thus foreign financing amounted to 3.7 percent of gross domestic saving and one-half of one percent of gross national product.

That Susan Strange neglects to relate foreign acquisitions of U.S. government securities to the balance of payments positions of foreign countries is revealed by her statement that neither of the "locomotive economies" (Germany and Japan) borrow abroad "for official financing." Germany and Japan were, until 1979, in balance of payments surplus and were lending, not borrowing, abroad. It is noteworthy that Germany, now that it has a sizable current-account deficit, is apparently welcoming inflows of foreign funds and has borrowed directly from Saudi Arabia.

I turn now to the treatment of interest rates and exchange rates, skipping over the presentation of data on the expansion of foreign exchange holdings and Eurocurrency markets, which in my view do not tell us very much about American power.

On exchange rates, Susan Strange attributes to the United States, if I understand her correctly, "the polarization of weak and strong currencies," between which the United States was able to rest comfortably. Just how Washington created severe inflation in Britain and Italy and price stability in Germany and Switzerland is a mystery. I don't regard this polarization into what were called vicious and virtuous circles as evidence of American power.

Nor do I agree with Paul Fabra on the cause and effect relationship between the appreciation of the Swiss franc, deutsche mark, and yen and the "deflationary effects on their economies." On the contrary, I believe that the slow economic expansion of Germany, Japan, and Switzerland in 1977-1978 generated their large current account surpluses, which in turn explain the upward movement of their exchange rates. I would turn the causation around.

The United States is also identified as the instigator of high interest rates in the 1970s. I believe this is historically inaccurate--look at German interest rates in 1973. But what is the relevance? I suppose the point is that the United States has more power over interest rates abroad than other countries have over U.S. interest rates. One cannot quarrel with this proposition, but one can ask what benefit the United States derives from this asymmetry. Again, I ask, what are the uses of power?

Susan Strange is struck by the ability of the United States to get others to support the dollar. She finds it paradoxical that Germany "comes to the aid" of the dollar more readily than it supports weaker currencies in the European Monetary System. The mystery is easily dispelled if one regards intervention in foreign exchange markets not as an aid to the issuer of the currency that is purchased but as an effort of the intervening country to dampen the rate of appreciation of its own currency. Early in the paper, Susan Strange emphasizes that monetary power should not be confused with the value of currencies. But later she appears to believe that supporting the dollar was in the American interest and that actions by Germany in this respect demonstrate the existence of American power.

I skip over the data on bond issues and direct investment. They do indeed demonstrate the importance of the U.S. economy and of its currency in the monetary system.

Finally, and "most significant of all," the monetary system is said to have been "deeply affected by the outcome of the choice between energy consumption and energy conservation." The United States consumed rather than conserved. That is true but the most recent data on petroleum consumption (and it is that rather than energy consumption in general that matters) seem to indicate that the United States may not be doing so badly. In any event, once again I have trouble following the analysis and relating it to power. How did the United States gain? Perhaps we are being told, at this point, that even the United States is powerless in the face of the oil crisis.

The German arrest of hyperinflation in 1923 is presented as one of several examples of how power over events may be regained and the international system redeemed. Yet, I thought the major thesis of the paper, as its title suggests, is that the United States is "still an extraordinary power." Thus the concluding paragraph strikes me as something of a non sequitur.

Let me repeat that though I find fault with the economic analysis of this paper, I do not disagree with its main thesis that the United States is not a pitiful and weak monetary giant. If we agree on that proposition, where do we go from there?

REJOINDER • *Susan Strange*

The once-divorced, it seems, find mutual comprehension far harder to achieve even with the best will in the world, than green young lovers. So politics and economics that, in the salad days of political economy two centuries ago, spoke and understood a common language, now seem to have the greatest difficulty in communicating with each other across the barriers that have grown up between them. And this seems true even when--as with my two discussants--there is evident goodwill and a genuine wish to enter a dialogue.

Bob Aliber's economism, for example, leads him to think about power in so narrow and bounded a way that he is honestly unable to see how the evidence I put forward in the paper might be relevant to the question, Has the United States really lost power? In the first place, to define power merely as a stock of favors (or favors and threats) to be used to induce responses from others, as if power were so many cookies in a cookie jar, is really rather simplistic. And secondly, what I am primarily concerned with is not international power so much as transnational power, or to put it simply, less the power of A to get B to act, than the power of A to manipulate, to direct or neglect the system as to oblige B to react, either in a particular way, or to present B with new and perhaps unpleasant difficult choices. Thus, few Europeans, still less Third Worlders, could accept his assumption that because every state has a central bank, all central banks have an equal sovereign power to control their money supply and to insulate themselves from external destabilizing forces. That has hardly been the experience of recent years. What I am trying desperately--and apparently unsuccessfully--to communicate to him is that when foreign central banks accumulate inconvertible dollars they do so because the power and influence of the United States over the system, the regime, the referee of the game--call it what you will--in some sense obliges them to do so.

Bob Solomon's complaint that the paper does not say enough about the uses of power again makes a similarly restrictive and quite unreal assumption about the nature of power, that power is only exercised with express and deliberate intention to produce a given reaction, response, or result--if you cannot prove intention, you cannot prove the existence of power. Power, I should hardly have thought it necessary to explain (especially to people who have exercised it) is more often used unintentionally than intentionally; and ultimately, whatever the means, it is used to allocate values in whatever system or organization people operate, and to allocate these values in favor of certain groups within the system rather than with disfavor to others. So, my answer to his question is that the United States has used the power it had in the system firstly to allow the forces of the market to rule (and corporate profits to be collected), and thus to allocate a greater value to the efficiency of the system in creating wealth (for some) than to either its stability or its equity. The choices made in Washington in the 1960s and 1970s--shortsightedly in my opinion for the enlightened interest of the United States itself--gave first priority to immediate national goals and too little attention to the long-term viability of the entire system and to the need to win the consent of the governed.

My indicators were not intended to show that the United States <u>depended</u> on foreign financing, merely that the possession of power (over the <u>running</u> of the system more than directly over the actions of others) is recognizable--as in all political systems--by the enjoyment of privilege. Who salutes whom is an indicator of army rank, even though superior officers do not <u>need</u> to be saluted.

It <u>is</u> also recognizable by the proven capacity to make changes in the rules of the game; by the capacity to license or restrain the major operators--in our case, the big multinational banks; and by the ability--which need not necessarily be exercised all the time--to inflict costs and impose risks and make others make the necessary unpleasant adjustments to change and shock. What it seems especially difficult for Americans to grasp about the international monetary system as it actually functions is its essential asymmetry in respect of each of these indicators of power. If American economists would just make the effort to put themselves in the shoes of, say, Belgium or Sweden, it would help them understand a little more about the nature of power in and over the system.

All I was trying to suggest was that there were some economic indicators (I did not refer to political or military ones, though these too exist) that suggested that though the United States may have abdicated power to the forces of the market, and though other states (Germany, Japan, China, Saudi Arabia) have become wealthier, yet the United States has by no means lost altogether or irrevocably either its authority over those market forces nor its preeminence in an essentially asymmetrically interdependent global political economy.

GENERAL DISCUSSION

The general discussion was concerned primarily with the definition and measurement of power in the international system. Keohane commented that a basic difficulty in political analysis is that power is not as fungible as money. Different uses of power require different sources of power, and different indices for its measurement. Strange, he said, relies on a revealed power analysis that cannot tell us much about changes in the level of power. This requires an analysis along the lines of Aliber's idea that monetary power reflects the ability to give gifts. Others pointed out that not all ends of power require expenditures. The United States, for instance, could reduce its petroleum consumption via taxes. Some argued that U.S. inability to follow this course reflected political limits on the ability of the government to gain resources. Explanation of such limits, it was suggested, is a central part of the political analysis of economic policymaking.

II

Domestic Politics, Openness, and the Political Economy of Monetary Policy

INTRODUCTION

In this section we turn our attention to the influence of domestic politics and openness on policy. Both papers deal explicitly with the interaction between domestic political pressures and the economic outcomes achievable in open industrial economies. They argue that by constraining domestic choices and opportunities, international factors play a decisive role in governing the institutional and behavioral structure.

The first paper, by Stanley Black, professor of economics at Vanderbilt University, examines the political and social environment within which economic policy is conducted. Such conditions affect decisions involving the policy regime--for instance the choice of exchange rate arrangements, or the choice of an antiinflation strategy relying on monetary rules as opposed to one relying on a union-based wage policy--which are the basis for more specific policy actions. He argues that "actual outcomes in most industrial countries can best be understood in a game-theoretical context, in which business, labor, and political leaders are each struggling to achieve a preferred outcome and in which none of these necessarily has the ability to impose its preferred outcomes on others."

To this end he develops an analytical model of an open economy in which stabilization policy can have short-run impacts on unemployment, real wages, and the balance of payments. He then examines a series of possible outcomes for situations characterized by differing degrees of dominance for labor, management, and the fiscal-monetary authorities. Black concludes with an application of his analysis to the recent experience of several major industrial countries in response to the series of external disturbances which have confronted economic policymakers in the 1970s.

Black's paper is discussed by Peter Katzenstein, associate professor of government at Cornell University, and Alan Stockman, assistant professor of economics at the University of Rochester. Katzenstein finds Black's basic focus on the relative bargaining strength of business and labor and the autonomy of central banks difficult to apply consistently to the major OECD countries. Black, for instance, characterizes the United States, West Germany, and Japan as having a cooperative bargaining environment. Yet organized labor is strong in Germany and conspicuously weak in Japan, while the Japanese central bank has little autonomy from the government compared with the Bundesbank. Katzenstein goes on to suggest that the relationships between labor, business, and government may depend, in addition to political strength, on the economic context in which countries operate, particularly their openness. He also cautions that political bargaining among the actors will be over the future distribution of power as well as the distribution of material benefits as measured by, say, real wages.

Stockman, in his discussion, suggests that a model of conflict resolution must include the institutional environment in which economic decision makers find themselves as well as their objectives. This environment includes the constraints upon actions of economic agents as well as the effects of actions. Conflict among agents results not only in policies, but also in rules that become part of the institutional environment. Furthermore, policies and rules will both become parts of a package of government programs. This raises two basic problems in the type of model used by Black. First, it is hard to distinguish government actions that are simply favors to specific groups from those rules that, by providing an institutional framework for further interaction, may benefit all concerned. Second, the effects, both economic and political, of a package of rules and policies is more difficult to determine than is the impact of a single isolated policy action.

In the second paper of this section Thomas Willett and John Mullen of the Claremont Graduate School examine the interaction between various possible exchange rate regimes and the likelihood that macroeconomic policy will have an inflationary bias. They begin by observing that evaluation of the inflation bias in a policymaking process must be conducted in relative rather than absolute terms. A process can be called inflation biased only if it results in higher rates of inflation than those desired (for instance) by the informed median voter. But Willett and Mullen argue that differences between short-run and long-run inflation-unemployment trade-offs, combined with myopic perceptions of voters and short time horizons of policymakers do lead to such bias.

Given the existence of an inflation bias, the exchange rate regime affects the significance of the bias from both a short-run and a long-run perspective. In the short run, Willett and Mullen argue, the (inflationary) price effects of expansionary monetary policy are likely to show up more rapidly under flexible rates than in a closed economy: "This would tend to steepen the short-run inflation-unemployment trade-off and thus to reduce the magnitude of the inflationary bias resulting from excessively short time horizons and political business cycle behavior." There is a shorter lag between the desirable (but temporary) real effects of an inflationary policy and its undesirable price effects. Consequently, even if voters are myopic it is less likely that policymakers will realize political gains from such policies. Under pegged rates, on the other hand, inflation bias might be worse than in a closed economy. This would be the case if the bias is a reflection of an inflation-consumption (rather than an inflation-unemployment) trade-off, since expansionary policy will temporarily raise domestic absorption (above the closed economy level) due to the development of a trade deficit.

In the long run, however, the constraints on macroeconomic policies may be quite different. Under permanently pegged rates, the long-run average of each nation's inflation is constrained by the world average of national rates. Willett and Mullen observe, however, that in the absence of close coordination of policy between nations, there may be a tendency toward excessive global inflation if pegged rates do produce short-run incentives for expansionary policy in individual countries.

Willett and Mullen do not conclude from their analysis that the existence of flexible exchange rates is sufficient to eliminate a substantial inflationary bias. Rather, they see flexible rates as making a marginal contribution in reducing such bias in policymaking, and they believe a constitutionally mandated monetary rule offers the most effective method for exerting antiinflationary discipline on national governments.

J. David Richardson, from the University of Wisconsin, in his discussion of Willett and Mullen, emphasizes several points in the paper with which he is in agreement. He is somewhat skeptical, however, of their preference for a constitutionally mandated monetary growth rule as a method for encouraging discipline among policymakers. Richardson suggests that nations that choose the discipline of a constitutional rule would presumably also behave responsibly without one. Instead, he suggests policies to increase public information--for instance, near immediate disclosure of policymaking deliberations--and education. He goes on to discuss several possible areas into which the Willett and Mullen analysis might be extended. One such area is the supply side of the economy; for instance, the exchange rate system surely affects the path of real wages. Another desirable extension would be to examine the relationship between the exchange rate system and the growth of external currency banking.

The second discussant of Willett and Mullen is Lucas Papademos of Columbia University. He applauds their willingness to examine the interactions between economic and political factors, while disagreeing with some of the specifics of their analysis. He suggests, to begin with, that myopia and misinformation on the part of the voting public, emphasized by Willett and Mullen as a source of inflation bias, are less important than several other factors, among them the excessive claims of competing interest groups on the limited financial resources of the government, the inflexibility of wages, the effects of higher energy prices, and the role of groups that have a vested interest in continuing inflation. He also suggests that the electorate does learn from past mistakes, implying that the appearance of myopia may be temporary. Papademos goes on to argue that Willett and Mullen may exaggerate the extent to which flexible exchange rates promote discipline over inflation-biased policy. He is careful to point out, however, that he does not see any system of fixed rates as a source of effective discipline, either. He ends his comment with several observations on the efficacy of a constitutionally mandated monetary rule, suggesting that such a rule does not offer a painless panacea for inflationary woes.

PAPER 4 • *Stanley W. Black*

Strategic Aspects of the Political Assignment Problem in Open Economics

INTRODUCTION

Economists of my generation (the 1960s) were brought up on a macroeconomic paradigm that involved the intersection of an aggregate demand curve with an aggregate supply curve [this is "what Rip Van Winkle knew when he went to sleep" in 1963, according to Gordon (1976)]. Fortunately for us, the many developments in the theory of inflation and unemployment during the 1970s, including the role of expectations, the natural rate hypothesis, and internal labor market theories can all be accommodated in this paradigm, with a certain amount of pulling and stretching of the supply curve (see Morley 1979, Chap. 4). For example a strongly monetarist theory of inflation can be built on a short-run upward-sloping supply curve that slopes upward only because workers are mistaken in their price-level expectations. When unanticipated monetary expansion raises aggregate demand and prices, some additional real output is forthcoming as workers see only the higher nominal wages and not the correspondingly higher prices. But this expansion evaporates in a puff of inflation as price expectations are revised upward. Other sets of behavioral assumptions can likewise be accommodated in this diagram, including institutionalist "cost-push" theories built on upward shifts in the supply curve.

But the economists' paradigm, whatever the behavioral assumptions behind it, rests on the assumption of <u>given</u> governmental policies, in particular monetary policies. Thus the monetarist conclusion, that control over the growth in the money supply is a necessary and sufficient condition for control over inflation, is built into the analysis. The implication is that any continuing cost-push elements of inflation can be made so painful in terms of unemployment and lost output that they will be squeezed out by monetary stringency.

This really begs the question of <u>why</u> monetary authorities choose differing rates of monetary expansion at different times and in different countries. The political theory of the business cycle has been developed to explain how and why vote-maximizing politicians may manipulate government spending and money creation in order to increase their chances of maintaining or achieving political power (See Nordhaus 1975; Gordon 1975; and Lindbeck 1976). The analytical contributions to this literature typically examine a set of political and economic constraints on politicians, which are assumed to enter into a voting function that is to be maximized. A large number of interesting and relevant factors have been introduced as constraints, including the slope of the short-run Phillips curve, the behavior of inflationary expectations, the degree of centralization in wage bargaining, the costs and benefits of raising revenue via the inflation tax, the political power of labor unions vs. rentier groups in the economy, the ideological stance of labor unions, the degree of independence of the central bank, and the degree of myopia and/or memory of voters concerning the harmful effects of temporarily beneficial policies (Gordon 1975).

In previous work (Black 1979) I have focused on the economic and political constraints and the policies chosen in particular cases, rather than on a general analysis of politicians' behavior. My work stressed the importance of differences in the sets of constraints in different countries, paying attention to detail in a group of five industrialized countries. I found that politicians in different countries would not only wind up choosing different rates of inflation because of the different constraints they faced, but they would even choose different policy regimes, such as reliance on a pegged exchange rate, a union-based wage policy, or a monetary growth rule to provide a central consistent basis for macroeconomic policy.

Such choices amount to picking different rules of thumb for macroeconomic policy, depending on the likely stability and success of the particular rule chosen in a given political and economic environment. This was described as a "political" assignment problem, in analogy to Mundell's (1962) assignment of policy rules based solely on economic relationships. The likely success of a given rule depends on the effective modes of power relationships in the country in question, whether dominated by a labor oriented political party ("socialist"), a business oriented party ("conservative"), or neither. The first of these probably could not rely on an independent monetary authority to achieve inflation targets because of the strength of the full employment commitment. The second, in contrast, could not feasibly use a union-enforced wage policy as an element of a macroeconomic policy. A conflict mode of relationship might rule out any successful consistent policy rule.

Both my earlier analysis and my recent experience in government suggest that a multipolar analysis of the sort just described provides a more realistic and perhaps more useful analysis of the political dimensions of the macroeconomic problem than either the economists' paradigm or the vote-maximization process described earlier. The aggregate supply and demand diagram assumes that government is an exogenous force with tools of economic policy that can be manipulated by the economist at will. The vote-maximizing model of political behavior recognizes that economic policy is actually determined in an interactive process involving politicians interested in their own survival and the political and economic constraints they face. As such, it is a substantial improvement on the simple economic model. Nevertheless, it clearly attributes both too much power and too much cleverness to political leaders, at least to those of the caliber seen in most countries recently. It also assumes that the private sector does not take account of predictable actions of political leaders, thus leaving it open to Lucas's (1976) critique of policy models.

In this paper, I intend to argue that actual outcomes in most industrial countries can best be understood in a game-theoretical context, in which business, labor, and political leaders are each struggling to achieve a preferred outcome and in which none of the three necessarily has the ability to impose its preferred outcome on the others. Differences in policy rules and outcomes in different countries may thus be attributed to differences in the relative bargaining strengths or the ability of the participants in this process in different countries to enforce threats, as well as differences in preferences concerning inflation and unemployment. Failure to agree on cooperative solutions may lead to higher rates of inflation and/or unemployment, as business and labor each seek to protect its real profit and wage position in an environment buffeted by oil price shocks and worldwide inflationary pressures. This will provide, I believe, a more realistic and more interesting analysis of the factors influencing macroeconomic policy. Furthermore, it deals effectively with Lucas's critique.

The next section of the paper introduces a simple one-period model of an open economy, which is drastically stripped down to enable the central policy issues to be explored with a minimum of complicating detail. The model assumes a small, open economy producing only traded goods and nontraded labor services under competitive market equilibrium conditions. The wage rate is thus analogous to the price of nontraded goods in the Salter (1959) model, while the price of traded goods varies directly with the price of foreign exchange. The purpose of the equilibrium version of this model is to provide a point of reference, a lodestar to which disequilibrium solutions must eventually return. But since the analysis concentrates on stabilization policy, the relevant time period is the short run of approximately one year. Therefore the model is enriched to allow disequilibrium solutions involving unemployment, balance of payments surpluses or deficits, and shifts in real wages due to exercise of market power in bargaining situations. In the long run, such disequilibria would be expected to affect the growth of real income, capital, or labor input, assumed constant in the short run. Several variants of the model are outlined, with varying degrees of capital mobility, market power, and disequilibrium in goods and labor markets. The stabilization policy problem is described as the management of the level of aggregate demand so as to achieve short-run internal and external balance with reasonable price stability.

The third section then sets up a series of game-theoretical solutions to the stabilization policy problem, characterized by differing degrees of dominance by one or another of the contending parties--labor, management, and the fiscal/monetary authorities. The fourth section suggests how the analysis can be used to discuss recent experience in various industrialized countries.

EQUILIBRIUM IN THE GOODS AND LABOR MARKETS
The Basic Model with a Flexible Exchange Rate

The crucial issues at stake in macroeconomic policy in an open economy can be seen in a specialized case of the Salter model of traded and nontraded goods. It is assumed in this paper that the economy produces only goods that are traded in world markets, at prices that are given to the economy in question. Thus problems of monopoly power in world markets and the terms of trade effects of exchange rate changes are ruled out of the analysis. On the other hand, the economy may produce and consume both exportable goods and importables.

In addition, nontraded labor services are produced and consumed in the domestic economy, both directly in the form of services such as construction, government, education, and personal services, and indirectly in the production of traded goods. The two key price variables in this model are the wage rate W, as the price of nontraded goods, and the exchange rate E, since the domestic prices of traded goods vary directly with the price of foreign exchange, given world market prices ($P=EP^*=E$, assuming $P^*\equiv 1$).

Production conditions can be represented by the curve PP in Figure 4.1, which indicates how labor services can be used either directly for

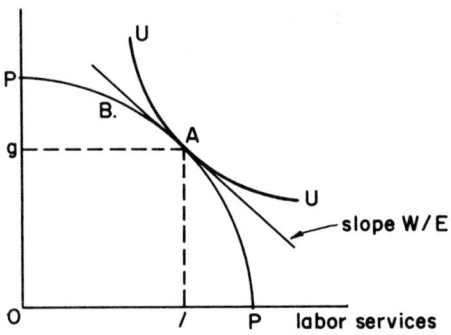

Figure 4.1

consumption or indirectly to produce goods for domestic consumption or export. Profit-maximizing producers will hire ℓP units of labor to produce Og amount of goods; Oℓ units of labor will be consumed directly in the home economy. Neoclassical production conditions with a fixed capital stock are assumed. The price line that is tangent to PP at point A has slope equal to the relative price of labor in terms of goods W/E.

Domestic demand for each of the two commodities in the model is assumed to depend on relative prices, real income, and real money balances. These conditions are reflected in the indifference curve UU of Figure 4.1, whose location depends upon tastes, holdings of real money balances (which yield services as means of payment), and the level and distribution of real income. Money income is equal to the value of production of goods and services plus the excess of government spending over taxes.

In this initial version of the model, no international borrowing or lending is allowed, and the exchange rate is assumed to equilibrate the market for foreign exchange. Therefore, the exchange rate is determined where the domestic demand for traded goods is equal to the domestic supply, as is the case at point A in Figure 4.1. The demand for money must also equal the supply as determined by the monetary authorities and the government budget deficit for full equilibrium in the model. These conditions are more fully sketched out in the first section of the Appendix, the last section of this paper.

Equilibrium conditions in this economy can be determined by examining each market in turn. It is convenient to do so in Figure 4.2, which portrays equilibrium conditions in each of the three markets in terms of the rate of change of wages $\dot{w}$ and the rate of depreciation of the domestic currency $\dot{e}$ (and the implied given rate of growth of the money supply $\dot{m}$). These are all rates of change from the (assumed given) previous levels of W, E, and M.[1]

As is shown more formally in the Appendix, equilibrium in the market for labor services, for a given rate of increase in the money supply, implies that as the rate of wage increase rises along the ℓℓ curve, the rate of depreciation must rise even more. This decline in the real wage is required to offset the fall in the direct and indirect demand for labor that results from a decline in the real value of money balances. Similarly, equilibrium in the market for traded goods requires that a more rapid rate of increase of traded goods prices along the gg curve be offset by an even larger rise in

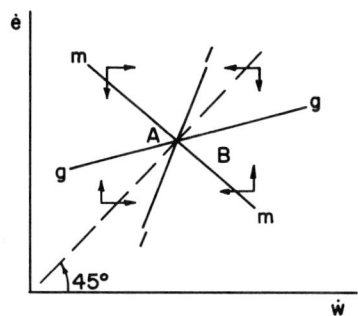

Figure 4.2

the rate of wage increase, again to counter the fall in demand resulting from a decline in the real value of money balances. Finally, in the money market, more rapid wage inflation must be balanced with slower inflation in traded goods prices to keep the overall inflation rate consistent with a given rate of increase in the money supply along the mm curve. Walras's law implies that all three curves must intersect in a single point, since zero excess demand in any two markets implies zero excess demand in the third.

Because the demand and supply functions have been assumed homogeneous in all prices and money, equilibrium in the basic model must occur along the 45° line in Figure 4.2, where the rates of increase of both prices ($\dot{w}$ and $\dot{e}$, and hence their weighted average $\dot{p}$) equals the rate of growth of the money supply, as is shown formally in the Appendix. This condition is described as purchasing power parity, since it implies that the exchange rate moves to offset the differential between the rates of increase of domestic prices ($\dot{p}$) and foreign prices.

The $\ell\ell$ curve in Figure 4.2 represents conditions of <u>internal balance</u>, where the demand for labor is equal to its supply and there is no pressure in this market either to accelerate or decelerate the rate of inflation. To the right of the $\ell\ell$ curve, there is excess supply of labor (unemployment) tending to lower the rate of wage increase, while to the left there is excess demand for labor.

Since the world price of traded goods is given to the country, any excess supply or demand for these goods can be satisfied in the world market. Therefore, the gg curve represents conditions of <u>external balance</u> in the foreign exchange market. Above the gg curve the supply of foreign exchange exceeds the demand, leading to a fall in the rate of depreciation (or an appreciation) of the domestic currency. Conversely, below the gg curve there is a deficit in the current account, which in the absence of capital flows leads to faster depreciation. As is evident from the arrows in Figure 4.2, the markets will stabilize the rate of inflation at point A under these conditions.

Shifts in Income Shares through Market Power, Unemployment, Payments Imbalances, and Taxation

Clearly, a "neutral money" model of the sort just laid out has little to say on the political economy of inflation. Indeed, the model only becomes interesting as it is modified to allow for the possibility that labor, business, and government in their struggle over income shares can accelerate the rate of inflation. There are several ways in which the model can permit shifts in relative prices and therefore income shares.

The equilibrium version of the model is based on the assumption of competitive domestic markets for goods and labor. As is well known, these conditions are modified if either labor or business succeeds in exercising monopoly power in labor or product markets. The bilateral monopoly problem in labor markets is shown in Figure 4.3. The traded goods sector demand for labor N^t slopes downward because of diminishing marginal productivity, while the supply of labor to the business sector $\bar{N} - N^d$ slopes upward. If business is able to exert monopsony power, it can calculate marginal cost MC from the supply curve and set the real wage at B so as to maximize profits at a rate below the competitive real wage C. On the other hand, labor unions with monopoly power would seek to set the real wage at a point such as L, which maximizes the real value of labor income. Since the previous real wage is taken as given in this short-run analysis, movement toward levels B or L in Figure 4.3 will imply observation of points above or below the 45° line in Figure 4.2. Thus, exercise of monopoly power by unions can shift the $\ell\ell$ curve to the right and, by raising costs for business, shift the gg curve down. The result is a rise in the real wage and a decline in the profit share. This process may be facilitated if labor can induce government to provide generous unemployment benefits or public employment for the workers who become unemployed in this process. The reason the latter condition can be helpful is apparent from Figure 4.1. If the higher real wage shifts desired production to the southeast along PP, there will be unemployment and excess demand for traded goods, unless government policy succeeds in shifting the pattern of demand to favor direct use of labor services.

Conversely, if business is able to exercise monopsony power in the labor market, it can shift the gg curve up and the $\ell\ell$ curve to the left, raising the profit rate and lowering the real wage. Again, this process would tend to move production to the northwest along the PP curve in Figure 4.1, generating excess demand for labor and a balance of payments surplus, unless government policies succeed in shifting the pattern of demand as well.

A second way in which the market equilibrium of Figure 4.2 can be disturbed is by disequilibrium in either the labor market (unemployment or unfilled vacancies) or the traded goods market (a trade surplus or deficit, financed by capital flows or reserves). In Figure 4.1 this would be shown by demand conditons producing a desired consumption point such as B that does

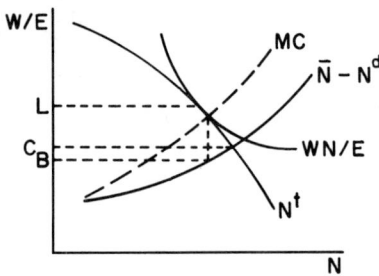

Figure 4.3

not coincide with the production point A. With demand at B, for example, there would be unemployment in the labor market and a trade deficit.

As argued more formally in the second section of the Appendix, under these conditions we may define disequilibrium $\ell\ell$ and gg curves that intersect off the diagonal of Figure 4.2 and correspond to various degrees of excess supply or demand in the two markets. For example, disequilibrium at a point such as B in Figure 4.1 implies a capital inflow in order to finance an increased availability of traded goods. This would shift the gg curve downward relative to equilibrium in that market, allowing a temporarily lower price of foreign exchange. Similarly, unemployment would be consistent with a rightward shift in the $\ell\ell$ curve relative to equilibrium, permitting a higher real wage, at least temporarily. Thus an unemployment, deficit point such as B in Figure 4.2, will correspond to a similar point in Figure 4.1.

A third way in which the real wage can be influenced is through direct government policies to influence the demand for goods and labor services, either through differential taxation or expenditure policies. For example, expansion of labor-intensive government services will tend to shift the equilibrium in Figure 4.1 to the southeast along PP, as would an increase in excise taxation on goods. Conversely, increased social insurance taxation or increased tariffs and subsidies on traded goods would tend to lower the real wage. In Figure 4.2, these policies would shift the $\ell\ell$ and gg curves' intersection as before.

A fourth way to influence the real wage and profit shares is to promote depreciation of the exchange rate through expansionary aggregate demand policy, while attempting to hold the money wage steady through incomes policy. The fall in the real wage would eventually generate a balance of payments surplus. The monetary counterpart of the surplus would, of course, be an increase in international reserve holdings. Failure to sterilize the influence of the reserve change on the domestic money supply would naturally undermine the ability to hold money wages on a steady course. Depreciation would involve moving vertically upward from point A in Figure 4.2. Now consider a policy to generate excess demand with a pegged exchange rate and rising money wages, leading to a deficit with unemployed labor horizontally to the right of point A in Figure 4.2. In this case the deficit could be maintained only as long as reserves held out or foreign loans were available. Thus manipulation of aggregate demand in conjunction with restraint on one or another of the price variables can influence income shares, at least in the short run. Obviously, an extended squeeze on profits or real wages will affect the supply of labor or capital, assumed constant above.

A fifth means of influencing income shares is through squeezing some group that exists on fixed incomes, such as a rentier class. More rapid inflation would reduce such a group's share of national income, leaving more available for both labor and capital.

The government itself can increase its share of national income through inflation, as progressive taxation in nominal terms raises the real tax burden on the private sector. This phenomenon (explored in the third section of the Appendix) affects both labor income through income taxation and profits through the understatement of depreciation allowances based on historical costs. The gains obtainable by business or labor by increasing prices or wages will thus be limited, on an after-tax basis, by the increasing government share of national income, as long as tax brackets are not indexed. Indeed, this factor provides an ominous incentive for the government to favor more rapid inflation.

Finally, there is the well-known Keynesian possibility that the supply of labor (or capital) may respond positively to a mild increase in the rate of inflation of wages (and prices), at least in the short run, due to money illusion, mistaken expectations, or long-term contracts. This phenomenon, which may be measured by the slope of the short-run Phillips curve, provides another reason for various groups in society to promote an increase in the rate of inflation with the intention of improving real income. The slope of the long-run Phillips curve is widely agreed to be much steeper than that of the short-run curve, in the neighborhood of full employment, but both curves may be rather flat at high rates of unemployment. Therefore, expansionary Keynesian policies can only be effective at relatively high rates of unemployment when the rate of inflation is reasonably low. Under these conditions, expansion of demand is unlikely to raise the rate of inflation very much.

Capital Mobility and Exchange Rate Expectations

The basic model given above, even with the modifications suggested in the preceeding section, omits a crucially important aspect of the macroeconomic management of open economies--the international mobility of capital under conditions of floating exchange rates. There are basically two approaches in the literature to this problem, depending on whether domestic and foreign bonds are assumed to be perfectly or imperfectly substitutable for each other.[2] This paper will take the imperfect substitutability approach, on the grounds of its greater empirical relevance. The basic assumptions are that not all exchange risks are coverable and that investors are risk averse, in the face of uncertainty concerning the expected future spot exchange rate. In this situation, the demand for foreign assets is an increasing function of the (uncertain) expected return on them, as compared to the domestic interest rate, $r^* - r + \dot{f}$, where r^* is the foreign interest rate, r the domestic rate, and $\dot{f}$ the expected rate of increase of the price of foreign currency over the relevant investment horizon. Equivalently, the supply of foreign loans in domestic currency is an increasing function of the expected return $r - \dot{f}$ less the foreign rate of interest r^*.

Under these conditions, an economy can run a current account surplus or deficit, but only at the cost of attracting financing or lending abroad via changes in interest rates and the exchange rate. With perfect capital mobility, on the other hand, any amount of external lending or borrowing can be easily arranged, and the uncovered parity condition $r=r^*+\dot{f}$ will hold.

As shown in the fourth section of the Appendix, the asset market equilibrium yields a relationship between the nominal wage rate and the price of foreign currency with the same downward sloping properties as the mm curve of Figure 4.2. A rise in the money wage reduces the real money stock, raising the domestic interest rate, and the lessened relative attractiveness of foreign assets reduces the price of foreign exchange. Thus, the mm curve of Figure 4.2 can continue to serve, now representing the combinations of the wage rate and exchange rate that represent equilibrium in the asset market.

A current account surplus, by increasing the net stock of privately owned foreign assets, lowers their price directly by increasing supply relative to demand and indirectly by raising domestic interest rates due to the wealth effect on the demand for money. The result is that the asset market equilibrium curve mm in Figure 4.2 shifts in toward the origin with a current account surplus, implying appreciation in the exchange rate. Conversely, a deficit shifts the curve out, leading to depreciation. These results include the effect of changing exchange rate expectations through $\dot{f}$, since an increase in the exchange rate will affect the expected rate of increase $\dot{f}$, depending on the behavior of expectations. Rational or regressive expectations would reduce $\dot{f}$, while adaptive or extrapolative expectations would increase it, ceteris paribus.

The upshot of this analysis is that external imbalance is still represented by the gg curve in Figure 4.2, even with capital mobility, since to its right the current account deficit leads to depreciation and to its left the current surplus leads to appreciation. Therefore the simple model with no capital mobility will not lead us far astray as long as capital mobility is less than perfect. On the other hand, perfect capital mobility implies that any current surplus or deficit can be easily financed at existing exchange and interest rates, so the mm curve remains unaffected by the current account. Only monetary variables or changes in real income can be expected to cause it to move in that case.

A MODEL OF CONFLICT
Objective Functions for Business, Labor, and Government

The macroeconomic problem as described in this paper involves finding rates of wage increase, depreciation of the exchange rate, unemployment, balance of payments surplus or deficit, monetary growth, and government deficit that are consistent and in some sense meet the objectives of each of the three groups concerned. "Consistent" means supported by the market equilibrium conditions of Figure 4.2, as modified by shifts and short-run factors such as exercise of market power, unemployment, and balance of payments deficits or surpluses.

The objectives of each group can be stated in terms of rates of growth of real after tax income, presumably anticipated over the future and discounted back to the present. Since the paper focuses on issues of conflict between each group, the trade-off of present versus future income will be brought in only where necessary. As shown in the fifth section of the Appendix, the rate of growth of real after tax profits in the production of traded goods will rise with the rate of increase in their prices ($\dot{e}$) and fall with an increase in the rate of change of wages ($\dot{w}$). Furthermore, one can expect the average tax rate on business profits to increase with the rate of inflation, if depreciation is based on historical cost data and the real value of the deduction shrinks with inflation.[3] As shown by Figure 4.3, there is an optimal rate of reduction of real wages from the existing level, because of diminishing returns to the increasing use of labor. Figure 4.4 shows an "optimal" combination of wage and price increase from the business viewpoint at point B, well above the 45° line. The elliptical shape and positively sloped semi-axis of the profit indifference curves are based on the argument that the "profit" dimension (northwest-southeast) is more important than the "inflation" dimension (northeast-southwest). Greater antipathy to inflation would be shown by circular, rather than elliptical, curves. As business moves on an indifference curve from the tangency point to the northeast in Figure 4.4, the benefits of lower real wages are first offset by higher inflation and then, turning back to the left of the 45° line through B, by lower profits due to diminishing returns to labor. Moving to the southeast along the back side of the curve, lower inflation compensates for excessively low real wages.

Similarly, labor's objectives in terms of the growth of real after tax income are depicted by means of the elliptical indifference curves centered about point L, below the 45° line. The benefits of increases in the real wage also run into diminishing returns due to reduced employment

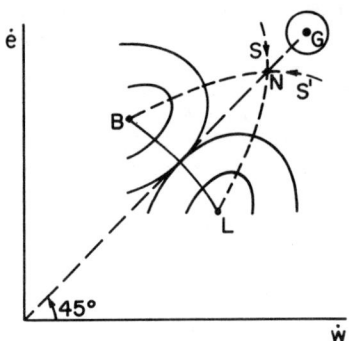

Figure 4.4

opportunities, as shown in Figure 4.3, leading to an optimum fall in the real wage at L. Higher inflation reduces real after tax income due to progressivity in the tax schedule, offsetting the benefits of higher real wages as labor moves to the northeast along an indifference curve.

The government bureaucracy, on the other hand, benefits equally from tax revenues generated by wage and profit inflation. In the long run, there will also be diminishing returns to government revenue from inflation, as capital and labor both withdraw from taxed pursuits. The bureaucrats' preferences are thus shown as the circular set of indifference curves centered at point G, with an optimum rate of inflation well above that of the private sector. Of course, the political leaders whose reelection depends on the private sector may have somewhat different preferences, being slanted more toward points B or L depending on their primary constituency.

There may be a fourth group, such as a rentier class or an unemployed underclass, which does not benefit from higher profits or higher wages but has to pay the higher prices out of a fixed money income. Such a group will have indifference curves centered at the origin of Figure 4.4.

Cooperative and Non-cooperative Equilibrium

If labor and management can bargain cooperatively to set the rate of money wage increase and the rate of price increase at rates that satisfy their own preferences as well as possible, they will choose some point along the contract curve, the solid line joining points B and L in Figure 4.4. The actual point achieved would depend on the relative bargaining power of the two parties, on their ability to enforce the terms of such an agreement, and on their influence over the macroeconomic variables determining the intersection of the $\ell\ell$, gg, and mm curves in Figure 4.2. There is a crucial consistency problem between the bargaining equilibrium and the market equilibrium. Only a certain combination of monetary expansion, exchange rate depreciation, balance of payments deficit or surplus, and level of unemployment will allow the achievement of a given bargained outcome, at some point along the contract curve BL. Both the monetary and fiscal authorities must also cooperate. Examples of inconsistency between bargaining equilibrium and market equilibrium would include Germany in 1974, when the central bank refused to ratify an "excessive" bargained wage increase, and France in 1975, when the high, government-sanctioned wage increases were inconsistent with the appreciating exchange rate.

It is, of course, quite likely that a cooperative bargaining equilibrium is not so easy to achieve, even between the two parties, business and labor. For instance, labor may not believe in the willingness or ability of business to hold the rate of price increase to the agreed level, especially in highly open economies. Similarly, business may not trust labor to hold to its agreement, particularly in countries where unions are weak (as in France) or where union contracts cannot be enforced in the courts (as in the United Kingdom). Noncooperative equilibrium can be found by tracing out the dashed reaction functions passing through points B and L in Figure 4.4.[4]

The reaction function for business is obtained by finding the optimal rate of price increase for each rate of wage increase offered by labor. This is found where the real after tax profit indifference curves are tangent to the vertical. Similarly, labor's reaction function represents the optimal wage increase for any given rate of price increase, where the after tax real wage indifference curves are tangent to the horizontal. The Nash-Cournot noncooperative equilibrium is found where the two reaction functions intersect, at point N. Clearly, the result of such behavior will be far higher inflation, on the assumptions of this analysis. Again, however, the achievement of a point such as N depends on the acquiescence of the monetary and fiscal authorities.

Under the chaotic conditions that can lead to noncooperative equilibrium, it is quite possible that one or another of the social partners could adopt a leadership role, with the other party then adapting along its reaction function. This would lead to a Stackelberg equilibrium, either at point S where business optimizes along labor's reaction function or at point S', where labor optimizes along business's reaction function (See Fellner 1949, Chap. 3).

Policy Rules and Institutional Structure

According to the line of argument in the introduction to this paper, the monetary and fiscal authorities in different countries might be expected to adopt different types of policy regimes or policy rules, depending on the relative strength of different groups in society and the institutional structure. The stage has now been set for such an analysis to be presented.

It is assumed that business and labor, and perhaps government employees, play the roles laid out for them above. Market conditions are as described in the second section of the paper. What should be the objectives of the monetary and fiscal authorities in choosing policy rules? The assumption here is that two types of equilibrium are desirable--real equilibrium, involving internal and external balance close to the 45° line of Figures 4.2 or 4.4, and financial equilibrium, involving a stable, and therefore low, rate of inflation, perhaps in the neighborhood of the contract curve BL of Figure 4.4, perhaps lower. Real equilibrium is desirable to promote the growth of capital and personal income in real terms, one of which will be damaged by a move in either direction from the 45° line. Foreign borrowing is assumed to be a costly means of allowing external balance to be achieved off the diagonal, due to imperfect capital mobility. Financial equilibrium is desirable to avoid the distortions of behavior due to rapid (and variable) inflation.[5]

Thus the monetary and fiscal authorities might be given an additional set of indifference curves centered on the diagonal between points B and L in Figure 4.4.[6] Their choice of policy, however, must be considered in the light of their political bargaining strength vis-à-vis business and labor. For the monetary and fiscal authorities have political masters in every country, although the immediacy of political control varies dramatically from case to case.

Consider, for example, the case of the labor-dominated government with a strong commitment to full employment and weak concern over capital formation and inflation. Assume also that the monetary authority is subservient to the finance ministry, rather than having a degree of "independence" from political control. Thus the authorities are unable to assert preferences different from those of labor. In such a case, despite any desire for real or financial equilibrium, the monetary and fiscal authorities are likely to be forced to ratify either a labor-dominated cooperative outcome with a rise in the real wage or a highly inflationary, noncooperative outcome.

Several policy regimes or "political assignments" have been tried under such circumstances, with varying degrees of success or failure. A pegged exchange rate, by preventing the price of traded goods from rising, brings the external balance problem swiftly into conflict with the inflationary or high real wage outcome. The gold standard "rules of the game," which would require deflation with an external deficit, would of course reinforce such a policy regime by ensuring that the mm and gg curves intersect at the pegged exchange rate and frustrate the objectives of labor. But given the assumption of political dominance by labor, the gold standard rules seem unlikely to be adopted. Nevertheless, the pegged rate option has been chosen by many European countries, and even more less-developed countries, as a target toward which monetary and fiscal (and therefore wage) policy can aim.

A second possibility is reliance on labor's strength to impose its own desired rate of wage increase or perhaps an even more "responsible" wage norm, in conjunction with controls on prices and exchange market intervention to prevent the exchange rate depreciating beyond target. This policy was followed by the Labor government in the United Kingdom during the "Social Contract" period of 1974-1976, but with little success. A key problem seems to be the difficulty of convincing foreign lenders of the sustainability of the policy, especially when significant foreign borrowing is required. Under such conditions the mm curve of Figure 4.2 shifts out, leading to excessive depreciation and undercutting the wage policy.

A third possibility, which essentially gives up on financial equilibrium in order to ensure at least an approximation of real equilibrium, is to adopt a "crawling peg" for the exchange rate, tying its movement to the rate of increase of domestic costs (wages). This will keep the outcome in the neighborhood of the 45° line, but without controlling inflation. Either a wage norm or monetary growth rule would be required to stabilize inflation.

A fourth possibility is agreement on a mutually acceptable change in the real wage through an incomes policy of the Scandinavian type. Here the social partners attempt to calculate the allowable increase in the real wage based on productivity change in the traded goods sector plus the increase in the world market price of traded goods. If both parties take the real wage change as given in bargaining over the money wage, an outcome in the cooperative range BL of Figure 4.4 is guaranteed.

A second interesting case of political assignment arises when there is a conservative political party with ties to business, weak or at least cooperative labor unions, and a strong, independent monetary authority. Under such conditions, the monetary authority could plausibly insist on a monetary growth rule to limit inflation despite unemployment that might be generated. Holding the mm curve at or near the contract curve BL will reinforce the likelihood of a cooperative, reasonable noninflationary settlement. If labor were to go on strike successfully seeking higher wage gains, the monetary authority could hold tight to its target, simply allowing the unemployment that results from a solution to the right of the ℓℓ curve in Figure 4.2. The perceived weakness of union negotiators in this type of environment could be expected to lead to negotiated settlements along the contract curve relatively closer to the business optimum point B then to point L. Balance of payments surpluses and relatively high growth of employment and capital stock might be the resulting outcome, as well as slower growth of real wages.

The analysis of this paper can be used to examine several different institutional factors in the inflation process. For example, in several countries relatively weak monetary authorities and powerful labor unions have allowed inflation to become entrenched. Under these conditions, indexation of wages is very likely to be adopted to protect real wages.[8] Labor does not, of course, give up its desire to increase real wages, nor do employers faced with higher real wages alter their responses. But full indexation in the form $\dot{w} > \dot{p}$ implies that only outcomes below the diagonal in Figure 4.4 are conceivable. This automatic reduction in the bargaining power of business makes it more willing to consider the adoption of other policies that will limit inflation, such as pegging the exchange rate. Both Belgium and Italy have moved in this direction, arguing that a floating exchange rate would involve a "vicious circle" in which wages and the price of foreign exchange will spiral upward without benefit to either the foreign balance or real wages.

An alternative application of the analysis involves comparison of countries with similar political alignments but differing antipathy to inflation, such as those with and without a memory of hyperinflation.[9]

RECENT EXPERIENCE IN INDUSTRIALIZED COUNTRIES

In several recent writings I have examined the economic policy behavior of a group of industrialized economies, including Canada, France, Germany, Italy, Japan, Sweden, the United Kingdom, and the United States.[10] During the 1970s these countries have been faced with several major external disturbances, including the sharp increase in international reserve holdings in 1970-1972 due to the breakdown of the Bretton Woods system, the resulting simultaneous worldwide inflationary boom of 1973-1974, the tripling of oil prices in 1974 and their doubling again in 1979, the worldwide recession of 1974-1975, and the renewed inflation of 1979-1980. The ability to cope with these shocks has become the litmus test for economic policy in the 1970s.

Each of these shocks can be portrayed in the basic model of this paper, with some reinterpretation. The infusion of reserves from abroad will raise the rate of growth of the money supply and the mm curve, if not counteracted by restrictive monetary measures. Inflation in world prices of traded goods raises the domestic prices of traded goods and the gg curve, for any given exchange rate (since $P = EP^*$). Thus a fall in the price of foreign exchange E can offset any rise in world prices, if domestic wages and money growth can be kept from rising along with P^*. An increase in the price of imported oil worsens the terms of trade, which in the Salter model used here implies an inward shift in the production possibilities curve along the traded goods axis in Figure 4.1. The result is to raise the price of traded goods relative to nontraded goods, requiring a fall in the real wage in Figure 2, as the gg and ℓℓ curves shift up.

It is clear that differences in institutional structure and the bargaining power of different groups in society can have major impact on the ability to respond effectively to these shocks. Countries with weak monetary authorities found it difficult to ward off excessive monetary expansion arising from the influx of reserves during 1970-1972, especially as many countries were at the time emerging from the 1970-1971 recession. Only a few countries with floating exchange rates, such as Germany and Japan, were able to mitigate the effects of the 1973 worldwide inflation through exchange rate appreciation. The members of the EEC snake pegged to the deutsche mark also gained some protection from inflation, as their exchange rate appreciated with the mark.

Coping with the oil price increase put special focus on the ability to adjust to lower real wage rates. This possibility was greatest in countries with cooperative bargaining environments and without indexation of wage rates, such as the United States, Japan, and Germany, although the United States fumbled its opportunity to adjust by holding down domestic oil prices. Canada and the United Kingdom, as actual or potential oil exporters, saw improved terms of trade arising from the oil price increase, and in both cases real wages rose significantly in 1973-1975. Both countries were forced to retrench in 1975. In France, Italy, and Sweden, on the other hand, wage inflation accelerated sufficiently to prevent the required decline in real wages. Cooperative labor bargaining broke down in all three cases, in France due to political accommodation associated with the 1974 presidential election, in Sweden and Italy due to the political strength of the unions. The phenomenon of "real wage resistance" reflects labor's bargaining power and willingness to ignore inflation.

If one examines the differences in inflation rates and unemployment rates among the major industrialized countries in the 1970s, one is struck by the similarity of the external disturbances and the diversity of the outcomes. Closer examination of individual countries suggests that differences in economic policy and institutions for setting wages, prices, exchange rates, and monetary policy can explain much of this diversity. But it is necessary to proceed in a careful, step-by-step manner, looking at each individual year's outcome, before stepping back for the broad generalization. That process cannot be undertaken here, for lack of space. But a few examples can be given.

Let us consider Japan in 1975, after the oil price increase exposed external vulnerability. The rate of wage increase was brought down from over 25 percent in 1974 to 10 percent, through a centralized system of wage bargaining and a long tradition of consensus politics. Unemployment hardly rose at all, given the Japanese system of avoiding layoffs. Only in France and Germany did wage increases also slow down slightly in 1975, in both cases at the cost of much higher unemployment. The Deutsche Bundesbank had set an internal monetary growth target of 8 percent in 1974, and the rapid rate of wage increase conflicted sharply with it, leading to rising unemployment in both 1974 and 1975. In France, the government had chosen an unrealistic exchange rate target and restrictive policies to support it. When the rate of wage increase refused to fall below 15 percent per year, the exchange rate target was dropped.

Another interesting case is the United States, under contrasting political leaders. Despite the apparent similarity of the rhetoric of Gerald Ford and Jimmy Carter, while in office the Republican Ford sought to restrain inflation at the cost of a gradual recovery in unemployment from the 1974-1975 recession. The Democratic administration sought to accelerate the growth of the economy and succeeded in significantly lowering unemployment, but at the cost of sharply higher inflation. The political shift in emphasis is clearly evident, despite Carter's later adoption of restrictive policies when inflation ran out of control.

Another example of political changes leading to different outcomes is the shift from the British Conservative government's effort at wage restraint in 1973 to the Labor government's "Social Contract" policy of 1974. The resulting dramatic explosion of inflation was only contained in 1976-1977 when foreign borrowing to finance the external deficit became harder and harder to obtain. The International Monetary Fund was used as a scapegoat to enforce stringent wage guidelines, slower monetary expansion, and fiscal restriction, eventually bringing a significant slowdown in inflation but rising unemployment. The alternation between business oriented and labor oriented governments in the United Kingdom has yet to impose order on chaotic wage and price setting institutions, leaving the present Conservative government again facing noncooperative bargaining outcomes.

CONCLUSION

There seems little room for doubt that political economy and the political assignment problem as discussed in this paper have a major role to play in explaining why there are such large differences in the observed macroeconomic performance of different countries. It seems reasonably clear that broadly successful macroeconomic policy can be formulated in a wide variety of social and economic environments, if a firm and consistent focus on real and financial equilibrium is maintained. Obviously enough lapses from such control lead to inflation and/or recession.

The particular policy approaches chosen to implement macroeconomic control have varied significantly between countries, in large part because of political, social, and institutional differences. Some types of policy have been particularly unsuccessful, such as the combination of wage norms and floating exchange rates in a labor dominated economy such as the United Kingdom. Similarly, the combination of a pegged exchange rate and politically accommodative wage and monetary policy proved inconsistent for France in 1975-1976 and for Sweden in 1977. The problem for the political leaders and monetary and fiscal authorities is to find the particular combination of policies that will solve the problem they face, taking account of the political and economic realities confronting them.

APPENDIX

The Basic Model

Using lower case letters to represent logarithms, the direct demands for labor services and goods in the given time period are

$$n^d = m_1(e - w) + m_{2y} + m_3(m - p) = -\alpha w + \beta e + \eta_1(p + y) + \Theta_1 m \quad (4.1)$$

$$t^d = t_1(w - e) + t_{2y} + t_3(m - p) = \gamma w - \delta e + \eta_2(p + y) + \Theta_2 m \quad (4.2)$$

where the sum of the elasticities in each equation equals zero, by homogeneity in prices and money. The (logarithm of) the money wage is w, the price of foreign exchange is e, the price level is $p = \mu w + (1 - \mu)e$ using expenditure weights, real income is y, and the nominal money supply is m.

The demand for money equation in the basic model is

$$m - p = \phi y - \lambda \dot{p} \tag{4.3}$$

Assuming the production function for goods is $T(N, K)$, its logarithmic derivative is

$$\dot{t} = a\dot{n} + b\dot{k} \qquad a = WN/ET; \; b = KT_k/T$$

the supply function (with a given capital stock) is $T^S(W/E)$, with derivative

$$\dot{t}^S = a\psi(\dot{w} - \dot{e}) \qquad \psi = T_n/(NT_{nn}) < 0 \tag{4.5}$$

and the indirect demand for labor is $N^t(W/E)$, with derivative

$$\dot{n}^t = \psi(\dot{w} - \dot{e}) \tag{4.6}$$

Money income is, in the absence of government deficits,

$$p + y = \log(W\bar{N} + \pi) \tag{4.7}$$

where profits in the goods-producing industry ($\pi = ET - WN$) have derivative

$$\frac{d\pi}{\pi} = (\dot{e} - a\dot{w})/(1 - a) \qquad \text{using } \pi = (1 - a)ET. \tag{4.8}$$

The equilibrium conditions in the market for goods and labor services are (in terms of levels, rather than logarithms):

$$N^d = N^S = \bar{N} - N^t - \bar{N}^g \tag{4.9}$$

$$T^d = T^S - \bar{T}^g, \tag{4.10}$$

where $\bar{N}^g$ and $\bar{T}^g$ are government purchases.

Substituting from (4.1) - (4.8) into (4.9) - (4.10) yields a solution for the levels of the wage rate and the exchange rate in each time period. The equilibrium rates of change are found by differentiating with respect to time, yielding

$$- \alpha\dot{w} + \beta\dot{e} + \eta_1(\dot{p} + \dot{y}) + \theta_1\dot{m} = -\psi(N^t/N^S)(\dot{w} - \dot{e}) \tag{4.11}$$

$$\gamma\dot{w} - \delta\dot{e} + \eta_2(\dot{p} + \dot{y}) + \theta_2\dot{m} = a\psi(\dot{w} - \dot{e}) \tag{4.12}$$

where

$$\dot{p} = \mu\dot{w} + (1 - \mu)\dot{e} \tag{4.13}$$

$$\dot{y} = 0 \tag{4.14}$$

the latter from differentiating (4.7), using (4.8) and (4.13). Substituting (4.13) and (4.14) into (4.11) and (4.12) yields the rate of change equilibrium condition:

$$\begin{bmatrix} a_1 & a_2 \\ a_3 & a_4 \end{bmatrix} \begin{bmatrix} \dot{w} \\ \dot{e} \end{bmatrix} + \begin{bmatrix} \Theta_1 \\ \Theta_2 \end{bmatrix} \dot{m} = 0 \qquad (4.15)$$

where

$a_1 = - + n_1\mu + \psi(N^t/N^s) < 0$

$a_2 = \beta + n_1(1 - \mu) - \psi(N^t/N^s) > 0$

$a_3 = \gamma + n_2\mu - a\psi > 0$

$a_4 = -\delta + n_2(1 - \mu) + a\psi < 0$

In the labor market (4.15) yields the $\ell\ell$ curve of Figure 4.2 and in the goods market the gg curve, with slopes respectively greater and less than unity, as shown in Figure 4.2. Similarly, differentiating (4.3), and using (4.13) yields a downward-sloping mm curve, which must, by Walras's Law, intersect the $\ell\ell$ and gg curves at a single point. By inspection of (4.15), the sum of the columns of the left-hand matrix and the coefficients of $\dot{m}$ add up to zero, by the homogeneity condition. Therefore, the equilibrium solution lies on the 45° line in Figure 4.2, where $\dot{w} = \dot{e} = \dot{m}$, which may be described as the purchasing power parity condition.

Disequilibrium in Labor and Traded Goods Markets[11]

Equations (4.9) and (4.10) can be modified to allow for unfilled vacancies V (unemployment, if negative) and a net export surplus X:

$$N^d = N^s + V = \bar{N} - N^t - \bar{N}^g + V \qquad (4.9')$$

$$T^d = T^s - \bar{T}^g - X \qquad (4.10')$$

Thus V and -X correspond to the horizontal and vertical distances between points B and A in Figure 4.1. The $\ell\ell$ nd gg curves of Figure 4.2 that intersect on the 45° line obtain when V and X remain equal to zero. But if vacancies (unemployment) or the current account surplus (deficit) are allowed to change, the effects of such disequilibria must be added to the equilibrium conditions in the first section of the Appendix. If it is assumed that initial $V = X = 0$, the equation (4.11) should have the term $\dot{V}/N^s$ added to the right-hand side, while equation (4.12) should have $-\dot{X}/T^d$ added to its right-hand side. The same terms should be added to the right-hand side of equation (4.15).

The result of adding disequilibria to the goods and labor market is to allow any condition of external and internal imbalance in Figure 4.1 to be represented by a disequilibrium $\ell\ell$, gg intersection in Figure 4.2, off the 45° line.

Taxation and Government Expenditures

Assume that taxes are levied on wage income and profit income according to the tax rate schedules $\tau(W\bar{N})$ and $\sigma(\pi - D)$. Then the rate of change of after tax wage income is $[(1 - \tau')/(1 - \tau^*)]\dot{w}$, where τ' is the marginal tax rate and τ^* is the average tax rate on wage income and $(1 - \tau')/(1 - \tau^*) < 1$. Similarly, the rate of change of after tax profits is $[(1 - \sigma')/(1 - \sigma^*)](d\pi/\pi)$, where σ' and σ^* are the marginal and average tax rates. The rate of change of government revenue is then

$$[\tau/(\tau + \sigma)] (\tau'/\tau^*)\dot{w} + [\sigma/(\tau + \sigma)] (\sigma'/\sigma^*) (d\pi/\pi) \qquad (4.16)$$

where $\tau/(\tau + \sigma)$ is the share of government revenue coming from taxes on wage income. The government's budget constraint is

$$WN^g + ET^g - \tau(W\bar{N}) - \sigma(\pi - D) = \Delta M + \Delta B. \qquad (4.17)$$

Capital Mobility and Expectations

Assume there are at any point in time existing stocks of three assets, money M, domestic bonds B, and foreign bonds with domestic currency value EH, where total private wealth is $A = M + B + EH$. The demands for these three assets are assumed to be:

$$M/P = m(r, y) \qquad (m_r < 0, m_y > 0) \qquad (4.18)$$

$$B/A = b(r, r^* + \dot{f}, y) \qquad (b_r > 0, b_{r^*} < 0, b_y < 0) \qquad (4.19)$$

$$EH/A = h(r, r^* + \dot{f}, y) \qquad (h_r < 0, h_{r^*} > 0, h_y < 0) \qquad (4.20)$$

For simplicity, substitution between domestic and foreign assets is assumed to be entirely in terms of domestic versus foreign bonds.

The ratio of (4.20) to (4.19) yields the portfolio balance condition, which is for convenience assumed independent of income.

$$EH/B = k(r, r^* + \dot{f}) \qquad (k_r < 0, k_{r^*} > 0) \qquad (4.21)$$

We may solve (4.18) for the domestic interest rate and substitute into (4.21) to find the price of foreign currency that clears the asset market, given existing stocks. Over time, these stocks will change through flows generated by the current account of the balance of payments according to

$$dH = X + r^*H \qquad (4.22)$$

From (4.18) an increase in the money wage raises the demand for money and therefore the domestic interest rate. From (4.21) this will reduce the demand for foreign assets and the price of foreign exchange, yielding a downward-sloping curve in Figure 4.2 that takes the place of the mm curve. A sufficient but not necessary condition for the negative slope is $d\dot{f}/de < 0$. Furthermore, this curve shifts down as an increase in the stock of foreign assets $dH > 0$ reduces their price E.

Objective Functions for Business, Labor and Government

Real after tax profits are $[\pi - \sigma(\pi - D)]/P$ and their rate of change is

$$\frac{1 - \sigma'}{1 - \sigma^*} \frac{d\pi}{\pi} - \dot{p} = \frac{a + \mu(1 - a)}{1 - a} - (\dot{e} - \dot{w}) - \frac{\sigma' - \sigma^*}{1 - \sigma^*} \frac{\dot{e} - a\dot{w}}{1 - a} \qquad (4.22)$$

If labor's share $\underline{a}$ falls as the real wage falls, there are diminishing

returns to increasing goods prices relative to wages $(d^2\log \pi/de)/w^2 < 0$.
Real after tax wage income is $[W\bar{N} - \tau(W\bar{N})]/P$ and its rate of change is

$$(1 - \mu)(\dot{w} - \dot{e}) - [(\tau' - \tau^*)/(1 - \tau^*)] \dot{w} \qquad (4.23)$$

Here, there are diminishing returns to wage increases as τ' increases.

The tax revenue accruing to the government is $[\tau(W\bar{N}) + \sigma(\pi-D)]/P$ in real terms. Using the result (4.16) in the second section of the Appendix and assuming for simplicity that the tax shares $\tau/(\tau + \sigma)$ are equal to the shares of wages and profits in national income and that the tax elasticities σ'/σ^* and τ/τ^* are equal, the rate of change of real govenment revenues is

$$[(\tau' - \tau^*)/\tau^*] \dot{p} \qquad (4.24)$$

which increases with inflation. Since the marginal tax rate is increasing, there appears to be no natural limit to the increase in government receipts. In reality, the rising tax burden can be expected to reduce the supplies of capital and labor or divert them to nontaxable uses, thus reducing taxable income.

NOTES

The paper has benefited substantially from comments by Peter Katzenstein, Samuel Morley, Alan Stockman, Willard Witte, and Akio Yasuhara, though all responsibility remains with the author.

1. Some might prefer to restate the argument in terms of finite differences, using $\hat{e} = \Delta E/E$, instead of $\dot{e} = dE/E$, etc.

2. See Dornbusch (1976b) and Branson (1979) for these two approaches. For an earlier development of the imperfect substitutability case, see Black (1973).

3. Other tax distortions arising from inventory profits and windfall gains on debt will tend to be eliminated by the shift to LIFO accounting and rising nominal interest rates.

4. For noncooperative equilibrium concepts, see Fellner (1949); Hamada (1974, pp. 13-33); Luce and Raiffa (1957, Chap. 5).

5. See Fischer and Modigliani (1978) for a catalogue of the problems due to inflation.

6. The authorities are assumed to have separate goals from the bureaucracy. Alternatively, we might consider two sets of indifference curves in $(\dot{m}, \dot{p})$ space, one for the monetary-fiscal authorities close to the origin and one for the private sector farther out along the diagonal. With elliptical indifference curves that are flatter in the inflation dimension, both the contract curve and noncooperative outcomes would involve stagflation $(\dot{m} < \dot{p})$.

7. I am indebted to Avinash Dixit for this point. See Edgren et al. (1973) for the Scandinavian model.

8. For a comprehensive discussion, see Braun (1976).

9. For example, Peter Katzenstein in his comments has suggested comparing Sweden and Austria.

10. Five of these were studied in Black (1977) and in Black (1979), while all eight were covered in Black (1978). See also Sachs (1979b) and other references cited therein. These papers provide a more complete background for application of political assignment analysis.

11. This section was added in response to comments by Alan Stockman.

DISCUSSION • *Peter J. Katzenstein*

Political Explanations of Economic Policy

   This paper breaks new ground in the economic modeling of political reality. In recent years economists and political scientists have paid attention to the political business cycle both as a consequence of capitalist democracies and as a cause of some of their instabilities. In contrast, with the help of the tools of economic analysis and game theory, this paper scrutinizes instead the bargains struck among business, unions, government bureaucracies, and central banks. The paper is a plausible extension of Professor Black's prior writings on the subject. It seeks to eliminate the tension involved in modeling the behavior of countries while at the same time rendering a descriptive verbal analysis of political actors and policy choices within countries.
   Writing from the perspective of political science I can add little to the technical parts of the paper. That I can follow the lucid discussion is one of the features of this paper that I admire without regretting that I do not command the tools necessary to evaluate its technical aspects. Instead these comments will focus on the insights we gain from an application of the paper's main categories--the bargaining strength of business and labor and the institutional autonomy of central banks--to some of the policy choices and political experiences of the 1970s. The discussion proceeds by setting forth these categories in the abstract and examining how they are applied in the paper; suggesting, within the paper's framework, an alternative classification of some of the OECD member states; reflecting on the inconsistencies inherent in that alternative classification; and, finally, dissenting sharply from economistic thinking about policy and politics.
   This paper explains policy choice in terms of the relative strength of business and labor as well as the degree of autonomy that central banks enjoy in their relations with political authorities. It distinguishes between two extreme situations. Where unions are strong and the bank is dependent, policy will try to achieve high growth in real wages and full employment while risking higher rates of inflation and lower rates of capital formation. Conversely, where business is strong and the bank is autonomous, policy will try to achieve a low rate of inflation and higher rates of capital formation at the risk of higher rates of unemployment and lower rates of real wage growth. A variety of policy instruments (or "political assignments") exist that could achieve these objectives--pegged exchange rates, a crawling peg or wage restraint in the first instance, and a strict monetary policy in the second.
   Unfortunately, this lucid framework is not fully applied to the political choices of the major OECD countries on questions of economic

management. In fact, the paper shies away from the task of consistently applying the categories of analysis that it has developed to the political reality that it seeks to understand. Britain's and Canada's policy choices are, for example, explained in terms of resource endowment rather than political variables. Yet differences in resource endowment do not appear central to the paper's game-theoretical framework.

This illustrates a general problem. When the paper turns to an examination of how the OECD countries have adjusted to lower real wage rates in the 1970s, it groups these countries by a variable not previously discussed. The United States, West Germany, and Japan, it is argued, exhibit a "cooperative bargaining environment" permitting a reduction in real wages; France, Italy, and Sweden are distinguished by a noncooperative environment and "real wage resistance." It is very difficult indeed to link this classification to either the relative strength of business and labor or to the autonomy of central banks, the two key variables developed throughout the paper. In sharp contrast to West Germany, organized labor in Japan is conspicuously weak in both politics and policymaking; yet at the same time labor's demand for full employment and high real wage growth is met more closely in Japan than in the other two countries and, indeed, in most countries of presumed labor strength. Analogously, both France and Sweden resisted real wage reduction in the mid-1970s even though the centralized Swedish labor unions are among the most powerful in the OECD while the fragmented French ones are among the weakest. Difficulties arise as well when we think about the autonomy of central banks. In sharp contrast to Japan, West Germany's Bundesbank enjoys a very substantial measure of autonomy from the federal government. Explaining the two countries' successful low inflation policy after 1973 in terms of exchange rate appreciation glosses over a puzzle which puts in question the critical importance that the paper attaches to the relative autonomy of central banks. Analogously, the Italian central bank probably enjoys a considerably greater measure of autonomy than do the central banks of France and Sweden. In short, the link between the two principles of classification--the degree of cooperation among political actors in adjusting to real wage reduction on the one hand and the power or autonomy of different political actors on the other--is nonobvious. Furthermore, numerous inconsistencies between how the OECD countries should be grouped following the paper's theoretical framework and how in fact they are grouped appear when the paper moves to the task of political analysis.

Is it possible to improve the political analysis within the paper's main framework? Do real world cases exist which vary greatly in the relative strength of labor and business and the degree of autonomy enjoyed by monetary authorities, thus lending themselves to a testing of the paper's propositions? In Western Europe there do seem to exist at least two cases, Austria and Sweden, where the unions are very strong, where central banks enjoy only limited autonomy from the government, and where, as predicted by the paper, policy tries to achieve high growth in real wages. Yet despite these similarities Sweden has tolerated much higher levels of inflation than has Austria and has chosen devaluation rather than appreciation of its currency as a way to bring the various conflicting demands on policy into harmony. Conversely, Switzerland and West Germany have strong business communities, relatively autonomous central banks, and, as predicted by the paper, a commitment to low inflation buttressed by appreciating currencies and a willingness to tolerate temporary, sharp declines in real wages. Yet while Switzerland has eliminated more than 300,000 jobs in the 1970s, its visible unemployment is negligible; in contrast West Germany's reduction in jobs, though smaller in relative terms than across the border, has resulted in a comparatively sharp increase in the number of unemployed in the 1970s. Thus, when applied to the analysis of the political realities of the 1970s, the framework generates a number of anomalies which should lead us to reexamine, rather than replace, its categories of analysis. In Austria, for example, the political strength of labor can be gauged by the gradual implantation of a Social Democratic regime, and in Sweden by its ability to shape political discourse even when the Social Democrats are out of power. In West Germany the political strength of the business community remains formidable despite a Social Democratic government, while in Switzerland business is strong because of its absence. The categorization of political systems is a tricky task. Since classifications by electoral or ideological criteria into Left and Right are often misleading, it is hardly surprising that a classification according to the strength of different political actors, interest groups, and social formations also encounters serious problems.

Perhaps one of the ways to improve political analysis is to reject the paper's assumption that countries as dissimilar as Sweden and the United States can both be classified as "small, open economies". Is it possible that differences in degree (economic openness) create differences in kind (political structure)? Austria's openness to and dependence on West Germany's economy has left its Social Democratic policymakers, even those who initially had doubts, with hardly any other choice but the pursuit of a hard currency policy. And the traditional openness of Swiss labor markets made it easy to export unemployment. In short, one could argue that the economic context in which countries operate dictates their strategic policy choices. The weakness in this formulation of the problem lies in an economic determinism that short-circuits political analysis altogether.

Instead, open and vulnerable economies may encourage a merging of the bargaining power of different political actors and of the institutional structures in which they operate. The paper's two key variables thus might be not independent but interdependent. The "neocorporatism" and "consociationalism" so distinctive of the small European countries appears to confound attempts at simple classification. The institutional fabric of Austria's political economy diminishes the power of the business community. Conversely, Switzerland's institutions attach more political weight to the Left than one might expect given the overwhelming political advantages which the business community enjoys in that country. The "Peace Agreements" signed between business and labor in both socialist Sweden and capitalist Switzerland in 1937-38 are examples of a transformation of the distributional struggles imitated after 1945 in the other rich, small, European states as well. Conditioned by their exposed position in the international economy, an institutional variant of capitalism has appeared that defies easy classification into Left or Right, business dominated or labor dominated systems of power. With the recent growth of interdependence and dependence, an increasing sense of vulnerability may encourage similar tendencies in some of the larger industrial states. The problems that this paper's framework encounters when applied to the political events and policy choices of the 1970s lies, I would argue, in part in these underlying political changes and transformations of capitalist economies.

These changes and transformations cannot be captured with economic assumptions about politics and policy. I am willing to grant that parsimonious explanation must rely on strong--and that means wrong--assumptions. That, after all, is the secret of all elegant theories. The paper's key assumption is that group behavior is oriented towards maximizing or optimizing rates of growth of real after-tax incomes, anticipated over the future and discounted back to the present. Without relinquishing the paper's theoretical structure, this assumption could be revised to take account of political changes in the real world. Important among these changes in the 1970s is the growing concern of unions with maintaining employment levels for their own constituencies as well as other segments of the labor force. More importantly, the view of policy choice as an instrument used in the achievement of economic objectives is profoundly apolitical in discounting the elementary fact that political struggles over any policy question involve not only the achievement of particular objectives but also reflect a struggle over the distribution of power in society. The form that this struggle takes may appear "chaotic" or "cooperative". But the consequences of struggle for a country's capacity to make future choices are at times profound. Indeed, in its economistic assumptions, which transform government bureaucracies into economic actors, the paper reveals in stark form a mode of analysis that in my opinion obscures the most important events and changes in the contemporary political economy.

Although I am very much attracted to the framework that this paper develops for its analysis of distributional struggles, in the end I react to it as did the late Hans Morgenthau to the intellectual advances of modern social science in the field of international relations. These advances, he is reported to have once argued, run the risk of methodological or theoretical overkill; at times scholarship is in danger of spending too much time sharpening the saw and too little time cutting down the tree.

DISCUSSION • *Alan C. Stockman*

INTRODUCTION

Stanley Black's paper on "Strategic Aspects of the Political Assignment Problem in Open Economies" is a welcome attempt to understand the political process underlying government policies in open economies. His paper suggests a game-theoretical explanation of the conflict between various special interest groups. I do not believe, however, that his particular model lives up to the high standard that he has set forth in his paper or provides a satisfactory explanation of conflict resolution within the general framework that he proposes. There are really two levels of discussion in his paper. First, there is a general framework for the analysis of political behavior in terms of cooperative or noncooperative games. Second, there is the specific application of this framework to a model of an open economy. I will comment on these in order and then return to the first issue.

THE ANALYSIS OF POLITICAL CONFLICT

According to Mike Darby, George Stigler once told Milton Friedman, "Milton, whenever you say that inflation is caused by excessive monetary expansion, I assume that means you don't really want to discuss the issue." The "economists' paradigm" that Black criticizes at the beginning of his paper is therefore partially a straw man: economists do not always treat government behavior as exogenous, but sometimes have tried to model and explain the actions and policies of governments.

Economists have recognized that understanding <u>why</u> the government follows some pattern of behavior may be important for understanding the consequences of that behavior, just as understanding the reasons for private behavior may help us understand the meaning and consequences of that behavior. For example, economists observe that many nominal wage rates are contractually fixed for certain periods of time. But if this fixity is not "exogeneous" but instead is the consequence of an optimal contract that allocates risk in an optimal way (e.g., from risk averse workers to less risk averse owners of firms), then, as Barro (1977) has pointed out, the implications for macroeconomic issues are entirely different. Similarly, it is important to understand the reasons for the government policies we observe. If a government policy is part of a tie-in-sale, or "package" of policies, then its consequences may be judged entirely differently than they would be in isolation. An example of this may be provided by the conflict between the results of McPherson's (1972) and Pincus's (1977) studies of tariffs in the United States. While the former study found little relation between political power and tariff protection, the latter study looked at a period of time when these tariffs were less likely to be part of a complicated package of implicit taxes and subsidies to various industries, and came to very different conclusions. Similarly, if a "benefit" is provided to a special interest group, then in order to determine the full effects of this "benefit" we may want to know whether it was the outcome of a political process whereby the special interest groups for government favors against other interest groups and whether this competitive process dissipated all of the interest group's rent. In other words, the interest group "paid" for the benefit until the marginal cost equaled the marginal benefit: were the average costs and benefits different from the marginal costs and benefits, or did the special interest group end up with "zero profit" from the government favors?[1]

Black's paper emphasizes at the beginning the distinction between the particular choices made at particular times by politicians or the government, such as a particular monetary growth rate in a particular year, and general rules of behavior or policy regimes, such as monetary growth rate rules or exchange rate systems. This important distinction has been made by others, e.g., Buchanan and Tullock (1962), in a related context. Unfortunately, Black's paper does not exploit this distinction to its full advantage, as we shall see.

An analysis of the conflict between various interest groups should presumably begin with a statement of the objective function of each group and the constraints under which each group operates. These are never explicitly stated in the paper. Political entrepreneurs might maximize utility of various commodities such as wealth and reputation where these commodities are "produced" by the political entrepreneur by combining inputs such as time, market goods, and environmental characteristics such as the opinions and strengths of various special interest groups. Such a model might be set up along the lines described in Becker (1974). If the market marginal rates of substitution between the goods, that is, their prices, are taken as given to each individual, then the analysis could proceed with a perfectly competitive environment. A game-theoretical environment would be appropriate if interest groups are not price takers, as in Black's bilateral monopoly setup. In that case, interest groups and politicians presumably anticipate and respond to the expected actions of others. Since the development of these response functions requires more sophistication on the part of agents than the price-taking assumption, I find Black's remark that the vote-maximizing model attributes "too much cleverness to political leaders" puzzling. A game-theoretical model attributes (appropriately, I think) a great deal of cleverness to political leaders, particularly those who turn out to be successful at their trade.

INTEREST GROUP COMPETITION IN AN OPEN ECONOMY

The economic model of an open economy used to generate conflict in Black's paper is a modification of the standard Salter model with a traded and a nontraded good. The modification is that the model is written in terms of rates of change rather than levels. This is unobjectionable for describing the change over time in an equilibrium in the model, but it is not appropriate to infer from this formulation that agents' preferences can be expressed in terms of rates of change of economic variables. The indirect utility functions of people in the model depend on the level of wealth and the levels of various prices (of the traded and the nontraded good). A diagram like Figure 4.2 could be drawn to illustrate the equilibrium in terms of the levels of prices.

Of what use is this model in helping us to understand political conflict? The answer implicitly given in the paper is that it isolates special interest groups and can help us understand the policies that would benefit or hurt each group. The paper gives several examples. First, it notes that a model with neutral money has little to say on the political economy of inflation. This, of course, depends on whether one includes in the definition of "neutrality" the requirement that there be no wealth redistribution. If so, then the point is correct, but we did not need the Salter model to tell us that. Next, the paper seems to confuse the neutrality of money and the endogeneity of money. The paper says that the model would become interesting if interest groups can, in the process of pursuing their goals, affect the rate of inflation. This is an issue of endogeneity of money. Money growth might be endogenous in this way because, say, inflation is part of an optimal tax structure in the absence of nondistorting taxes. Yet money might be completely neutral in the model.

Next, the paper lists several ways in which income might be redistributed through the political process. First, there is monopoly in product or labor markets. Clearly government redistribution through conferring monopoly power appears to be an important empirical issue, though redistribution through the collection of all government programs may be very different, as noted above, from the redistribution effects of a particular program. Yet the former redistribution is what is relevant to special interest groups facing an all or nothing decision from government.

Second, the distribution of wealth can be altered directly through taxation and expenditure programs. These can include policies the paper lists separately, such as taxation by inflation of fixed, nominal income streams and by bracket creep if income tax rates are graduated and nonindexed. The paper also lists as possibilities two items that I fail to understand as methods by which the government can influence the distribution of wealth: disequilibrium and money illusion. Are these government policies?

The Salter model of trade presented in the paper does not seem very useful in providing insights into the nature of conflict between special interest groups. Indeed, the only aspect of the model that is carried into later sections of the paper is the notion of a bilateral monopoly problem between workers (who supply the nontraded services and inputs into the traded good production) and capitalists (who supply capital to the traded good industry and are residual income claimants in that industry). A richer model might identify possible coalitions among several groups in society and allow for more interesting patterns of competition and cooperation in obtaining government favors of various kinds. Coalitions of this kind have been discussed in empirical work on the effects of various regulations, e.g., the recent work by Landes on the effects of maximum hours laws (1980).

The paper's model of conflict, summarized in Figure 4.4, may puzzle many readers, as it did me. Why not represent the set of possible solutions to the bilateral conflict in terms of an Edgeworth Box? Instead, the paper represents it in Figure 4.4 in a diagram with prices (rates of change again) on the axes. In the case analyzed in this paper, I do not think that the representation makes much difference. But generally there would be a problem with using an Edgeworth Box, once it is recognized that competition among the special interest groups uses real resources and affects the size and shape of the box. Unfortunately, a diagram with prices on the axes cannot be used to illustrate these changes in the supplies of goods to society net of conflict costs or the effects of government programs that affect the welfare of special interest groups through means other than changing prices (such as direct redistribution programs). Conflict resolution cannot be represented in a diagram like this because there is no one-to-one correspondence between prices and entitlements to goods.

I find it difficult to understand the indifference curves in Figure 4.4 because it is not clear what is being held constant. One's first impression is that there is no "optimal" relative price for either group, short of infinity, since either group would always prefer a higher relative price of the good of which it is a net seller. Then there would be no points B and L in the figure. But sales fall as the relative price of a product rises and so each side has an optimum relative price. But this is a relative price; both sides would be indifferent to a doubling of all nominal magnitudes. It would therefore appear that points B and L should not be points at all, but lines out of the origin with a slope representing the optimal relative price. Of course, it may be that some other nominal magnitude is held constant in this diagram, e.g., the money supply. But then, of course, both sides would benefit from holding more real money balances, so that the optimal B and L would lie on the lines out of the origin but arbitrarily close to the origin. If no nominal magnitudes are implicitly being held constant in the diagram, then there is obviously no contract curve since there is no locus of tangencies of indifference curves that are lines out of the origin. In that case we can tell from the model neither the equilibrium resulting from the conflict nor the social optimum.

Since conflict using real resources that could be used in alternative ways is wasteful, one would expect society to invest real resources in constitutional-level decisions that would establish general rules or policies to minimize future losses from social conflicts. Hayek (1948, 1967, 1976) has argued that the common law serves this purpose. Rules that serve this purpose may lie behind the adoption of Schelling points to aid in conflict resolution (see Friedman 1980). The adoption of general rules to apply in all situations regardless of the transitory interest of individuals raises interesting problems associated with time inconsistency (Strotz 1956), such as how individuals can commit themselves in advance to rules that, if adopted, make everyone better off.[2] The issue of general rules versus particular actions, mentioned at the beginning of Black's paper, could have been useful when discussing the particular case of conflict considered in the paper.

MODELS OF CONFLICT AGAIN

A model of conflict resolution must describe not only the objectives of agents but also their environment--the effects of their actions and the constraints upon their actions. We might imagine agents (individuals or groups whose internal organization we ignore) being endowed with initial characteristics that we can list in a vector and call "power." These characteristics would include initial endowments of goods, abilities to perform various tasks (including physically taking goods from others), etc. One might imagine a set of institutional constraints under which each person finds himself, or one might imagine people in a Rawlsian initial state, behind a veil of ignorance, and investigate their choice of institutions. Depending upon the institutional framework and the distribution of power in society, various actions will have various consequences on an individual's consumption of the commodities that enter his utility function. Entitlements to these commodities are "produced" by the individual, through his "actions" that combine his time, market goods, and characteristics of other people (their power) as in Becker (1974). The individual's environment is described partially by "production functions" that show the results of these actions for various combinations of inputs, including the distribution of power. These actions affect not only current but also future entitlements to goods for the agent. Agents choose actions to maximize utility. But they may also choose <u>rules</u> which become part of the institutional environment. Choices of rules can be thought of as constitutional-level decisions. Agents may also choose <u>policies</u>, which are general strategies for behavior within the given set of rules. An action is then a specific realization of a policy under specific conditions. The actions that are actually undertaken depend not only upon the distribution of power in society but upon the institutional framework, which influences optimal policies. Since actions may require the use of real resources, and may influence the amount of resources society has both now and in the future (through influences on incentives to produce), some institutional frameworks will be superior to others. Inferior institutional frameworks would be those that result in actions (and hence conflict resolutions) that produce Pareto-inferior allocations or that produce results that would be unanimously unacceptable to agents behind the Rawlsian veil of ignorance.

An institutional framework, however, constrains agents' actions and requires real resources to enforce. The solution to the time-inconsistency problem is therefore costly. Agents may use the government as a vehicle for undertaking actions that are not part of the set of actions agreed upon to enforce the institutional framework. Agents obviously have an incentive to disguise such actions as part of the agreed upon role of government. Consequently, it may be difficult to distinguish what actions of the government are simply part of the enforcement of an institutional framework and what are only instruments of private actions for private gains. An example is provided in Thompson's (1979) discussion of the national defense argument for aiding certain industries: Thompson argues that what appear to be a set of government programs favoring certain groups are actually part of an optimal institutional framework.

CONCLUSION

These comments indicate that it is difficult to use existing models of political behavior and conflict resolution to interpret real world events for two reasons: first, it is difficult to distinguish government programs that are part of an optimal institutional framework from those that are simply favors to special interest groups; second, it is difficult to determine the consequences of the package of government programs in contrast to the effects of a single program. Yet attempts by agents to generate favors from the government will usually involve compromise and coalitions with other interest groups, and hence will usually produce packages of programs rather than single programs in isolation. Consequently, I do not feel comfortable with the kinds of interpretations of real world events given at the end of Black's paper. I cannot suppose there is labor-dominated government as Black does without wondering why government is labor dominated; what compromises were traded in what other areas for support in some particular areas?

So despite the many insights in Black's paper, I am unable to conclude that we yet have a satisfactory model of conflict among special interest groups that we could use to think about the "political assignment problem" or that we would dare use to investigate the real world with much confidence. Nevertheless, his recognition of the social costs of conflict and of the trade-offs facing individual agents in obtaining political benefits makes his paper an interesting contribution to the collection of work on these issues.

NOTES

1. David Friedman (1980) has pointed out that better-organized interest groups, who are better able to avoid free rider problems among their members and are most likely to obtain government favors, are the groups that are most likely to compete away all their expected gains from the government programs. The more severe the free rider problem, the less likely a group will obtain the favorable program, but the greater the gain to the group (that is, to the free riders in the group) if the program is instituted.

2. Steve Landsburg has suggested to me a puzzle that illustrates a time-inconsistency problem. A being from outer space has come to visit earth, and is bestowing on every earthling a gift. The gift is the right to come into the being's spacecraft and choose the contents of one or both of two boxes. One box contains $1000. The other box contains either nothing or one million dollars. You do now know which box is which, but you may choose either box or both boxes. The being, however, has analyzed the personality of each earthling. If a person's character would lead him to choose only one box, then the being places a million dollars in the second box; if the person's character would lead him to choose both boxes, then the being places nothing in the second box. Fifty million earthlings have gone before you for their gift; the being has correctly analyzed each of their personalities. It's your turn. Will you choose only one box or will you choose both?

REJOINDER • *Stanley W. Black*

I appreciate Peter Katzenstein's thoughtful and provocative comments. I would simply respond that I did not intend the game-theoretical analysis in the paper to explain <u>all</u> of the differences in behavior between countries. Rather, it seems to me to explain an additional source of difference going beyond those represented by differences in economic structure and the disturbances hitting an economy. Thus differences in size and openness, as well as resource endowment, are intended to be included within the scope of the model.

GENERAL DISCUSSION

GENERAL DISCUSSION
In the general discussion several people suggested that Black's basic mode of analysis might benefit from further disaggregation. Distinguishing between debtors and creditors, for instance, would permit coalitions between other private sector groups. Similarly, a disaggregation by sector would permit cooperative behavior of labor and business in specific sectors. Others suggested that the basic hypothesis of conflict theories like Black's--that is, tracing inflation to interest group struggles over distribution--is simply incorrect. Inflation is a very unreliable way of redistributing income. Interest groups battle instead over tariffs, taxes, and other things.
Inflation, it was suggested, has resulted from policymaking errors that reflected misplaced belief in the notion of a stable Phillips curve trade-off between inflation and unemployment. Solomon pointed out that inflation was present prior to World War II and that the postwar inflation has been episodic, not steady as a Phillips curve explanation might suggest. Several

political scientists argued that economists tend to focus only on "peacetime" inflation. But the postwar period has been one of continuous international tension. Models that leave out the international situation, they contend, can't explain reality. In response it was noted that in prior periods "war" was a temporary situation after which a return to price stability and pegged exchange rates was widely expected. In the current situation, by contrast, cold war is a permanent phenomena and belief in price stability no longer exists.

discretionary government policies through constitutional amendments outlawing budget deficits and/or placing limits on the proportion of GNP devoted to government spending, the existence of such biases is a matter of controversy among leading economists (see, for example, the contrasting views of Arthur Burns 1979a and Paul Samuelson 1979).

In an ideal democracy, with a well-informed and farsighted public and institutional arrangements that secure an equal weighting of each citizen's interests, the public would receive the levels of government spending, taxation, and inflation that were desired by the average (median) voter. It is useful to think of deviations from this ideal as occurring through two main channels or sources of bias. One is the unequal weighting of interests so that, for example, small, well-organized groups of special interests win out in the political process over the preferences of larger but less-organized groups such as consumers. The other occurs when short-sighted and/or ill-informed members of the public vote out of office politicians who do not cater to their misperceived interests. In the terminology of the public choice literature, the first channel causes deviations from median voter outcomes, while the second leads to deviations between actual and informed median voter outcomes.[4] It is, of course, possible for both types of biases to operate at one time.

In this paper, we will be particularly concerned with the second type of bias, both because it is the one that will be most affected by alternative exchange rate systems and because we suspect that it is probably the most important source of potential inflationary bias. (On the other hand, we expect that the first source may be more important with respect to the possibility of excessive government spending.) In our judgement a strong case can be made that the relative flatness of the short-run, inflation-unemployment trade-off in response to less than fully anticipated changes in macroeconomic policy, combined with a bias toward an "excessively" short time horizon in the operation of the political process and a desire for full employment, has been a major cause of the escalation of inflation in the Western world over the past two decades. With expansionary macroeconomic policies, a disproportionate amount of the desirable effects of expanded output and employment show up first; while the costs of higher inflation are more heavily concentrated in later periods. With contractionary policies, just the reverse is the case. If the political process does indeed operate with an excessively short time horizon from the standpoint of a reasonable range for social rates of discount, the result is a bias toward expansionary overcontractionary policies. This has shown up perhaps most persistently in the failures to carry through to successful completion antiinflationary policies. Time and again contractionary policies are adopted, but tend to be abandoned under heavy political pressure because the initial effects of the program have increased unemployment too much and have not reduced inflation enough. On the expansionary side, there are political incentives to exploit favorable short-run inflation-unemployment trade-offs as well as to validate supply shocks and cost-push pressures. No doubt some portion of our higher rates of inflation in recent years have been due to underestimates by economists of the longer-run inflationary effects, but even where these are estimated correctly by experts, as long as the views of the public are not dominated by rational expectations, there is political advantage in exploiting the difference between short-run and long-run inflation-unemployment trade-offs, which results in both excessive volatility and higher rates of inflation than would occur with an informed median voter benchmark. This bias will be greater, the flatter is the short-run Phillips

This has most commonly been presented in terms of the discipline argument for fixed exchange rates, a topic that remains the focus of a great deal of debate. Now what is particularly interesting is not that there has been a conflict or different weighting of objectives among different economists. That is certainly an everyday occurrence. It is rather the terms under which the discipline debate has taken place.

While here and there questions about the direct conflict between these two objectives have been raised, usually these issues have not been explictly joined. Most discussions of the discipline issue take it as desirable to have external discipline over domestic financial policies, but raise questions about whether fixed or flexible exchange rates provide better discipline. In other words, where the discipline argument for fixed rates is taken on by advocates of flexible rates, it is usually on the grounds that in reality pegged rates give less discipline and flexible rates give more discipline than had been suggested by advocates of fixed rates such as Robbins (1954) and Viner (1956). For example, Haberler accepted the view that "The imposition of financial and wage discipline is, after all, the most important advantage that can be claimed for a system of stable exchange rates" (Haberler 1964, p. 20), but concluded that reserve flows and exchange controls often undercut the immediate discipline of pegged rates and that the depreciation of flexible rates might well exert a stronger disciplinary force on domestic policies (see also Friedman 1953; Johnson 1970). Other arguments included the points that the adjustable peg system of Bretton Woods did not exert the same amount of discipline as a genuine, fixed rate gold standard and that in an inflationary world environment, fixed exchange rates would force the importation of inflation rather than stability (on this see especially Yeager 1968 and 1976).

What tends to be missing from these discussions are compelling arguments as to why external discipline over domestic developments is desirable. This is a point that is more often assumed than argued. In many cases the rationale appears to be that anything that reduces inflation is desirable, combined with references to the historical record of the mismanagement of paper money by governments or beliefs that fixed rates would help hold wage pressures in check.[3] In other words, control of inflation is assumed (often implicitly) to be the only or at least the most important objective of policy. Such arguments make sense only from the standpoint of a particular individual's value judgment about what the rate of inflation should be. They do not recognize the possibilities that the majority of citizens are getting the rate of inflation that they demand.

A more refined view argues that discipline is necessary to keep inflation from being "excessive" but the meaning of excessive often is not made clear. Is it excessive from the standpoint of the preferences of a particular individual or is it excessive from the standpoint of some collective standard of the "public interest"? Occasional references to various inflationary biases suggest that the latter concept is sometimes in mind, but generally little careful analysis of the courses of bias is given.

Apparently such tendencies are generally taken to be self-evident. But are they? What are the bias-free norms or benchmarks by which policies should be judged? And if biases are found what is the best way to reduce their incidence? To what extent should one directly try to change the processes that give rise to bias, versus adopting a second-best approach of imposing constraints that will limit the operation of the bias, and what are the most promising methods under each approach?

As is indicated in the recent discussions of proposals to discipline these factors has been formally shown to create inflationary biases as well as macroeconomic instability in models of the political business cycle. Perhaps more importantly, they also create incentives for a greater degree of inflationary validation of shocks and disincentives for carrying out antiinflationary policies.

A steepening of the short-run trade-offs resulting from the adoption of flexible exchange rates would reduce (although in general not eliminate) these biases. These effects will be stronger, the more open the economy in terms of both trade and capital flows, and the greater any tendency for exchange rate overshooting. With fiscal policy, the effects will be less strong; and it is possible, although we do not think likely, that the incentives for fiscal policy-induced political business cycles could be increased.

With pegged rates, the political incentives for an inflationary bias will be greater in open than in closed economies. It isn't clear that short-run inflation-unemployment trade-offs will be influenced because balance of payments deficits will dampen the increase in domestic employment as well as inflation, but it is argued that the real income-inflation trade-off would be improved and that this would lead to increased incentives for overly expansionary policies.

Alternative pegged rate systems may have quite different effects on the longer-run constraints placed on domestic macro policies. For example, adjustable pegged rates do not present a long-run constraint and in fact may be likely to maximize the incentives to inflate. It is argued that even the discipline of permanently pegged rates would only keep countries from inflating more rapidly than the world average, which in turn, would be biased upward by the incentives to export inflationary effects in the short run.

We conclude that while a good deal more research is needed for us to be completely confident about these questions, it seems likely that for countries like the United States, the best approach to reducing the degree of inflation bias is the combination of flexible exchange rates and a constitutionally mandated monetary growth rule.

INFLATIONARY BIASES AND INDEPENDENCE VERSUS DISCIPLINE AS OBJECTIVES FOR EXCHANGE RATE REGIMES

There is a long history of discussion of the relationship between exchange rate regimes and domestic macroeconomic policies. One of the most interesting aspects of this literature is the extent to which the question of desirable exchange rate systems has been approached from two quite distinct normative points of view and the relatively little amount of attention which has been devoted to attempting to reconcile or at least understand the interrelationship between these points of view. From one perspective, the focus has been on how to remove or reduce the balance of payments constraint on domestic macroeconomic policies so that these policies could be aimed at promoting the stability and growth of the domestic economy. Given this objective, and balancing the benefits of increased domestic policy independence against possible costs, such as the possible discouragement to international trade and investment from exchange rate changes, the question has been, what is the best form of exchange rate system?[2]

Coexisting with this independence approach, however, has been an also widely held point of view that exchange rate systems should be judged from exactly the opposite standpoint. The question is, How well do alternative international monetary regimes "discipline" domestic financial policies?

PAPER 5 • *Thomas D. Willett and John Mullen*

The Effects of Alternative International Monetary Systems on Macroeconomic Discipline and Inflationary Biases

INTRODUCTION AND SUMMARY

This paper argues that despite the long history of debate about financial discipline and alternative exchange rate regimes, several important points have not been sufficiently clarified. There has been relatively little explicit debate about the conditions under which it is desirable to have balance of payments discipline. Relatively little integration has characterized two traditions in balance of payments writings. One tradition assumes that it is desirable to free domestic macro policies from the dictates of the balance of payments. The other assumes that a balance of payments constraint is necessary to hold domestic inflationary tendencies in check. Most of the debate over discipline has been over whether fixed or flexible rates would give more discipline, not whether external restraints were desirable. We argue that to establish a case for adopting fixed exchange rates to generate balance of payments discipline, it needs to be shown not just that inflation would be less under fixed rates, but that the resulting amount of inflation would be closer to what is desired on the basis of some democratic norm, i.e., that it offsets or reduces inflationary policies present in the democratic process.

We believe that a reasonable case can be made that there are inflationary biases in our current political arrangements that lead to rates of inflation higher than would be desired by the informed median voter given the relationships between inflation and the real side of the economy. We question, however, whether the adoption of pegged exchange rates is the most effective method of reducing or offsetting this bias. We make a distinction between two different types of discipline effects, short-run effects on political incentives to engage in "excessively" inflationary policies, and the longer-run constraints of the need for balance of payments equilibrium.

In previous debates those who have argued that there is greater discipline under flexible rates have tended to focus on the former concept, while those who have favored fixed rates have tended to focus on the latter. No matter whether reserve losses or exchange rate depreciations give prompter and more forceful signals to the public, by speeding up price relative to output adjustments flexible exchange rates will increase the steepness of the short-run, inflation-unemployment trade-off in response to variations in monetary policy. We believe that a major cause of inflationary bias is the difference between the short-run and longer-run inflation-unemployment trade-offs resulting from less than fully anticipated changes in macro policies combined with an "excessively" short average effective time horizon on the part of government officials and the general public.[1] The presence of curve, and the less farsighted is the voting public.[5]

As will be argued in the following section, by steepening the short-run inflation-unemployment trade-off, flexible exchange rates may reduce the magnitude of this bias, reducing the degree of both the disproportionate short-run relative to long-run benefits of expansionary policies and costs of contractionary policies.

Of course, there is no general agreement that we have in fact suffered from inflationary biases. In models that assume rational expectations throughout the economy, there will be little or no systematically exploitable inflation-unemployment trade-offs and hence no reason for there to be an inflationary bias from this source over the long run. Similarly, if everyone voted in this manner, there would be no scope for other biases resulting from deviations from informed median voter outcomes. We are in the very early stages of empirical investigation of these issues and there is currently scope for a wide range of opinion among reasonable people. Our own view is that while learning behavior on the part of the public is quite important and the rational expectations approach has highlighted quite important considerations, there is still considerable scope for inflationary biases that result from rational ignorance. We believe that the range of possible government behavior is sufficiently broad, and that changes in government practices are sufficiently reversible, that governments usually face differences in the short-run and long-run effects of policies, so that less than fully anticipated policy changes will continue to occur for a long time, if not indefinitely. Furthermore, while major participants in the financial markets have substantial self-interest incentives to be highly informed with respect to economic policy developments, the typical voter does not. There is a private good/public good distinction that makes greater ignorance on the part of potential voters quite rational (after all, what is the probability of a particular individual's vote influencing the outcome of an election?).[6]

Also, from the standpoint of our questioning of the traditional discipline argument for fixed exchange rates, such an argument is relevant only if biases do in fact exist. So to the extent that rational expectations are or become dominant in the economy and the polity, the general interest discipline argument for fixed exchange rates disappears. Thus, in the remainder of this paper we consider the discipline arguments with respect to alternative exchange rate systems under the circumstances in which they might be relevant, i.e., that there is an exploitable, short-run inflation-unemployment trade-off.

There are two basic approaches to reducing the operation of biases in the political process. One is to attempt to directly correct the causes of bias. The second approach assumes that this first best approach is too difficult to implement, and focuses instead on placing constraints on the outcome of the process. Thus, for example, with respect to the possibility of government overspending, the first approach stresses increasing the information and political participation of the public and revising institutional arrangements that give disproportionate political power to special interests [for examples of such proposals, such as randomly elected legislatures, see Mueller (1979); Mueller, Tollison, and Willett (1972, 1976)], while the latter approach focuses on constitutional limitations on budget deficits and the share of government spending and taxation in the economy. In other words, the choice is between trying to revise incentive structures and placing constraints on the outcomes of the existing incentive structures.

We believe that proposals for fixed exchanges as a disciplinary device should be viewed as belonging to the latter category, while arguments that flexible rates increase discipline by making the inflationary consequences of policies more quickly apparent belongs to the former category.

The next section considers the effects of pegged versus flexible exchange rate systems on the incentives to inflate resulting from differences between short-run and longer-run inflation-unemployment trade-offs. In the last section the role of pegged exchange rates as a constraint on inflationary policies is considered.[7]

THE EFFECTS OF PEGGED VERSUS FLEXIBLE EXCHANGE RATES ON THE UNCONSTRAINED INCENTIVES FOR EXPANSIONARY AND CONTRACTIONARY POLICIES IN OPEN ECONOMICS

Monetary Expansion under Flexible Rates

Under flexible exchange rates a given increase in the money supply will have greater effects on both inflation and output over the medium term than under pegged exchange rates. The accompanying exchange rate depreciation will both raise the price of internationally traded goods and stimulate domestic employment on Keynesian multiplier grounds through an increase in exports relative to imports. In effect, while some portion of the domestic stimulus spills out onto other countries under pegged exchange rates, it tends to remain more fully bottled up with the country of origin under flexible rates.[8] By itself, however, this doesn't tell us anything about the incentives for political business cycle behavior. All it says is that to achieve a given amount of stimulus one needs to turn the monetary policy dials more under pegged than under flexible exchange rates. What we need to know to draw implications for political business cycle behavior is whether alternative exchange rate regimes will have different effects on inflation and unemployment from those that would occur in a closed economy.

We don't believe that one can confidently predict effects over the medium or long run. Only recently have researchers begun to focus explicitly on the question of how international sector considerations can influence medium-term inflation-unemployment trade-offs (see, for example, Argy and Salop 1979; Bilson 1979; and Witte 1979). Most of the earlier models adopted Keynesian fixed price assumptions, and we need to know a great deal more about both impact and feedback effects in multisector models.

We believe, however, that one can answer this question with respect to short-term effects. The empirical evidence suggests that while the effects of unanticipated policy changes affect domestic prices only rather slowly, we find that foreign exchange markets tend to react rather quickly. Thus under flexible rates, monetary expansion will lead to quite rapid exchange rate depreciation, and the evidence suggests that the pass through from exchange rate changes to the prices of internationally traded goods is also fairly prompt.[9] Thus there seems to be a strong presumption that the effects of monetary expansion will begin to show up much more rapidly on domestic wholesale prices and consumer prices under flexible rates than under pegged rates or closed economies. Under pure rational expectations, this impact effect would have little if any effect on the rate of price adjustment in domestic sectors, but to the extent that mark-up pricing and adaptive expectations are present in domestic sectors, they would speed up the rate of adjustment in domestic sectors as well (see Pigott, Rutledge, and Willett 1980). It should also be remembered that impact effects will be much broader than indicated by the share of imports and exports in the GNP as the prices of import substitutes and domestic prices of export goods and those using imported inputs will be influenced directly. Wage indexing would also contribute to the speeding up of inflationary effects.

Note that such a scenario would not automatically imply that floating rates would have been an additional cause of domestic inflation in any meaningful sense, but it would lead to a speeding up of the price effects of inflation. This would tend to steepen the short-run, inflation-unemployment trade-off and thus reduce the magnitude of the inflationary bias resulting from excessively short time horizons and political business cycle behavior.

This result is complemented by an analysis of the speed of adjustment of employment effects. As has been recently emphasized by a number of writers, because price elasticities in the foreign exchange market are likely to be quite low in the short run, the initial effect of a depreciation is likely to be a worsening of the trade balance as measured in foreign currency. These J-curve effects suggest that depreciation could actually have contractionary rather than expansionary effects in the short run.[10]

Such a result is not inevitable, because while the trade balance will initially worsen in terms of foreign currency it will not in real terms nor necessarily in terms of domestic currency. It is not clear how these conflicting developments should be weighted (for discussion on this question, see Sweeney and Willett 1976a). Likewise, as Dornbusch has pointed out (1976b), to the extent that the initial worsened trade balance is financed out of domestic saving rather than consumption, the effects will not be contractionary. While we do not think that the current state of analysis makes it clear whether the initial effects of depreciation will actually be contractionary (on this, see also Dornbusch and Krugman 1976, and Casas 1978), we think that there is a strong presumption that the additional expansionary effects on output will not occur as rapidly as the effects on prices.

As a consequence it seems quite safe to conclude that flexible exchange rates will increase the steepness of the short-run inflation-unemployment trade-off in response to unanticipated domestic monetary expansion and hence reduce the incentives for political business cycles. The magnitude of the reduction would be greater, the more open the economy in terms of both trade and capital flows (the greater the capital mobility, the greater the exchange rate depreciation), and the greater the direct feedback effects from exchange rate changes to domestic prices.

The conclusion that flexible exchange rates give fewer incentives to use monetary policy to engage in political business cycle behavior could be reinforced by any direct effects on public attitudes over and above the effects on inflation under the different regimes. The extent that exchange rate depreciation gives a clearer direct signal to the public of perhaps overly expansionary policies than do reserve losses under pegged exchange rates could further reduce the incentives to inflate. Gottfried Haberler has been one of the leading proponents of this view. Harry Johnson (1970, p. 105) has argued in a similar vein.

> The record since World War II speaks poorly for the anti-inflationary discipline of fixed exchange rates. The reason is that the signal to governments of the need for anti-inflationary discipline comes through a loss of exchange reserves, the implications of which are understood by only a few and can be disregarded or temporized with until a crisis descends; the crisis then justifies all sorts of policy expedients other than the domestic deflation that the logic of adjustment under the fixed-rate system demands. Under a

flexible-rate system, the consequences of inflationary government
policies would be more readily apparent to the general population, in
the form of a declining foreign value of the currency and an upward
trend in domestic prices; proper policies to correct the situation, if
it were desired to correct it, could be argued about in an atmosphere
free of crisis.

For similar comments see Friedman 1953, pp. 428-29.
Note that Johnson is talking here primarily about discipline under fixed
versus flexible rates in terms of the adequacy of the early warning signals
that they give, rather than in terms of long-run constraints on policy. It
is interesting that advocates of floating tended to focus on this former
aspect of the question--the incentives not to deviate from "correct"
policies--while advocates of fixed rates were forced to rely more on the
long-run constraint argument, a topic to which we will turn in the following
section. First, however, we need to consider several further questions about
the incentives for inflationary biases under different circumstances.

Fiscal Expansion under Flexible Rates

Monetary and fiscal policy may have substantially different short-run
effects on the behavior of flexible exchange rates (for recent policy
discussions on this, see Dornbusch and Krugman 1976, and Willett 1978b).
While monetary expansion unambiguously leads to exchange rate depreciation,
pure fiscal expansion, by bidding up domestic real interest rates, will
induce a capital inflow rather than outflow. This will dampen the amount of
exchange rate depreciation and with sufficiently high capital mobility can
even give rise to an appreciation. Thus our conclusions about the effects of
monetary expansion on the steepness of short-run Phillips curves would not
necessarily carry over to the case of fiscally induced expansion.

If the economy behaves more closely to Keynesian than monetarist
principles and international capital mobility is quite high, the use of pure
fiscal policy could exaggerate rather than diminish the incentives for
political business cycle behavior under flexible exchange rates. Our own
suspicion is that there is a sufficiently monetarist component to the
operation of most economies, and that international capital mobility is not
sufficiently above critical levels, that the general presumption toward a
reduced inflationary bias for monetary policy under floating rates is not
reversed by the possibility of different effects from the use of fiscal
policy. The establishment of this conclusion with a high degree of
confidence would require a great deal more technical research, however.[11]

Effects of the Degree of Openness on the Effects of Expansion under Pegged
Rates

How does taking international consequences into account under pegged
rates lead to differences from the traditional closed economy analysis of
political business cycle considerations? In operational terms this question
becomes, How does the degree of openness influence the incentives for such
behavior? It does not seem obvious that the degree of openness will
influence inflation-unemployment trade-offs under pegged rates. While
increased imports will hold down the amount of inflation that accompanies a
given amount of domestic expansion, the increase in imports also implies that
the proportion of the expansion in aggregate demand that is spent on
domestically produced goods and services will also decline. It doesn't seem
clear that the ratio of price to employment effects would be substantially

altered.

We believe that there is a presumption that the degree of openness will increase the incentives for inflationary bias, however. The reason is that unemployment is not the only aspect of the real side of the economy that will influence political behavior. Changes in profits and real wages, for example, are also important factors. In a closed economy all of these factors tend to move together in response to changes in macro policies. Thus expansion tends not only to reduce unemployment but also to increase profits and real income of workers, etc. In discussing policy aspects of inflation-unemployment trade-offs, changes in unemployment are usually taken (at least implicitly) as a proxy for a whole array of real effects (see for example, Nordhaus 1975, pp. 171-72).

In an open economy, however, changes in the unemployment rate may not be a good proxy for changes in real incomes. A trade deficit increases domestic absorption above domestic output, leading to an increase in the real value of current income as compared with a situation of balanced trade.[12] Both price and domestic employment effects will be less for a given degree of policy stimulus, the more open the economy, but there is no particular presumption about the effects on the slope of the short-run Phillips curve. The country running a disequilibrium trade deficit is, however, living beyond its means and is subsidizing current consumption through foreign borrowing or drawing down reserves. This will improve the current real income-inflation trade-off at the expense of worsening it in later periods when the disequilibrium trade imbalance must be reversed.[13] This would increase the incentives for an expansionary bias along the same lines as a lessening of the slope of the short-run inflation-unemployment trade-off.

Effects on the Incentives for Disinflationary Policies

It should also be noted that this temporary increase in real income due to a disequilibrium trade deficit before an election would be likely to increase the costs of disinflationary policies after the election. In many recent analyses the traditional assumptions of downward inflexibility of nominal wages are being replaced by assumptions of downward inflexibility in real wages. While the empirical evidence suggests that such an assumption is not tenable in its extreme form, there does seem to be a great deal to the idea of downward real wage resistance in the sense that increases in real wages are likely to ratchet upward the positions of expectations-augmented as well as nominal short-run Phillips curves, thus increasing the unemployment costs of achieving any given lower inflation rate. Under such circumstances, the temporary artificial boost to real wages generated by a trade deficit may be particularly pernicious in terms of contributing to the political incentives for validating a wage-price spiral.

With flexible exchange rates on the other hand, the political difficulties of reducing inflation should be less than in the case of either a closed economy or an open economy under pegged exchange rates. The biggest difficulty in pursuing disinflationary policies is that it tends to take so long before one begins to see any substantial progress in lowering the rate of increase in domestic prices. This adds to the criticisms that management policies no longer work, and contributes to the pressures to abandon restrictive monetary and fiscal policies.

With a well-functioning foreign-exchange market, however, the adoption of more restrictive macro policies is likely to lead to an appreciation (or at least a reduction in the rate of depreciation). Inverting the analysis in the section on Monetary Expansion under Flexible Rates, we see this will have a relatively rapid antiinflationary effect on the prices of internationally traded goods and may also contribute to slowing the rate of increase of domestic wages and prices without having any very substantial initial adverse influence on domestic employment. Thus in contrast to the effects of pegged exchange rates in open economies, flexible exchange rates should speed up the beneficial effects of disinflationary policies and increase the probability that they will be continued to a successful conclusion.[14]

BALANCE OF PAYMENTS CONSTRAINTS UNDER ALTERNATIVE INTERNATIONAL MONETARY REGIMES

Any system of pegged exchange rates will have the effect of increasing the incentives for political business cycles as discussed above, with the size of this effect an increasing function of the degree of openness of the economy and the amount of international reserves and/or borrowing capacity available to sustain balance of payments deficits. Alternatives to pegged rate regimes may have quite different effects, however, in terms of the longer-term constraints that they place on macroeconomic policies.

On these grounds, a true gold standard with a commitment to avoiding trade barriers and exchange controls would provide the maximum binding constraint, although it must be remembered that macro policies will be constrained to the rate of global gold production, which may be erratic and could produce either inflationary or deflationary pressures.[15]

Under such a system with discretionary macro policy in the short run, the long-run average of each nation's macro policies would be constrained by the world average of national macro policies. But these in themselves could contain a substantial inflationary bias. Countries would be influenced by the average national rate of bias, and while this would still constrain some countries, it could force higher rates of inflation on others. Furthermore, as discussed in the previous section, the tendency of balance of payments deficits to improve short-run inflation - real income trade offs for individual countries would cause countries undertaking independent individual actions to perceive trade-offs that were more favorable than were collectively feasible. Under such circumstances, decentralized national decision making would be further biased toward excessively expansionary policies and the problem of global inflationary bias would be even greater than on the basis of closed economy considerations alone.

The problem of inflationary bias would be even greater under regimes where the pegging of exchange rates and avoidance of controls is not permanent. While the discipline of genuinely fixed rates has often been ascribed to the Bretton Woods adjustable peg system, this is clearly inappropriate. Devaluation was clearly viewed as being politically costly under the Bretton Woods system, but when national price levels became substantially out of line with those required for balance of payments equilibrium, the result was often controls or devaluation rather than deflation.

As long as a government's time rate of discount is not infinite, the incentives for "excessively" expansionary policies will be less, the higher the longer-run costs that current policies imply. In this regard, the deflation required by permanently fixed rates is likely to be the greatest discouragement for countries on the flexible rate side of optimum currency area criteria, i.e., for those (such as the United States) for which deflation is more costly than devaluation. Next in terms of incentives would be an adjustable peg because of the political costs that would be involved over and above the direct economic effects of devaluation.[16]

Heavily managed floating would be perhaps the system with the greatest inflationary bias, as heavy intervention could substantially limit the depreciation of exchange rates in the short run (say, before an election) and could be gradually reduced and then reversed after the election with less political trauma than would be generated by a sizable discrete devaluation under an adjustable peg. This consideration suggests the desirability of strong international surveillance of exchange rate policies under managed floating that goes well beyond the avoidance of blatant beggar thy neighbor policies such as occurred during the 1930s (for recent discussions and references to the literature on alternative approaches to international surveillance of exchange rate policies, see Artus and Crockett 1978; Willett 1977, Chap. 4, and 1978b).

A crawling peg would also not provide strong incentives, especially if combined with a high level of international liquidity. The initial rate of depreciation could be sharply limited while the balance of payments deficit generated could later be reduced primarily through the downward crawl of the currency rather than through contractionary macroeconomic policies. Of course the differences in the extent to which differential longer-run costs would restrain the amount of excessive preelection stimulus would depend negatively upon the time rate of discount incorporated in political decision making.

CONCLUDING COMMENTS

This paper argues that the traditional debate over the desirability of balance of payments discipline over macroeconomic policies frequently failed to pay attention to the domestic biases that might justify the need for such discipline or to distinguish clearly between two different senses of discipline. One is the influence of alternative exchange rate regimes on the propensity to engage in "excessive" inflationary policies. The other is the influence of the gold stock or requirements for balance of payments equilibrium as a long-run constraint on macro policies. While the analysis presented here points to the need for a great deal more research before definitive answers can be reached (if then), the available evidence suggests to us that there do indeed tend to be net inflationary biases generated by political processes in the Western industrial countries (as judged by the informed median voter benchmark).

In our judgment however, this does not present a convincing case for pegged exchange rates for countries that otherwise should adopt flexible rates on optimum currency area grounds. Our analysis suggests that pegged rates would generally increase the incentives for an inflationary bias, while under most types of pegged rate regimes, the long-run constraint of the need for balance of payments equilibrium would not eliminate a global inflationary bias. Our analysis of effects on differences between short-run and long-run inflation-unemployment trade offs resulting from macro policy changes needs to be supplemented by consideration of the incentives for validating different types of disturbances through monetary expansion along the lines of Paper 9, by Dale Henderson (although including price as well as output effects). The effects that alternative exchange rate systems may have on the generation of disturbances (if, for example, wage-push pressures are more likely under pegged or flexible exchange rates) also need to be examined. We do not believe, however, that such analysis will undercut our tentative conclusion that pegged exchange rates are not likely to be an effective means of substantially reducing inflationary biases.

For that matter, however, neither do we think that the adoption of flexible exchange rates is sufficient to eliminate a substantial inflationary bias. In other words, our analysis leads us to reject the traditional discipline arguments for pegged exchange rates on antiinflation grounds. We believe that the adoption of flexible exchange rates makes only a marginal contribution toward reducing the inflationary bias in macroeconomic policymaking, especially in relatively large, closed economies like that of the United States.

Likewise, while we applaud efforts to improve the information of the electorate, we are doubtful that such efforts will be fully successful. Short of very substantial revisions in our domestic political institutions, we thus see a constitutionally mandated adoption of monetary growth rules as the most effective method at the present time for exerting antiinflationary discipline on national governments (and on wage-and price-setting units).[17] Such a policy should be likely to be at least as durable as an attempt to return to a gold standard and would not leave the rate of monetary growth to the vagaries of gold discoveries or balance of payments developments. The adoption of such a rule would of course impose economic costs as well as benefits. Optimal discretionary policy would obviously be more desirable, but the policy history of the past two decades makes us increasingly sympathetic to arguments for monetary growth rules.

NOTES

This paper, of which Willett is the primary author, draws upon a larger study under way by the authors on inflation-unemployment trade-offs and balance of payments discipline under alternative international monetary systems. Financial assistance for this project from the General Electric Foundation and the Center for the Study of Law Structures at Claremont Men's College is gratefully acknowledged, as are helpful comments by Randall Hinshaw, Leon Hollerman, and Richard Sweeney on an earlier draft.

1. See, for example, Lombra (1979).
2. See, for example, Johnson (1970, pp. 91-92). This is how the question was frequently posed. Of course, depending upon their causes and their relationships with other economic and financial variables, exchange rate changes may promote rather than hinder the efficient allocation of resources, and the relative costs and benefits of different exchange rate systems may vary tremendously from one economy to another based on the considerations discussed in the literature on the theory of optimum currency areas. For recent discussions of these topics and references to the literature, see Tower and Willett (1976), and Willett (1980a).
3. For further discussion of and references to this literature see the expanded version of this paper (Willett and Mullen 1982).
4. For a review of and references to this literature see Amacher, Tollison, and Willett (1975, 1976).
5. See, for example, Nordhaus (1975); MacRae (1977), Hirsch and Goldthorpe (1978); and Willett and Mullen (1982).
6. For recent discussion and references to the rational expectations and political business cycle literature, see Hibbs (1977); Frey (1978); and Santomero and Seater (1978). On the role of rational expectations our own views closely approximate those of Fellner (1979) and Haberler (1980). On the incentives for rational voter ignorance and nonparticipation and resulting implications for certain types of economic policies, see Amacher,

Tollison, and Willett (1975) and Willett (1980a).

7. As David Richardson notes in his comment on this paper, our distinction between the effects of alternative exchange rate systems on the incentives to inflate versus longer-run constraints on outcomes is overdrawn, as it assumes that optimal reserve positions do not enter directly into the utility functions of policymakers. Conceptually we accept the argument that reserve levels should enter policymaker utility functions and hence would have short-run as well as longer-run effects. However, we believe that over a wide range these short-run effects are quite weak, sufficiently so as to make our view of reserves as a long-run constraint a useful assumption. For discussion of this point and references to the literature, see Willett (1980b).

8. Of course this bottling up will not always be complete under floating. For more detailed surveys and references to traditional literature on international transmission and insulation and the effects of the degree of capital mobility and alternative monetary systems on the effects of monetary and fiscal policy in open economies, see Cooper (1976), Sweeney and Willett (1976b), Tower and Willett(1976), Willett (1976), and Mussa (1979).

9. See, for example, Goldstein (1980), Hooper and Lowrey (1979), and Solomon (1980), and references cited in these works.

10. The J-curve effect refers to behavior of the trade balance (exports less imports) following depreciation or devaluation of a nation's exchange rate. Because trade elasticities tend to be lower in the short run than the long run, the immediate effect of a depreciation/devaluation may be a worsening of the trade balance. This is because the physical flows of exports and imports change slowly while the value of imports in domestic money terms rises immediately. As the elasticities move toward their long-run values, however, exports rise in real terms while imports fall and the balance of trade improves. Graphically, the behavior of the balance of trade, which at first falls and then rises, looks like a J.

11. In earlier studies of whether the degree of international capital mobility was sufficiently high for pure fiscal expansion to lead to an appreciation of the dollar, the evidence was mixed, not appearing to be either strongly above or below the threshold value. (See Willett 1976 and its appendix by Victoria Farrell, and also the recent analysis of Kenen 1978).

12. Absorption is the total domestic expenditure on final consumer goods and services and on "real" investment, including expenditures on imported goods and services. When there is a balance of trade deficit (surplus), absorption or spending will exceed (fall short of) national income. For a more detailed explanation, see Yeager (1976).

13. Maintenance of a pegged rate under these circumstances would also avoid the adverse terms of trade effects which would be likely to accompany exchange rate depreciation. (Of course a country's terms of trade do not logically have to worsen as the result of exchange rate depreciation, but this appears to be most commonly the case.)

A depreciation accompanying expansionary policy will also affect the real wealth of the domestic economy. Real wealth may rise or fall depending, among other things, on the extent to which domestic residents have diversified their wealth among assets from different countries. Since the effect of a depreciation on real wealth is, in general, uncertain, nothing specific can be said about how the relative incentives to inflate under different exchange rate regimes would be influenced by a real wealth effect. For recent discussions of terms of trade and wealth effects, see Tower

(1975), Tower and Willett (1976), Isard and Porter (1977), and Deardorff and Stern (1978).

14. This analysis has been undertaken on the assumption that the foreign exchange markets are dominated by stabilizing speculation, which moves exchange rates immediately to their medium-term equilibrium path. Tendencies for exchange rate overshooting in response to monetary policy changes would strengthen these conclusions (see Willett and Mullen 1982).

15. For discussion of various possible types of gold standards, see Yeager (1976) and the references cited therein.

16. For discussion of these political costs, see Marris (1970), and Willett (1980a).

17. On the case for making the adoption of monetary rules a constitutional issue, see Yeager (1962) and Buchanan and Wagner (1977). From our perspective there is little rationale for the current enthusiasm for proposals for constitutional amendments to balance the federal budget. While it can be reasonably argued that the option of deficit financing does contribute to biases for overspending and excessive inflation (see, for example, Buchanan and Wagner 1977), balanced budgets would not be sufficient to eliminate these biases. If one really wants to constrain such biases it would be much more effective to adopt constitutional limitiations on government spending and the rate of growth of the money supply. Each of these should stand independently on its own merits, to limit perceived overspending and to constrain perceived excessive monetary growth. At present we personally find the evidence to be somewhat more persuasive for support of the second than of the first of these proposals.

DISCUSSION • *J. David Richardson*

Willett and Mullen's paper is stimulating and rewarding, due especially to its abundance of insightful and sensible observations. Several deserve added emphasis, or should be conditioned in various ways, and the first part of these comments addresses them. The second part of the comments outlines additional considerations in assessing the effects of exchange rate systems on macroeconomic discipline.

I find it very useful to distinguish, as the authors do, between two ways that changing the exchange rate system might discipline policy authorities. First, it might alter their incentives to choose responsible policy, illustrated in the paper by the fact that the slope of the short-run Phillips curve varies with the exchange rate system. Second, it might alter the constraints facing any policy choice, illustrated in the paper by the unavoidable need to maintain positive official reserves in exchange rate systems featuring official intervention.[1] Thus a change in the exchange rate system alters both the carrots and sticks perceived by policymakers. One should therefore be wary of arguments defending some particular exchange rate system as providing maximal carrots only, or maximal sticks only. In this regard, I don't think it is helpful for the authors to identify the incentive/carrot effect with discipline in the short run and the constraint/stick effect with discipline in the long run. Policymakers are always tempted to exploit the short-run Phillips curve, even while approaching long-run equilibrium; and ongoing official reserve losses always constrain behavior, even before they become excessively large.

Willett and Mullen also have interesting observations on the discipline provided by an informed electorate in a democracy. One implication of these observations is that the government would be more disciplined in a "meritocracy" than in a democracy, where "merit" is determined by information and where policy decisions match the preferences of the median informed voter. I would condition the authors' implied enthusiasm for informational meritocracy somewhat, recognizing that decision making by the well-informed may not be as economically desirable, nor as disciplined, as straight democracy in situations where the well-informed have acquired market power and act aggressively. This is a simple application of the antimonopoly argument, but it acquires practical force if we agree that the market system generally rewards the well-informed with market power.

A third of Willett's and Mullen's observations should be set in bold type in all textbooks and taped to the typewriter of economic journalists. Pegged exchange rates generally do discipline governments, but they "discipline" them to inflate at roughly the average global rate--and that is a two-edged sword. Pegged exchange rates discipline profligate governments that would otherwise inflate at above average rates; but they also "discipline" (penalize) "virtuous" governments that would otherwise have chosen less inflation than they reluctantly import under pegged rates. The first kind of discipline leads to lower national inflation under pegged rates; the second kind of discipline leads to higher national inflation under pegged rates. It is not at all clear that the first effect will dominate the second, as much of the literature supposes. And the authors even give some good reasons why the global inflation around which national inflation clusters will be itself higher under pegged exchange rates than under more flexible systems.

A fourth observation that the authors might highlight with greater clarity concerns the efficiency of discipline. Suppose one could determine that of all exchange rate systems, pegged rates discipline policy most desirably. The authors point out that finding this would nevertheless not necessarily provide any grounds for preferring pegged rates to other exchange rate systems. Pegged rates might not provide the desired amount of discipline in a first-best way; other means might provide it better. Now it may seem tortured to eschew pegged rates in this case because they would be a second-or third-best system for attaining discipline. But, on the contrary, it is a very practical and sensible stance. Second-best systems are to be rejected because they waste resources and create undesirable side effects. If discipline is the goal, let us attain it in the most efficient (first-best) way. Efficiency is after all just a principle of conservation of resources and elimination of unwanted by-products.

Willett's and Mullen's ideal (first-best) method for encouraging discipline turns out indeed not to be any particular exchange rate system. It is a constitutionally mandated rule for monetary growth. I am less sanguine than they, however, about the feasibility and wisdom of "rules" in this matter. My presumption is that the government of a nation that would choose the discipline of a constitutional amendment would also behave responsibly in the absence of such a rigid rule. And the government of a nation that defines responsible behavior as using its policies flexibly to satisfy its constituents would be irresponsible to encourage such a constitutional amendment.

If not rules for monetary growth or for exchange rate systems, then what do I prefer as an ideal (first-best) way of encouraging discipline? Since the problem is in considerable measure aggravated by lack of information, misleading information, and woolly thinking about macroeconomic policy and its consequences, I favor rather direct means of providing information and education. For example, one might desirably legislate full and near immediate disclosure of policymaking deliberations, with supporting forecasts and data. Or it might be worthwhile militating for increased attention to economics in public school curricula--surely there are as many external social benefits to an economically well-informed citizenry as to a grammatically, historically, or hygienically well-informed citizenry.

Since Willett's and Mullen's paper is part of a larger, ongoing piece of work, it seems fair also to mention a few areas for extension.

First, the authors might profitably expand the set of macroeconomic goals on which they focus. Their paper reflects the literature on the political business cycle by considering only two goals, low unemployment and low inflation. It then emphasizes the short-run trade-off between them and examines how fast the short-run Phillips curve converges to the long-run Phillips curve under alternative exchange rate systems. Yet today, an increasingly prominent third macroeconomic goal is a high and adequately rising standard of living. Its fundamental indicators are, of course, real wages, real rates of return, capital formation, technological change, and growth. But the paper provides very little discussion of the effect of alternative exchange rate systems on these economic variables. For example, one can argue that wage-push pressures might be greater, the more flexible the exchange rates. As the authors show, asset-market-determined changes in exchange rates have pronounced, and frequently magnified, short-run price effects. It seems reasonable that wages would be similarly affected, since workers' perceived value of escalator-clause insurance will rise with price volatility, and such clauses will become widespread. Increased wage-push pressures in turn could undermine government commitments to pursue disciplined policies.

To elaborate on this proposed extension, there seem to be good behavioral reasons why real wage stickiness would vary directly with exchange rate flexibility. Then any exogenous negative shock to real wages (e.g., OPEC oil pricing), or any exogenous or induced attempt to raise them, could create undesirable supply-side consequences that would not characterize less flexible exchange rate systems (because real wages would be less rigid). To the extent that macroeconomic policy successfully ratified demands for increased real wages in the short run, real returns to property, education, innovation, and managerial expertise might fall, causing temporary declines in capital formation and technological advance. But even temporary declines cause the trajectory of real standards of living to be lower through all future time. If expected real wages were based on the former trajectory, there would be a new (endogenous) reason for increased real wage demands in the future. The process could clearly repeat itself ad infinitum in a vicious circle of inconsistent claims to real income streams and declining productivity and growth. The scenario just described suggests that a useful complement to the authors' thorough treatment of the demand side would be an examination of how exchange rate systems affect the supply-side.

One final extension that seems worthwhile is to examine how exchange rate systems increase the likelihood and growth of external currency banking. Since such banking is essentially just unregulated intermediation and liquidity creation, it represents in itself a "discipline" on government financial policy. As a means of avoiding government regulation, it will presumably enhance macroeconomic performance if government regulation is less disciplined and responsible than private (bankers') behavior, and diminish macroeconomic performance if government regulation is more disciplined and responsible by comparison. Obviously, government regulation of banking has different effects in different times and places, checking the excesses of the market in some and tempting policymakers toward their own excesses in others. The way this relates to exchange rate systems is as follows. The stronger is a government's commitment to its exchange rate target and the heavier is the intervention the government employs in reaching the target, the larger the stock demands for official reserves, one source of external currency deposits, are likely to be and the more confining will be controls over international capital movements and exchange transactions, controls that have sometimes increased the incentives for external currency banking to grow.

NOTES

1. The rigidity of this constraint is undermined, however, by increasing government access to commercial bank loans for balance of payments financing. This access effectively allows official reserves to become negative; that is, it allows positive net official indebtedness.

2. There can obviously be too much discipline as well as too little, just as for any other good or service.

DISCUSSION • *Lucas Papademos*

Inflation, the International Monetary System, and Macroeconomic Discipline

INTRODUCTION
   Three facts and three propositions have greatly influenced both theoretical analyses and popular discussions of macroeconomic policy in recent years. The facts are: (1) the acceleration of inflation and its persistence even during periods of high unemployment; (2) the large supply (oil) shocks that have hit the world economy since 1973; and (3) the gradual adoption of a system of relatively flexible exchange rates following the breakdown of the Bretton Woods system in 1971. The propositions are:
(1) perfectly anticipated macroeconomic policy cannot affect "real" economic variables such as aggregate output and employment; (2) unanticipated macroeconomic policy can influence the path of aggregate output and employment but, on the whole, activist policies tend to destabilize rather than stabilize the output fluctuations induced by various kinds of demand and supply shocks; (3) a major source of the macroeconomic instability and the "inflationary bias" that characterizes many modern economies can be attributed to the politically motivated "fine tuning" of the economy by the government, which in turn partly reflects the short-sighted attitudes of both the government and the public.
   These propositions have been employed by economic observers in various attempts at analyzing and interrelating the above mentioned facts. One interesting contribution is the paper of Thomas Willett and John Mullen. They examine how alternative exchange rate systems can impose "discipline" on domestic economic policies by affecting the sources of the inflationary bias that characterize modern economies. Their analysis takes into account how "rational" anticipations of macroeconomic policies by the public alter the inflation-unemployment trade-off a government can exploit under alternative international monetary systems and constrain a government's ability to stabilize economic fluctuations and/or generate political business cycles. Their conclusions are novel and rather controversial. They argue that flexible exchange rates provide a better system for controlling worldwide inflation because (1) such a system will discourage governments from pursuing short-sighted policies that overstimulate the economy or from engaging in political business cycle behavior, and (2) it may help accelerate the disinflationary effects of restrictive macroeconomic policies. This conclusion is at variance with the traditional proposition that a system of fixed exchange rates provides a better mechanism for enforcing discipline over domestic macroeconomic policies because it requires governments to face the constraint imposed by the balance of payments equilibrium and/or the threat of currency devaluation. Willett and Mullen conclude their analysis

with the proposition that the most effective means of exerting macroeconomic discipline and eliminating the inflationary bias inherent in government policies is the adoption of a system of flexible exchange rates combined with a constitutionally mandated monetary growth rule.

The major conclusions of the Willett and Mullen paper cannot be considered as valid in general, although some of the underlying premises are justifiable under certain circumstances. In this note I question the validity of certain explicit or implicit assumptions that underlie their thesis and criticize their reasoning which suggests that a system of floating exchange rates will discourage the kind of policies that they perceive as the cause of the accelerating inflation of recent years. Although my views reveal a disagreement with the major propositions and policy implications of their analysis, I would like to state at the outset that their paper is a useful and stimulating contribution to the literature on the political economy of international monetary relations. It examines a number of important and relevant issues in macroeconomic policy by taking explicitly into account the often neglected interactions between economic factors and political forces, and it enhances our understanding of how alternative exchange rate systems affect the formulation of politically motivated macroeconomic policy. My discussion is organized around three main topics: (1) the major factors underlying the inflationary bias of modern economies and the issue of macroeconomic discipline; (2) the implications of alternative exchange rate systems on a government's incentives to generate political business cycles or, more generally, on the public's implicit demands for myopic inflationary policies; (3) the desirability of a constitutional amendment that restricts monetary growth.

THE ISSUE OF DISCIPLINE AND SOURCES OF INFLATIONARY BIAS

The relative advantages of alternative international monetary systems have been the subject of continued debate for many years. The question of which system is most efficient and effective is still unsettled and generates a variety of opposing and strongly held views. These disagreements can be partly attributed to differences in assumptions regarding the functioning of markets and differences in the criteria by which the performance of an exchange rate system is judged. But they also reflect the fact that the functioning of the international monetary system depends upon elements whose character is more political than economic.

An important criterion employed in evaluating an exchange rate system is the degree of "discipline" it imposes on domestic economic policies. The traditional view is that a system of fixed exchange rates provides the most effective mechanism for restraining excessive inflationary policies. Although this view is widely held, it is not universally accepted. As Willett and Mullen point out, a number of economists have previously suggested that a system of flexible exchange rates can provide a better disciplinary mechanism because the depreciation of the foreign value of the currency that results from expansionary policies provides an early and visible <u>signal</u> of imbalance, which can lead to prompt corrective actions (Friedman 1953; Johnson 1970). Furthermore, these economists argue that fixed exchange rates impose only a long-run constraint on domestic financial and wage policies because the loss of exchange reserves can be offset in the short run, thus allowing a continuation of inflationary policies until the loss of reserves becomes critical.

The advocates of the potential disciplinary effectiveness of flexible exchange rates have failed to demonstrate that the early warning signals provided by such a system would actually lead countries to reverse their policies; they have also failed to specify the norms that determine the extent to which actual policies deviate from the desired ones. Indeed, since different countries can and do select different macroeconomic objectives explicitly or implicitly and since a system of flexible exchange rates allows each country to pursue its objectives with maximum independence, it is unclear that the "early warning signals" would (or should) have any effect on domestic policies. Willett and Mullen extend the arguments of the earlier advocates of the disciplinary effects of a system of flexible exchange rates by examining how this system affects the forces that lead a country to pursue policies that result in inflation higher than the "bias-free norm" that would be chosen by that country's "average (median) voter." Thus conceptually their analysis consists of two parts: identifying the sources of inflationary bias in modern economies, and examining how alternative international monetary systems affect the magnitude of the prevailing biases.

A main proposition, which underlies the Willett and Mullen approach to macroeconomic discipline, is that the most effective means for reducing the inflationary biases inherent in the political-economic process is by influencing the causes of the bias rather than by constraining the consequences of the process generating the bias. I tend to agree with this proposition. I disagree, however, with the Willett and Mullen assessment of the major sources of inflationary bias and with their analysis of how a system of flexible exchange rates can reduce the bias.

The most important source of inflationary bias, according to Willett and Mullen, is that "short-sighted and/or ill-informed members of the public vote out of office politicians who do not cater to their misperceived interest." This "causes a deviation between actual and informed median voter outcomes." I label this kind of bias the "myopia and amnesia syndrome." A special form of this bias can be labeled "the political business cycle effect." The "myopia and amnesia syndrome" is a bias that reflects the interaction of two characteristics of public behavior and two aspects of the inflationary process. It reflects the presumed fact that a large fraction of the electorate operates with a very short time horizon (a high positive rate of time preference) and a rather weak memory. It also reflects the fact that the short-run inflation-unemployment trade-off is very flat and that there is a substantial lag in the inflationary (deflationary) effects of expansionary (contractionary) policies. A myopic public tends to demand more expansionary policies than a farsighted, well-informed public because it discounts heavily the future inflationary consequences of such expansionary policies. Eventually these consequences are experienced and the public demands corrective disinflationary actions. But its myopia makes it impatient with the very gradual deceleration of inflation and the high costs of unemployment induced by the recession. The public then tends to favor, or at least not to object to, a reversal of policies that often leads to overexpansion, in part because of public amnesia regarding the delayed costs induced by such overshootings.

The inflationary bias generated by this syndrome is greater, the flatter the short-run inflation-unemployed trade-off. The magnitude of the bias can be measured by the difference between the long-run inflation target considered optimal by the well-informed, far-sighted, median voter and the inflation rate toward which the economy gravitates as a result of myopic tendencies. Standard models of the inflationary process suggest that this biased state is given by the point of tangency of the short-run trade-off and the indifference curves implicit in the public's welfare function that evaluates the costs of excess inflation and unemployment.[1] In general, the biased state will not be stable.

The myopia and amnesia syndrome is a necessary condition for the existence of political business cycles but it is not a sufficient one. Governments may decide to exploit the apparent shortsightedness of part of the public in order to maximize their votes by generating electoral business cycles, fueling an economic expansion before an election and engineering a contraction immediately after to offset the inflationary costs. If governments manipulate the economy for purely political considerations they will tend to aggravate the inflationary bias and the instability induced by the public's behavior. Governments, however, may be unable or unwilling to engage in political business cycles, as I will discuss below. If they act passively, simply responding to public demands, the net inflationary bias will exist because of persistent public misperceptions. But governments also have the option, and some would argue the responsibility, to educate the public and pursue farsighted, socially optimal policies. To sum up, the magnitude of the inflationary bias considered by Willett and Mullen depends upon two factors: the fraction of the electorate that persistently exhibits the myopia and amnesia syndrome, and the extent to which governments are willing and able to generate political business cycles. The first factor can be considered as determining the demand for this inflationary bias, the second factor as determining its supply.

The proposition that the major source of the inflationary bias experienced by most countries in recent years can be attributed to the myopia and amnesia syndrome or the political business cycle game is not convincing. Although this kind of bias does exist and although specific inflationary episodes can be related to the politically motivated manipulation of aggregate demand, I doubt that these factors can account for a substantial amount of the increase in the average inflation rate in recent years for two broad reasons: the effects of this bias cannot be permanent and are highly uncertain, and other sources of inflationary bias exist, which, in my opinion, are of greater significance and consequence. More specifically, the reasons can be summarized as follows.

Although part of the public may be shortsighted in specific circumstances and forgetful of specific events, the majority of the electorate learns from past mistakes and it is able to foresee the future costs and to discount the short-run benefits of temporary overexpansionary policies. In the sixties and early seventies this was probably not true, partly because the public lacked the experience after a long period of low and fairly stable inflation. In recent years, however, as opinion polls amply demonstrate, the majority of the electorate considers inflation "public enemy number one" and is very cynical and apprehensive about governmental manipulations of the economy. These arguments are supported by the results of a recent comparative empirical study of the public's political response to economic fluctuations (Hibbs 1980c). It is found that the public weighs heavily the experiences of many past periods in making current political judgments (the rate at which the public discounts past economic performance in making political judgments is estimated to be 0.22 for the U.S. and 0.11 for the U.K. and West Germany). Moreover, this study verifies that public aversion to inflation relative to unemployment changed substantially from the 1960s to the 1970s, thus creating an unfavorable political climate for the pursuance of inflationary policies.

The ability of governments to engage successfully and systematically in the political business cycle game is rather limited. The previous argument suggests that the possiblity of profitable exploitation of public attitudes declines as the public becomes better informed about the nature of the inflationary process and thus less myopic. More generally, "rational" anticipations of systematic cyclical stabilization attempts by the government will reduce appreciably their effects, especially the disinflationary effects of a recession. It is thus not surprising that most of the available empirical evidence is not particularly favorable to the political business cycle hypothesis.[2] This does not necessarily imply the absence of an inflation-unemployment trade-off in the short run as implied by the strict version of the "rational expectations" hypothesis. Such a trade-off will exist even when agents attempt to forecast rationally. One reason, pointed out by Willett and Mullen, is insufficient or incomplete information available to the public about government policies and their effects on the economy. But a short-run trade-off will exist even when expectations are strictly "rational" and the public knows precisely the future course of monetary and fiscal policies; the reasons are the nonauction nature of labor and many product markets, the associated fact that wage and price adjustments are constrained by overlapping contractual arrangements, and the presence of stochastic, intersectoral shocks in heterogeneous labor and product markets.[3] Nevertheless, the <u>existence</u> of such a trade-off, even under "rational" expectations, does <u>not imply</u> that such a trade-off is <u>exploitable</u>, especially by the fairly regular and thus easy to anticipate pattern of electoral cycles. On the contrary, the "rational" anticipation of such policies in the presence of wage and price inflexibilities can result in an effective horizontal short-run trade-off, at least when unemployment is above its equilibrium, virtually eliminating the inflationary benefits of the contractionary part of the electoral cycle (Papademos 1979). Moreover, the political business cycle game cannot be particularly effective because of the uncertainty regarding the stability of economic relations and the future course of "exogenous" economic variables such as energy prices. The 1980 election year offers a glaring example.[4] But if the "demand" and "supply" of myopic policies cannot account for much of the current inflationary bias, what are alternative causes of this bias?

There exist a number of causes of the inflationary bias in the world today and one main carrier that sustains and validates them into an inflationary fact. I will discuss briefly four alternative sources of bias, which can be labeled political, structural, external, and institutional. The means that creates (or permits) inflation is, of course, the excessive growth in the money supply. Most economists would agree today that, in a broad sense and in the long run, inflation is a monetary phenomenon. The majority of the public also seems to accept the proposition that money creation is a major factor behind the current inflation.[5] But the fact that money growth is a necessary factor for the existence of persistent inflation does not <u>really</u> answer the question of why most countries have accepted higher inflation, or, alternatively, why most countries have been pursuing a policy of "excessive" monetary growth.

One fundamental cause of the inflationary bias is political or sociopolitical in origin. It results from the excessive claims of special interest groups on the limited financial resources of the government and/or from conflicting social objectives. Each specific group demands more in terms of "services" and at the same time it attempts to minimize its own tax contribution to public finances. The society as a whole demands greater allocations for national defense, welfare programs, and other government services, but is unwilling to accept the implicit financial obligations, partly because different groups emphasize the relative importance of different goals. And governments, which attempt to satisfy all the needs of all the people all the time, often find that the partial monetization of the resulting deficits is the least painful means of financing them, at least for a while. The critical question in this hypothesis is how the sociopolitical and economic structure of a country affects the degree of monetization of government deficits. The answer to this question should help explain the tremendous disparity of inflation rates around the world.

A second source of inflationary bias is structural in nature. It exhibits itself in the observed flatness of the short-run inflation-unemployment trade-off, and it reflects primarily the apparent inflexibility of wages in the presence of slack labor markets.[6] It may also reflect the effects of "rational" anticipations of government policies that are committed to the goal of full employment and that are subject to the political constraints discussed above.[7] This source of inflationary bias is not, of course, a cause of inflation, but it explains the difficulties faced in reducing inflation once under way and the unwillingness of both the government and the public to pursue contractionary policies that have extremely gradual effects on inflation while requiring substantial sacrifices in terms of unemployment.

A third source of inflationary bias in recent years can be related to the dramatic increases in energy prices. Again the "oil shocks" by themselves cannot be a cause of persistent inflation, since they affect only the relative price of energy (or the rate of change in the terms of trade). But the oil shocks have induced substantial temporary accelerations of inflation, which have not been totally offset in most countries because of the presence of the two above mentioned types of bias.

Finally, another source of bias seems to develop gradually as inflation persists in economies where markets are imperfect or nonindexed to inflation. A certain constituency develops with a vested interest in seeing inflation persist or at least decelerate slowly. This constituency includes governments that take advantage of the resources generated by the "bracket creep" as well as homeowners and businessmen who count on inflation for reducing the real cost of their debts. One would expect this bias to be temporary as financial instruments become indexed to inflation and as a result of public protests. But the inflationary experience in many countries over the last ten years is not encouraging.

THE EFFECTS OF THE EXCHANGE RATE SYSTEM ON THE SOURCES OF INFLATIONARY BIAS

The effectiveness of an exchange rate system in imposing discipline on domestic macroeconomic policies depends upon its ability to reduce or contain the causes of the inflationary bias and/or to constrain the outcomes of the process that generates the bias. Willett and Mullen offer two main arguments in support of their thesis that a system of flexible exchange rates is more conducive to macroeconomic discipline than a system of fixed exchange rates. The first, which they emphasize, is that flexible exchange rates will be more effective in reducing the inflationary bias that results from the demand by the public and the supply by the government of myopic inflationary policies. Their second argument is that a system of flexible exchange rates will facilitate a government's attempts to disinflate the economy by effectively increasing the speed with which inflation declines in response to a restrictive monetary policy. Both of these arguments are based on the proposition that in the short run the ratio of the price effect to the output effect of a monetary stimulus is larger under flexible exchange rates than under alternative exchange rate systems. In other words, flexible exchange rates imply a steeper effective short-run inflation-unemployment trade-off in response to a change in the money supply. The basic reason is that a monetary expansion results in a rapid depreciation of the exchange rate, which promptly affects the (domestic currency) prices of internationally traded goods, thus increasing the domestic aggregate price index, which in turn affects the determination of wages. And although the exchange rate depreciation will eventually lead to an increase in aggregate output by inducing an increase in net exports, this output effect is very gradual because of the low price elasticities of exports and imports. The depreciation of the exchange rate may even have a contractionary (J curve) effect on output in the short run, although this is not necessary for the Willett and Mullen argument. All that is necessary is that there be a steeper short-run trade-off, which will "reduce the inflationary bias resulting from excessively short time horizons and political business cycle behavior".

A number of considerations, however, suggest that the above conclusion is unwarranted. First, the relative steepness of the short-run trade-off under flexible exchange rates is a short-run phenomenon. And, as Willett and Mullen admit, the nature of the trade-off in the medium run is not well understood. Furthermore, the concepts of the short run and medium run are not well specified. If the impact effect of an expansionary policy is short lived and the slope of the trade-off in the intermediate run is not as unfavorable, a government that plans to induce a preelection expansion may be successful by simply initiating its plans earlier. Clearly, a better understanding of the nature of the trade-off in the intermediate run is necessary before we can draw any conclusions. Second, the steepness of the trade-off that results from an expansionary monetary policy under flexible exchange rates results primarily from the immediate depreciation of the exchange rate. But if the monetary expansion is expected to be temporary, to be followed by a monetary contraction immediately after the election, it is unlikely that the exchange rate will depreciate appreciably. Indeed, "rational" anticipations of the simple electoral cycle game would discount completely the effects of a temporary preelection acceleration of the money supply. A third point concerns the role of fiscal policy. As Willett and Mullen recognize, a fiscal expansion will not result in a steeper trade-off and may actually lead to a flatter one since the exchange rate may appreciate as a result of capital inflows induced by higher interest rates. Now it is my impression that most governments engage in the political business cycle game by employing fiscal policy more than monetary policy. This is both because of purely political considerations (tax cuts and special project grants are always popular) and because of the shorter lags in the effects of fiscal policy on aggregate output. If fiscal policy is the popular instrument and if its short-run inflationary impact is not adversely affected by a flexible exchange rate system, there is no reason why this system will reduce this source of bias. On the contrary, a government could engage in the political business cycle game more successfully under a system of flexible exchange rates ("rational" expectations notwithstanding). It could employ expansionary fiscal policy, starting say six to nine months before an election, to stimulate output with minimum inflationary side-effects and then, just a few months before the election, pursue a contractionary monetary policy, inducing a sharp appreciation of the exchange rate to contain the inflationary pressures. (The output effects of monetary policy would occur conveniently with some lag after the election.)

The second argument advanced by Willett and Mullen regarding the superiority of a system of flexible exchange rates, which rests on the proposition that the steeper short-run trade-off will increase the speed with which inflation declines in response to a restrictive monetary policy, is more persuasive than the previous one. The apparent flatness of the short-run trade-off, especially when the unemployment rate is higher than the value consistent with full employment, has been a major source of difficulty in disinflating the economy, not only for the obvious reason that it implies an extremely slow deceleration of prices, but because it tends to discourage both the public and the government from pursuing a costly policy that does not seem to work. This is what I referred to earlier as a structural source of inflationary bias. If a system of flexible exchange rates helps to accelerate the initial disinflationary impact of a restrictive policy by speeding up the deceleration of prices relative to wages, it may help break the momentum of inflation and condition favorably inflationary expectations. Although this is a plausible thesis, the magnitude of the effects are not certain and require further investigation. It is worth pointing out that the effect of flexible exchange rates on the inflationary process works primarily by <u>shifting</u> the short-run trade-off rather than by actually affecting its slope (this is the reason that I have referred to this effect as a change in the <u>effective</u> slope of the trade-off faced by the monetary authority). Strictly speaking, the slope of the trade-off reflects the effects of labor market conditions on the wage-setting process. These effects may be fairly insensitive to the adjustment of prices in the short run, as, for example, implied by the Phelpsian model of wage adjustments. In this case the short-run effects of exchange rate changes on a subset of prices will not have a substantial impact on the economy's "underlying average inflation rate."

To recapitulate my discussion of the Willett and Mullen thesis, I agree with their underlying hypothesis that influencing the sources of the inflationary bias inherent in the political-economic system is ultimately a more effective means of imposing macroeconomic discipline than constraining the consequences of such a bias. But I disagree with their proposition that a system of flexible exchange rates will provide a better mechanism for controlling the forces responsible for the acceleration of inflation in recent years. I have argued that the major sources of the inflationary bias experienced by most countries cannot be attributed to any great extent to the myopic demand for inflationary policies by the public and the supply of such policies by governments pursuing the political business cycle game. Even if this is the major source of inflationary bias, it is unlikely that the flexible exchange rate can eliminate it or even reduce its effects; although flexible exchange rates can have a beneficial effect on the dynamics of a disinflationary policy, the magnitudes of such effects are uncertain and require further study.

The recent experiences with flexible exchange rates strongly suggest that such a system has not been successful in discouraging the forces behind the steady increase in worldwide inflation. On the contrary, it is not difficult to construct an alternative scenario that explains how the system of flexible exchange rates has provided the monetary authorities of many countries with the safety valve of unconstrained monetary accommodation when they were confronted with the strong sociopolitical and structural causes of inflationary bias discussed earlier and the unprecedented and persistent supply shocks. And although a policy of <u>partial</u> and <u>temporary</u> monetary accommodation is a justifiable and appropriate response to unanticipated large disturbances, a policy of "inflating and floating" cannot offer a permanent and stable solution to a society's economic problems. Indeed, under a system of flexible exchange rates, there exists a possibility of a "vicious circle" of price and exchange rate adjustments that could aggravate an inflationary spiral.[8] The potential for such a dynamic instability is greater in countries with a large foreign sector, strong labor unions, and widespread wage and price indexation agreements. These are the same countries in which the forces of inflationary bias discussed earlier are likely to be stronger, thus increasing the pressures for monetary accommodation, which in turn foster this instability. Flexible exchange rates, by removing the discipline imposed on the monetary authorities under fixed exchange rates by the threat of reserve losses or devaluation tend to facilitate, if not encourage, policies of monetary accommodation.

A system of flexible exchange rates <u>by itself</u> cannot provide a sufficient mechanism for imposing discipline on domestic macroeconomic policies. Nor is it likely to provide the effective signals or disincentives to discourage the major sources of inflationary bias. If "discipline" is the primary criterion for choosing an exchange rate system, a system of fixed exchange rates based on a uniform standard such as the gold standard or a uniform world currency under the control of an international monetary authority will provide a more effective means of constraining worldwide inflationary pressures. It is important to emphasize, however, that I am not suggesting that any system of fixed exchange rates provides an effective disciplinary mechanism. The gold exchange standard or reserve currency system, which supplements gold reserves with foreign exchange convertible into gold at a fixed price, is not conducive to discipline, as the experience of the fifties and sixties demonstrates. Since under a gold exchange standard, world reserves are augmented by the deficits of reserve currency countries, the discipline imposed by such a system tends to encourage reserve countries to pursue inflationary policies since they can finance their deficits by increasing their liabilities rather than by decreasing their reserves; as the proportion of the monetary liabilities of the reserve currency countries rises in relation to the stock of gold reserves, the gold exchange system becomes progressively unstable. Only a pure gold standard or a controllable, uniform international currency provides for an automatic adjustment mechanism that cannot be altered by the independent actions of the monetary authorities of individual countries. The pure gold standard has the additional advantage of enforcing the price stability implied by the "impartial and impersonal force" of the stock of world gold reserves; but for the same reason, it is subject to the criticism that it requires price-level and employment adjustments in response to arbitrary and random fluctuations in the available quantity of a single commodity, and that it is not a totally equitable system since it favors gold-producing countries. An international monetary system based on a uniform currency is free from such criticisms, but it requires the establishment of a strong international monetary authority with the ability to exercise more discipline than the sum of its parts. Of course, both a gold standard and a uniform currency system imply the total abdication of monetary control by the individual countries, and also imply an adjustment mechanism that may require deficit countries to accept a period of substantial unemployment and surplus countries to tolerate a period of inflation. The independence of national policies is an important goal of many countries that obviously conflicts with the establishment of a viable system of fixed exchange rates. Nevertheless, if the overriding goal of an international monetary system is the control of worldwide inflation, a system of fixed exchange rates based on a uniform currency under the steady but not rigid control of an international monetary authority offers an effective mechanism of inflationary control.

A CONSTITUTIONAL AMENDMENT TO LIMIT MONETARY GROWTH?

In the concluding section of their paper Willett and Mullen propose, as the only effective means of eliminating the inflationary bias of the economy, the combination of flexible exchange rates and a constitutionally mandated monetary growth rule. This proposition, which does not follow directly from their previous analysis, stems from the realization that although flexible exchange rates are more appropriate than fixed rates for reducing the size of the inflationary bias they discuss, nevertheless the magnitude of this bias can still be unacceptably high. A fixed monetary growth rule, of course, can succeed in enforcing domestic monetary discipline under freely floating rates. It obviously cannot control world-wide inflation unless all countries abide by such a rule--but if they are willing to do so they will be willing to accept a uniform world currency. The advantage of a money growth rule combined with freely floating rates is that it allows an individual country to choose its own long-run inflation target with maximum independence from the rest of the world. The adoption and enforcement of a constitutionally mandated monetary growth rule, however, does not offer a painless panacea for the inflationary woes of a country and it need not succeed in eliminating the sources of inflationary bias.

If the control of inflation is the only goal of macroeconomic policy, then it is both necessary and desirable that a monetary growth rule be adopted under a regime of flexible exchange rates. If, however, full employment and output growth are considered equally important objectives of macroeconomic policy, it is unlikely that a rigid monetary rule can provide the best means of conducting monetary policy. A fixed monetary rule can succeed in stabilizing the economy only if the economy is sufficiently flexible to adjust promptly to the constraints imposed by the fixed rule. Unfortunately, the apparent inflexibility with which wages and prices respond to excess unemployment implies that a fixed rule can result in undesirable outcomes in the presence of certain types of disturbances. The recent experience with large unanticipated supply shocks suggests that a fixed rule providing for insufficient monetary growth in the presence of an external inflationary disturbance will result in a prolonged period of underutilization of productive capacity with only a gradual deceleration of the price level. Under such circumstances, a socially desirable macroeconomic policy, which weighs the costs of temporarily higher inflation relative to the costs of excess unemployment and lost output, would imply a partial and temporary monetary accommodation of the supply shocks.[9] It is unlikely that a permanent monetary growth rule will be consistent with such a policy.

In addition to the fundamental issue associated with the stabilizing properties of a fixed monetary rule, there exist important conceptual and technical problems that can seriously hinder its successful implementation. In modern economies with well-developed financial markets, the choice of the money supply to be controlled by a fixed rule is not obvious, for there exist a variety of monetary assets with almost indistinguishable characteristics of liquidity and risk, which can be easily substituted for transactions balances. And in a world of uncertainty regarding the stability of economic behavior and the evolution of financial markets, it is not possible to control all monetary aggregates simultaneously employing the limited number of available instruments of monetary control. Financial innovations undermine the stability of the historical relationships between aggregate output and various monetary aggregates as well as between these aggregates and the instruments of control. Furthermore, these historical relationships are not independent of the actual policies pursued by the monetary authorities in the past and, consequently, their stability cannot be guaranteed in the future under alternative policies. On the contrary, it can be expected that a policy that stabilizes the rate of growth of a particular monetary aggregate will tend to undermine the predictability of its relationship to aggregate income. The problem of choosing and accurately controlling a monetary aggregate requires further study.[10] The monitoring and controlling of monetary aggregates constitutes an important element of monetary policy, but incorporating into the constitution an arbitrary fixed monetary growth rule is a little premature.

Of course, it can be argued that a monetary growth rule, especially one sanctified through a constitutional amendment, will become an effective means of exerting macroeconomic discipline by conditioning the expectations of the public, thus improving the flexibility of the price mechanism and the stability of financial market behavior. Inflationary expectations will be permanently tied to the fixed rate of monetary growth, appropriately adjusted for changes in the rate of growth of real output and velocity. Workers will learn, through trial and error, that they must promptly constrain their wage demands if they are to avoid a period of prolonged unemployment, and both workers and firms will shorten the length of their contractual arrangements to enhance their ability to respond to random shocks. This is a possible but rather improbable outcome in a society that cannot manage to reconcile the political and social forces underlying the inflationary bias in its economy. In all likelihood, a constitutional amendment forcing the economy into a monetary straitjacket will not succeed in establishing macroeconomic discipline. It will only succeed in converting future monetary crises into constitutional crises.

NOTES

This article was written while Lucas Papademos was a visiting economist at the Federal Reserve Bank of Boston. The opinions expressed do not necessarily represent the views of the Federal Reserve Bank of Boston or of the Federal Reserve System.

1. For an analysis of the effects of myopic preferences on optimal antiinflation policy, see Modigliani and Papademos (1978). The implications of a myopic electorate in a model of the political business cycle are examined by Nordhaus (1975).

2. Nordhaus's (1975) initial study found support for this hypothesis in only three out of the nine countries he examined. And although he reported that the evidence for the United States was consistent with the hypothesis, the empirical tests reported by McCallum (1978) were unfavorable.

3. The implications of the existence of overlapping wage contracts for the existence and nature of the inflation-unemployment trade-off are analyzed in Fischer (1977a), Taylor (1980a, 1980b), and Papademos (1979). For a more general discussion on the role of stabilization policy with "rational" expectations, see Fischer (1980) and Taylor (1980b).

4. The unanticipated strength of the economy in the second half of 1979 (due primarily to a temporary decrease in the saving rate) and the 1980 OPEC oil shock forced the Carter administration to pursue restrictive policies resulting in a dramatic increase in unemployment just a few months before the election. This is hardly the policy pattern predicted by the theory of the political business cycle.

5. New York Times, April 27, 1980.

6. For a discussion of the causes of this kind of bias, see Tobin (1972).

7. See Cagan (1978) and Papademos (1979).

8. See Bilson (1979) for a discussion and a model of the "vicious circle" hypothesis.

9. The nature of optimal antiinflation demand policies with illustrations from the experience of the 1970s are examined in Modigliani and Papademos (1978).

10. For a collection of recent studies examining these issues, see Controlling Monetary Aggregates III, published by the Federal Reserve Bank of Boston (1980).

GENERAL DISCUSSION

GENERAL DISCUSSION

The general discussion of Willett and Mullen centered on two issues. One concerned the matter of explicit, constitutionally mandated or internationally agreed upon rules as means of disciplining policy decisions. It was observed that two questions are involved here: first, What will be the effects of a rule? and second, Will a rule be obeyed? In the latter regard it was pointed out that the German constitution gives the Bundesbank great independence, but it is widely recognized that in some situations this independence must give way. Robert Aliber recounted his experience with rule-making in the Aliber family. Rules would be established in a sort of constitutional convention, sometimes with monetary payments as an incentive to their acceptance. Eventually, the rules would break down, usually as a result of some new circumstance (say, boyfriends). This would lead to a crisis and a need for a new form of rules. From this experience he drew several conclusions: No rule is going to work for a long period; unforeseen events will cause breakdown. When this happens we do not start de novo. New rules must be conditioned by existing attitudes concerning the credibility of leaders and the rules they promulgate.

The second issue discussed was the empirical relevance of political business cycles. Susan Strange suggested that it is an idea that is specific to the United States; other democratic systems lack the predictable timing of elections required. Keohane added that there is no empirical support for such behavior outside the United States, and even in the U.S. data there is not much. Hester contended, however, that politicians will certainly respond to economic problems in ways that will improve their own positions. Goldstein suggested both views might be consistent with a world in which politicans "would--if they could--but they can't." Policymakers might like to manipulate economic fluctuations to their own benefit, but in fact are unable to do so.

III

Making Monetary Policy in the United States

INTRODUCTION

Reflecting the confluence of political and economic factors, understanding what policymakers do or fail to do and why is difficult under the best of circumstances. Moreover, the development of useful theoretical and empirical analyses of the policy process is not enhanced by studies that abstract from salient features of the environment within which policy is made or by the natural tendency of policymakers to cover their trails (and tails). The three papers in this section attack these problems directly.

Few statements have been more frequently quoted over the years than Milton Friedman's famous declaration that "inflation is always and everywhere a monetary phenomenon" (1970, p. 24). However, as Ira Kaminow, former senior advisor at the Federal Reserve Bank of Philadelphia, points out, our understanding of inflation is incomplete if we relate excessive money issue to inflation without at the same time specifying the forces that contribute to rapid monetary growth. Accordingly, Kaminow begins by briefly examining the distinctions between and relationships among the so-called proximate and ultimate (or fundamental) causes of inflation. He argues that "a completely adequate inflation theory must explain how the fundamental forces are transmitted to the money supply and how these fundamental forces mix with monetary institutions and endogenous behavioral functions to generate a pattern of money supply dynamics similar to actual empirical observations."

Kaminow critically examines several frequently mentioned ultimate causes of inflation, such as federal budget deficits or the wage-and price setting behavior of the private sector, and argues that one cannot make a persuasive case that such factors systematically affect money growth. This conclusion, which was discussed extensively at the conference, and Kaminow's belief that "the ultimate causes of inflation are so fundamental to our social and political system that it is hopeless to count on changes in the fundamentals as a realistic strategy to slow inflation," lead to an investigation of the role of some technical and procedural aspects of monetary policymaking in explaining the dynamics of money growth.

Kaminow concludes, based on a model of money growth presented in the paper, that Federal Reserve procedures, particularly "base drift," were a dominant technical influence on money growth over the 1970s. In particular, base drift allowed policymakers to close the gap between publicly announced money supply targets and actual money growth by implicitly moving the targets toward actual money growth. Of course, Kaminow recognizes that procedures themselves can be endogenously related to other factors. He points out that "a plausible explanation of the adoption of base drift. . . is institutional self-defense of the monetary authorities against attempts by the Congress to establish performance criteria." This theme, developed in detail in Kane's paper, is a cutting edge of the political economy of policymaking; whether or not technical adjustments in policy procedures can alter economic outcomes depends to a considerable degree on whether procedures have ever or can ever sever the relationship between ultimate and proximate causes of economic fluctuations.

Both Thomas Mayer and John Woolley, the discussants of Kaminow's paper, like the questions Kaminow has posed. However, they find his emphasis on the technical aspects of policymaking misplaced. More specifically, Mayer queries that "to explain long-run inflation, doesn't one have to explain what determines M^T [the target rate of monetary growth]? If the political theory is right, political pressures are likely to operate by affecting this target rate and, hence, it should not be left unexplained." Moreover, if policymakers understand and appraise the significance of base drift, then actual monetary growth reveals the preferences of policymakers, and the publicly announced procedures and targets, as suggested by Kaminow, represent institutional defenses erected to fend off, resist, or confuse social, political, and economic forces.

Woolley, taking a more general tack, argues that "unless it can be shown that the behavioral model is independent of other actors (more distant causes), then the behavioral model does not adequately reveal possible avenues for reform." Skeptical of the notion of policymaker independence, Woolley observes that "no prudent political actor can ignore the possibility that reactions to his policy decisions might damage the future ability of his organization to achieve policy goals, nor can he safely ignore rapidly changing political and social conditions, if ignoring them entails significant cost to him."

Any constraints flowing from the political-social environment may, of course, be exacerbated by uncertainty surrounding both the economic outlook and central features of the analytical foundations governing policy routines and procedures. Woolley mentions the ongoing debate over the specification and stability of the demand for money as an example of the latter and asks, "What are the consequences for the conduct of monetary policy of substantial dispute among economists about a matter as central as the demand for money?" Understanding the resulting tension between appearance and reality in a complex policymaking process, emphasized by Mayer and Woolley and reflected upon by Wallich in his paper, may help to reconcile policymaker calls for caution in decision making with policy critic charges of myopia.

In a comment submitted after the conference, Thomas Willett and Leroy Laney argue that Kaminow's "results for the United States are neither so robust as to leave no scope for other explanations, nor are some of the most important of these alternative hypotheses inconsistent with the operation of the proximate causes on which he focuses." Drawing on a larger multicountry study of the causes of inflation via their effect on the money supply process, they report that "while the results vary quite a bit from country to country (as would be expected). . . they do suggest rather strongly that, taken together, underlying variables [e.g., government budget deficits, wage increases, changes in international reserves, and import price increases] had a good deal of explanatory power with respect to inducing monetary accommodation." They go on to argue that "positive analysis which indicates that political factors have had a substantial impact on money supply behavior in the past does not logically imply the normative view that the only way to obtain more prudent rates of monetary growth in the future is to try to influence these particular underlying factors." Logically prior to designing

Introduction

an alternative to the present system, however, is a recognition that monetary policymakers have played a political role in the broadest sense of that term. Reforms that ignore this role may alter the appearance but not the reality of policymaking.

The several themes that emerge from Kaminow's paper and the discussion of it by Mayer, Woolley, and Willett and Laney, set the background for the paper by Edward Kane, Reese Professor of Banking and Monetary Economics at Ohio State University, which examines the political milieu within which the Federal Reserve functions. Kane emphasizes the fact that "Federal Reserve goals. . . are hammered and shaped on the anvil of national politics," and that "no logically coherent strategy exists for promoting every macroeconomic goal at the same time." As a result, "macroeconomic goal formation is inevitably a political process of trade-offs, in which the economic interests and political clout of different groups of citizens are, along with the timing of the next election, carefully weighed and balanced." This, Kane argues, is the essence of Fed policymaking. It means that "policymaking requires tough choices not between good and evil, but among alternative goods. These alternative goods differ in the speed with which benefits develop and their distribution across the populace." The unavoidable conclusion is that the proximate determinants of Fed actions are political rather than economic.

Kane argues that the perspective summarized above is the key to understanding the often intractable relationship between the appearance and reality of Fed policymaking. More specifically, he believes that "disguised politics transform the appearances of contemporary Fed practices, processes, and reasoning into the opposite of underlying realities." This transformation, which helps to explain the low correlation between the Fed's rhetoric and its record, is an ongoing, dynamic process: "The Fed shapes and reshapes both itself and its policies--cosmetically and fundamentally--to accommodate and to manipulate political and economic developments that impact on its nominal task." Unfortunately, understanding this process is frustrated by the "deliberately muddled trail" left behind. Clearing the trail is the main focus of Kane's paper.

The macroeconomic and policy implications of Kane's hypothesis are striking. He argues that the Fed's independence is grossly exaggerated: "By the accommodating year after year of cumulative fiscal deficit, the Fed has come to function like a chaperone at a fraternity party. It legitimizes the process without changing it very much. Time after time, Fed officials accept the contradictory policy assignment of singlehandedly bringing inflation and unemployment down to satisfactory levels and, time after time, they stoically accept the blame when these impossible goals fail to materialize." With the Federal Reserve a willing scapegoat, Kane suggests that "inflation will not slow appreciably until the constituency against inflation becomes a political majority."

Kane's paper is discussed by Allan Meltzer, a leading monetarist and cofounder (with Karl Brunner) of the Shadow Open Market Committee--a private and informal organization which regularly develops specific proposals relating to the formulation and implementation of United States monetary policy and makes other recommendations regarding various aspects of the domestic and global economic situation. Meltzer generally accepts Kane's hypothesis. He does note, however, that institutional arrangements can matter more than Kane seems to imply. As Meltzer puts it, "Often an institutional facade is created, then takes on a life of its own and restrains subsequent actions."

Reinforcing a central feature of Kane's argument, Meltzer suggests that the role of monetary policy and the Federal Reserve in producing a redistribution of income via inflation warrants more emphasis in discussions of political economy. Invoking the median voter model, Meltzer argues that such redistribution should be expected if the Fed is subject to political pressures that are ultimately traceable to the electorate and if the decisive (median) voter in that electorate earns less income then the mean income recipient. Meltzer also suggests that the resulting incentive to redistribute income may help to explain why many government benefits are indexed, while the tax system is not. Given this analytical framework, Meltzer, like Kane, is not sanguine about the likelihood of the Fed taking action by itself to reduce the secular rate of inflation.

There have been many previous conferences focusing on past, present, and future policy choices and actions. But far too often they have in reality been diatribes rather than dialogues. Policymakers, noting the perennial disagreements among the "experts" and the wide gap between "theory" and "practice," felt they could safely ignore such gatherings. Our distinguished group of participants worked hard to avoid such an outcome. To complement their efforts, a conscious attempt was made in planning the program to bridge the gaps separating policymakers, policy advisors, and academics (who often play the role of policy critics). Henry Wallich, since 1973 a member of the Board of Governors of the Federal Reserve System, and before that Professor of Economics, Yale University, and consultant to many domestic and international organizations, graciously agreed to assess the complex relationship between policy research, policy advice, and policymaking. Having been a productive researcher and "supplier" of economic advice in earlier stages of his career, and more recently a "demander" of such advice, he was particularly well qualified to address this topic.

At the outset Governor Wallich notes that economists and policymakers are frequently disappointed with each other. Is the problem, Wallich asks, that economics promises more than it can deliver, or is it that policymakers for a variety of relevant (or irrelevant) reasons are unreceptive to outside advice? Discussing the latter, Wallich candidly admits that "policymakers are always under pressure to put the urgent ahead of the important. Thus, they underinvest in economic advice, both from academics and from their own staffs." At an analytical level, this tendency is accentuated by the fact that "economics . . . rarely points unambiguously toward any particular policy, either in the long run or the short." It is further exacerbated by the policymakers' perception of weakness in the various analyses they receive: "This weakness on the side of academic supply can be seen in the diminishing credibility of many Keynesian propositions, the observed limitations of monetarists' ideas as they are increasingly implemented by policy, and the remoteness from reality of rational expectations theory."

Recognizing that economists (as well as policymakers) are not value free, and that there is hardly any conceivable view that is not backed by some economist, Wallich argues that policymakers face a severe "filtering" problem internally and credibility problem externally. Such problems are exacerbated, according to Wallich, by the tendency for the profession to have a consistently negative attitude regarding policy, and by the fact that "academic economists do not have to live with their mistakes, and some of them, therefore, are prone to understate the degree of uncertainty attached to their analyses." As Wallich notes, "The policy mistakes of academics are buried in dead storage files in some warehouse. The mistakes of policymakers are republished monthly in the nation's major economic time series."

Introduction

Thoughtful comments on Governor Wallich's paper are provided by William Dewald, editor of the Journal of Money, Credit and Banking, one of the two leading academic journals specializing in monetary theory and policy, and Allan Meltzer. Dewald focuses his initial remarks on Wallich's observations concerning the quality of information available to the policymaker, the strategy used in conveying such information, and how the policymaker typically reacts to the wide and varying spectrum of professional opinion available. Dewald takes particular exception to Wallich's suggestion that a policymaker is "safest" if he avoids the extremes of professional opinion and chooses intermediate positions. According to Dewald, "There are no 'democratic' principles in science." Put more forcefully, "There is no knowledge in the Equal Ignorance Principle." Reflecting on Wallich's observation that policymakers typically underinvest in economic advice, Dewald notes that "to know you don't know is the beginning of wisdom," and wonders "whether policymakers might not serve their own interests by remaining ignorant, for with added knowledge go added responsibility and perhaps added accountability." Dewald recognizes that if the Federal Reserve were to move boldly it could subject itself to severe political pressures from the private sector, the Congress, and the administration. The resulting lack of incentives to act, consistent with the thesis advanced by Kane in Paper 7, and an "abiding emphasis on the short-run rather than long-run consequences of their actions" go a long way, in Dewald's view, toward explaining the failure of policymakers to consistently contribute to economic stability.

Meltzer, in a comment submitted after the conference, observes that "major changes in policy frequently follow, rather than lead, informed public opinion." To illustrate, he notes that "the acceptance of Keynesian policy, the floating of the dollar, the recent acceptance of medium-term economic strategies and rejection of fine tuning in Britain, and the adoption of the volunteer army are examples of major changes that were influenced by economists whose views were not well received, and that were often scorned as unacceptable or infeasible by 'responsible' officials." The remainder of Meltzer's remarks are directed specifically at Wallich's use of the recommendations he received in 1975 as an example of the poor advice policy makers often receive from monetarists and Keynesians. Quoting extensively from the recommendations developed by the Shadow Open Market Committee at the time, Meltzer, as well as Dewald, argues that subsequent events have strongly confirmed the appropriateness of their preferred policies.

PAPER 6 • *Ira P. Kaminow*

Politics, Economics, and Procedures of U.S. Money Growth Dynamics

INTRODUCTION
   In the 1960s, the key debate over inflation's causes turned on whether it was monetary or nonmonetary forces that generated increases in the price level. Those who carried on the classical tradition argued that trend inflation was determined by the rate of money issue. Those who adopted the Keynesian position explained inflation as a response to cost-push, demand-pull, or similar nonmonetary forces.
   As the 1970s unfolded, the debate changed its outward appearance without changing its fundamental character. Those sympathetic to the classical view began to emphasize the (old) idea that the monetary theory of inflation, while true, was incomplete. It is not enough to pin trend inflation on excessive money issue without a better understanding of the forces that make for rapid growth in money. So they began to discuss the (nonmonetary) causes of the money growth trends that led to inflation. The focus shifted to money as the <u>proximate</u> cause of inflation with the understanding that there are nonmonetary factors that play a more fundamental role in causing inflation.
   The Keynesian tradition underwent a similar change in emphasis. It was generally conceded that in a proximate sense inflation is a monetary phenomenon. Demand-pull, cost-push, or other pressures would be inflationary only if validated by adequate monetary growth.
   While it appears on the surface that the two traditions have come closer together, the harmony is largely illusory. If there is no longer substantial disagreement over the proximate cause of inflation, the policy and theoretical relevance of the relation between money and inflation remains as controversial as ever.
   The new criticism of the causal link between money growth and inflation is that the link is so obvious and so lacking in content as to be of only incidental use in advancing our understanding of the ultimate inflation process. The truly interesting issues according to the critics are in the ultimate, not the proximate, causes of inflation. R. J. Gordon (1975, p. 808), for example, writes:

> It is not enough, in short, for economists to issue the facile judgement that inflation would end if governments would simply reduce the growth rate of the money supply, because this recommendation unrealistically ignores the reaction of constituents prepared to vote against politicians who carry out such a policy.

For similar sentiments, see Keohane (Paper 1) and the Hickman quote therein. For Gordon, therefore, it is the will of the electorate, not excess money growth, that is the interesting and significant cause of inflation. Other writers attribute inflation ultimately to such economic, political, and social forces as inequality of income distribution (Goldthorpe 1978), government spending (Buchanan and Wagner 1977), the decline of U.S. power (Keohane, Paper 1), excessive demands on the economy pressed through the political process (Hirsch 1978), and low productivity growth (Freund 1980).

It is true, as many argue, that the causal link between money and inflation borders on the tautological. Indeed a number of standard dictionaries actually <u>define</u> inflation as, for example, "undue expansion or increase in the currency of a country, esp. by issuing paper money not redeemable in specie" (Random House 1956). But for all its self-evident character, the inherent link between inflation and money growth remains extremely important in explaining and perhaps influencing the inflation process. Some modern critics may be guilty of minimizing the value of the link in understanding and controlling the inflation process.

Difficulties in Establishing Sharp Distinction between Proximate and Ultimate Causes

For one thing, the distinction between proximate and ultimate causes can easily be overdrawn. Behind every so-called ultimate cause of inflation is a cause more ultimate than that. To say, for example, that the government cannot lower money growth because the populace will, in that event, vote the government out, merely moves us one link back on the causal chain. What influences voter behavior? Perhaps ignorant voters do not accurately weigh the benefits and costs of inflation. Then how do we explain the ignorance? There is a never-ending layering of successively more ultimate causes. Indeed, the process can turn back on itself. Thus, voter ignorance may influence government money stock objectives. But, is it impossible that behind voter ignorance is a governmental process that encourages economic illiteracy among voters? In the United States, the Federal Reserve responds to political pressures, but also plays an influential and authoritative role in educating the public on inflation's causes and consequences. The Fed could, in the interests of preserving its institutional interests, mislead the public regarding its role in inflation.

More generally, we should not reject out of hand the view that the monetary authority has as much an independent role in the money creation process as broader political and sociological forces. The extreme version of a totally passive monetary authority that is implicit or explicit in much of the literature on the political economy of inflation is an untested hypothesis. Returning to the U.S. example, the Federal Reserve is at least nominally independent, and its traditions and personnel, its wisdom and ignorance, its institutional objectives and maximizing behavior may all exercise a significant and at times a dominant independent influence on money growth.[1]

The Money Supply Link as a Policy Tool

If inflation is linked ultimately to money creation, then regardless of its basic cause, inflation may be amenable to solution through reform of the monetary authority. Inflation may result, for example, from the pressure of excessive demands made on the economy through the political process. But if this is so, it may be possible to redesign monetary arrangements to sever the links between political pressure and the money supply. Indeed proposals have been made to sever these links through significant changes in the money creation process. A return to the gold standard and legal or constitutional limits on money growth rates are frequently discussed examples.² The importance to practical economic policy of being able to design a noninflationary money supply process can hardly be overestimated. Some phenomena that have been suggested as the ultimate causes of inflation are so fundamental to our social and political system that it is hopeless to count on changes in them as a realistic strategy to slow inflation. Unless we can redesign the money control mechanism, the only recourse may be to wait patiently for less inflationary patterns of social and political dynamics to assert themselves.

It may, of course, be that the fundamental inflation forces are so powerful as to overwhelm any domestic monetary system or any attempt to change the monetary system. It is significant to note, for example, that broad inflation trends in the United States prior to the 1950s seemed to transcend the details of the money supply process. Despite wide variations in U.S. monetary arrangements over time, inflation was largely a wartime phenomenon. This may suggest that war or other fundamentals will cause inflation regardless of the monetary system currently in force. But it may not. And we will not learn anything about the feasibility of controlling inflation directly through monetary policy unless we study the money creation mechanism with as much care as we search for the prior causes of inflation.

The role of money as a meaningful cause of inflation has exceedingly pertinent policy implications for the U.S. inflation. In October, 1979, the Federal Reserve revised its money control procedures as a key part of its antiinflation program. This revision was a waste of time and effort if the ultimate cause of inflation goes deeper than and ultimately dominates mere policymaking technique.

The Money Supply Mechanism and Tests of Inflation Hypotheses

The idea that inflation is a monetary phenomenon suggests crucial scientific tests of any and all so-called fundamental political or sociological theories of inflation. If it is political and popular forces that ultimately generate inflation, these forces must somehow press on the money creation mechanism. A completely adequate inflation theory must explain how the fundamental forces are transmitted to the money supply and how these fundamental forces mix with monetary institutions and endogenous behavioral functions to generate a pattern of money supply dynamics similar to actual empirical observations.

In a context not altogether dissimilar to ours (although not specifically related to the question of inflation), F. A. Hayek (1967, p. 13) used the example of the theory of evolution. The theory of natural selection, like theories of inflation, is designed mainly to explain broad patterns of observed phenomena rather than to make precise predictions of new classes of yet unobserved and entirely novel phenomena.

> Disputes which have arisen in the course of the growth of the theory of evolution have thus significantly turned not so much on facts but on such questions as <u>whether the postulated mechanism can account for the evolution having taken place in the time which has been available</u>. And the answer has frequently come, not from the discovery of new facts, but from purely deductive arguments such as the mathematical theory of genetics, while experiment and observation did not quite keep up with the mathematical theory of selection [emphasis added].

This suggests a strategy for helping us choose among alternative "ultimate" explanations of inflation. According to Hayek, the theory of evolution is incomplete and subject to less powerful tests without a detailed specification of the mechanism through which environmental forces bear on individual organisms to influence evolution of the group. Mathematical models of genetic change and the implications of such models for the dynamics of evolutionary change significantly strengthen tests of natural selection. If we view the impacts of the political and social environment on inflation as analogous to the impacts of the physical environment on the evolution of organisms, then the money creation process is the mechanism analogous to genetic transmission and change. A complete theory of inflation, subject to strong scientific testing, requires models of the money creation process as the theories of evolution require genetic models. It can then be postulated how the social, political, and broad economic environments impinge on inflation through the money creation process.

As in the case of evolution, inflation theories must specify transmission mechanisms formulated as precisely as possible so that we may be better able to choose among alternatives.[3] Hayek (1975) makes the point that social science will never generate theories with as much precision as the physical or biological sciences. But it is clear that the more precisely a theory is formulated the more it is exposed to the possiblity of rejection and therefore the more confidence with which it can be held if not empirically rejected.

The main purpose of the present paper is to indicate by example how we need to go about modeling a dynamic money supply creation process as an essential feature to be embedded in any complete model of inflation. The key is to develop a model that throws off analytic solutions or is subject to simulation experiments that tell us whether observed money supply dynamics could have been generated with plausible behavioral and policy parameters. At the minimum, we should be able to identify from such a model which parameters are key in determining the inflation process. At the maximum, we could identify institutional innovations that might turn the inflation process off without having to resort to major political or social overhaul.

The next section of this paper discusses, by way of illustration, certain frequently suggested fundamental causes of inflation. The third section presents a mathematical model of the money supply dynamics suggested in this section. The fourth section discusses numerical estimates of the model. The implications of the model for understanding the inflation process are discussed in the fifth section, and conclusions appear in the last section.

ILLUSTRATIONS OF FUNDAMENTAL CAUSES OF INFLATION

Before we proceed to the main exercise of the paper, it will be useful to review three alternatives that seek to identify the "ultimate" motivation for the postwar rise in money growth rates in the United States. This might allow us to be a bit more specific in the nature of the task that lies ahead for those of us who would like to develop a truly comprehensive theory of inflation.

Fiscal Policies

A number of economists[4] and public policy analysts have identified the rapid increase in federal government expenditures as a principal cause of postwar U.S. monetary expansion. The argument is simple: the government has an incentive to finance part of its growing expenditures through the issuance

of non-interest bearing debt (currency and member bank reserves). This
allows the government to deceive the public about the true cost of its
operations. So current officeholders gain the advantage of providing
increased services without suffering the political costs associated with
raising taxes or floating interest bearing debt. A more recent version of
this argument claims that the government has an interest in generating
inflation apart from the seigniorage gains. Inflation generates "bracket
creep" and other distortions in the tax structure that raise real tax
revenues. This gives legislators an opportunity to pass vote-getting
reductions in statutory rates while keeping real revenues at or above
original levels.

The argument remains imcomplete and indeed unconvincing until some
plausible and specific transmission device can be suggested that links
elected officials' hypothesized (and largely untested) inflation and money
growth preferences to the money supply creation process. It is implausible
in the U.S. case, for example, to postulate a direct link through which the
Federal Reserve is ordered to supply currency and bank reserves to finance a
stated share of federal expenditures. A slightly more reasonable suggestion
hypothesizes a link between government borrowing and interest rates. During
periods when the government runs large deficits, it enters the credit market
to borrow. This runs up interest rates and the Federal Reserve pursues a
policy to lower rates to their original levels. That is, the Fed buys
Treasury securities with bank reserves. The effect is to monetize the new
debt. Whether large government debt raises interest rates is a matter of
some controversy. The controversy involves first the debate over liquidity
preference (supply and demand for money) versus loanable funds (supply and
demand for credit) as theories of interest rate determination. Only if
interest rates are determined in credit markets will (ceteris paribus) an
increase in outstanding government debt put upward pressure on rates. If
rates are determined in the money market, there is no reason to expect that
nonmonetized deficits will raise rates and so motivate monetary expansion.[5]
On the contrary, under a liquidity preference model, constancy of rates is by
hypothesis determined strictly by monetary growth. Second, the controversy
involves the question of whether the government credit financing represents
net new credit demand. If citizens correctly anticipate future tax
obligations, they could be prepared to buy the new government debt at
existing interest rates in anticipation of using the proceeds at maturity to
pay off personal tax obligations that will come due when the national debt is
retired.

The point here is not so much that the proposed transmission mechanism is
controversial. The point is that we have not been told explicitly what we
need to believe about the policy response function, the rationality of
taxpayers, and the determinants and dynamic pattern of short-term interest
rates in order to go from historical timing and magnitude of government
deficits to the observed historical pattern of money growth.

Accommodative policies

A second suggested explanation of postwar monetary acceleration presumes
that the authorities have accommodated upward price and wage movements.[6] The
argument was originally proposed in the case of wage demands and has recently
been extended to commodity price shocks, particularly to energy price
increases. The proposed transmission mechanism envisions labor demanding and
getting high wage settlements. These wage settlements raise the real wage
and consequently increase unemployment. The monetary authorities follow

expansionary policies in order to restore economic growth. The oil price version of the argument notes that oil price increases are similarly accommodated by monetary expansion (see Keohane, Paper 1).

The most intriguing question raised by this transmission mechanism is whether the system has a stable equilibrium. On the surface it would appear that the system is highly unstable. Wage demands, for example, lead to money growth and inflation, which in turn lead to further wage demands. Indeed intuition suggests that the simple wage demand/money spiral explains too much. Is there a plausible monetary response function and wage settlement function that would have led to only 7 or 8 percent trend money growth in the thirty-five years since the end of World War II? One might expect that once the spiral got rolling, there would soon be no limit to the acceleration in money growth. Once unions learned that wage settlements would be eroded by monetary growth, demands would become limitless. If the system worked mechanistically, the monetary authorities would be forced to accommodate exponential growth in wages with exponential monetary growth. The hypothesized transmission based on accommodative monetary policies also raises significant questions about the willingness of employers to systematically grant real-wage settlements above market-clearing levels unless they too anticipated a near instantaneous return to the equilibrium real wage via price increase.

It is clear we must go beyond casual assertions to more testable specifications of the path from high real-wage demands to high money growth. Again, the point to be made here is not that accommodative policy responses are necessarily incapable of explaining observed money growth patterns. It is certain that a suitably sophisticated and complex model can be developed that will do the job. But would such a model be plausible or forced? Would it be reasonably simple and general or full of "dummy variables" and repeated post hoc explanations of "special factors"?

Monetary Policy Technique

A third class of "ultimate" causes of monetary expansion concerns central bank procedures and institutions. The idea here is not that fundamental forces foisted inflation on the system but that technical policy procedures led the authorities to excessive money issue. One such explanation for the United States describes a Federal Reserve policy rule based on achieving a target interest rate. The presumption is that the target rates tend to be below market rates. These below market interest rate targets lure the Fed into an excessively expansionary monetary policy. In the first instance, interest rates are lowered by increasing money. But as money expands, inflation expectations grow. This increases the inflation premium built into interest rates, and drives nominal rates back to and eventually above their original levels. Higher interest rates generate a further pull toward expansionary, low-interest policy which, in the short run, moves interest rates down but in the longer run pushes them to new heights.

The set of institutional procedures in force until October 6, 1979 can be linked to excessive monetary expansion; it is this transmission mechanism that is modeled in some detail in the present paper.

A MODEL OF MONEY GROWTH

The idea that monetary control is an essential condition of inflation control was recognized by the Federal Reserve as well as other central banks in the early 1970s. The Fed began to establish money growth targets and to explore operating procedures to achieve those targets. Until October 1979, the basic control instrument employed by the Federal Reserve was the Federal funds interest rate (the interest rate charged on interbank loans of reserves). The rate would be moved up or down as money growth was exceeding or falling short of target. By raising (or lowering) the interest rate, money demand and therefore the money stock was reduced (or increased). The Federal funds rate was replaced as the instrument of policy by nonborrowed reserves on October 9, 1979.

The pre-October 1979 regime was widely criticized because the Federal Reserve did not allow sufficient movement in the interest rate to quickly restore money growth to target. Moreover, it was sometimes argued that the authorities were not sufficiently familiar with the economic and monetary system to determine the correct setting of the interest rate necessary to achieve the desired money growth rate. But even if the procedures did not yield adequately fine monetary control they were not obviously inflationary. So long as target overshoots and undershoots were treated more or less symmetrically, there was no obvious reason to expect an expansionary bias. It is interesting in this regard that during the decade of the seventies money growth exhibited no particular trend. There was, however, significant positive serial correlation in money growth - a persistent decline after 1972 and an equally persistent increase from 1975 onward. Over much or all of the seventies, the Fed clearly aimed at long-run growth in the narrowly defined money stock (M1) of roughly 5 or 6 percent per year. Yet M1 growth went from about 8 percent in 1972 to 4½ percent in 1975-1976 and gradually up to 8 percent in 1978-1979. The purpose of this paper is to develop a model that will help determine whether monetary control procedures alone could have explained the observed pattern of money growth without resort to more fundamental causes.

Evidence that control procedures adequately explain money growth patterns is not meant to rule out the existence of more fundamental influences. To the contrary, as was pointed out above, every cause has a more ultimate cause. If technical control procedures account for money growth patterns, the next item on the agenda (not dealt with at length in the present paper) might be to explain the reason those particular procedures were adopted. But that is precisely the point. To identify the feature of Fed procedures that influences money growth trends allows us to better focus the search for the next cause back in the chain. Such identification will help us choose among alternative fundamental influences on the basis of the extent to which each is consistent with the particular procedures chosen.

The question now is to determine whether there is anything in the technical procedures of the seventies to explain the absence of trend and strong positive serial correlation of changes in money growth. The answer is yes. A reasonable model of economic behavior combined with a fairly specific model of the Fed's procedures shows that the combination could plausibly have generated the observed pattern. Whether, and the extent to which, one accepts Fed procedures as adequate to explain the major movements in U.S. money growth in the seventies depends on views regarding the relationships among several behavioral and policy parameters and the course of exogenous factors.

In order to characterize broad Federal Reserve policy procedures we turn to estimates of these procedures in Kaminow (1979a). That paper estimates the reaction function of the Federal Open Market Committee (FOMC) over forty-two months during the period 1975 to 1978. It was over this period that Federal Reserve procedures reached something of a high point in institutionalization and specificity as a result of House Concurrent Resolution 133. Resolution 133 was passed in March 1975 and required the Fed to adopt monetary and credit growth objectives for twelve-month periods. Prior to Resolution 133, the Fed had used internal monetary growth objectives of six-month duration. Procedures before March 1975 were similar but not identical to those adopted afterwards. The paper took as its null hypothesis that the FOMC behaved as it said it did in official descriptions of policy behavior. As the paper points out in some detail, those descriptions of policy did not include a noteworthy role for any "fundamental" considerations. Monetary policy was almost exclusively a technician's game. A succinct description of the way the Fed viewed its own procedures can be found in the FOMC's Record of Policy Actions for the June 1978 meeting.

> It was noted in the discussion that the Committee's objectives for the monetary aggregates were embodied in the one-year ranges established at quarterly intervals and that the adjustments made from time to time in the Federal funds rate were intended to increase the likelihood that the longer-run growth rates would fall within these ranges.

Thus, the Federal funds rate was perceived as an instrument designed to achieve money growth targets. Monetary growth was seen as the Fed's major throttle to control economic activity. But targets for money growth rates were set more or less mechanically. The money growth target adopted in April 1975 called for growth in M1 within the range 5.0-7.5 percent per year. By the end of 1978, this range had been gradually lowered to 4-6½ percent. The midpoint of the target growth range was reduced four times, each time by ¼ percentage point.

In my 1979 paper, I show that during the period 1975-1978 the Fed moved the Federal funds rate in proportion to the difference between the observed money stock (narrow (M1) measure of money) and the target level for the corresponding month. Specifically, the funds rate was raised (lowered) by about 30 basis points per month for each percentage point by which the money stock exceeded (fell short of) the middle of its target range.

About a dozen economic variables were included in various combinations in the funds rate reaction function to determine whether the Fed responded to measures of economic performance. These variables included unemployment, growth, and inflation variables measured in levels and first differences. Current and past observed data were used as well as Fed Staff projections. In no case did any of these measures explain any of the funds rate movement in equations which included the deviation of M1 from its target. I take these results as evidence that technical rules, more or less mechanically applied (the R^2 was 0.5), dominated monetary policymaking over the period in question.

I propose now to combine this reaction function with a simple model of the economic behavior of the general public. The model of public behavior presumes an underlying money demand function such that the equilibrium nominal interest rate is determined by the combination of a liquidity and an expectations component. The hypothesized temporal response of interest movements to an increase in money growth is this. Immediately upon expansion in the money stock, real balances increase (that is to say, price-level changes lag behind money stock changes). This drives the interest rate down because real money balances exceed real money demand. However, as the price level rises over time in response to the original monetary expansion (inflation is determined by the money supply), real balances fall back toward their equilibrium level and the real interest rate (consequently) rises back toward its equilibrium. Additionally, to the extent that monetary expansion generates expectations of price increases, the nominal interest rate rises to reflect an inflation premium.

One can imagine the rich dynamic that is developed by the interaction between the hypothesized policy reaction function and implicit money demand function. Suppose the monetary authorities decide to expand monetary growth. In the first instance this will cause the authorities to lower the target rate of interest. The new lower target rate will be achieved by expansion in bank reserves and consequently in the money stock. The monetary expansion keeps the interest rate down only for a time. Prices, and therefore the interest rate, rise. Then, the Federal Reserve expands bank reserves to keep the interest rate on target, but soon discovers that monetary growth exceeds target. The Fed, following its reaction function, raises its interest rate target to choke off money demand. The ultimate outcome of this interactive process is beyond ordinary intuition. Whether money growth in such a system explodes or collapses, remains near target or tends toward a stable equilibrium around some other money growth rate, is by no means immediately obvious. Nor is the response of the equilibrium of such a system to a shift in money demand. It is not clear either whether the success of this system depends on the accuracy of the Federal Reserve's model of the economy and financial markets. If the Fed does not know what interest rate is consistent with achieving its monetary targets, can the procedures described herein lead to explosive money growth on account of consistent over/or underadjustments in the interest rate?

In order to answer these and similar questions, we write down a system of differential equations (the complete derivation is in a technical appendix available from the author). For analytic convenience the system is written in a linear form in logarithms.

The Fed's response function:

$$\frac{dr}{dt} = a(M - M^T) \tag{6.1}$$

That is, the change in the interest rate (r) depends on the excess of the observed money stock (M) over the target money stock (M^T).

The temporal motion of the nominal interest rate within the market is given by

$$\frac{dr}{dt} = \alpha \frac{d}{dt}(m - M + P) + \frac{d}{dt}\dot{P}^e \tag{6.2}$$

The first term in (6.2) reflects the liquidity effect. The interest rate depends on the excess of real money demand (m) over real money balances (M - P). The α is a speed of adjustment parameter. In equilibrium m - M + P is zero. The second term is the change in expected inflation and captures the inflation premium.

The third equation describes the temporal motion of prices.

$$\frac{dP}{dt} = \pi(M - P - m) \tag{6.3}$$

The price level is hypothesized to adjust so as to equate the supply and demand for real balances. That is, the price level rises if real balances exceed real money demand. We postulate a simple adjustment mechanism through which P rises (falls) in proportion to excess real balances. The speed of adjustment is given by the coefficient π.

If we equate equations (6.1) and (6.2), dr/dt drops out and the system can be written as two differential equations in dM/dt and dP/dt. We take the population to be rational in the sense that expectations of inflation $\dot{P}^e$ are equal to the actual realized inflation rate. Inasmuch as the system is entirely nonstochastic, rationality implies that inflation is perfectly anticipated. Solution of the system yields a number of conclusions. First, the money stock is stable around its target if α exceeds π. The intuition of this condition is clear. The motion of r given by (6.2) is determined by offsetting liquidity and inflation-premium effects. An increase in the money stock reduces the rate as a result of the liquidity effect but tends to push the rate up through its impact on inflation expectations and consequently on the inflation premium. The system is stable if an increase in the money stock, in the first instance, lowers the interest rate. The second result of the solution to the differential equation system is that the conclusion of stability of money growth around target is entirely invariant with respect to the size of the Fed's response coefficient a, so long as it is positive. Moreover, the stability result is invariant with respect to money demand. Regardless of any changes in the demand for real balances, the money stock tends to return to its target level.

There is nothing in the qualitative solution of the system (6.1)-(6.3) to generate a persistent deceleration or acceleration of money growth from target. If the Federal Reserve followed the procedures described, we should expect money growth to remain near target or at least reveal a tendency to move toward target. In order to provide a plausible explanation of the decline in money growth from 1972 to 1975 and the increase from 1975 to 1978, we need to add to the system one more feature of Fed operating procedures that characterized the 1970s-base drift.

Recall that Federal Reserve operating procedures called for resetting the money growth target path each quarter. Empirically, there was a great deal of continuity in target money growth <u>rates</u> established from one quarter to the next. Revisions in the growth rate ranges never changed by more than ½ percentage point between adjacent quarters and the change was usually less. However, the target growth paths measured in levels of the money stock were subject to substantial movement because the base level from which the target growth rate was measured was the actual money stock of the preceding quarter instead of the targeted level. If the base level happened to be high, the target path was high; if the base level happened to be low, the target path was low.

The base drift feature of Federal Reserve procedures is illustrated in Figure 6.1. Each triangular section represents the target growth range adopted by the FOMC at the meeting specified. The dotted lines represent the midlines of the growth ranges. By construction, floor, ceiling, and midpoint growth rates did not change from target to target. Thus, for example, each illustrated target path corresponds to growth rate ranges of 4 to 6½ percent per year. Measured in terms of growth <u>rates</u>, therefore, policy was unchanged from target period to target period. However, because actual money growth rates exceeded target growth rates, and because of base drift, there was a steady upward drift in the targeted levels of the money stock as illustrated. In the absence of base drift, the target path midline would have been extended from the preceding targeted midline rather than from the actual level of the money stock. With the path of money illustrated, in the absence

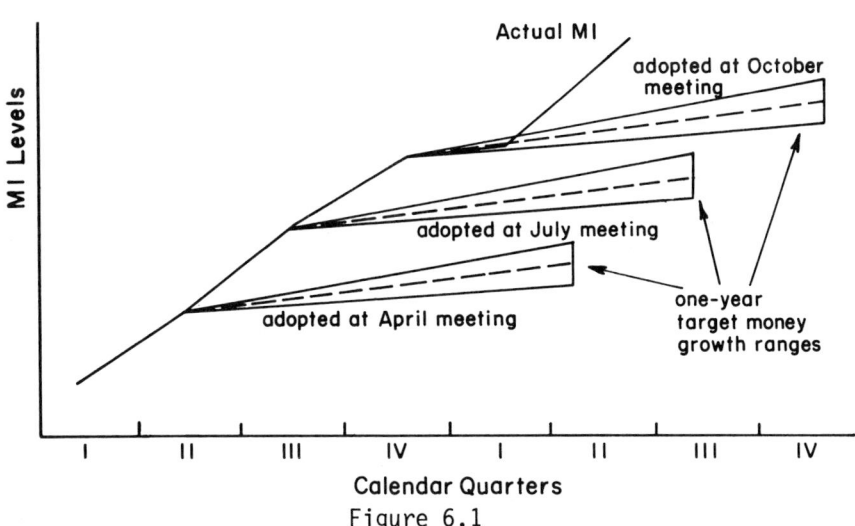

Figure 6.1
Illustration of base drift.

of base drift, constant target rates of growth would have meant much larger deviations of actual money growth from target money growth.

An analytic solution to the system (6.1)-(6.3), which incorporates base drift, provides a number of interesting conclusions that deviate sharply from those reached in the absence of base drift. The most significant impact of the base drift feature of monetary procedures is that money growth trends are determined by initial conditions at the time procedures are introduced and are permanently influenced by any shifts in real money demand (m). If m remains stable, the money stock asymptotically approaches an equilibrium growth path that is parallel to the original target path but above or below that path by a distance proportional to the initial excess demand for real balances. The equilibrium path for money will change over time according to changes in m. If, for example, there is a once and for all permanent upward shift in the demand for real balances equal to 10 percent of the money stock, the target growth path will gradually shift up in successive target setting periods toward a new equilibrium path. Money stock growth will then be stable around the new path. During the adjustment from the old to the new equilibrium path, observed money growth rates will exceed targeted rates as the money stock approaches the new path.

While the new path will lie above the parallel to the old path, it will not in general shift up by the same amount as the upward shift in m. Indeed, as we discuss in the next section, with empirically plausible parameters, the target path will shift by a smaller amount than the shift in money demand. If, as seems entirely reasonable, m has a long-run growth trend, the system will generate a long-run upward drifting base so that observed money growth trends will tend to exceed target growth rates.

NUMERICAL ESTIMATES

Whether, and the extent to which, application of the reaction function we have described can plausibly account for money growth trends observed during the seventies is an empirical question. The major qualitative prediction of the model is that we can expect deviations from money growth targets to depend on changes in the demand for real balances. The Fed can be expected to undershoot its targets when growth in real money is declining and to overshoot when growth in money demand is increasing. In other words we hypothesize that Fed policy accommodates shifts in the demand for real balances. To the extent that the demand for real balances depends on the level of economic activity, therefore, base drift leads to a procyclical policy. There is nothing, however, in the model we have described that should lead to a long-run expansionary bias.

The broad outline of money growth in the 1970s is consistent with the theory that Fed policy is procyclical. Money growth declined relative to target until the trough--and somewhat beyond in 1974. Then the actual money growth began to accelerate relative to target growth, reaching a peak differential in 1978-1979.

One can develop more specific tests of the hypothesis by calculating numerical values for the shift in the target growth path associated with changes in real money demand. We take our time unit as a quarter. In order to convert the Fed response estimate in Kaminow (1979a) to a constant elasticity of response as modeled here, suppose the Fed funds rate is 6 percent; then the estimate of a 30 basis point per month response to a 1 percent deviation from target means a = 15. Similarly if the funds rate is 12 percent, a 30 basis point per month response means a = 7.5. We consequently use the values of 15 and 7.5 as brackets for the plausible range on a. The parameter α indicates the elasticity of response of the interest rate to a change in the excess demand for real balances. If we take the interest elasticity of the demand for money to be less than unity, then $\alpha > 1$. For illustration we make our numeric calculation for $\alpha = 2$ and $\alpha = 5$ corresponding respectively to interest elasticities of 0.5 and 0.2. Finally, π indicates the quarterly rate of adjustment of the price level to its equilibrium. We make illustrative calculations for π = 0.05, 0.1, 0.25.

The Table 6.1 shows the impact of a percentage change in the demand for real balances on the height of the Fed's new money growth target path under alternative assumptions for the parameters a, α, and π. The "response elasticity" is the percentage response of the level of the equilibrium target growth path to a shift in real money demand. Thus, the response elasticity means this: if the demand for real balances increases by 10 percent of the money stock, and if the response elasticity is .25, the equilibrium target money growth path will rise by 2½ percent of the money stock. Approximately half this rise will take place in the first six quarters. Therefore, a once and for all 10 percent upward shift in money demand would add a total of 2½

TABLE 6.1. Elasticity of response of target money growth path to changes in real money demand

a	α	π	Response Elasticity
7.5	2	0.05	0.25
7.5	2	0.10	0.22
7.5	2	0.25	0.19
7.5	5	0.05	0.42
7.5	5	0.10	0.29
7.5	5	0.25	0.28
15.0	2	0.05	0.28
15.0	2	0.10	0.09
15.0	2	0.25	0.09
15.0	5	0.05	0.20
15.0	5	0.10	0.22
15.0	5	0.25	0.16

percent to money growth, of which 1½ percent would take place in the first six quarters.

We leave it to the reader to evaluate, on the basis of individual views regarding the course of changes in real money demand and the appropriate values of the parameters (a, α, and π), the extent to which base drift explained movements in the money stock during the seventies. Our purpose here is not to provide a definitive answer to the question, but to demonstrate how the mathematics of money growth (recall the Hayek quote regarding the mathematics of genetics) should be used to develop more specific testable hypotheses.

IMPLICATIONS

If one accepts base drift as a dominant technical influence on the course of money growth over the 1970s the question presents itself as to why the Federal Reserve allowed base drift to creep into its procedures. This question should be recognized as an inquiry into the next, more "fundamental," cause of money growth, as we discussed earlier in the paper. We have merely rephrased the question from "Why did money grow the way it did?" to "Why did the Fed include base drift in its procedures?" Presumably, if we better focus the question, we should arrive at a better answer. A wide variety of "fundamental" explanations that may be broadly consistent with money growth trends may turn out to be inconsistent with the selection of base drift as part of the Fed's operating procedures. Is base drift a reasonable procedure to adopt if one's objective is to accommodate wage demands or monetize the debt?

An official justification for base drift was articulated by Governor Henry Wallich in May 1976. Wallich explained:

> Various critics have argued that this base drift for the calculation of growth rates causes the actual rates of growth over several quarters to differ from the specified range even if the range were maintained unchanged from quarter to quarter. The procedure, it has been charged, makes the actual movement of the aggregates a random walk.
>
> In the light of the historical record, this criticism lacks substance. Base drift over successive quarters in the last year has been relatively small. Moreover, such quarterly moves have been largely mutually offsetting. . . .
>
> If deviations from the ranges were to become large, some cognizance of that fact would, of course, have to be taken in the setting of new ranges in the light of the recent growth of the aggregates in addition to changes in the economy and the outlook that have occurred meanwhile.
>
> Techniques could be visualized that would compensate for base drift above or below the midpoints of earlier ranges. Growth ranges could be modified in such a manner as to get back on the original track at some specified point in time, assuming that this track had remained appropriate in the light of the economic outlook. Alternatively, in addition to stating the new ranges of growth on the new base, those same ranges could be recomputed in terms of the old base. Either method, however, would tend to be confusing to many members of the public and would add little to deliberations of the FOMC, which in any event has access to these and other calculations.
>
> Moderate base drift in any event has little meaning, given the looseness of the relation of the monetary aggregates to the ultimate

objectives--GNP, employment, and price stability. It is these ultimate objectives, of course, which primarily concern the monetary policymaker in the setting of long-run growth ranges.

Thus, in May of 1976, it was the view of at least one member of the FOMC that base drift was merely a technical problem that could and would be offset if it got out of hand and if circumstances so dictated. By 1978, however, trend money growth rates had accelerated much above target and the Fed in fact had made no adjustment. Within the Federal Reserve the base drift problem was increasingly seen as a more serious problem than had originally been envisioned. A number of internal staff memoranda critical of base drift had begun to circulate along the lines of Poole (1976). This is to say, base drift allowed the Fed to forgive past overshoots and undershoots, so that policy errors were allowed to cumulate.

External observers also began to see the problem as serious and in the Humphrey-Hawkins Full Employment and Balanced Growth Act, an attempt was made to legislate against base drift. The Fed was required to set fixed-base targets for one year out so that quarterly revisions in the base were henceforth prohibited. This reduced base drift from a quarterly to an annual phenomenon. My experience within the Federal Reserve indicates that there was substantial support for this element of the Humphrey-Hawkins legislation, which would reduce the magnitude of the base drift problem.

To go beyond Governor Wallich's official 1976 justification of base drift, we might ask the question, did the Fed have an ulterior, unstated motive to introduce base drift? Two possible answers suggest themselves. First, it was widely believed by critics of base drift that it was instituted to reduce the need for substantial interest rate adjustments. By permitting the money target to "catch up" to the actual money stock each quarter, fewer adjustments in the Federal funds interest rate were necessary. The Fed, of course, had a rather lengthy history of reluctance to move interest rates too quickly.

A second possible justification of base drift relates to institutional self-preservation. By virtue of Concurrent Resolution 133, the Fed was required to specify its own performance standards. That is to say, the Fed was asked in advance to set out explicitly its money growth objectives. In the absence of base drift, actual money growth could deviate by substantial amounts from target. With base drift, there was an automatic correcting mechanism that kept the money stock near target, or more precisely, it kept targets near the money stock. Base drift can be seen in this regard as part of a broad pattern. The Fed responded to the Concurrent Resolution in a number of ways. Even before Resolution 133 was passed, the Fed lobbied for an understanding that its money growth objectives were merely guides. As time progressed, the Fed would be permitted to deviate from target as incoming information dictated. Second, the Fed refused to refer officially to its money growth ranges as targets. Note, for example, the quotation from an official Fed document on p. 308. The reference is to growth ranges and, significantly, not to _target_ growth ranges. Third, the Fed stated its targets in terms of a _variety_ of different measures. This had the advantage of being on or near target for at least one measure of money growth.

Thus, a plausible explanation of the adoption of base drift (and hence of money growth patterns of 1970s) is institutional self-defense of the monetary authorities against attempts by the Congress to establish performance criteria. Conclusions regarding the plausibility of base drift as an instrument to achieve other objectives such as accommodating wage or price movements, monetizing the federal debt, or other ultimate social, political, and economic goals are bound to be controversial assertions one way or the other. It is my view, however, that attempts to justify use of base drift as a device to achieve these broader objectives are likely to be forced and unpersuasive.

CONCLUSION

A substantial literature has begun to develop to the effect that the notion that inflation is a monetary phenomenon is trivial in the sense that it is not helpful either as an analytic or policy tool. The basic causes of inflation transcend the money stock, which itself is subject to more fundamental forces. Such a view is a scientific (testable) hypothesis that predicts a link between fundamental forces and money supply growth. The burden rests on advocates of this view to postulate the link and to predict as precisely as possible the expected pattern of money growth.

In this paper, we have postulated an alternative hypothesis. At least over the recent past, U.S. money growth patterns have reflected, in part or in whole, particular details of Federal Reserve operating procedures. These procedures do not necessarily reflect broad social or economic forces. Instead they may reflect the views and concerns of Federal Reserve officials. As such we conclude that it may well be possible to successfully address the inflation process by revising operating procedures of the Fed as was done in October 6, 1979. If these new procedures lead to a sustained slowing in money growth a serious question will be raised about the validity of so-called fundamental theories of inflation.

NOTES

The author wishes to thank conference participants, particularly Raymond Lombra, for many helpful comments. He accepts responsibility for all remaining errors. The views represented in this paper do not necessarily reflect the views of the management of the Government Research Corporation.

1. The idea that details of institutional arrangements and the actions of policymaking agents in maximizing their own objective functions can influence policy has recently been discussed in a number of papers. In regard to macroeconomic policies, see, for example, Preston and Rolnick (1980), Black (Paper 4), and Kane (Paper 7). For a closely related area, see the literature on the so-called political business cycle, for example, Nordhaus (1975).

2. See, for example, Willett and Mullen (Paper 5), Friedman and Friedman (1980), and the 1980 platform of the National Republican Party.

3. It may be instructive to those of us who are searching for practical solutions to inflation that the most practical (for good or bad) insights that have come from the natural-selection/genetic-change nexus have come from altering genetics (genetic engineering), not from altering fundamentals of the environment. Rather than try to change organisms by changing the environment (a scheme that would no doubt work given a sufficient number of generations), we have had more success intervening directly at the "proximate" or transmission level, which in the inflation context, is analogous to the money creation mechanism.

4. See, for example, Buchanan and Wagner (1977), Friedman and Friedman (1980).

5. My purpose here is not to reopen an old debate on the equivalence or

lack of equivalence between loanable funds and liquidity preference. For the reader who is convinced the two theories amount to the same thing, the point made in the text is incorrect. I, however, am persuaded by Tsiang (1966) that the two theories are equivalent only in full equilibrium. In a dynamic setting, they yield different results.

6. See, for example, Moore (1979) and Freund (1980).

DISCUSSION • *Thomas Mayer*

Explanations of inflation can be divided into two types. On the one hand, there is the political or sociological approach. This approach assumes that there exist no significant technical problems in controlling inflation, and that our failure to do so must, therefore, be due to the "constellation of forces," that is, to the fact that those who gain from inflation have more political power than those who lose from inflation. By contrast, the economic approach can take either of two forms. It can suggest that inflation is not intentional but is due to technical errors in monetary and fiscal policies. Alternatively, it may explicitly, or more frequently implicitly, be based on the argument that, regardless of the "ultimate" cause of inflation, the relevant problem is to understand the mechanisms by which inflation is generated.

Such agnosticism about the fundamental cause of inflation can be defended on several grounds. One is to argue that we understand much more about economic processes than about political processes and should focus our discussion on that which we understand.

The other justification is to say that an effective antiinflation policy is more likely to emerge from an understanding of the mechanism by which inflation is brought about than by knowing which groups are responsible for it. This is so because, unless these groups can either be shamed into abandoning their support for inflation, or can be convinced that inflation is not really in their own interest, they will continue to push for inflationary policies. By contrast, if the mechanism by which they generate inflationary policies is exposed, it may be possible to stop them in their tracks. Thus, it is possible that the reason why the proinflation group may get its way even if it has less political power than the antiinflation group is that the antiinflation group does not understand the way in which the inflation is brought about. Once it understands this, it can take the lever used to generate inflation away from the inflationists. For example, if inflation results from the workings of a political business cycle, Congress could impose a stable monetary growth rate rule on the Fed. Another such possibility exists if the antiinflation group could form a dominating coalition with another group that, while not caring so much about inflation, through the base drift trick.

Hence, it seems that if the Fed did not have the base drift mechanism available, we would have had just as much inflation as we actually did. In this way, base drift is not a <u>significant</u> causal element in the inflation. It also follows from this that the use of base drift cannot be employed to test the political theory of inflation. Suppose that the Fed wants to expand the money stock too fast because of political pressures. It could do this either via base drift or by changing the announced growth rate.

Turning to Kaminow's formal model, he explains the interest rate as a function of the gap between the actual and the target rates of monetary growth, M^t. This is plausible, and Kaminow's empirical estimates here are very useful. But to explain long-run inflation, doesn't one also have to explain what determines M^t? If the political theory is right, political pressures are likely to operate by affecting this target rate and, hence, it should not be left unexplained. One possibility is that M^t is a negative function of the previous inflation rate; i.e., that the Fed reacts against excessive longer-run inflation. But it <u>could</u> also be a positive function. The Fed might want to prevent excessive unemployment by financing the underlying rate of inflation, and may determine this rate by looking at the past inflation rate. But whatever the sign of the equation that actually links M^t to the past inflation rate, it does not seem useful to treat M^t as a constant. And I suspect that if M^t were made a function of the inflation rate, it is quite possible that the solution of Kaminow's equations might change.

It might also be useful to introduce asymmetries into the model. Given the usual attitude of Congress, a restrictive policy is more costly to the Fed than is an expansionary policy. Furthermore, if prices are more inflexible downward than upward, then a series of random errors in monetary policy can account for secular inflation.

Another point about Kaminow's model relates to his finding that "the Fed can be expected to undershoot its targets when growth in real money demand is declining and to overshoot when growth in money demand is increasing." This is not <u>necessarily</u> bad. It depends on whether the overshoots and undershoots are due to shifts in the IS or LM curves.

All in all, I am much more impressed by the significance of the question that Kaminow has raised than by his answer. But then raising the right question is often more important than giving the answer.

NOTE

1. In any case, the idea that one should eschew more direct explanations of a phenomenon in favor of more basic and "fundamental" explanations is primitive. All chemical phenomena can be reduced to physical explanations, but this does not mean that chemistry should be rejected as "superficial."

wants for some reason to take the lever of power that is used to generate inflation away from the inflationists.

A third possibility is that the proinflation group is so powerful because, like advocates of a tariff, the gainers from inflation are easier to organize than the much more diffuse losers who do not find it worth their while to be manning the ramparts against inflation all the time. But if there exists a single mechanism that is used to generate inflation, such as discretionary monetary policy, then it may well be worthwhile for the inflation losers to organize a temporary coalition that eliminates this lever.

Hence, even _if_ inflation is not primarily due to errors, the economic approach to inflation should not be considered naive because it focuses on "surface phenomena," rather than getting at the "underlying cause."[1]

Kaminow's paper therefore deals with a very worthwhile question when it asks by what mechanism inflation is brought about. This also provides a possible way of testing the political approach. Consider, for example, a specification of this approach that argues that inflation results from the fact that producer groups have captured certain government agencies such as the Departments of Labor and of Agriculture. Unless it can be shown that these departments have some effect on monetary policy, this explanation of inflation can be rejected.

But, unfortunately, the answer that Kaminow gives, that it is base drift that is the culprit, is not a useful point on which to focus in the long chain of causation that leads to inflation. To see this, consider the distinction between situations in which an agency is constrained by the available means, and situations in which it is not. If there are several ways to skin a cat, all equally costly, and one of these ways is eliminated, then just as many cats as before will lose their skins. One must, therefore, ask the question: Supposing the Fed is prevented from using base drift, as is partly the case under the Humphrey-Hawkins Act, does it readily have available other means that allow it to reach the same money stock as it would have reached with base drift? In principle, the Fed can, obviously, simply adjust its announced growth rate to reach any money stock target it wants. So one must ask whether juggling the growth rate is so much more expensive for the Fed that, when it has to do this rather than use base drift, it will follow a less inflationary policy. Would it really be so costly for the Fed to pursue its policy openly by changing the announced growth rate, rather than to do so surreptitiously by keeping the growth rate stable and applying it to a shifting base?

One possible cost of not using base drift, but just changing the growth rate instead, is that doing so _could_ perhaps generate Congressional criticisms. But would it? If it does not rely on base drift the Fed would have to raise its growth rate targets during the expansion, which is the time when, at least in the past, the Fed has tended to overshoot its money stock targets. This is a time when interest rates are high and rising, and Congress is not likely to object to a speedup of the money growth rate. Conversely, in the absence of base drift, the Fed would have to lower its announced money growth rate targets in recessions, but since interest rates are then falling, Congress is not so likely to criticize the Fed so strongly. On the whole, it does not seem that the Fed has much to lose in Congress by giving up base drift.

The Fed has to be concerned not only about Congressional criticism, but also about criticism by the financial and academic communities and by foreign central banks. But these are all sufficiently knowledgeable to have seen

DISCUSSION • *John T. Woolley*

It's All Proximate

INTRODUCTION

In "Politics, Economics, and Procedure of U.S. Money Growth Dynamics," Kaminow addresses one of the most important issues of interest to students of inflation today: How best to go about understanding the ways in which policy and politics cause inflation. Unlike those contemporary analysts focusing on political or sociological sources of inflation, Kaminow argues that there are important advantages in focusing first on policymakers and their actions before taking political and sociological factors as the central objects of analysis. The main arguments he marshals for this position are two. First, as a matter of policy reform, altering the behavior of a well-defined group of policymakers should be easier than altering very basic characteristics of our social and political lives. Second, as an intellectual question, any satisfactory understanding of inflation must include the money supply mechanism and show how other factors influence it. Thus, it is appropriate to begin an investigation at that point. Kaminow then goes beyond these arguments to stake additional claims. He argues that moving beyond the behavior of immediate policymakers to examine prior pressures on them puts us into an infinite regress of cause and effect of which we cannot hope to make good sense. Thus any approach other than his cannot be as neatly bounded for research purposes. Further, he hopes to demonstrate that a sufficiently adequate explanation of the money supply process need not go beyond an examination of the behavior of immediate policymakers.

Kaminow has taken on a task of obvious importance. I find his first two arguments quite plausible and indeed, at first glance, quite persuasive. I shall argue, however, that both are flawed by conceptual difficulties. These conceptual problems gravely undermine the more extended arguments Kaminow makes. He also encounters problems demonstrating that his model of the behavior of the immediate policymakers is persuasive. I shall comment first on the conceptual problems, then on the results Kaminow presents.

CONCEPTUAL PROBLEMS

The central focus of Kaminow's analysis is what he calls the money control mechanism or the money supply mechanism: "The main purpose of the present paper is to indicate by example how we need to go about modeling a dynamic money supply creation process as an essential feature to be embedded in any complete model of inflation." Kaminow's frequent references to the Federal Reserve suggest that he refers to that organization when he says "money control mechanism," etc. He takes this to be, as I shall call it, the least distant cause of monetary policy - and thus, in the long run, of inflation. The apparent analytic goal is to isolate the behavior of this least distant cause and, if possible, to show what changes at that level might be effective in reducing inflation.

There is a fundamental conceptual problem in this approach: unless it can be shown that the behavior being modeled is independent of the behavior of other actors (more distant causes), then the behavioral model does not adequately reveal possible avenues for reform. That is, if one acknowledges, as Kaminow does, that there <u>are</u> other distant causes, even though we do not yet fully understand how their influences are transmitted to the least distant cause, then the behavior of the least distant cause in some sense embodies the effects of those prior causes. This means, quite simply, that one cannot exclude the effects of more distant causes merely by modeling the behavior of a group of proximate policymakers. Nor can one say to what extent that behavior can be altered independent of those more distant causes.

The case of the Federal Reserve is not adequately dealt with by Kaminow's observation that there is not "a direct link through which the Federal Reserve is ordered to supply currency and bank reserves to finance a stated share of federal expenditures." The behavior of the Federal Reserve is not unaffected by political and social forces merely because it is not the object of direct orders by other political actors. Further, it is not adequate to suggest that the Federal Reserve has "at times a dominant independent influence on money growth." Problems of identifying the effects of distant causes are not resolved by noting that the Federal Reserve system is occasionally independent - whatever that may mean. No prudent political actor can ignore the possibility that reactions to his policy decisions might damage the future ability of his organization to achieve policy goals, nor can he safely ignore rapidly changing political and social conditions if ignoring them entails significant costs to him.

Kaminow nowhere convincingly argues that the Federal Reserve is <u>not</u> often, or even usually, affected either by the preferences of other actors or by other distant causes. Therefore, we cannot accept his premise, namely, that he is modeling <u>only</u> the least cause of monetary policy. One cannot successfully exclude the effects of more distant causes merely by refusing to discuss them.

It may be objected that I ignore Kaminow's findings that no variables other than changes in the intermediate target (monetary aggregates) explain movement of the Federal funds rate instrument. Through this finding, it might be argued, Kaminow does create the presumption of independence. This, however, is not persuasive. Two important questions are not addressed, both going to the heart of the issue of independence. The first has to do with reasons for selecting the targets, and the second has to do with the kinds of constraints placed on adjustments of the instruments. Why were alternative targets <u>not</u> chosen? Why were interest rate ranges constrained as they were? Both of these are important in describing the actions of policymakers, and they are particularly likely to be the points at which other causes are manifested.

Kaminow criticizes possible explanations of inflation that focus primarily on more distant causes. His point is that others have failed to specify adequately the mechanism by which these causes can affect the money supply mechanism. This point is simultaneously one that other analysts should take very seriously <u>and</u> that should be recognized as a potentially harmful diversion.

I agree with Kaminow's position that a truly satisfactory account of the role of distant causes of inflation would include a discussion explaining why monetary policy authorities are unable to resist those forces. However, the failure, or inability, to develop a fully specified model should not lead us to reject other kinds of investigations too quickly. On the one hand, it is possible to make quite meaningful scientific statements about the relationship of cause and effect without fully specifying all the mechanisms in between (even accepting the dubious assumption that all the mechanisms could ever be specified). On the other hand, given the obvious importance of certain recent developments, e.g., OPEC, it seems rather artificial to insist that such factors should, or even could, be excluded from a study of inflation, pending development of a more fully specified model. Can we satisfactorily focus only on the behavior of policymakers as if the outside world hardly existed?

Kaminow has not, I submit, successfully excluded more distant causes from his analysis. The work is not, as he claims, a test of an "alternative hypothesis" to the one that inflation is primarily accounted for by more distant causes. The way the monetary authority relates to the external world may or may not be explicitly examined by analysts, but ignoring it does not make it go away. At the same time, monetary authorities may well contribute an autonomous boost to inflation for various reasons. Kaminow is correct to note that this fact is ignored by those who fail to discuss seriously the relationship of their more distant causes and the money supply mechanism.

THE NUMERICAL EXERCISE

The heart of the paper is a mathematical model intended to illustrate that observed behavior of the money stock can be accounted for adequately by a model of the least proximate causes of monetary policy behavior. The effort is ingenious. Both as an exercise in dynamic modeling and as a transparent introduction to the basic elements that economists believe should be included in a specification of the money supply mechanism, this work should be of interest to political scientists who are concerned with these problems. Moreover, Kaminow also models the "base drift" phenomenon, which, we later learn, is an element of Federal Reserve political strategy, not a necessary element of monetary policy technique. It is a good example of explicitly incorporating a distant cause of policymaking, as discussed above. I should hasten to add, of course, that the author tries valiantly not to discuss it in such terms.

The exercise is disappointing for the author's failure to argue that his model adequately "fits the facts" - or that it does better than competitors' models. It may be democratic to "leave it to the reader" to decide whether or not the model works, but one might fairly expect somewhat more guidance from the author at this critical point. This is doubly disappointing since Kaminow has offered this exercise as an instructive example of how to go about modeling the monetary mechanism. As it is, a political scientist inclined to try to incorporate a model of the monetary mechanism has no particularly persuasive reason to adopt Kaminow's.

If I might engage in a bit of speculation, Kaminow's unwillingness to address this point suggests an interesting observation about the context in which the Federal Reserve acts. It is my impression from casual exposure to recent exchanges among economists that there is a lively discussion as to exactly what has been happening, if anything, to the demand for money (e.g., Goldfeld 1976; Hafer and Hein 1979). The complexities of the issues under debate may be such that we should excuse Kaminow for being unwilling to take a definitive stand on the matter.

However, if it is true that this issue has been under considerable dispute, then another issue of some interest is raised. What are the consequences for the conduct of monetary policy of substantial dispute among economists about a matter as central as the demand for money (see Wallich, Paper 8)? One presumes that a condition for this continuing dispute is the existence of sharply competing theoretical positions or of the lack of convincing empirical support for the dominant position, or both. What the Federal Reserve believes about such a question must surely be important for monetary policy, and must, in Kaminow's model, be embedded in the parameter $\underline{a}$ in equation (6.1). If the Federal Reserve's actions reflect the uncertainty among economists about these matters, then clearly again distant causes are represented in Kaminow's model. What does it mean for the fight against inflation if there is uncertainty about a basic element of the relevant theory? What adjustments in modeling would be required by that uncertainty?

CONCLUSION

As we would expect from an economist who has spent considerable time observing the Federal Reserve from a high staff position, Kaminow provides a paper that is sensitive to the tension between appearance and reality in a complex policymaking process, and that shows a policymaker's attentiveness to the importance of routines and procedures in shaping decisions. It is of obvious interest that someone with Kaminow's experience believes strongly that inflation in the 1970s can be understood primarily as the consequence of the Federal Reserve's technical procedures rather than the political and social context with which the Federal Reserve has to contend. I do not agree with that conclusion, and I have argued that Kaminow has not been able to meet the conditions that would be necessary to make his case persuasively. Nonetheless, I can only applaud any effort to further our understanding of inflation if it contributes, as Kaminow's does, to clarifying the problems researchers face in analyzing sources of inflation in the contemporary world.

COMMENT • *Thomas D. Willett and Leroy O. Laney*

Technical versus Political Causes of Monetary Expansion

In his interesting paper and oral presentation at the conference, Ira Kaminow presented a strong attack on those who have stressed underlying political determinants of money supply expansion. He argues that for the United States the major factor behind the escalation of monetary growth in the 1970s has been technical deficiencies in Federal Reserve operating procedures, the combination of interest rate targets and base drift that nullified the need to correct for errors in hitting money supply targets. We find Kaminow's analysis and empirical evidence to be quite plausible. It is a further helpful confirmation of some rather widely held views about the proximate causes of U.S. monetary policy.

We do not understand, however, the reason for Kaminow's strong attack on explanations that focus on the possibility of more underlying causes for the behavior of monetary authorities. His results for the United States are not so robust as to leave no scope for other explanations, nor are some of the most important of these alternative hypotheses inconsistent with the operation of the proximate causes on which he focuses. We do not wish to defend every analysis that relates inflation to underlying political variables. As Kaminow charges, there certainly have been examples of sloppy and confused thinking in this area, and there is a great deal more research to be done. But we believe that there has already been a good bit of careful analysis that escapes Kaminow's charges that this literature has not clearly spelled out the channels through which these underlying political variables will influence monetary behavior, and that these hypotheses have not been investigated empirically. To the contrary, there has been a good deal of empirical analysis along these lines in recent years published in respectable journals. (See, for example, Parkin 1975; Gordon 1977; and Willett and Laney 1978). As is indicated in this literature, and in several comments made at the conference, there are political considerations that underlie, at least in part, monetary authorities' traditional concerns with attempting to minimize fluctuations in interest rates. Furthermore, it is easy to see how one of the most commonly discussed underlying variables, the central government deficit, induces monetary expansion at least partially through the monetary authorities' attempts to mitigate the upward pressure that deficits put on interest rates. Indeed this linkage is mentioned in Kaminow's paper. Thus the accommodation of budget deficits hypothesis is quite consistent with Kaminow's findings. Likewise, while we believe that the major rationale for accommodation of wage-push pressures is concerned with avoiding unemployment, it would not be surprising for increased wage bills to put some upward pressure on interest rates that would induce monetary accommodation via that channel.

Of course, as Kaminow quite rightly stresses, the proof of the pudding is not in spelling out hypotheses, but in investigating their consistency with the facts. We are nearing completion of just such a project for the American Enterprise Institute (Laney and Willett 1982), which investigates, for the major industrial countries over the postwar period, the statistical explanatory power of several major hypotheses about the causes of inflation via their effect on the money supply process.

Our findings have some relevance to a number of questions that were discussed during the conference. While the results vary quite a bit from country to country (as would be expected), and also depend upon the particular specification of the equations, they do suggest rather strongly that, taken together, underlying variables had a good deal of explanatory power with respect to inducing monetary accommodation. For the four main hypotheses concerning pressures for monetary accommodation that we investigated, the following order of importance was found in general across industrial countries: central government budget deficits, wage increases, changes in international reserves, and import price increases. Only for the last did we find little evidence of significant effects over the postwar period.

With respect to the debate over how much of the rapid monetary expansion in the early 1970s was due to the huge U.S. balance of payments deficits and international liquidity explosion of that period, we found that the effects were significant (supporting Keohane's focus on this development), but that they were less important than domestic considerations [see Laney and Willett (1980b) and Willett (1980b)]. In other words, we found the world economy to be not so highly integrated that international monetary developments dominated national considerations over this period. But in the aggregate the international liquidity explosion did induce more rapid monetary expansion than would otherwise have occurred (on the order of 10 to 20 percent of the monetary expansion in the non-U.S. industrial countries during 1970-1972).

As with many other studies, our investigation of political influences on monetary policy yielded mixed results. Our findings for the United States were particularly interesting, however (see Laney and Willett 1980a).

A Federal Reserve reaction function, specifying several ostensibly purely economic forces as independent variables, explains a relatively high proportion of changes in M1 over the years 1960 through 1976, an interval during which periodic political influences on U.S. monetary authorities were alleged to operate. In fact adding a dummy variable, representative of a presidential electoral cycle set equal to minus one in the perhaps more inflation-conscious first two years of the four-year presidential term and plus one in the last two when more stimulatory unemployment reducing action is called for politically, did not yield significant results. (Several other variables hypothesized to be descriptive of a presidential cycle were the subject of experiment, but these also did not demonstrate any statistical significance.)

But this does not mean that changes in the U.S. money supply were not influenced by political factors during these years. One of the independent variables, the high-employment federal deficit, included to capture the response of the central bank to monetize federal debt because of upward pressure on interest rates, has a quite significant statistical relationship to the above presidential electoral cycle variable. Since this variable appears more important than any of the other "economic" factors in our basic money supply reaction function, it is certainly possible that the money supply process feels the impact of politics through this channel. If this high employment federal deficit is itself regressed upon several variables hypothesized to influence it, including the electoral cycle variable, the coefficient on the latter may be taken as a rough measure of that part of the high employment deficit attributable to incumbent presidential politics.

Separating the observed high employment deficit into "election-induced" and "election-adjusted" components in this fashion, the equations reported in Table 6.2 apply (see the footnote in the table for identification of variables, reasons for inclusion, and explanation of statistics.) In equation (6.1), the election-induced component of the deficit is statistically quite significant, providing some evidence of Fed responsiveness to politically motivated government spending or taxation changes along with its response to such changes not associated with politics and other economic incentives. While the coefficient on the election-induced component of the deficit is larger than that on the remainder of the deficit, suggesting the possibility that the Fed response to the former was not only significant but was even of a greater magnitude than the normal deficit-financing response, the t-statistic measuring a statistically significant difference in the two coefficients is very weak. (The t statistic judging whether 0.64 represents a statistically significant upward shift from 0.45 here is only $t = 0.98 > 0.88$ critical value at the 80 percent level using a one-tailed test.)

In equation (6.2), however, the coefficient on a dummy variable set equal to 1 in 1972, 0 otherwise, in the equation explaining the deficit is added to the election-induced component. This was done because 1972 has been singled out as extraordinary both for politically motivated fiscal stimulus and the degree of cooperation between the executive branch and the Fed (see, for example, Maisel 1973 and Tufte 1978 for an analysis of political-economic interaction during 1972). In this case the coefficient on the election-induced component of the deficit is more strongly significantly different from that on the residual election-adjusted component (with $t = 2.11 > 1.83$ critical value at the 95 percent level using a one-tailed test).

These results clearly point to some influence of politics on monetary policy over the interval. And while more evidence is necessary to prove the case conclusively, there is even some suggestion that the Fed's response to politically induced fiscal policy was greater than its reaction to the nonpolitically related federal deficit.

We should also like to stress our disagreement with Kaminow's assertion at the conference that the philosophy of those who stress ultimate political causes of monetary expansion is that little can be done to exert better direct control over the money supply. While this is undoubtedly the view of some, it is certainly not ours (nor, we suspect, that of many other researchers). Positive analysis that indicates that political factors have had a substantial impact on money supply behavior in the past does not logically imply the normative view that the only way to obtain more prudent rates of monetary growth in the future is to try to influence these particular underlying factors. Perhaps greater resistance is required on the part of the Fed itself, regardless of the consequences. Our results complement work such as Kane (Paper 7), which emphasized that the current degree of independence of the Federal Reserve system has not been sufficient to keep it from operating in a substantially political manner. It therefore can be argued that we need reforms that recognize this political role and

TABLE 6.2. The reaction function (1960-1976) with high-employment deficit separated into calculated election-adjusted and election-induced components (dependent variable = $\Delta M1$)

Equation	Constant	ΔM_{t-1}	Δy_t^e	$(y_a - y_p)_t$	Δp_{t-1}	W_{t-1}^d	DEA_t	DEI_t	$\bar{R}^2$	D-W	S.E.
(6.1)	1.42 (1.32)	0.56 (6.53)*** [0.57]	49.99 (4.24)*** [0.35]	-0.45 (-4.45)*** [-0.49]	-0.88 (3.27)*** [0.25]	223.22 (4.39)*** [0.57]	0.45 (6.37)*** [0.78]	0.64 (3.34)*** [0.27]	0.95 (41.57)	2.30	1.37
(6.2)	1.57 (1.72)	0.56 (7.81)*** [0.57]	47.92 (4.75)*** [0.34]	-0.40 (-4.44)*** [-0.43]	-0.68 (-2.64)*** [-0.19]	201.33 (4.51)*** [0.52]	0.40 (6.16)*** [0.68]	0.71 (5.49)*** [0.36]	0.96 (56.71)	2.09	1.17

Note: Independent variables: ΔM_{t-1} = change in M1 in previous year; Δy_t^e = capital investment commitments component of the diffusion index of leading economic indicators, included to capture procyclical accommodative response of the Fed to incipient changes in economic activity; $(y_a - y_p)_t$ = actual minus potential output in manufacturing, included to capture countercyclical response to slack economic activity relative to potential; Δp_{t-1} = change in CPI inflation rate in previous year, included to capture response to accelerating inflation; W_{t-1}^d = detrended real wage level, included to capture wage validation response of monetary authority due to concern about unemployment; DEA_t = election-adjusted component of the high employment deficit, included to capture crowding out pressure due to higher interest rates; DEI_t = election-induced component of the high employment deficit, included to capture politically motivated fiscal policy; $\bar{R}^2$ the coefficient of multiple determination adjusted for degrees of freedom; D-W = the Durbin-Watson statistic; S.E. = the standard error of the regression.

The t and F statistics are in parentheses; standardized beta coefficients are in brackets. A one-tailed test is utilized to measure statistical acceptability of t statistics for coefficients signed as theoretically hypothesized; * indicates significance at 90 percent level, ** at the 95 percent level, and *** at the 99 percent level.

make elected officials more directly accountable for monetary behavior, or alternatively it can be argued that the Fed must adhere to more binding monetary rules that will reduce the influence that these political and economic pressures traditionally have had on the rate on monetary growth. It is possible that actions taken in October 1979 are a step in the direction of less discretionary central bank response to both purely economic and political pressures.

REJOINDER • *Ira P. Kaminow*

I shall skip the opportunity provided by this reply to defend my paper against the thoughtfully prepared comments of the discussants. Instead, I would like to make the point that while the discussants have a substantive disagreement with me, they have not accurately characterized the disagreement nor seen its implications.

The generally accepted theory of inflation postulates a positive relationship between the supply of money and the rate of inflation. Much of the literature on inflation begins with this theory and then takes a step that, if perceived at all, is perceived as innocuous: money growth, at least in a proximate sense, is the cause of inflation. This step, in the context of the search for the ultimate causes of inflation, is in fact an unsupported leap. The theoretic relationship between money and inflation no more implies that money growth is the cause of inflation than it implies that inflation is the cause of money growth. That is to say, as we search for inflation's causes, it is logically possible that we will learn that there is a causal behavioral link running from certain social or political parameters to a particular pattern of inflation rates. The rate of growth of money necessary to achieve the equilibrium inflation pattern would then be mechanically "solved" by the system. The logical sequence of events in this scenario goes from fundamental causes to inflation to an implied money growth path. Thus, the understanding that money growth is the cause of inflation is not a logical consequence of the theoretical link between money growth and inflation. It is instead a scientific statement that has content in the sense that it is logically subject to refutation.

It is precisely this issue that I seek to exploit in my paper. What I seek to do is to take the money-is-the-proximate-cause-of-inflation story at face value. I do this by presuming that there is a behaviorally interesting link between the fundamentals (whatever they are) and the money supply, which runs through the money creation process but not through inflation. That is, money growth is determined at least partially (in the paper, exclusively) in a behavioral way, not mechanistically implied by a behaviorally determined inflation rate.

I believe the fundamental argument my critics have with my paper is that they are not willing to accept the view that money causes inflation as literally as my paper implies. I believe they would feel more comfortable with the view that inflation is the cause of money growth. Thus, for example, theories of monetary accommodation to wage pressures, government deficits or import price increases (as suggested by Woolley, and Willett and Laney) are theories that posit a relationship between fundamentals and inflation rates, with the monetary authorities supplying whatever stock of money is necessary to achieve a politically or socially determined inflation rate. I suspect also that Mayer is closing in on the same sort of point when he suggests, "It seems that if the Fed did not have the base drift mechanism available, we would have had just as much inflation as we actually did." Inflation, in this view, is not determined by what the monetary authority does. Rather, what the monetary authority does in substance is implied by the politically or socially determined inflation rate.

Whether money growth causes inflation or inflation causes money growth is by no means a trivial matter. The more strongly one believes that "monetary policy authorities are unable to resist those (political) forces," as Woolley does, the more strongly one believes that the inflation rate is ultimately determined as the solution to a political or social system and the less expectation there can be that restructuring the monetary mechanism will reduce inflationary pressures. If a firm monetary rule yields a rate of inflation unsatisfactory to the political system, the rule will likely be broken.

In summary, I believe the issue that divides us is not, as Willett and Laney suggest, that I "attack . . . explanations that focus on the possibility of more underlying causes for the behavior of monetary authorities." It is the opposite. I urge explanations that focus on the more underlying causes for the behavior of monetary authorities. The discussed alternative is to focus on underlying causes of inflation, with the behavior of the monetary authorities being trivially determined by the inflation rate. It is the paper's premise that the behavior of the monetary authorities can be modeled in a nontrivial way. Consequently, authorities' use of base drift raises interesting questions about their motivation. The alternative view--that the authorities are merely technicans providing enough money to validate the inflation generated by the political or social system --finds base drift a mere technical detail easily replaceable by some alternative detail. Pay your money and take your choice.

GENERAL DISCUSSION

GENERAL DISCUSSION

Many of the participants elaborated on the themes raised and examined by Kaminow and his discussants. Several noted that Kaminow's paper could be viewed not so much as a set of arguments identifying the explanation of excessive money growth but rather as illustrative of the type of research economists and political scientists need to conduct to better link up the so-called proximate and ultimate causes of inflation. Many agreed that specifying how aspects of the Fed's procedures contributed to excessive money growth was a useful first step. It was suggested, however, that behind the procedures (or proximate causes) lie the more fundamental causes. Kane noted that the banking committees in Congress, and their staffs, generally understood the ramifications of base drift. This being the case, why did Congress put up with it? Kane suggested such procedures evolve as the self-interests of the parties involved combine to alter the appearances of policy (monetary and fiscal) relative to the realities of policy. Extending Kane's argument, Susan Strange viewed base drift and its relationship to Concurrent Resolution 133 as indicative of the Fed's willingness to legitimize a transparent, symbol-laden process that suited the political needs of Congress and the president.

There seemed to be general agreement that the Fed's procedures were designed to facilitate some form of political and economic accommodation over at least the short run. It was noted that most economists agreed that it was certainly within the Fed's power to control monetary growth over a 3-6-month period. Since the Fed apparently did not exert such control, some wondered whether the failure to accommodate over the longer run--perhaps the litmus test for the existence of meaningful central bank independence--was possible in a democracy in the absence of an inflationary legacy such as Germany's.

PAPER 7 • *Edward J. Kane*

External Pressure and the Operations of the Fed

INTRODUCTION
   Fed goals do not hatch full formed like Athena from the brow of Zeus. They are hammered and shaped on the anvil of national politics by artisans who never cease to reheat and touch up their work.
   Nor is any particular macroeconomic goal absolutely good. Reputed macroeconomic public enemies such as unemployment, inflation, stagnation, and payments imbalance are neither entirely bad for the national economy nor bad at all for every sector. Unemployment probably retards inflation and strengthens the balance of payments; inflation reduces repayment burdens borne by debtors and encourages many types of investment; economic stagnation makes it easier to preserve the quality of the physical environment; and international payments imbalances lower the cost of living, reduce shortages, and generate profits for importers.
   No logically coherent strategy exists for promoting every macroeconomic goal at the same time. Policies meant to promote one goal tend to interfere--either in the short or the long run--with efforts to achieve at least one other. Typically, the difference between macroeconomic good and macroeconomic evil depends principally on how political power is distributed. Macroeconomic goal formation is inevitably a political process of trade-offs, in which the economic interests and political clout of different groups of citizens are, along with the timing of the next election, carefully weighed and balanced.
   Elected and appointed politicians use constitutionally granted market power to resolve, to their personal and professional satisfaction, sectoral conflicts over the distribution of economic resources. Fiscally underrestrained sectoral demands on government resources combine with cyclically shifting electoral payoffs to incumbent politicians to induce accommodative monetary policies that squeeze private-sector real incomes and impose a politically induced overlay on the ordinary business cycle. In the United States, the trade-offs made in formulating monetary policy are seldom openly admitted either by elected politicians or by Federal Reserve officials. Surreptitious politics clouds the process of central-bank goal formation and encourages Fed officials to describe their decisions in a ludicrously sanctimonious kind of code. To understand the workings of the Federal Reserve System, one must learn both to sort out political events affecting Fed policy decisions and to crack the several codes in which political communication takes place.
   This paper develops the hypothesis that political events--not economic events--are the proximate determinants of Fed actions. It focuses on the

elaborate system of contacts, threats, rewards, and punishments by which incumbent politicians in Congress and in the executive branch transmit monetary policy instructions to the Fed. Four main classes of relevant political events can be discerned: impacts of individual sectors on incumbent politicians; incumbents' impacts on Fed officials; Fed dealings with incumbent officials and individual sectors, including those that comprise the operative constituency against inflation; and internal Fed dealings: transactions among Fed officials and with and among component staffs. The analysis offered here concentrates on events of the second and third type.

To maintain the unfavorable trends in inflation and in the foreign exchange value of the dollar that the United States has experienced during the last fifteen years, U.S. politicians had to revise institutional arrangements for selecting monetary policy priorities. Incumbent federal politicans and political appointees preferred to ratify excessive sectoral demands on government fiscal resources in the short run, relying on taxation levied covertly by inflation to rebalance sectoral demands over the longer run. Moreover, incumbents found that they could at least occasionally curry votes by pursuing slight preelection improvements in macroeconomic indices at the expense of substantial postelection deterioration (Gordon 1975; Nordhaus 1975; Tufte 1978). To carry out these policies, incumbents had to persuade Fed officials to monetize a succession of federal deficits. Political pressure on the Fed fostered monetary policies that allowed incumbents to take credit for distributing current sectoral benefits and for bringing about short-run decreases in unemployment without requiring them to accept consonant blame for the inflationary consequences that these policies generated over the longer haul.

Analysis of the political economy of Fed decision making suggests that the Fed's role in this process of blame displacement is carefully scripted. Underlying this hypothesis is the principle that adjustments in Fed procedures and structural arrangements must be politically optimal at the time they are made. By revealed preference, authorities with jurisdiction (i.e., incumbent politicians or top Fed officials) have rejected other feasible approaches as less desirable than those chosen. Over time, legislation amending the Federal Reserve Act and extending the Fed's stabilization responsibilities via the Employment Act (and amendments thereto) have produced a U.S. central bank very different from the one originally conceived. This legislation, while undermining the Fed's ability to carry out its primordial assignment of acting as a roadblock to short-sighted economic policies, has left the Fed just enough apparent autonomy to provide incumbent politicians with a plausible scapegoat for all untoward macroeconomic events. By accommodating, year after year, a cumulative fiscal deficit, the Fed has come to function like a chaperone at a fraternity party. It legitimizes the process without changing it very much. Time after time, Fed officials accept the contradictory policy assignment of singlehandedly bringing inflation and unemployment down to satisfactory levels, stoically accepting the blame when these impossible goals fail to materialize. That intelligent observers continue to be swayed by Fed promises is a phenomenon for which (in contrast to P.T.Barnum) modern theories of expectations formation have no good answer.

FED APPEARANCES VERSUS FED REALITY

The place that the Federal Reserve System holds today in the macroeconomic policy formation process calls to mind Chesterton's conception of politics as the art of not telling the truth without actually lying. To decipher the Federal Reserve Act and most official Fed statements, one needs to recognize that key words have come to mean almost precisely the opposite of what they would mean in ordinary discourse. For example, Fed independence is now a code word for Fed political subservience and a Fed stock certificate no longer represents anything more than a nonmarketable, fixed-coupon bond of indefinite maturity.

In all too many cases, disguised politics transform the appearances of contemporary Fed practices, processes, and reasoning into the opposite of underlying realities. Fed fiction begins with its legal form of organization as a quasiprivate corporation. Formal ownership of Federal Reserve stock certificates by so-called "member" banks makes the Fed look suspiciously like a bank-owned corporation. In reality, the Fed operates as an agency of the federal government. Fed staff members see themselves as government employees, and members of the Fed's Board of Governors are appointed by the president of the United States subject to the consent of the Senate. Fed stockholders have no proxy decisions to make and no beneficial interest in Fed earnings.

Every Federal Agency Pursues an Identifiable Self-Interest

Federal agencies are, first and foremost, political institutions. They are created by revocable laws passed by Congress that assign them specific functions intended to benefit the common good. Political appointees are put in charge, largely in consideration of prior service to the party in power or to some powerful elected official. Career civil servants tend to stay on through political changes, but whenever an incoming president pushes the rival party out of office, an agency's leadership is replaced at the first convenient opportunity.

Agency performance is loosely monitored by the electorate and by elected officials to whom the agency is accountable. Good performance reflects credit to the president and/or the Congress. Hence, it spells long life, increased scope, substantial autonomy, and larger budgets. Poor (especially scandalous) performance threatens an agency's leaders, life, scope, autonomy, and budget. However, this political reward and punishment process operates with a long and capriciously unpredictable lag.

Every government agency strives not only to do and be judged good, but to do as well as it can. Interpreted in the narrowest of economic terms, this statement asserts only that agencies (just as firms and consumers) are optimizing entities that act to maximize the realization of given goals subject to institutional and technical restraints. But interpreted broadly, the statement is subject to a cynical distinction. With lagged responses to agency performance, the words "good" and "well" may refer to different sets of goals and restraints. The "good" in the main clause remains the elements of the common good that constitute the agency's nominal task, but the subsequent "well" may refer to agency managers' perception of their own or the agency's near term self-interest, as limited by the political reward system (Acheson and Chant 1973).

Especially in economic policymaking, the common good--like beauty--lies in the eye of the beholder. Policymaking requires tough choices, not between good and evil but among alternative goods. These alternative goods differ in the speed with which benefits develop and in their distribution across the populace. Labeling such choices political ones in no way places them beyond the purview of economic analysis.

Trade-offs made between short-run and long-run benefits and between benefits and burdens to be visited on various special interests are the very essence of Federal Reserve policymaking (Maisel 1973). Federal Reserve officials do not merely set marginal policy benefits equal to marginal policy costs. They invest a great deal of effort both in identifying--as far as they can in an uncertain economic and political environment--what political, bureaucratic, and economic benefits and costs apply and in selling their final policy choices to relevant clienteles.

Although the Federal Reserve Act conveys a passive image, the Fed is not a mindless, monetary policy robot that Congress switched on one day in 1914 and that (with a recall for rewiring in the 1930s) has operated dutifully and independently ever since. If the Fed is to be viewed as a robot, it should be viewed as an adaptoid. The Fed shapes and reshapes both itself and its policies--cosmetically and fundamentally--to accommodate and to manipulate political and economic developments that impact on its nominal task.

This adaption can be seen clearly in the range of innovative approaches that Fed officials have developed both for impacting on financial market participants and for neutralizing outside criticism (Borins 1972; Weintraub 1978). The range of operational policy weapons wielded by the modern U.S. central bank contrasts vividly with the few crude tools the authors of the Federal Reserve Act meant to place in its hands.

Federal Reserve "Independence" Is Greatly Exaggerated

Although the Federal Reserve is generically just another federal agency, it is a species unto itself. Bureaucratically, the Fed enjoys a set of formal privileges that in the short run insulate its budget from partisan incursion and its highest officials from the threat of dismissal.

Federal Reserve governors are granted a degree of autonomy surpassed only by the Supreme Court, in the form of long terms of appointment and an independent source of operating funds (Burns 1978). The seven members of the Federal Reserve Board enjoy 14-year terms in office, staggered to make it hard--at least in theory--for a president (in his maximum eight years in office) to dominate the board by threats of nonreappointment. Moreover, neither the president's Office of Management and Budget nor the Congress can influence Federal Reserve decisions through the conventional discipline of the budgetary process. The Federal Reserve is chartered as a quasiprivate corporation with first call on the interest that accrues on its portfolio of over $125 billion in U.S. Treasury and agency securities.

At best, this special bureaucratic shielding works only in the short run. Unlike Supreme Court justices who are appointed for life, Federal Reserve governors must concern themselves with postseparation career planning. Unless they are appointed at an advanced age, they must regularly review alternative job opportunities. This need to consider their future career profiles increases the separation rate and the number of partial-term appointments available over time. Governors appointed to unexpired partial terms are particularly susceptible to reappointment pressure.

Moreover, in the long run, successive presidents and Congresses must be persuaded to maintain the statutory armorplate. Fed officials possess a narrow political base. What political strength they have is drawn from the Fed's client banks, backed up by constituencies against inflation and for bank regulation. On the issue of inflation, popular allegiance has been weak and becomes even weaker when and as a recession develops. This is when the Fed--whose previous antiinflationary policies inevitably take the blame for surging unemployment--is most vulnerable. In boom and recession, Fed officials must struggle in Congress to turn aside or to soften bills (such as H.R. 7001 in the 1980 Congressional session) that threaten to chip away at various pieces of the Fed's suit of armor. The necessity to campaign continually for the preservation of Fed autonomy makes Fed officials far more submissive to the short-run political interests of incumbent presidents and congressmen than they care to admit.

Debate about the desirability of an independent Federal Reserve system proceeds from a dangerously false premise. The Fed is approximately as independent as a college student whose room and board is financed by a parentally revocable trust fund. Some conflict will be tolerated, but the limits of the benefactors' patience must always be kept in mind.

Just as other federal agencies, the Fed is fully accountable to representatives elected by people (Board of Governors of Federal Reserve System 1974, p. 3). The difference lies in the intricate pattern of accountability and in the precise rewards and punishments elected officials are able to manipulate. Although dissatisfied politicians can't discipline recalcitrant Fed officials by forcing their dismissal or even by cutting next year's budget, they can and do restrain them by threatening to make unfriendly new appointments and to take back various elements of the Fed's vaunted independence.

Therefore, in addition to coping with the System's nominal responsibilities for economic policy and for facilitating the flow of domestic payments, Federal Reserve officials worry about avoiding public confrontations and preserving the System's structural autonomy. Each regime wants to bequeath to its successors an agency at least as strong in structure as the one they inherited. No regime wants to be recorded as gaining a string of Pyrrhic policy victories for which the System itself is made to pay dearly in the long run.

POLITICAL EVENTS AND FORCES INFLUENCING FED DECISIONS

As scientists, economists are interested in observable phenomena. Unfortunately, external influences on the Fed and Fed reactions to these influences leave a deliberately muddled trail behind them. How to read this trail is the focus of this paper.

Political action for and against the Fed emanates from many sources and occurs along a broad spectrum of events. Presidential scoldings, special-interest attacks or pleas for help, and formal votes to approve or to reject legislative proposals are merely the most visible of these events. Private interests and elected officials work at the day to day task of influencing Fed officials by subtle means. These less dramatic tools include promises of jobs, public praise, use of rumors and trial balloons, informal meetings, hearings on legislative recommendations of various kinds, and redistribution of bureaucratic privileges.

Congress and the president impact on Fed officials formally and informally through the link of their shared responsibility for macroeconomic and financial events. Private interests act through governmental agencies sensitized to their needs, through the press, and through channels of social and economic contact.

A Framework for Assessing Incumbent Self-Interest

In the tradition of Anthony Downs (1957), we may conceive of elected officials as managing a production process, whose inputs consist of their own time, wealth, and office budgets and whose output is the probability of reelection. For a congressional incumbent, at least four intermediate products enter the reelection-probability production functions:

1. A record of individual achievement in office, as perceived by consitituents. This record may be decomposed into different elements of constituent service (broadly considered).
   a. Service to the constituent business community in sponsoring important legislation or in shepherding it toward enactment
   b. Positions and votes taken on important issues, as reflected in favorable ratings by special interest groups, including so-called public interest groups
   c. Casework for individual constituents in dealing with the federal bureaucracy, e.g., in clearing claims for lost veterans' pensions or social security checks and following up constituent appeals against denials of benefits
   d. Providing responsive answers to opinionated mail from irate constituents
   e. Name recognition:--keeping his or her name before constituents in as many ways as possible
2. The prestige which the office and particular mix of committee assignments currently enjoys
3. The size of the campaign budget
4. The short-term performance of the national economy, as represented (say) in Okun's "discomfort index," which sums the current rates of inflation and unemployment

Holding hearings on legislation threatening to impose new congressional controls on Fed procedures enhances incumbents' ability to influence Fed thinking about what adjustments in the monetary aggregates would prove desirable.[1] It also elevates the status of service on a banking committee and, if legislation is enacted, raises the chairman's and committee members' record of achievement (Woolley 1980). In addition, raising manifold possibilities for restructuring Fed regulatory powers triggers greater involvement by bank and savings and loan lobbies, increasing the flow and selectivity of campaign contributions from these institutions' political action committees (PACs).[2]

Statutory Framework within Which the Fed Operates

Fed officials' legal authority to make macroeconomic policy decisions on their own is contained in two frequently amended pieces of legislation: the Federal Reserve Act (1913) and the Employment Act of 1946. Proposed readjustments in the scope of Fed autonomy and responsibilities under these acts can be manipulated as a system of rewards and punishments, to increase or to diminish the prestige and quality of life enjoyed by Fed bureaucrats.

The President. As the hub of the executive branch, the office of the presidency provides numerous points of contact with Fed officials. Presidents can steer Fed decision makers in the direction they desire by holding out carrots of accommodation or by beating them with administrative sticks.

Appeals for policy coordination serve as tasty carrots. The ideal of assisting in the design of unified macroeconomic policies plays directly upon the ego of Fed officials by promising to enlarge their scope of activity. Governors and staff representatives may be invited to participate in policy formation over a broad field of economic issues with top officials from the Treasury, State Department, Commerce Department, Council of Economic Advisers, and Office of Management and Budget. Given that governors are drawn from a pool of predominantly idealistic and public spirited persons who see their service as a personal sacrifice made for the greater good, such appeals and opportunities are hard to resist.

The president appoints members of the Federal Reserve Board (FRB) and designates one member to serve as chairman. Economists widely regard the FRB chairmanship as the single most powerful economic policy post in the federal government. However, because a chairman's power is predicated on the cooperation of a majority of other board members, a president can punish an FRB chairman by appointing "difficult" but loyal persons to the board when and as vacancies arise. Less formally, he can make life in Washington uncomfortable in many ways for any set of government officials who stubbornly refuse to bend toward his view of the common good. Since such pressure should increase board turnover, it can reinforce the president's appointment power precisely when it promises to be most useful.

Every chairman is anxious to influence new appointments to the board. In the 1970s, when accelerating inflation drove levels of compensation for competitive positions in the private economy far above board salaries, board turnover soared. President Carter's first three and a half years saw six resignations. This turnover magnified the president's leverage on his FRB chairman and, early in Volcker's chairmanship, may have been used to make appointments specifically intended to blunt a politically uncomfortable policy thrust.

During the 1950s and 1960s, Fed officials were publicly called on the carpet by two different sitting presidents (Truman and Johnson) for resisting broad macroeconomic policy recommendations. The first such incident (in early 1951) cost Chairman McCabe his job, although two months later (see Clifford 1965) it led to an accord with the Treasury that strengthened the Fed. On the other hand, the second incident marked the high-water mark of Fed power, after which Chairman Martin never publicly challenged a president's economic policies again. In 1972, Chairman Burns permitted an election-year spurt in the monetary aggregates that assisted President Nixon's reelection campaign (Kane 1974a). In July 1975, President Ford pointedly celebrated his birthday with the board. Under Carter, beginning with the presidential press conference of November 1, 1978, the Federal Reserve Board chairman began to appear at the president's side to pledge in advance Fed support for the latest changes in Presidential economic policy strategy.

This increased receptiveness to shows of presidential attention reflected in part the Fed's increasing need for presidential support both to stop the inflation-accelerated exodus of member banks from the System and to fend off the accelerating congressional criticisms of its policies. As Fed problems became embodied in the concrete form of individual bills that would either extend or limit the Fed's powers, it became important to have the ability to call on a presidential <u>veto</u> in the clutch.[3]

Congress. Congressional power over the Fed also resides in ability to grant or to withhold rewards (legislative changes that Fed officials want) and to impose punishments (legislative changes that they don't want). Besides simple praise, the class of congressional rewards consists principally of two items. First, Congress could allow the salaries of Fed governors (which are currently constrained by those of Cabinet officers) to move as freely as those of the Reserve Bank presidents (which are tied instead to salaries received by local commercial-bank presidents). More competitive salaries for members of the Board of Governors would strengthen the Fed politically. It would increase the board's prestige and reduce its turnover. It would permit top staff salaries to be more competitive as well. Second, Congress could increase the degree of Fed authority over nonmember banks and savings institutions. Through the 1970s, Fed officials were especially anxious to gain the power to set reserve requirements for nonmember depository institutions.

Congressional restraints on governor salaries strongly limit the population of individuals for whom FRB service poses an attractive career opportunity. For individuals of a given age, salary levels for FRB governors are more adequate for academics and career bureaucrats than for lawyers and bank executives. Similarly, low current salaries are less unattractive for youngish individuals, who can extract substantial implicit income by planning to parlay board service either into the name recognition required to campaign for elective office or into many years of higher-paying jobs in the private sector. Recently, Congress has taken action to reduce the present value of even this implicit or steppingstone income. The Ethics in Government Act of 1978 (as amended in May 1980) applies specifically to FRB members and serves to restrict their postseparation employment even more than the stringent "Boy Scout rules" the Fed adopted in 1973. Postemployment conflict-of-interest restrictions are especially severe for board members who fail to serve out the (possibly partial) term to which they were appointed. They are prohibited for two years from taking a wide class of jobs in the financial industry. Moreover, since the early 1960s, the board's own rules have prevented sitting governors from earning outside income from speaking fees. Taken together, congressional and in-house restrictions on FRB members' ability to earn explicit and implicit income make it hard to recruit competent governors with broad experience and make it uneconomic for all but a narrow class of FRB members to plan to serve more than a fraction of a full fourteen-year term.

Accelerating inflation tends to reduce the after-tax real value of governors' salaries and to increase the differential burden of reserve requirements on member banks. By letting the membership problem fester through the 1970s, Congress kept Fed officials under constant pressure. The Fed's fundamental membership problem was that declining membership (which for economic reasons was concentrated among small- to medium-sized banks) simultaneously reduced and narrowed its political base. This undermined Fed clout with Congress by impairing its ability to rally widespread bank lobbying activity in support of its policies. To close the Fed's longstanding political wound, in March 1980, Congress extended Fed-imposed reserve requirements to nonmember institutions, but permitted reserve balances to be held in the form of correspondent balances at member banks. This legislation denies the correspondent-balance option to all banks that were members on July 1, 1979. To establish incentives to restore the blood the system lost in the years prior to July 1, 1979, the Fed proposes to administer the statute by requiring a 100 percent passthrough of correspondent-held reserve balances to Fed accounts.

Although the class of congressional deprivations is virtually unbounded, recent threats have focused on the following issues:

1. Expanded Congressional oversight of decisions made by the Federal Open Market Committee, FOMC. Starting in 1975, the Fed was required to

report quarterly (now semiannually) to the congressional banking committees on interim FOMC policy targets for the next twelve months and, since February 1979 (under the Humphrey-Hawkins amendment to the Employment Act), to square these targets verbally with administration plans. Related controversy has centered on the number and identity of the targets reported, on the desirability of simultaneously reporting interim targets, on whether the Fed should adopt a monetarist strategy, and on the contents and timely release of FOMC minutes, including the possibility of opening FOMC meetings under the Government in the Sunshine Act.

2. Reducing Fed budgetary autonomy. Congressman Wright Patman's overarching objective was to force the Fed to obtain its operating funds from annual appropriations from Congress. He urged retirement of Fed stock and regular audits of Federal Reserve accounts and policies by the Government Accounting Office, GAO. In 1977, a GAO audit was finally established, but the scope of the audit was limited to the Fed's bank supervisory functions. H.R. 7001 sought to redeem Fed stock and to end Federal Reserve bank presidents' membership in the FOMC.

3. Full-cost pricing for Fed banking services. This is now required by 1980 legislation. Although intended nominally to help private banks compete more effectively with Federal Reserve banks in the market for correspondent services, it affects the Fed's ability to tailor offers of implicit interest to the advantage or disadvantage of individual banks.

4. The propriety of having Federal Reserve bank directors and Board Chairmen lobby members of Congress. Although lobbying expense is legal for the Fed, government agencies that are restricted to congressionally appropriated funds are disallowed from spending funds in this way. This issue is designed to restrain the political activity of Fed officials.

5. Realigning the four-year term of FRB chairman to coincide with that of incoming presidents. This would ensure each new president a chance to place his own person in this top policymaking post. Although it incorporated a one-year delay, such a bill passed the House in 1980.

6. Extending the need for Senate confirmation to cover Reserve Bank presidents (because they are potential member of the FOMC) and to require new confirmation for an FRB chairman who had been confirmed previously as a board member. The first part of this proposal (which has not been enacted) would reduce the FRB's power to select Reserve Bank presidents and would allow Congress to screen all members of the FOMC. The second part addressed a loophole that could have allowed the president and the FRB to make an end run around the process of congressional screening. Since 1977, it has been necessary for all FRB chairman and vice-chairman to be explicity confirmed in their posts.

7. Broader representation of women, minorities, and regional nonfinancial interests on F.R. bank boards and on the Board of Governors itself. For example, in May, 1980, before granting approval of Lyle Gramley's appointment to the FRB, the Senate passed a resolution decrying "Eastern" domination of recent board appointments. Except that this issue impinges slightly on presidential and Fed officials' freedom of appointment, it is essentially symbolic.

8. Transferring the Fed's supervisory authority over member banks and bank holding companies (BHCs) to a new agency, which would consolidate in a single office all federal bank regulatory functions, including those currently exercised by the U.S. Comptroller of the Currency and the Federal Deposit Insurance Corporation (FDIC). By segregating the locus

of monetary control from that of bank and BHC regulation, this change would deprive the Fed of a major element of leverage over credit policy at individual banks (Kane 1973).
9. Pressures to allocate credit in favor of specific sectors. These range from proposed bailouts of troubled industries, cities, and firms to proposals meant to provide better access to credit for small businesses and would-be homeowners. These pressures for sectoral relief constrain the Fed's ability to impose sharp or sustained increases in nominal interest rates on the macroeconomy.

One consequence of the assault in 1975 by post-Watergate freshman legislators on executive branch autonomy and on the congressional seniority system was an intensification of interest in reassessing Fed officials' rights and duties (Kane 1975; Weintraub 1978). Prior to Wright Patman's being stripped in 1975 of the House Banking Committee chairmanship, he had perennially pushed these same issues without effect. In the rush to build can-do records, his successor Henry Reuss, and his Senate counterpart William Proxmire (who succeeded John Sparkman in the same year), transformed what had been widely perceived as Patman's personal vendetta against the Fed into a careful reevaluation of congressional oversight responsibilities.

Since 1975, Fed officials have found themselves besieged simultaneously on many fronts. Month after month, House and Senate banking committees and subcommittees have held hearings to consider a series of bills that would either strengthen the Fed by relieving its membership problem or weaken it by chipping away at one or another of the Fed's special bureaucratic privileges. Few weeks pass in which a contemporary Fed chairman does not spend time preparing or delivering testimony for committee hearings. Legislation passed during this era has reduced the Fed's ability to keep internal procedures and debates from public scrutiny.

Beyond the Statutory Framework: The Scapegoat Hypothesis

As a matter of legislative formula, the Fed is "merely a creature of Congress" in the same sense that Mary Shelley's fictional green monster was a "creature of Frankenstein." In both cases, the issue is whether the "creator" can ever truly bring the creature back under control.

Although a few congressmen and senators work very hard for this result, one can legitimately question whether the Congress as a whole has any taste for the task (Kane 1975; Roberts 1978; Weintraub 1978; Woolley 1980). In practice, the ponderous multilayered structure of congressional decision making and the economic naivete of the great preponderance of elected officials provide effective limitations on congressional ability to dominate a reluctant Fed. Members who cannot to any great extent interpret current macroeconomic information fear the possibility that a Fed chairman's election-year counterattack might tar them with the label of "inflationists," while the slowness and unwieldiness of Congress itself virtually insure that its influence even on quarter-to-quarter decisions by the Fed will prove more apparent than real.

At election time, incumbent congressmen find it extremely convenient to be free to blame the economic ills of the country on the "misguided" policies of an "independent" Federal Reserve system. A skeptic would say that the knowledgeable congressional leaders consent to small adjustments in Fed powers and responsibilities just often enough to keep the activist reformers among them hard at their job of reminding Fed officials of their accountability to Congress.

As this suggests, congressional dealings with the Fed have levels of meaning quite different from their surface appearance. Many of the most important transactions occur away from the public eye. The most palpable transactions take place when Fed witnesses testify at open hearings of congressional committees. A closely related type of encounter takes the form of sparring in the press and on TV over the severity and causes of alleged macroeconomic problems and the workability of reputed "solutions." Such public transactions are theatrically disputatious. They involve a great deal of posing and game playing, some of which is carefully rehearsed. Harsh exchanges are sometimes initiated solely for symbolic effect, to assure some troubled Fed or party constituency that its plight (which in most cases will continue to be neglected) has not been forgotten.

Private meetings occur frequently at the staff level. When necessary, congressional and Fed staff members negotiate legislative compromises for their principals, but in most cases they meet merely to exchange analysis and information about matters of "mutual interest." These meetings are generally friendly ones, but reluctance, resistance, and hostility are not unknown. In top-level contacts, persuasion is applied and deals are sealed. Fed officials lobby key congressmen and senators much as other special interests do, except that they are severely limited in the kind of inducements they can offer. Still, with what they have to work with Fed officials try--just as private contractors and other federal agencies do--to build up a coterie of friendly congressmen and senators.

In open forums, congressional criticisms of Fed policy vary predictably over the business and electoral cycles. At the top of a boom when unemployment first begins to increase, legislators focus on the Fed's "inhumane" willingness to sacrifice unemployed workers to the cause of slowing inflation and on the tendency of monetary restraint to reduce the flow of credit to small businesses and participants in housing markets (builders, construction workers, and would-be homeowners). Although these sectors tend to lobby for low interest rates at all times, a guilty suspicion exists that the social costs of using tight money to fight inflation falls disproportionately on them, and on the automobile industry as well. Reinforcing this view is a perennial complaint that, no matter how tight money becomes, loans of "low social value" somehow get made. In times of recession when unemployment is high and inflation begins to relent, congressional critics tend to accuse Fed officials of aggravating and then aborting the previous boom instead of keeping the economy moving along on a smooth path of "sustainable growth." They demand that the Fed relent in its "pathological" concern with fighting inflation and assist troubled firms or cities and fight singlemindedly the now-pressing problem of unemployment. Especially in election years, congressmen tend to continue this pressure until long after the recovery has begun and strong inflationary pressure has built up once more. As the recovery solidifies and turns into an inflationary boom, the foreign exchange and gold value of the dollar weakens and monetary policy is discovered to have been too easy for too long. At this stage, Fed officials are ceremonially urged to tighten up monetary discipline. The intertwining cycles run on and on, but this brings the analysis full circle.[4]

Although at each point of the cycle Fed officials offer ritualistic defenses against each charge, they cannot fail to recognize that political benefits accrue to them from allowing incumbents to use the Fed as a scapegoat. Bearing such criticism patiently contributes to the stereotype of Fed decisions as a continuing series of policy errors, but Fed officials are compensated by the survival of the unique bureaucratic privileges the Fed enjoys.

Lesser Sources of External Pressure on the Fed Officials

Almost everyone has an opinion about the state of the national economy and what could be done to improve it. Some opinions are better informed and less self-serving than others, but all of them are affected by the owner's perspective as an interested member of various political and economic groups. Perspectives on many macroeconomic issues differ markedly between creditors and debtors, between workers and employers, between jobholders and the unemployed, between landlords and tenants, between a product's producers and its consumers, between bureaucrats and the public that pays their salaries, between Fed staff economists and their counterparts in academe, and between incumbent politicians and those seeking to unseat them. The best-articulated opinions come from the business, financial, and foreign central-banking communities and from various elements of the economics profession.

Central bankers in other countries. As the events of October 6, 1979, and Fed documents (e.g., Board of Governors of Federal Reserve System, 1974) testify, Fed officials maintain important points of regular contact with the international central-banking community. The detailed features of these connections adapt to the flow of political and economic events, with structural changes becoming clear only after the passage of time (Coombs 1976; Solomon 1977). The Board of Governors and New York Reserve Bank are linked formally to counterparts in Europe, Canada, and Japan through a network of daily telephone calls and through face-to-face meetings held under the aegis of various international organizations. The principal organizations are the Bank of International Settlements (which except in August, conducts monthly meetings in Basel), the International Monetary Fund (which holds a high-level meeting once a year in one or another major world capital), and the Organization for Economic Cooperation and Development (headquartered in Paris).

Since the tribe of central bankers is genetically encoded to resist inflation, they operate as an explicit part of the constituency against inflation. Just as any domestic interest group, the central-banking community seeks to impact politically on incumbent U.S. politicians. They do this primarily through their powers of persuasion and their power to improve or to worsen the dollar's standing on foreign exchange markets.

As the world's major reserve and vehicle currency, the dollar is inherently vulnerable to speculative attack. Fed officials labor long and hard to maintain an assured capacity to coordinate central-bank intervention against any large scale flight from dollars. For this reason, as the dollar has weakened secularly, the foreign central-banking community has gained more and more leverage over Fed officials and, through them (at least on occasions--such as October 6, 1979--when the dollar is highly vulnerable), over U.S. politicians as well.

Domestic business and financial community. Because monetary policy affects the income statements and balance sheets of every kind of business firm, managers and stockholders strive energetically to communicate their policy perspectives to Fed officials. Whereas most members of Congress openly confess their inability to make sense of macroeconomic developments, spokespersons for the domestic and international business and financial communities profess to understand economic events and policies perhaps too well. On the symbolic level, businessmen regard the Fed as a restraining force in federal policymaking and the chairman as a spokesperson for their view of the public interest. Many lobby simultaneously against inflation and big government and for measures to strengthen the dollar and to grant relief to their own troubled industries. They firmly expect the Fed to value these same goals. In return, they support the Fed in its struggles with Congress to maintain its "independence" and urge the retention of "proven" Fed leaders when an unsympathetic president has a chance to make a change.

This mutuality develops partly because Fed officials and executives are of the same social class. Top and middle managers at the Fed are alumni of the same schools, live in the same types of neighborhoods, and float in the same executive labor pool as those in the private economy. Between this pool and the Federal Reserve, regular interchange occurs in both directions. In particular, stints of employment at the Fed add gloss to a career as a securities dealer or commercial banker. For this and the following list of other reasons, dealers and bankers influence Fed policies more than any other industry groups.

1. <u>They serve as sources of information about the distribution of policy burdens that may help guide open-market policy in the short run.</u> First, banks and dealers bear the initial impact of open-market policy. Their impressions of how that policy is working and their observable reaction to Federal Reserve actions are important pieces of distributional information. Monitoring these responses provides feedback that can be used to guide short-run policy adjustments and to evaluate long-run issues concerning the appropriate institutional framework of monetary control.

Officials that manage the Fed's open-market account in New York describe the ease or difficulty with which banks and dealers can adjust to policy actions as the "tone" or "feel" of the money market. For years, this subjective tone or feel occupied an untoward and politically sensitive central place in the FOMC's assessment of whether or not its policies were realizing its intentions.

2. <u>Banker and dealer interpretations of events can contribute to the system's understanding of its own policies.</u> One element of Fed stabilization policy is to discover more about how its policy instruments actually work. To produce better effects, Fed officials need better theories of how its instruments link up with intermediate targets and goals. Although one may debate how well Fed officials learn from experience, evolutionary changes in FOMC strategy have developed as pragmatic adaptions to lessons taught by past mistakes.

From a research perspective, each business-cycle turning point begins a fresh scientific experiment from which to learn something new about how monetary policy works. Bankers' and dealers' self-interest makes them keen (if biased) observers of these experiments. By publicizing their developing forecasts and critical insights, bank and securities-industry analysts (such as Henry Kaufman) can put a great deal of pressure on the FOMC.

3. <u>Regulator-regulatee symbiosis.</u> To some extent, regulators tend to think of regulatees as customers or clients whose approval needs to be cultivated. Prior to the 1980 extension of Fed reserve requirements to nonmember banks, this tendency exemplified itself in Fed discussions of its membership problem. Membership in the system is wholly voluntary for state-chartered banks. Even though national banks are required to join the system, their ability to convert to a state charter made even their continued membership a quasivoluntary decision. This "exit option" gave member banks leverage they could use to soften Fed supervisory and regulatory policies. Persistent

failure to respond to widespread banker criticisms could embarrass Fed officials by reducing the very reach of the system. To keep at least a semblance of an exit option open, commercial banks lobbied successfully against instituting compulsory membership per se.

This clientele orientation explains a parallel tendency for regulatees and regulators to view themselves as victims of a common enemy: the unreasoned demands of well-intentioned but naive legislators. Far more often than not, U.S. banking firms and their federal regulators stand together for or against proposed reforms in banking regulation.

Such solidarity is useful to both parties. In backroom legislative showdowns, bankers have considerable political power. They pointedly contribute funds to the election campaigns of state, local, and national candidates, giving special attention to the needs of candidates who serve on banking committees. More subtly, some congressmen and senators have been induced to make investments in bank stock. Such holdings create an unavoidable conflict of interest, by linking industry profits with the legislators' personal financial welfare.

On the other hand, in dealing with issues that capture the public's imagination, bankers' grasping (if not villainous) image in American folklore puts them at a severe disadvantage. With the general public, the media, and most politicians easily confused about how financial markets and monetary policy work, it is hard for bankers to argue the economic merits of their own case. Their obvious self-interest makes observers skeptical of their motives and arguments.

A political fire storm develops whenever bankers make cumulative increases in their prime rate,[5] even when anticipated inflation is accelerating very quickly and prime rate increases merely defend banks' real incomes. In times of tight credit, borrowers whose loan requests are turned down tend to band together to blame refusals on bankers' greedy disregard for the national interest. The event of raising the rate on bank loans and reducing availability is taken as prima facie evidence of a banker conspiracy to exploit monopoly power. In the popular press, bankers' fiduciary responsibilities to stockholders and the risks and returns available on alternative assets are seen as pretexts for tightening credit terms rather than as causes.

Bankers' need for assistance in media politics and the Fed's inability to offer financial incentives impart a symbiotic character to their mutual relationships with Congress. When legislation is introduced to hold down bank interest rates or to channel bank loan funds toward or away from favored or disfavored classes of borrowers, sponsors inevitably seek to involve the Fed in administering the program.

When called to testify on the subject, Fed officials underscore the administrative difficulties and long-run economic problems that would almost certainly attend such control programs. Fed officials' willingness to help bankers resist gross regulatory incursions creates a political debt on which the Fed sometimes calls to resist attacks (often from the same regulatory activists) on its bureaucratic autonomy. On issues of Fed reform, bankers' solid lines of communication and influence into Congress and the administration can be used more openly. Bankers' less direct interest makes it easier for them to lay out the Fed's case. To argue convincingly that "good intentions" will produce bad effects, it is nice to possess hands that appear relatively clean.

4. <u>Points of formal contact</u>. Although of minor practical significance, business and financial interest have three points of formal contact with Fed

officials. These occur in the Reserve Bank Directorates, the Federal Advisory Council, and the Consumer Advisory Council.

Reserve Bank boards of directors consist of six persons (three bankers and three other persons actively engaged in commerce, agricultural, or industrial pursuits) elected by the member banks in that district (usually after considerable prior screening by Fed officials) and three "class C directors" appointed from the public at large by the Board of Governors in Washington. These regional boards meet regularly to "supervise and control" Reserve Bank operations. This gives a director many opportunities to exchange views on Fed policies with the Reserve Bank president, who represents the district in the FOMC.

Directors also elect each district's member of the Federal Advisory Council. This council meets at least four times a year with the Board of Governors in Washington, to confer about the economic outlook and any elements of Fed policies and operations its members wish to discuss. The council is specifically empowered to make oral and written representations on these matters and to collect information and issue policy recommendations as well. It (and a larger counterpart Consumer Advisory Council that focuses on consumer-related banking issues) are widely thought not to exercise important influence.

Economists. In policy debates, an economist's role depends both on the nature of the issues and on where he or she is employed. Labor and business economists function principally as advisors and advocates. After advising their clients of the advantages and disadvantages of current and prospective policies, they help their clients to state their side of an issue as clearly and as forcefully as they can. They may or may not have much role in deciding what stand their employer takes on a given issue. They may not even agree with the position they are called upon to represent.

On issues where political pressure or ideological bias predetermines their employer's stand, presidential, congressional, and Fed staff economists function in much the same way--the major difference being that they are expected to gather and process statistically a great many numbers to support their principals' case. Still, government economists feel a responsibility to their craft (nurtured by their academic colleagues) to represent their professional perceptions of the public interest to some degree as well.

On some issues and under some chairmen, Fed staff economists play a leading role in policy formation (Wallich Paper 8). As a matter of tradition, even on controversial issues Fed staff economists play an active and politically nonpartisan role in system decision making (Maisel 1973; Pierce 1979; Lombra and Moran 1980). Fed economists are jealous of this role and of their reputation for preparing for internal consumption an objective analysis of even the most controversial problems facing the Fed. When a chairman resists what staff members firmly believe to be the public interest (as, for example, when a chairman thinks of himself as the "best economist in the system"), the more adventurous among them may supply helpful arguments and data to dissident governors or district bank presidents. When board and FOMC decisions run seriously counter to their conception of the public interest, at least a few individual staff members will regard it as their right (if not their duty) to explain matters to their colleagues in the academic or banking communities. On rare occasions (and usually only after another job has been lined up), some have gone so far as to "leak" their independent analysis of a given issue to the press.

In most bureaucracies, habitual violation of administrative secrecy is tantamount to mortal sin. During the Burns era, a siege mentality, featuring a narrow view of proper staff lines of communication, took root at the Fed. But, though impaired, a more open, public-interest tradition survives among the professional staff. Many staff members remain eager to debate Fed policies informally with outside observers.

By fostering this tradition and engaging in such debates, academic economists pose an indirect influence on Fed decision making. Formally, the governors and their senior staff meet several times a year with a panel of distinguished academic consultants to discuss Fed policies and the national economic outlook. Informally, staff members exchange views with academic economists in professional assemblies and during looser contacts of a diverse sort. A particularly interesting forum is the Shadow Open Market Committee (SOMC) formed in 1973 by academic economists Karl Brunner and Allan Meltzer. The SOMC is a group of prominent monetarist economists who gather twice a year to evaluate Fed open market policy in the light of contemporaneous monetary policy recommendations of their own. Their goal is to produce academic criticism in which elements of "Monday morning quarterbacking" play a minimal role.

The media and Main Street. Because of what may be described as the "gross economic illiteracy" of the American journalistic establishment, the Fed and its political, business, and academic critics set the tone and dimensions of journalistic discussions of macroeconomic goal formation. For the most part, the press concentrates on what financial and governmental celebrities have to say. The space allocated to items of monetary policy news tends to be proportional to the public standing of the celebrity newsmaker and to bear little relation to the intellectual quality of the case developed. Journalists act as a channel for disseminating and explaining the positions of the contending parties rather than as agents for skeptically investigating and reconciling competing claims.

Contemporary economic journalism is almost completely an exercise initiated by--and focusing on--a media event or press release of some kind. This concentration on reportable events rather than on evidence and logical argument reinforces politicians' tendency to focus on the quick-to-develop effects of policies rather than on their long-run implications. To enhance their effect, distributors of official handouts often support their documents with individual background interviews. These are offered both to guard against embarrassing misunderstandings and to reward individual journalists for friendly reports in the past.

THE FED'S INTERNAL WORKINGS ARE ADAPTED TO ITS SCAPEGOAT ROLE

The Federal Reserve System is a political institution designed by politicians to serve politicians. Framers of the Federal Reserve Act deliberately dispersed jurisdiction over Fed actions among 12 regional (district) banks and a coordinating Board of Governors in Washington, D.C. Precise control over the Fed's various policy instruments is statutorily fractionated among 127 individuals: the nine-member boards of directors at each Reserve Bank, the twelve-regional bank presidents, and the seven governors. Intricate legislative formulas differentiate among bodies that may initiate policy actions and bodies that must review these initiatives. By these formulas, the chairman of the Federal Reserve Board appears as a governor only to be "first among equals" and not obviously more powerful than the president of the Federal Reserve Bank of New York, who also has a permanent place on the FOMC and whose salary (usually a reliable index of organizational authority) runs about twice that of the chairman.

Such contrived structural confusion must serve a political purpose. Government institutions evolve by natural selection, albeit without a genetic overlay. In bureaucracies, although change is often painfully slow, structural innovations occur principally as creative ways of relieving external and internal pressure on top management. Form follows function in the sense that organizational changes that serve continuing agency purposes survive while those that do not are eventually eliminated.

Elements of the Fed's bureaucratic structure are best seen as rational adaptations to ongoing and sporadic political pressures on the Fed's management team. As their principal functions, these adaptations serve to establish a cautious posture vis-a-vis incumbent politicians, to blur internal responsibility for controversial decisions, and to diffuse external blame for policy mistakes widely among system personnel.

Although the office of Federal Reserve Board chairman has come to occupy--in practice and over time--the predominant position in the hierarchy of the Fed, formally all Fed policy decisions are made jointly. Reinforced by the ambiguous formal dispersal of jurisdiction over the Fed's major policy instruments, the jointness makes it easier for Fed chairmen to let congressmen and senators blame them unfairly after the fact for whatever financial or macroeconomic developments their constituents dislike. The Fed's internal structure rolls the blame displaced from elected politicians into a thin film that spreads smoothly across a host of internal committees, councils, and boards.

The duality and ambiguity enshrined in the language of the Federal Reserve Act erect a uniquely confusing bureaucratic structure that makes the Fed appear both independent of short-run political influence and decentralized in its internal organization. The Employment Act of 1946, as amended by the Humphrey-Hawkins Act of 1978, enlarges the Fed's statutory mission while providing no specific guidance as to how Fed officials should execute politically sensitive trade-offs among conflicting goals. In accepting a series of impossible economic policy tasks, Fed officials set themselves up as shields for elected politicians, institutionally absorbing and distributing the blame for repeatedly choosing shortsighted policies. When the Fed fails to achieve its contradictory goals, how sharply these politicians and their successors attack (and whether or not they try to impose punitive damages) depends on the quality of Fed efforts to get along.

Being programmed to fail repeatedly at their policy assignments, Fed officials find it useful to express their intentions in a code that makes it hard for hindsighted critics to score cleanly. Fed officials consistently refuse congressional requests to identify their implicit short-term targets for inflation and unemployment. They won't even commit themselves as to which combination of the many values reported in their ranges of tolerable monetary aggregate growth rates they would most prefer. This obfuscation masks the Fed's openness to political influence and facilitates the formulation of quasicontradictory explanations both of the mechanics of their policies and of the rationale behind them. To protect the system from criticism and bureaucratic punishment, Fed chairmen are systematically led to employ their bully pulpit to miseducate the U.S. public about the macroeconomic consequences of alternative economic policies.

Why Does the Fed End Up Having a Procyclical Impact?

Despite the FOMC's progressive adoption since 1970 of countercyclical targets for monetary growth rates, U.S. monetary aggregates continue to move procyclically (Kaminow 1979a). In fact, in the presence of accelerating inflation, deposit-rate ceilings and the structure of bank reserve requirements and FDIC insurance premiums make observed movements in monetary aggregates understate the procyclical thrust of Fed monetary policy (Kane 1978). These regulations make the stock of money substitutes expand rapidly whenever interest rates rise.

In a now-classic piece, Brunner and Meltzer (1964b) show that the Fed's procyclical impact can be traced to "money-market myopia," i.e., to the Fed's obsessive concern with damping the size of short-run increases in nominal interest rates. What I wish to add to their analysis is the hypothesis that Federal Reserve officials aren't fooled into thinking that focusing on short-term interest rates is sound policy. I maintain that the political response system, driven by sectors that are ill-served by rising interest rates (including firms and individuals that consciously or unconsciously speculate against interest rate increases), makes it necessary for the Fed to follow nominal interest rates closely and to increase them less rapidly in the face of accelerating inflation than farsighted, independent policymaking would require (Kane 1980a). It is merely convenient internally and externally for Fed officials to rationalize their interest rate focus as they have.

Experience teaches that when the inflation rate varies over time, the policy effects of changes in the level of nominal interest rates becomes hard to interpret. Nominal interest rates treat loan repayments of future dollars as the equivalent in value of current dollars. But with inflation, future dollars have increasingly less purchasing power. To account for this, it is better to focus on real interest rates. These are nominal interest rates minus the anticipated rate of price inflation. For example, with 10 percent anticipated inflation, a 12 percent Treasury bond rate would pay only 2 percent real.

Although real and inflation-adjusted interest rates would measure the thrust of monetary policy more accurately, in the popular mind and in the popular press the Fed's chief task is to act as the arbiter of nominal interest rates. During times of monetary restraint, this adversary perception subjects the Fed to political pressures from sectors that are hurt by rising interest rates. These sectors' political action leads elected officials to resist increases in nominal interest rates.

Fed efforts to reassure its antiinflation constituency focus attention on observed changes in nominal interest rates and reinforce the mistaken popular notion that changes in the level of nominal interest rates are reliable indicators of the macroeconomic thrust of monetary policy. In times of gathering inflation, to placate the Fed's natural constituency in the business and financial communities, Fed officials tend to emphasize that they are fighting inflation with high and rising nominal rates of interest. However, unexpectedly accelerating inflation would push up nominal rates anyway. The issue is how hard the Congress and the administration are simultaneously pushing Fed officials to fight unemployment by expanding the money stock.[6]

Money market myopia is rooted in an underlying political and societal myopia with respect to the long-run and short-run consequences of economic policy. To end money market myopia, the fundamental need is not just to change Fed operating procedures and to disentangle the Federal Reserve System from excessively short-term political influences, but also to help the American public to understand who is responsible for bad monetary policy performance. Accountability for our economic policies, and for monetary policy in particular, should flow through to elected officials. What I find offensive in the current U.S. situation is that the Federal Reserve tries to convince people that it is independent. Every senator and congressman knows that the Fed responds to political pressures, as indeed every agency should under our system of government. Why should the Fed take the blame institutionally for mistakes of policy that are forced on it? The problem is not so much that the Federal Reserve fails to flatten out business cycles, but that it acts in ways that aggravate the cycle in economic activity. As a minimum, voters should insist that the Fed not be made to serve as a mechanism for injecting politically induced, procyclical influences that make business cycle swings wider.

Despite their efforts to do the best job humanly possible, given the political constraints they accept, Fed officials end up adopting policies that reinforce rather than offset cyclical influences. An important part of the difficulty is the emphasis Fed officials place on nourishing the false image of "the independence of the monetary authority within the structure of government" (Burns 1978, p. 381). In the 1970s, the desire to preserve this independence locked Fed officials into a "Caesar's wife" syndrome, in which they became more sensitive to political pressure than even a less "independent" central bank would need to be. They sought to avoid the controversy that would attend their making hard decisions about the sectoral distribution of income precisely in order to maintain a latent capacity to make such decisions at some unspecified future date. If Fed officials could accept openly either in their charter or in their hearts that they are fundamentally servants of the elected representatives of the people no different from any other bureaucrats, the electorate would have a fairer chance to punish inflationists and to reward farsighted economic statesmanship.

Because recurring sectoral and election-year pressures lead policymakers to adopt an inappropriately short-run horizon, somewhat longer terms of elected office might prove helpful. But frequent elections are not the major source of stop and go monetary policy. The ultimate sources are the exaggerated expectations that voters (as pressure groups) have as to what government can do for them economically and the lack of constraints on the ability of special interests to beg benefits from the federal government. In the final analysis, lawmakers register and balance the distribution and intensity of voter opinion. Inflation will not slow appreciably until the constituency against inflation becomes a political majority. For this to occur, interest groups must learn, as parts of a "constituency of the whole," that society's relying habitually and permanently on the government to improve on demand the lot of any individual sector produces in the long run not more wealth for some sectors but less for everybody.

FINANCIAL DISTORTIONS CAUSED BY RESCUE POLICY

Fed efforts to fight inflation often conflict with its responsibility to maintain confidence in the liquidity and integrity of private financial institutions. The politically ingrained tendency of sacrificing vital, long-run public interests to meet the short-run needs of vulnerable sectors emerges in the Fed's evolving policy of bailing out spectacularly distressed speculators.

Since 1965, when the U.S. rate of inflation first accelerated sharply, increased volatility of interest rates has made speculating on yield-curve movements a high stakes game. With each ratchet in the level of market interest rates, rather than letting losing speculators take their lumps, politicians have prevailed on the Fed to bail out a series of nationally publicized basket cases. Incumbents have done this because they are pressed by identifiable individuals to preserve their jobs and because they fear that losses incurred by lenders to notorious bankrupts may provoke a wave of failures, perhaps escalating into a full-scale financial panic. An interest group's vulnerability to rising interest rates goes a long way toward explaining the extent of its efforts to develop standby political influence. As in the trade off of future inflation for current improvements in the unemployment rate, the political benefits from saving troubled firms are immediate and perceptible, while the economic damage to incentives for risk bearing is more subtle and escalates slowly over time.

Over the last fifteen years, a national bail out policy for spectacularly unsuccessful speculators has developed in the United States. This policy has greatly altered the structure of financial incentives and financial institutions in this country. The distribution of anticipated, real, after tax rates of return (A-RATEs)' on alternative assets has been seriously distorted by these policies. Rewards to risk taking have been boosted by truncating realizable losses from large risky ventures, while ceilings on deposit interest rates have moved deposit institutions simultaneously to rely heavily on riskier nontraditional liabilities (Kane 1974b, and 1979b) and to attract deposit customers by barter (services and merchandise premiums) rather than by monetary rewards.

Politicians' propensity to effect industry rescues focused early on the deleterious effect of successive run ups in short-term interest rates on traditional thrift institutions (and for a while in 1974-1975 also on real estate investment trusts). From a financial point of view, savings institutions are just another set of interest rate speculators that borrow short to lend long. Efforts to protect their profit margins took the form of erecting an increasingly complex system of differential ceilings on deposit interest rates. The unintended, long-run consequences of these ceilings have been disastrous. The ceilings have blatantly loaded the costs of bailing out thrift institutions principally on the nation's smallest savers (i.e., households with less than a few thousand dollars in accumulated wealth), while driving more and more of the household savings that constitute thrift institutions' traditional business into unregulated and riskier channels (Kane 1974b). In hopes of earning a decent A-RATE, wealthier households have been led to substitute a mix of CDs and imperfectly diversified positions in the bond and stock markets for traditional deposit liabilities. Less wealthy households have diverted much of their savings from financial assets into physical assets, particularly housing (Kane 1980b). To increase the A-RATE on the acquisition of real assets, households have leveraged themselves heavily. Ironically, the conservative ideal of preserving accumulated wealth from inflation has driven U.S. consumers increasingly into debt, adding fuel to the nation's inflationary fires, generating a speculative housing boom that displaced business investment, and finally precipitating the March 1980 spread of controls into the area of consumer credit.

Implicitly, Fed officials have also committed themselves to bailing out large individual speculators on a needs basis. The record of specific Fed rescues runs from the Penn Central commercial paper default of 1970, through the 1974 rescue of Franklin National Bank's uninsured lenders, to the emergency loans granted separately to First Pennsylvania Bank and to the Hunt brothers in 1980. By placing an implicit government safety net under large scale, go-for-broke speculation, the Fed is encouraging aggressive bankers and wealthy individuals to pursue socially exorbitant risks. Moreover, the institutionalization of this rescue mentality shifts the costs of risk bearing from individuals to society and diverts managerial resources from competing in the marketplace for economic profits to competing in the political arena for government subsidies. The cumulative, long-run social costs of these policies do not enter any of the government's standard accounting systems, but they are becoming enormous.

SUMMARY STATEMENT

External pressure is to politics what arbitrage is to economics and finance. It is a force that explains how individuals and groups of individuals manage their affairs. As applied to the operations of the Fed, external pressure is a stress that helps Fed officials to decide what priorities to assign to conflicting macroeconomic goals.

In resolving any of the dilemmas of monetary policymaking, the key pressure points are Congress and the president. Every other group is subsidiary. To have a genuine effect, arguments for changing the operative set of monetary policy priorities must first impact politically on elected or appointed politicians.

Conceiving of the Fed as a willing scapegoat, whose task is to absorb guilt efficiently, explains very well the complicated, arbitrary looking structure of the Federal Reserve system. Most of the Fed's special bureaucratic features (its independence, its acceptance of contradictory policy assignments, and its murky lines of internal authority) and its incomplete policy strategies serve definite political ends. If one accepts the hypothesis that the Fed's main function is to serve as a policy scapegoat for elected officials, these apparent anomalies may be seen to be intelligible adaptations to recurring political pressures.

Fed officials desire good monetary policy performance even more than anyone else. With the best of intentions, they revise the structure of Fed decision making and modify procedures for conducting their operations and for monitoring their effects. However, as long as these changes have no perceptible impact on the relevant political forces, they can have precious little effect on the short-run compromises Fed leaders find it prudent to make among alternative policy goals.

On the other hand, the Depository Institution Deregulation and Monetary Control Act of 1980 does affect the balance of political forces. Because it removes an important source of external pressure on Fed officials, it is potentially far more important than the largely cosmetic past pledges of Fed allegiance to monetary aggregate targets. Extending Fed-administered reserve requirements to nonmember deposit institutions lessens the value of member banks' exit option and increases the Fed's ability to command their political support. This enhanced political muscle makes it politically feasible for the Fed to take more effective action against secular inflation in the 1980s than it has at any time during the last two decades.

NOTES

This paper brings together in a single source analysis developed earlier in Kane (1973, 1974a, 1974b, 1975, 1978, 1979a, 1979b, 1980a, 1980b). The author wishes to thank Benjamin Friedman, Benson Hart, George Kaufman, Allan Meltzer, Thomas Mayer, Anna Schwartz, and the editors of this volume for valuable comments on an earlier draft and to acknowledge the impact on his thinking of repeated conversations with Richard C. Aspinwall, Robert Eisenbeis, Raymond Lombra, and Edward J. McCarthy. All opinions expressed are those of the author and not those of the National Bureau of Economic Research.

1. Consider this statement about election year monetary policy by House Banking Committee Chairman Henry Reuss: "I think a build-up in the money supply during the Presidential election is a good thing. It would have helped in 1970, actually; but when you continued it into 1973 and made it worse, and continued in 1974, I and others did protest" (Committee Hearings, February 19, 1975, p.21).

2. The great spurt in the number of bills introduced in the last two Congresses (which approached 20,000 pieces of legislation in the 1979-80 Congress) suggests a larger strategy of shaking down PACs of all kinds.

3. In private correspondence, Stephen V. O. Clarke has emphasized that the importance to the Fed of maintaining friendly relations with the White House was appreciated even in the early 1920s. In a 1922 letter to Montagu Norman, Benjamin Strong wrote:

> In the face of a powerfully organized antogonism in Congress, the Federal Reserve System must, to a considerable extent, rely for its protection against political attack and interference upon the present administration...We cannot afford, practically or politically, to embark upon a course which ignores the policy of the administration, which would possibly antagonize the administration and place us in the position where we would be quite helpless to resist the repeated efforts which have been made in Congress to effect important and possibly vital modifications in the underlying principles of the Federal Reserve System (Clarke 1967, p.30).

4. It is instructive to compare the cyclical shifts in banking committee members evaluations of current monetary policies with contemporaneous Policy Statements put out semiannually by the nonpolitical Shadow Open Market Committee led by Karl Brunner and Allan Meltzer.

5. This is the lowest rate of interest that banks admit collecting on funds lent to their best business customers.

6. To put monetary policy effects in proper perspective in an era in which regulation-induced proliferation of deposit substitutes undermines the interpretability of alternative monetary aggregates, I wish the Fed would focus on changes in the level of real interest rates. To do this most effectively, the Fed would have to establish a regular survey of anticipated inflation rates over several different horizons. To let us track the net effects of monetary policy on lending, borrowing, and spending decisions, the survey should cover a stratified sample of financial and business decision makers. Reporting these data would force politicians and Fed officials to confront the issue of whether movements in anticipated rates of inflation are eroding or reinforcing the apparent impact of changing nominal rates of interest.

7. As a mnemonic, A-RATE stands for "adjusted rate" and is formed from the first letters of the appropriate adjustments, elongated for poetic effect by a silent E.

DISCUSSION • *Allan H. Meltzer*

Politics and Economics at the Federal Reserve

Ed Kane offers us some thoughtful propositions about the political economy of the Federal Reserve and a useful summary of his earlier work. As the title suggests, Kane emphasizes external pressures coming from Congress and the executive branch and outlines the way in which these pressures operate on the Fed. He finds that the Fed's political role is to act as a scapegoat, or buffer, between the public and the government. The Fed accepts the opprobrium for decisions over which it has limited influence in exchange for the appearance of independence.

Kane states three main, and several subsidiary, propositions. I will restate the propositions and comment on them. Then, I offer some suggestions for extensions.

One of Kane's main propositions is that the Federal Reserve is a political institution--part of the government. Related to this proposition, is Kane's view that Federal Reserve independence is greatly exaggerated. The truth, he believes, is that the Fed adjusts to accommodate political and economic developments.

Kane is generally correct, I believe. Policy without politics is hard to imagine. My main caveat is that institutional arrangements can matter more than Kane recognizes. Often an institutional facade is created, and then takes on a life of its own and restrains subsequent actions. The Bundesbank and the Swiss National Bank seem to have greater freedom than the Federal Reserve currently enjoys. Further, the Federal Reserve produced the deflations of the thirties and the early twenties with minimal interference from the rest of the government despite the presence of the secretary of the Treasury and the comptroller on the (then) Federal Reserve Board. I doubt that a repetition of these mistakes would leave the Fed in its present form.

Recent Federal Reserve chairmen--Burns and Miller--seemed eager to be part of the broader policy process. In an earlier day, Marriner Eccles was an active participant in the policy planning of the Roosevelt administration. Is independence irreversible, so that it cannot be reclaimed once it has been given up? Do the personalities who serve as chairmen have a more lasting influence on the institution than social scientists concede? Or, is there some more fundamental process at work? I am inclined to the latter view, but the influence of Burns on the inflation of the 1970s, of Eccles on the recession of 1937, or Riefler and Strong in the twenties, and similar examples from other countries leaves room for doubt.

Kane's second main proposition is that the Federal Reserve acts as a scapegoat bearing the brunt of criticism for fluctuations in prices, output, employment, and interest rates, particularly at election time. This is the price the Fed pays for its limited independence. In recent years, Congress has further restricted the Fed's authority, for example, by requiring more frequent reports but, Kane argues, Congress has stopped short of assuming control of Federal Reserve policy because it wants to retain a scapegoat.

How different is the Fed from other agencies? Congress does not control all government activities directly, and cannot get along without agents. When the public, or a significant segment of the public, desires a change in agency duties or actions, Congress responds. Recent changes ranging from environmental protection or health and safety to the deregulation of trucking and airline routes and fares suggests that Congress responds, albeit slowly, not just to the regulated and the regulators but to the public. The history of the Federal Trade Commission under Chairman Pertschuk shows one way in which the constraints operate.

Kane's view, that the Federal Reserve is an agent of the Congress or of Congress and the president, differs from a substantial part of the literature in political science and economics. There, much credence is given to the notion that bureaucrats determine policy and that agencies are relatively unconstrained. A good, formal statement of one version of this hypothesis is Niskanen (1971). Kane's view seems, to me, better founded.

A third proposition, loosely related to the preceding two, states that policymaking involves a choice about distribution of benefits. Kane notes the Federal Reserve's concentration on a narrow range of interest rates, their well-known money market myopia. This, he claims, benefits a vocal group of borrowers. Kane also notes the distributional effects of Regulation Q, the bail out of Franklin National Bank, First Pennsylvania Bank, and the Hunt brothers.

I believe that distribution is the feature that should receive most emphasis in discussions of the political process. One of the main ways in which political economy differs from economics is that voters choose to redistribute income. Decisions in the marketplace differ from decisions in the polling place because individuals in the polling place maximize subject to an additional constraint--the voting rule, which specifies who votes, how often a person votes, and what constitutes a majority. I will summarize the voting rule, following the well-established tradition of referring to the decisive voter.

It is easy to show that with universal suffrage and majority rule, the median voter is the decisive voter. What matters, qualitatively, is not whether the decisive voter is precisely at the median but whether he is to the right or left of the mean income recipient. If the decisive voter earns less income than the mean income recipient, he has an incentive to tax and redistribute.

This argument, developed more fully in Meltzer and Richard (1981), suggests that Kane has not pushed his hypothesis far enough. The Fed is an agent of Congress, but Congress and the president are agents of the public. The president, Congress, and the Fed do not respond instantly to changes in the decisive voter's demands, but they respond fast enough to retain the positions they occupy.

This line of argument suggests that the Fed produces inflation not accidentally but as a response to the decisive voter's desire for higher taxes on current incomes and on assets. Unanticipated inflation is a tax on wealth, but inflation is also a means of lifting people into higher tax brackets. Should we treat as accidental the fact that social security benefits, welfare payments, and Congressmen's expenses are indexed, but the tax system is not indexed? I do not think so. More importantly, the failure to index tax rates and willingness to index redistribution suggests an intent to increase the share of income redistributed.

Much of the Fed's action is purposeful. If we trace the gains and losses back to the voters, we may learn what the purposes are. To avoid misunderstanding, let me add that I do not think of Federal Reserve governors as careful calculators who count the votes in Congress and the electorate. Institutional arrangements, and high costs of monitoring, give agents some discretion. Also, many of the governors of the Federal Reserve do not have much substantive knowledge of the monetary process. A number of papers, most recently Lombra and Moran (1980), present a consistent view of Fed governors as not very well informed about the consequences of their actions. None of this should suggest that they are oblivious or ignorant of the political pressures for income redistribution.

Kane ends on a hopeful note. He believes that the recent legislative changes strengthen the Fed's control of its constituents and, thus, increase the Fed's ability to reduce secular inflation. I am not convinced. If we get lower inflation in the eighties, I believe it will be a result of voter choice--as in Britain--and not a result of more power at the Fed.

GENERAL DISCUSSION

GENERAL DISCUSSION

Most participants strongly endorsed Kane's analytical approach and conclusions regarding the operations of the Federal Reserve. There was considerable discussion of the process of political structuring, which shapes the environment within which policy decisions are formulated and implemented. It was noted that several studies suggest that the structural characteristics governing the formal, as well as informal, relationships between a nation's central bank and other sectors of the economy, including the government itself, appear to be systematically related to a country's economic performance. However, if the structure is endogenous, as is suggested in Black's paper, then legislating a set of structural (central bank-government-private sector) relationships conducive to achieving an improved economic performance is not straightforward.

Extending the discussion, some suggested that the move to flexible exchange rates in 1973 was in fact a structural change that altered the relationship between political pressures emanating from the Congress and the president and the reactions of the Federal Reserve. This theme, developed in the paper by Willett and Mullen, makes explicit the role of the market vis-a-vis the state (emphasized in Strange's paper) and the constraints imposed by making policy in an increasingly open economy.

Finally, several participants reflected on the relationship between

Kane's thesis and the fact that we seldom observe major changes in policy. Some also suggested that the Fed's willingness to be a "legitimizer" adds a type of stability to the political process while imparting instability to the economy. Since this is not what scholars have in mind when they speak of long-run, steady-state equilibrium, it is important to identify and analyze the conditions that lead the electorate to act and thus bring about modifications in existing arrangements. Obviously, ongoing developments in England represent the type of economic and political dynamics that deserve careful study.

PAPER 8 • *Henry C. Wallich*

Policy Research, Policy Advice, and Policymaking

THE NATURE OF THE PROBLEM
   Academic economists frequently express a desire to have a greater impact on economic policy and seem disappointed with what they appear to be achieving from the outside. Policymakers frequently are heard to say that they would like to get more help from academic economists, and seem disappointed with what they do get. Does economics promise more than it can deliver? Or, is the flow of communication less than adequate?
   There are indications that suggest that it is lack of communication more than lack of communicable substance that is at fault. For one thing, the role of economists in government is by no means diminishing. In my agency, the Federal Reserve Board, from which most of the empirical observations in this paper will be drawn, the role of economists is rising. Increasingly the members of the Division of Research and Statistics, some 150 economists, and those of the Division of International Finance, some 50 economists, are drawn into policy advice and operations. The same applies to many of the Federal Reserve Banks, with their economists. Also, at the higher levels both of the Federal Reserve and of government agencies generally, the role of economists as policymakers seems to have grown, although the condition prevailing in 1975, when four cabinet members, the chairman of the Federal Reserve Board, and the chairman of the Council of Economic Advisers were professors of economics, and only the secretary of state was a professor of political science, may have represented a temporary high point. The public's estimate of the ability of economists to predict and cope with economic situations and problems may have diminished in the light of recent performance. Nevertheless, popular interest in and newspaper coverage of economic matters still seems to be on the upgrade. The quality of economic reporting in the press has improved visibly.
   One possible reason for believing that economic inputs into policymaking are relatively neglected is that the allocation of time for such inputs is never a high priority, for either side. Academics may be reluctant to cut a class in order to participate in an important government meeting. Policymakers are always under pressure to put the urgent ahead of the important. Thus, they underinvest in economic advice, both from academics and from their own staffs.

SUBJECT MATTER AND OCCASION FOR ECONOMIC INPUT INTO POLICYMAKING
   Economic policy, and especially monetary policy, is strongly influenced, of course, by economic theory. Classical monetary thinking, Keynesianism,

and of late monetarism, have all shaped it, in different degrees at different times. There can be no question as to the importance of these basic inputs into policymaking.

Such basic inputs, naturally, differ widely for different policymakers. The government, in general, is not run by economists, but by a congeries of politicians, businessmen, lawyers, and diverse technicians, including economists. In the process of running the country, they become "men of affairs," if that had not been their role previously. On the Federal Reserve Board, the proportion of economists, of course, is higher than in most other government agencies. But it is never so high either on the Board or on the Federal Open Market Committee (FOMC) that its economist members would feel at ease becoming at all technical. No blackboard, to my recollection, has ever disfigured the splendid proportions of the Board Room at Constitution Avenue and 20th Street.

The contingent of lawyers and businessmen have a practitioner's background in various aspects of microeconomics--taxes, accounting, prices and wages, credit, and many others. With such a background, it is probably quite possible to vote intelligently on the FOMC, and to follow the discussion, although some grounding in macro concepts would be helpful. But as soon as macro concepts make their appearance we are apt to encounter the influence of Keynes's defunct scribbler, in the form of verities absorbed in college and not updated since. In Keynes's day, these verities dealt with the balanced budget, the gold standard, the public debt. Of today's men of affairs, very few, of course, predate the Keynesian revolution. Big deficits, high public debt, easy money, indifference toward inflation, and intolerance of unemployment are their intellectual heritage. Monetarist indoctrination from college days is still rare.

Today's men of affairs, moreover, are not dependent on intellectual baggage carried forward from the past. They absorb contemporary economics from their company economists, from organizations like the Committee for Economic Development and the Business Council, from congressional hearings and, of course, from the press, which today competently popularizes much academic output.

There is, of course, a wide range of doctrines that the man of affairs could assimilate and to which he could refer in speech and action with equal intellectual respectability. These doctrines aspire to objectivity and their originators would be chagrined to find them interpreted as manifestations of value judgments. It is precisely on grounds of value judgment, however, that the man of affairs is likely to pick his economics. He will identify Keynesianism with expansionism and monetarism with price stability. Even worse, he may come to identify Keynesians with left-of-center and monetarists and rational-expectations proponents with right-of-center politics, however wrong such identifications may be.

These broad perceptions do not necessarily apply in every individual policy decision. One may place great value on price stability and still favor a particular cut in the discount rate. More technical economics, especially in the area of forecasting, then assumes considerable importance. Every policymaker necessarily acts on expectations. The question is only whether these expectations are formed by casual observation or by systematic forecasting techniques.

The forecast presented by the Federal Reserve Board's staff, based on the Board's version of the MIT-Penn-Social Science Research Council (MPS) model modified by judgmental contributions, plays a powerful role in FOMC deliberations. Given the wide range of outside forecasts, the weight given to the Board staff forecast may well be excessive despite its good performance in comparison with other major macro models. Nothing is more sobering, in evaluating any single forecast, than inspection of an array of twenty or thirty widely differing forecasts of GNP, prices, and unemployment. The Reserve Bank presidents on the FOMC do have the advantage of being exposed to their own Bank's forecasts in addition to the Board forecast. Board members have a harder time forming their own quantitative projections.

As far as forecasts are concerned, the views of the major producers in any event are readily obtainable. How much weight any forecast should carry is debatable, particularly in the light of recent performance in the profession generally. Theory tells us that the more uncertain the forecast, the smaller should be the policy reaction. The growing acceptance of the belief that we do not know enough to fine tune the economy properly relates not only to our uncertainty about the effect of policy actions, but also to the uncertainty of the forecasts upon which these actions might be based.

All this adds up to saying that the input of economics on policymaking is pervasive and strong but that nevertheless it rarely points unambiguously toward any particular policy, either in the long run or the short. This gives great importance to the ability to form individual opinions, which, in turn, leads back to the need for continuing contact with the sources of ideas, a very important part of which has been past academic contributions. But the question that the policymaker today addresses to the theorist is, "What have you done for me lately?" The answer is that, after monetarist concepts and recommendations made their recent mark, not much that is new and powerful has been added to the theoretical base of monetary policymaking.

One reason for the present low level of economic inputs into monetary policymaking, therefore, may be that not many good new ideas have been around lately. This weakness on the side of academic supply can be seen in the diminishing credibility of many Keynesian propositions, the observed limitations of monetarists' ideas as they are increasingly implemented by policy, and the remoteness from reality of rational expectations theory. For new ideas in labor market analysis, which seem to have flowed well, there seems to have been inadequate demand on the government side. The needs of government for economic inputs, moreover, also come in waves. For instance, the Bank Holding Company Act amendments of 1970 created a strong demand for microanalysis of banking markets, but as it happened a large body of research in this field had been completed during the 1960s off which the bank regulators still are living. This clearly has implications for the kind and volume of economics produced within the Federal Reserve.

TRENDS IN RESEARCH ACTIVITY AT THE FEDERAL RESERVE

In recent years, there appears to have been a trend toward a reduction in research activity by the economic staff on the Federal Reserve, both at the Board and at the Reserve Banks. A greater proportion of research has become more directly policy oriented. The reason is not a reduction in the number of professional economists employed, which has remained roughly constant. It is, rather, that the Federal Reserve Board particularly has been handed a wider range of functions, and has had to meet increasing demands on existing functions. These have been met in good part by shifting staff time from research to policy advice and related operations. The Bank Holding Company legislation of 1970 brought a massive surge in activity in this area, through a bunching of applications for acquisitions. As these activities diminished, the International Banking Act, the Financial

Institutions Regulatory Act, and the Monetary Control Act began to make heavy demands on staff time.

Congressional staffs have increased massively, and this has led to an increase in congressional demands for reports, congressional correspondence, and the writing of testimony for appearances of board members before congressional committees. Economic developments such as floating exchange rates, the development of the Euromarkets, a larger number of international meetings, and growing interagency activities have added to the need for staff work in the international area.

All this has meant that at each staff level there is less time for the kind of research work that used to be done some years ago. Economists are drawn into policy work at an earlier stage in their careers than in the past. Some people like this and some do not. Many staff members have to work harder to maintain the academic credentials that economists hired from among the more talented graduates of the higher-ranked universities are normally concerned with.

I believe that similar cycles have occurred at other government agencies from time to time. Historically, this has sometimes been followed by a concentrated effort to restore a research component to staff activity by creating some new kind of research department. The circumstances that produce such a concentrated effort, which usually is a severe burden on the budget, may differ--a new agency head or evidence of inability to cope with agency problems or to keep up in bureaucratic infighting with other departments, are among the observable sources of impulse.

Occasional relief from budgetary squeezes plays a role. Different agencies may find themselves in different stages of this cycle. The same no doubt is true of different academic disciplines. It is my impression that in economics generally now the cycle is at a stage where demand for and expenditures on economists are relatively low. That is bound to affect the attractiveness of jobs in the economics area within government and the distribution of research between academia and government.

ACADEMIC VERSUS GOVERNMENTAL RESEARCH

The declining trend of research activity in certain government agencies raises not only the question of career attractiveness for those with a basic orientation toward academia, but the more fundamental one of the distribution of research between academia and government. The standard allocation is, of course, that basic research belongs in the universities and the research institutions and applied research in government, without anything like a rigid line being drawn. Obviously there is room for each in both places. The reduction in government research means that it would be desirable to have a larger volume of policy-oriented research done in universities. This shift seems to accord with the shift in priorities observable in National Science Foundation grants, which increasingly seem to stress applied research. But if, as seems to be the case, the foundations also are leaning increasingly toward "results," while the universities' own resources are clearly stretched more tightly than they used to be, the burden of cutbacks will fall heavily on basic research.

Concern about this trend has been expressed many times. Outside of economics the risks and costs of running out of basic research may well be much larger than in our field. Nevertheless, the trend is very worrisome. If it cannot be reversed or stopped, a possible antidote would be more rapid circulation of academics through government. The United States is fortunate in having a high degree of mobility between academia and government. If the trend is toward an imbalance to the disadvantage of basic research, a possible compensatory factor would be a more rapid return of academics from temporary government employment. The decline in the relative attractiveness of government employment for academics with a bent for basic research would encourage this, at the cost, of course, of frustrating the government's effort to attract more academic talent for operating and policy work. In any event, this "circulation" through government would remain a feasible prospect for only a small part of the economics profession and would be open to an even lesser degree to noneconomist academics such as political scientists.

DEMAND FOR AND SUPPLY OF ECONOMIC EXPERTISE

To make academic economists' inputs into government effective, both sides must understand their market. Academics as well as policymakers must understand clearly what academics have to offer. On both the supply and the demand side, considerable improvement in understanding is possible.

In the course of my own work, I have been on both sides of this market from time to time. Let me first lay out my past perplexities as an academic supplier to the government of what goes under the name of economic expertise, and then describe my present frustrations as a user of such expertise.

The academic adviser to government may see himself in the role of a Max Weber type, value-free expert, or as somebody pleading a point of view--in either case, he will have positions that he wants to defend and others that he wants to oppose. The difference between the Weber style and the other kind of expert is only that the first makes his/her case on technical grounds, while the second weights his technical argument with his values. In either case, the outside expert faces the problem of making the advice effective.

Advice is effective to the extent that it is accepted and to the extent that it affects the view and action of the advisee. The two effects normally are inverse to each other. The advice most likely to be accepted is to the effect that the advisee is doing the right thing and should go on doing it. By adopting the same point of view as the advisee, however, the adviser changes nothing. The farther the adviser's viewpoint moves away from that of the advisee, the greater the potential change that he can effect, but also the less the probability of acceptance. Effectiveness of advice can be defined as the distance from the advisee's point of view weighted by the probability of the advice being accepted. So measured, effectiveness is zero both when the adviser's point of view coincides with that of the advisee and when it differs so much as to have zero chance of acceptance. Somewhere in between there is a maximum. With some simple, but not implausible, assumptions about these relationships, we can conclude that the maximum occurs midway between the advisee's view and a totally unacceptable view.

Different advisers, of course, may have different utility functions and not all may derive maximum utility from maximum effectiveness of their advice. The yes-man will value acceptance of his advice above everything and therefore place his bets close to the viewpoint of the advisee. The congenital oppositionist will prefer to insist on his own point of view even if he is sure to be totally rejected. Aiming at the point of maximum effectiveness does mean, usually, shading one's own preferences and adapting them somewhat to those of the advisee, but it is this advisory strategy that has the biggest impact.

Choosing among these alternative strategies of advice requires, of course, that the adviser know the lay of the land pretty well, both as regards the policy issues involved and the political and other options facing the advisee. In practice, I have found very often that my advisee knew a great deal more about the issue than I did and that the things I did know were not necessarily applicable to his situation. Nevertheless, economics often supplies a good guide to policy. Competition, optimal allocation of resources, and the marginal principle can all be helpful in disentangling conflicting pros and cons. Economics does have something to offer even if its precepts do not always prevail.

The adviser is aided by the fact that the policymaker, in the last analysis, must boil down and simplify his problem in order to be able to act. At an early stage of the decision process, governmental deliberations typically dissolve into a welter of often unrelated details. But the human mind, and particularly that of a person with many decisions to make, cannot cope with all these complexities. In one way or another, some aspects of the problem are eliminated as unessential and others get elevated to a key role. On these the final decision then is made. If the adviser is able to focus on them, he has a good chance of being effective.

THE REALITIES OF POLICYMAKING

How does this process look from the point of view of the policymaker? Temperaments vary, from the self-confident operator who feels sure he is right, to the worrier who needs to rehash all options before he can make up his mind. It is the worrier who thus becomes an attractive advisee for the academic. The worrier will feel this need particularly if at one time he was an academic and is aware of the fact that he has not kept up with his discipline. Given the pace and workload of government, that eventuality becomes a virtual certainty within a very few years in office. Few things are more unnerving than the feeling that one has overlooked something that one ought to be aware of. By the same token, it is reassuring to touch base with an adviser who is on the frontier of thought, or simply to make sure that the expert does not know much more than the policymaker does. When one has touched all the bases in that way, one has become a kind of negative expert knowing that there is nothing new to know.

The policymaker's principal problems, with respect to receiving advice, are when, on what topics, and from whom to solicit it. The first two--when and on what--require some knowledge of the state of the art and the state of professional opinion on rapidly evolving situations. A congenital worrier can spend too much time learning that there is nobody who can help him. It is about the third--from whom--that he faces his most difficult decisions. Given the tested principle that there is no conceivable view that is not backed by some economist, the policymaker can proceed, of course, on the principle of "pick your policy, pick your adviser." Or he can pick a gaggle of advisers of predictably different views, which also makes him appear impartial and, having received conflicting advice, proceed to do what he wanted to do in the first place.

Assuming, however, that he is seriously interested in receiving advice, he needs to know a good bit about his advisers. In a world of value-free economists, he would be able to ignore ideology. In practice that would be naive. He, therefore, needs to know ideological biases very well if he wants to adjust for these and arrive at value free views. Likewise, he needs to understand the variance around the views which he is presented. Academic economists do not have to live with their mistakes and some of them, therefore, are prone to understate the degree of uncertainty attached to their analyses. For instance, in 1975 the Federal Reserve was advised by leading experts on both sides of the fence dividing monetarists and Keynesians that it should sharply raise the stock of money to make room for recovery. This was clearly high risk advice that in the light of subsequent history does not stand up well.

Much of the time, of course, advice from the two sides of the Keynesian-monetarist fence is conflicting (ignoring the fact that there are a few right-of-center Keynesians whose policies may come closer to those of the monetarists). In that case, the Board and the FOMC will be reasonably safe in the middle. If they duck in between, the two sides will be shooting at each other. Even more important than such balance between academic partisans is similar balance in the Congress. Monetarism has enjoyed a considerable vogue among politicians, understandably, since it tends to absolve them from responsibility for the consequences of poor fiscal policy. In that view, most of the responsibility rests with the Federal Reserve, which therefore tends to acquire some Keynesian leanings in self-defense. The difficulties of obtaining good advice may be particularly severe for the Federal Reserve because these difficulties reflect differences of view about macroeconomics. Differences on the relative evils of inflation and unemployment are wide, and they tend to be associated with different evaluations of the cost of dealing with either. It would be a rare adviser who believes that inflation could be dealt with at moderate costs but prefers expansion, or who sees the costs as enormous but nevertheless proposes to incur them.

At a micro level, as I have noted before, differences tend to become more technical. It becomes easier here to give "value free" advice. In some cases, nevertheless, there are more clearly defined constituencies on micro issues than there are on the broad issue of inflation versus unemployment. Frequently, in these cases, the division is between business and the consumer, or business and labor. Where clear partisanship is involved, the policymaker knows whose advice he is getting and will treat it, not as technical advice, but as ex parte.

In surveying the professional scene, one becomes aware of one peculiar anomaly. Relations between the Federal Reserve and the academic profession are not as cordial as one would wish them to be. The Federal Reserve is the professional home of large numbers of economists. It is probably the most "economically oriented" of all the Washington agencies. Its subject matter is the bread and butter of economic thinkers and practitioners. Nevertheless, economists have conspicuously abstained from treating the Federal Reserve as "their" agency in the way in which, one might say, large parts of the profession have identified with the fiscal policy process.

That the Federal Reserve should be a political whipping boy is understandable, perhaps even desirable. When the Fed acts as a buffer between the politicians and the printing press, it is fulfilling its proper function. This is not, however, its ideal role with respect to the economics profession.

The credibility of monetary policy with the public is damaged by comment from the profession implying that monetary policy is a simple matter that, with a little intelligence and goodwill, could reliably produce predictable results. Nor is the credibility of monetary policy strengthened by comment about a small number of individuals pursuing objectives that are not in the national interest and ignoring the needs of the people. The public is very much in need of information about the Federal Reserve, as frequent press comments on the mysteries of the Fed make clear. This purpose would be better served, however, by a less consistently negative attitude on the part of the profession.

THE POLICYMAKER AND HIS STAFF

The economic enlightenment that I have discussed so far comes to the policymaker from the academic consultant. In fact, the policymaker ordinarily receives a much larger input from the agency's staff, especially at the Federal Reserve. Much more can be said about the Federal Reserve's outstanding staff than can be encompassed in this paper. Because of its intellectual strength, it is by far the most important source of economic input into the Federal Reserve Board and FOMC. Even though its research function has somewhat declined of late, it reflects an enormous concentration of strength in the areas it covers, greatly exceeding the density of coverage of major topics that is possible even in the economics departments of leading universities. It is precisely, however, because the staff is not an economics department of a university that its intellectual influence on the advisees is of a peculiar nature.

The staff, being hierarchically organized, at the Board and within each Reserve Bank, tends to speak with one voice. Sometimes, of course, when there are significant differences among its members, such differences surface. Differences within the staff may show through in the various decision options that the staff usually produces on particular issues. In other circumstances, such options may represent structured alternatives not indicative of any particular positions within the staff. Board members can, of course, deal with individual staff members and learn their views, but, by the nature of its organization, the staff tends to resist systematic attempts by Board Members to infiltrate its decision processes. It may reasonably fear that such intrusion may affect the staff's objectivity or that it might interfere with the achievement of a single voice. It would also take away from work for the Board as a whole.

These bureaucratic imperatives carry over into the relations of the staff with academics, with whom most professional staff members can reasonably view themselves on an intellectual level. Given the great resources that the staff is able to throw into any particular investigation, the staff can reasonably assume that it has done, or at least could readily do, as much research on any point of major interest as single academics.

The staff, moreover, on many issues is guided by prior decisions of the Board. This is particularly true in the regulatory area. Once the Board has made up its mind, the staff's function becomes one of implementing and defending.

Much of the staff's work is in the public domain, through the large volume of reports, testimony, material prepared for open meetings, and individual publications by staff members. The staff, therefore, is by no means sheltered against the public gaze and against criticism from their professional peers. An important exception is material prepared for immediate monetary policy purposes. Confidentiality of this material helps to preserve the objectivity of the staff. It minimizes the staff's risk aversion that would no doubt limit some of its expressions of judgment if every word could be brought into the political arena. For the Board, confidentiality of staff forecasts and related advice is essential to maintain confidence in the professional quality of the staff's judgment. If staff reports and recommendations were to become a basis for political debate, policymakers' desires to obtain such materials would diminish and the risks to the Federal Reserve of publicly aired conflicts would increase.

For the outsider, all this may add up to an impression of inflexibility on the part of the staff. But that may well be an excessively subjective reaction. Not every bright new idea can be sure of the full welcome that its outside originator may feel it deserves. Moreover, continuing involvement with the ideas of outside academics on the part of staff members can make life as difficult for senior staff as involvement with individual Board members. That there is no suppression of thought is evidenced by the Board's liberal publications policy for staff members, including points of view that differ from those of the Board, so long as the Board's operations are not seriously prejudiced.

Bureaucratic tendencies toward a single staff position also reflect the operating responsibilities of the staff. The greater the responsibility to get things done and get them done on time, the less the opportunity to dawdle by the wayside in purely intellectual pursuits. All the greater is the need for deliberate efforts to seek academic inputs and to cultivate activities that will help staff members maintain the professional quality that they and the organization prize.

GROUP DYNAMICS

On major policy issues involving values such as the choice between more and less expansive policies, the general tendency of any well-known academic is usually predictable. It is easy for the policymaker, therefore, to elicit the kind of advice that he would like to receive. Groups of academics, nevertheless, seem to manifest subtle shifts in attitude that supply more objective policy guidance. This remains true even though the individual members of such a group may vary from time to time, so long as they are replaced by others of broadly similar outlook. The position of members of such a group relative to each other tends to remain the same. But the spectrum shifts, and that is highly significant for a policy point of view. It is the nearest thing to unanimity that a diversified but continuous group is likely to achieve.

Few things are harder for an academic than to confess error. The annals of advice that academic advisers have given to policymakers contain interesting exhibits of policies that fortunately were not adopted. But it is not customary to bring up old mistakes. The policy mistakes of academics are buried in dead storage files in some warehouse. The mistakes of policymakers are republished monthly in the nation's major economic time series.

In addition to gradual shifts in the direction of policy advice, there appear to be shifts in value judgments, such as the relative cost of inflation and unemployment. There also seem to be trends affecting the spectrum of opinion regarding the variables that should be empirical rather than ideological, such as the level of full-employment unemployment or its latter-day counterpart, the nonaccelerating inflation rate of unemployment. These shifts are part of the group dynamics observable in panels or rotating groups of policy advisers.

There are several groups in Washington to which these observations apply. They deal with macro policies as well as with other policy oriented topics at the Federal Reserve, at the Treasury, at Brookings, at the American Enterprise Institute, and no doubt among many others. These groups involve a considerable overlap of individuals and have a considerable degree of continuity of particular individuals. They all serve as a means of communication between academics and government officials, although they differ considerably in the emphasis on, respectively, new research and communication to government officials of existing research.

In some cases, a substantial effort is made at rotation of academic participants, with particular emphasis on bringing in younger members of the profession, who, very often, have new ideas to communicate. Experience nevertheless has shown that this communication is difficult. Lacking government experience, younger academics new in these groups do not find it easy to hit the right level of abstraction and relevance, and to put their ideas across clearly to people who surely are listening with a great deal of interest. The old hands have a considerable advantage in this respect and their ideas come across more clearly and easily. As a result, a frequency distribution of participants in such meetings reads pretty much like a standard list of the leading members of the economic departments of the leading universities, making allowance for the absence of distinguished names that are known not to have strong policy interests.

This situation is symptomatic of a much broader problem of communication between academics and government. There is willingness and interest on both sides. But the information, the knowledge of new ideas, does not flow smoothly. Broader, more frequent, and more intensive contacts are needed if government is to absorb all that academia has to offer. It seems in keeping with the trend of the times to suggest that this impediment will not be removed by some macro approach, but only by a multitude of painstaking micro efforts.

DISCUSSION • *William G. Dewald*

Federal Reserve Governor Henry C. Wallich has most impressive academic and public policy credentials. He's an obvious choice to appraise how well what academic economists know gets transmitted to public policymakers and vice versa. I commend the organizers of this conference for persuading him to present his views on the subject.

Governor Wallich's paper represents an attempt to generalize from his experience with policy adviser-policymaker relationships over several decades. It contains many sensitive reflections on both his interpretation of the quality of the information that is transmitted and the strategy of delivering it. Governor Wallich has been extremely conscientious in seeking the best advice he could get, both outside and inside the Federal Reserve. He works at it in a careful, evenhanded, and generally commendable way. But underlying his evenhandedness is the viewpoint, probably shared by other policymakers, that there is such a wide and varying spectrum of professional opinion on any economic policy issue that policymakers cannot rely on a consensus of professional opinion, but rather must generally sample the various opinions of advisers and then make up their own minds. Governor Wallich's paper repeatedly makes the point that the policymaker is safest avoiding the extremes of professional opinion and hewing to intermediate positions. He says that policymakers generally are their own best advisers inasmuch as they select the array of people who will advise them from outside or within their institutions and then split the difference of opinion among them. Though I've come halfway from Columbus to Washington to comment on Governor Wallich's paper, I don't know what to make of his idea.

Governor Wallich is clearly correct in interpreting policy advice as often being a mixture of values and knowledge. Yet insofar as knowledge is concerned, splitting the difference of opinion between alternatives makes no sense. There are no "democratic" principles in science. Our knowledge of how the economy works or, for that matter, how the government works is not predicated on majority opinion. Majorities may be important in wielding political power, and specifically in the politics of making monetary policy. But knowledge is something else. It depends on verifiable theories and on estimated probabilities of events. There is no knowledge in the "equal ignorance principle" that if there are conflicting alternatives, the best position is balanced between them.

To quote Governor Wallich, "Much of the time, of course, advice from the two sides of the Keynesian-monetarist fence is conflicting. In that case, the Federal Reserve will be reasonably safe in the middle. If it ducks in between, the two sides will be shooting at each other." Not necessarily! They could be shooting at a sitting governor, which is why I'm here.

The idea that disagreements among economists about the way the economy works give policymakers a free hand to proceed on the basis of their own common sense is all right if policymakers are not thereby absolved from responsibility. They alone authorize policy actions. This involves politics insofar as the effects of those actions help some people and hurt others. But it involves science insofar as the effects are predictable.

That the Federal Reserve as an institution agrees to a degree that knowledge matters is evidenced by its having hired literally hundreds of economists fresh from Ph.D. programs or candidacies for tenure in the nation's leading universities. These very talented economists estimate, simulate, and evaluate models of aggregate demand and supply, and macro and micro models of money, banking, securities, and foreign exchange markets. The research papers that emanate from some of these studies are published in professional journals such as the Journal of Money, Credit, and Banking. In the years I've edited it, Federal Reserve authors have represented 8 percent of the total. Some studies are published by the Federal Reserve. Others are not released for publication for a variety of reasons including confidentiality. (I wish some the JMCB published had been confidential. Where did Governor Wallich get the idea that only policymakers live with their mistakes?)

Despite the Federal Reserve's financial commitment to staff an economic research organization, it's not clear from Governor Wallich's remarks that the problem of getting scientific information to policymakers is much different from inside than from outside the Federal Reserve. He tells us why this happens. The policymakers are often so busy making policy that they don't have time to invest in information. Furthermore, they bring pressures to bear on the research staff, at least those high enough in the organization to bring the views of the staff to the attention of the Board, to become involved in the internecine work of policymaking.

Before I became editor of the JMCB, I published in it a review of Lee Bach's Making Monetary and Fiscal Policy (1971). He viewed the ignorance of policymakers about money and the monetary mechanism as the greatest hurdle to effective policymaking. To know that you don't know is the beginning of wisdom. Bach pleaded for more research to aid policymakers. But given my suspicious nature, I wondered whether policymakers might not serve their own interests by remaining ignorant, for with added knowledge would go added responsibility and perhaps added accountability.

Governor Wallich is perceptive in identifying that the strongest advocates of monetary growth control are not in the Federal Reserve but in Congress. In terms of specialization this is strange since at least the details of monetary policy are out of the bailiwick of its power and understanding. The Federal Reserve, which has essential monetary not budgetary powers, according to Governor Wallich "tends to acquire some Keynesian leanings in self-defense."[1] I don't think the politicians in Congress or the Board of Governors should get off so easily in ducking responsibility.

How can economic policy responsibility be made effective? One way is for policymakers to learn more about how instruments of policy within their influence affect the economy. In reviewing Bach's book I suggested that the Federal Reserve as one example is in a position to experiment to learn about market behavior in response to policy actions and that it ought to do it. What would happen to interest rates if the Federal Reserve rigidly controlled the growth of some monetary aggregate for a year? Even more radical, what would happen if it forced slower monetary growth from business cycle trough to peak than otherwise--the reverse of its historical pattern.

In my judgment, the real test of policy advice and policymaking is in devising a systematic monetary policy in advance and being judged by its effectiveness.[2] Perhaps in a democracy such a plan should be legislated rather than left to the discretion of the Federal Reserve. This would put a burden on the Federal Reserve to apply its knowledge about money and the monetary mechanism and incentives to improve its understanding. It would put a burden on Congress and the president to sign off on such a policy prescription and permit the Federal Reserve to implement the policy just as the administration does in the case of fiscal policy.

To apply this suggestion to the current policy debate, the evidence is overwhelming that there is no reason why, with the elimination of lagged required reserve accounting, the Federal Reserve could not maintain the growth in M1 at a target rate month after month. Further, the evidence is that a policy of monetary growth about equal to average real growth would keep inflation stable compared with the wild ups and downs of the past twenty years. I think that's a message that politicians would hear and respond to favorably. However, I suspect that for the Federal Reserve to make such a prediction risks something more than being wrong. It risks imposing some responsibility on Congress which, as Governor Wallich correctly discerns, is already dodging responsibility for inflation and the business cycle by blaming the Federal Reserve (see Kane, Paper 7). But legislating fixed monetary growth is a logical extension of the increased accountability that has been placed on the Federal Reserve by Congress in recent years. Going one step further, perhaps in addition to constitutional limits on government spending, constitutional limits on monetary growth need to be enacted. Peel's Act in 1844, which limited the fiat money issue of the Bank of England, wasn't a great success, but perhaps it's an idea whose time has come. Constitutional rules aren't needed where power and responsibility are wielded effectively. But twenty years of poor monetary policy, despite an enormous amount of information produced by the economics profession about the workings of the economy, is evidence that something other than a lack of knowledge is the culprit.

Governor Wallich and his colleagues in the Federal Reserve are highly intelligent and articulate politicians with the power and presumably the understanding, but without incentives, to do what has to be done to avoid inflation. As a consequence, despite good intentions, they have contributed to slow real growth, to the amplitude of the business cycle, and to a lot of other bad results because of their abiding emphasis on the short-run rather than long-run consequences of their actions.

For example, consider monetary growth control within narrow limits. Would it increase variability in interest rates or the equivalent, and if so, would that increased variability make real growth more variable? That's a fundamental question. The Federal Reserve has behaved as if the answer to this question is yes. But the evidential basis is not at all clear. Ray Lombra, who organized this conference and was a member of the Board of Governors' staff, recently appraised the state of knowledge about this issue, naturally in the JMCB (Lombra and Struble 1979), and concluded more or less that we don't know how much more short-term interest rate volatility would accompany steady monetary growth. They argued that even if there were strong tendencies toward increased volatility, private market makers in such circumstances have been found to exert a strong stabilizing influence. But a lot of uncertainty exists. Govenor Wallich doesn't know what would happen if the Federal Reserve controlled monetary growth within narrow bounds for an extended period. But it is important to know. So, Governor Wallich, how about getting off the fence and back in the field? To make the October 1979 revolution in FOMC operating procedures complete, why not fire the manager of the Federal Open Market Account, and hire the likes of Ray Lombra to hold M1 growth to an annual rate of 4 percent for fifty-two weeks? That's more than the FOMC has been delivering the past 6 months so the policy would be stimulative for the current recession and it would be antiinflationary for the longer run. If the new manager missed his target growth in any month, he should be instructed to add or subtract the missing money to next month's target and if average monetary growth in any twelve-month period were more than half a percentage point from target growth, you should fire the new manager and hire a statistician who understands the Central Limit Theorem.

NOTES

1. Marriner Eccles, Chairman of the Board of Governors of the Federal Reserve System in the 1930s and 1940s, was an outspoken champion of fiscal policy. Chairman Arthur Burns was a protagonist of wage-price controls in the 1970s to lower inflationary expectations, and Governor Wallich is one of the principal advocates of TIP--a program of differential tax rates to induce a cut in inflation.

2. In one of his specific examples of wrong-minded academic advice to the Federal Reserve, Governor Wallich says, "For instance, in 1975 the Federal Reserve was advised by leading experts on both sides of the fence dividing monetarists and Keynesians that it should sharply raise the stock of money to make room for recovery. This was clearly high risk advice that in the light of subsequent history does not stand up well."

I offer as a counterexample some advice I gave in 1975 and I was not alone. "In these initial hearings under Concurrent Resolution 133, it is safe to recommend that the Federal Reserve aim at no more than a 6 percent annual growth rate in M1 through mid-1975. If optimists are correct and the economy is bottoming out now, the rate might well be slowed a little in the second half of the year, but only after sure signs of recovery are recognized. If the economy continues to slide, 6 percent growth should be targeted again and again until the economy turns up. For the long run, however, a 6 percent M1 growth would likely be inflationary. Evidence to that effect led the Joint Economic Committee in 1968 to recommend that the Federal Reserve limit variation in M1 annual growth rates between 2 and 6 percent. Since real output has grown at about 4 percent annual average, this would be a rough long-term target for noninflationary monetary expansion, though changes in the structure of markets might require a somewhat higher or lower rate.

Any other relatively constant rate of growth in any monetary aggregate would likely improve economic performance. The historic problem with monetary policy is that monetary growth rates have been above average during expansions and below average at cyclical peaks and the early stages of recession, just the opposite of what would be reasonable. Four percent M1 growth would have protected the economy from the worst excesses of monetary policy historically, not only in the 1930s but in every post-World War II expansion and contraction. Secularly 4 percent monetary growth would have yielded more expansionary monetary policy actions in the slow-growth 1950s and early 1960s and less expansionary policies over the inflationary decade just past than actually experienced." (First Meeting on the Conduct of Monetary Policy Hearings before the Committee on Banking, Housing, and Urban Affairs, U.S. Senate, 1st Session, April 29 and 30, and May 1, 1975, pp. 47-48.)

COMMENT • *Allan H. Meltzer*

Wallich Fails a Reading Test

Academic economists, acting as economists, can summarize for policymakers what they know that is applicable to a problem and can indicate the consequences they expect to follow from proposed actions. A policymaker may not follow the advice of his academic adviser immediately, or perhaps ever, for many relevant or irrelevant reasons. A belief that the advice cannot be implemented politically, or a belief that the Congress would not approve of the change, requires a judgment by the policymaker.

Comparative advantage has a role in advising as in other exchanges. Henry Wallich ignores that role and, I believe, makes the additional mistake of equating maximum effectiveness with advice that "has the biggest impact" on current decisions.

I am much less certain. Lasting effects of economics on economic policy often require a prior change in policymakers. Major changes in policy frequently follow, rather than lead, informed public opinion. The acceptance of Keynesian policy, the floating of the dollar, the recent acceptance of medium-term economic strategies and rejection of fine tuning in Britain, and the adoption of the volunteer army are examples of major changes that were influenced by economists whose views were not well received, and that were often scorned as unacceptable or infeasible by "responsible" officials. Keynes's well-known comment on the role of the ideas of economists and philosophers makes this point. Keynes was careful to add that the effect usually comes slowly, after there is turnover in the group choosing policies.

Although I disagree with the main point of Wallich's advice to economists and regard as absurd his suggestion that the Federal Reserve is "safe in the middle" between conflicting recommendations, I will confine the rest of my comment to his misstatement about "monetarist" recommendations in 1975.

Wallich is incorrect when he writes, "[I]n 1975 the Federal Reserve was advised by leading experts on both sides of the fence dividing monetarists and Keynesians that it should sharply raise the stock of money to make room for recovery." The "monetarists" on the Shadow Open Market Committee urged the Federal Reserve to keep the growth rate of money in 1975 at the same <u>average</u> rate that had been held for the year ending June 1974. Excerpts from the committee's statement of March 7, 1975, including <u>all</u> references to the growth of money follow (emphasis added):

> The economy is now in the second quarter of a sharp business contraction following three quarters of mild contraction. The worsening is due to a sharp deceleration in the growth of the money supply from June 1974 to February 1975. . . .
>
> From December 1971 to June 1973, the money supply grew at an annual rate of 8.4 per cent. This excessive growth rate reinforced inflationary tendencies already at work. The 3-percentage point reduction in the monetary growth rate to 5.5 per cent in the year ending June 1974 was sufficient to produce the mild recession we experienced in the first three quarters of 1974, and to achieve a gradual dampening of inflation. Had the Federal Reserve maintained the 5.5 per cent growth rate in the year ending March 1975, the prospects of restoring full employment and gradually reducing inflation would be much better. The current recession would be much less severe. Instead, the <u>Federal Reserve cut the growth rate of the money supply a further 4 percentage points from June 1974 to February 1975 to only 1.5 per cent</u>. It is this drastic decline in monetary growth that accounts for the steep rise in the unemployment rate, the steep decline in industrial production, and the current generally depressed economy.
>
> There can be no doubt that the Federal Reserve did not intend to be so restrictive. The published record of the Federal Open Market Committee tells us so. The question is why the Federal Reserve has failed so miserably to achieve the target ranges of monetary growth it has set month after month since June 1974. . . .
>
> The fact is that it is the Federal Reserve's own operating procedures that account for the recent anomalously low rate of monetary growth. The Federal Reserve sets a money supply target growth rate but its

actual operations are carried out with a Federal Funds target rate. If the Federal Funds rate is pushed by market forces to a lower level than the target, the trading desk at the New York Federal Reserve Bank resists the pressure by reducing the growth of reserves below the level that would achieve the target money supply growth rate. . . .

We renew the recommendation made at our September meeting that the growth rate of money be held at 5½ per cent. However, growth should not start at that rate from the current low level. We recommend that the money stock be brought to the level it would have reached in March 1975, if our policy had been followed. A one-time increase in money--currency and demand deposits--to $290 billion should be announced and provided by April 15. This increase would put the money growth rate back on the path leading the economy toward full employment at lower rates of inflation than in recent years. . . .

If there is a large increase in the growth rate of money--to an 8 or 10 per cent permanent average in calendar 1975--the Federal Reserve will finance $10 to $12 billion of the federal government deficit. This will amount to an addition of approximately $25--$30 billion to the money supply. Inflation will accelerate in 1976 and 1977. If the growth rate of money is kept in the 5.5 per cent range we recommend, more of the federal government deficit must be financed by domestic saving and by foreigners. This method of financing the federal government deficit reduces the amount of real saving that becomes available to finance housing and private capital formation. . . .

The policy of crowding out private capital and housing the finance budget deficits is not attractive, but it is the least unattractive of the choices before us. In recommending this alternative, we emphasize that interest rates may and probably will rise to clear the market for credit. . . .

As noted, the large budget deficit to be financed in 1975 is likely to push interest rates up later in the year and attract foreign lenders, so the Federal Reserve's current concern will diminish. The Federal Reserve in this situation must guard against two dangers: (1) implementing monetary growth rates at 8 or 10 per cent, or higher, to finance the budget; (2) delaying or retarding the rise in interest rates and thereby increasing the growth rate of money above the target level it sets. If it does not guard against these dangers the Federal Reserve will, as in the past, be the main engine of inflation.

We will not achieve full employment, stable growth, and stable prices unless we stop shifting from excessive to inadequate to excessive monetary growth rates. By continuing stop and go policies, we guarantee that past experience will continue. High inflation will be followed by recession and recession by higher inflation.

If the Federal Reserve begins now to put money growth back on the path of a 5.5 per cent rate, we can look forward to recovery by the last quarter of 1975 and a sustained dampening of inflation. Long-term stability will require ultimately reducing the monetary growth rate to a lower level consistent with the growth of real output.

The reader can judge for himself. Money growth in 1975 was 4.6 per cent. The economy recovered, and the measured rate of inflation declined.

GENERAL DISCUSSION

GENERAL DISCUSSION

Several participants commented on Wallich's remarks suggesting policymakers were safe sitting on the analytical and empirical fence separating monetarists and Keynesians. Robert Aliber wondered whether or not the fence was n-diminsional, reflecting analytical, philosophical, and sociological disagreements between Democrats and Republicans, Congress and the president, large and small banks, banks and other financial institutions, and U.S. leaders and foreign leaders. Viewing policymaking in this way, some argued such conflicts act as an overlapping series of constraints that in effect "fence in" policymakers.

There was also a discussion of the so-called monetary rule--that is, a fixed (low) rate of growth in the money stock--advocated by Dewald in his comment on Wallich's paper (and by Willett and Mullen in their paper). Some observed that if the rule is such an appealing alternative to current policy then one must wonder why it has been so difficult to sell to the public and to policymakers such as Wallich. Recognizing that there can be "long and variable" lags in the diffusion of knowledge, several participants noted in response that although fiscal and monetary policymakers in the United States (as well as around the world) talk about monetary growth, there is still considerable confusion about the economic and financial implications of high versus low money growth as compared to high versus low nominal rates of interest. The tendency to equate "high" nominal interest rates with a "tight" monetary policy and "low" rates with an "easy" policy is still widespread.

Perhaps only a significant enhancing of the public's economic literacy or a severe deterioration in economic performance will create an environment conducive to a thorough reexamination of traditional policy approaches in comparison to various domestic and international policy "rules" and other more flexible alternatives.

IV

Financial Integration and Monetary Control

INTRODUCTION

The foregoing papers have focused on various aspects of the relationship between political economy and domestic and international monetary relations. A recurring general theme has been that the effects of increased political, economic, and financial integration--for example, the effects of an ever-expanding set of linkages among worldwide markets for commodities and financial assets--have been either ignored or, at best, imperfectly understood by both researchers and policymakers. The two papers and discussions in this final part of the conference proceedings develop this general theme by focusing analytically on some specific problems that "openness" and integration create in the financial area.

In the 1960s much ink was spilled in examining the merits and drawbacks of fixed as compared to flexible exchange rates. The debate became somewhat academic in 1973 when the last vestiges of the fixed rate system came apart and exchange rates began to respond more flexibly to changes in the underlying forces determining the international supply and demand for a particular currency in relation to other world currencies.

Over the last eight years casual observation would confirm that few nations have been willing to allow exchange rates to fluctuate freely in response to shifts in market supply and demand. Rather, countries have adopted a "managed" approach to the exchange rate, whereby they will intervene (i.e., buy or sell foreign currencies) so as to limit the depreciation or appreciation of the domestic currency in the short run. In the first paper, Dale Henderson, a senior adviser to the Board of Governors of the Federal Reserve system, examines the appropriate role of intervention policy in an open economy. The paper proceeds on the premise that disturbances that could produce economic instability can in principle be alleviated by an appropriate intervention policy. Using results derived from a carefully developed macroeconomic model, Henderson argues that in general it is not optimal for monetary authorities to rigidly fix the exchange rate or to allow it to fluctuate freely. More specifically, he shows that the optimal policy--a managed float--depends in a particular way on what information the authorities have concerning the structure of the economy and the sources of disturbances to which it is subjected. In a broader context, which includes the policies and reactions of foreign governments to intervention by the home government, Henderson identifies situations where countries have a mutual interest in intervening to reduce exchange rate variability and situations where they do not. Such findings advance our understanding of the possibility for conflict and coordination in international monetary relations.

The first discussant, Herbert Grubel, Professor of Economics at Simon Fraser University, compliments Henderson on the technical virtuosity of his paper and confirms the importance of the issues Henderson examines. Grubel's major reservation concerns the implications of Henderson's analysis for policy makers. While it is useful to show that a managed float can be optimal, the core of the problem, Grubel argues, is whether or not policymakers possess enough knowledge about the structure of the economy and the sources of disturbances to successfully implement such a policy:

> In the real world do, or can, economists ever know the causes of observed disturbances, together with the probability distribution of their being reversed or aggravated or offset by other disturbances? To be sure, guesses on these matters can be made, just as private market participants make them in their pursuit of profits. But in my view there is little evidence that policymakers can do better on average than private market participants, where actions are known to reduce the instabilities associated with random disturbances. It is exactly these reasons, together with the uncertainty over lags, which have led to the monetarist prescription for aggregates constant policies and letting relative prices, the interest and exchange rates, do the adjusting to disturbances.

The implication, of course, is that intervening could exacerbate rather than alleviate economic instabilities.

John Bilson of the University of Chicago is the second discussant of Henderson's paper. He finds himself uncomfortable with the conclusions of the paper, and traces this discontent to the "realism" of the paper's assumptions. For one thing, Henderson assumes that the foreign central bank pursues a monetary policy that holds its interest rate constant. As a result, claims Bilson, it is difficult to tell if the change in the exchange rate is due to the intervention or to the assumed reaction of the foreign central bank. On an even more fundamental level, Bilson is skeptical, for both theoretical and empirical reasons, of Henderson's assumption that wealth holders are risk averse, thus rendering domestic and foreign securities imperfect substitutes, as is required if sterilized intervention is to have any impact. Bilson concludes by suggesting that a preferable alternative to the type of interventionist policy supported by Henderson's analysis is one in which monetary policy aims at a stable and predictable monetary growth rate and intervention policy is guided by a publicly announced set of exchange rate forecasts.

The final paper in the volume, by Donald Hester, professor of economics at the University of Wisconsin, examines how increasing financial integration and an increase in the pace of financial innovation have affected the interpretation and control of the monetary aggregates. The aggregates have played an increasingly important role in the formulation and implementation of monetary policy in the United States and in other major countries such as England, Germany, and Switzerland. Such countries now set target growth rates for various monetary aggregates and manipulate their various policy instruments (e.g. open market operations, reserve requirements, and the discount rate) in pursuit of such "intermediate" targets. The presumption is that hitting these targets is conducive to achieving the central banks' final or ultimate inflation, unemployment, and growth targets. (An obvious corollary is that missing the intermediate targets, that is, the monetary aggregate targets, is likely to be associated with missing the final

Introduction

targets.)

Hester focuses in particular on various developments in the Eurodollar market and the domestic money market in the United States. In assessing the growing quantitative significance of these developments, he concludes:

> Innovations and regulatory changes are likely to have weakened the Federal Reserve's ability to control monetary aggregates and economic activity. Evidence about this suggestion is necessarily indirect. The problem is rather like watching generally reliable dials in the control room of a nuclear power plant; one cannot legally or physically observe the reactor directly. Nevertheless, available evidence strongly suggests that vibrations within the monetary reactor are becoming more severe; more control rods and a different reactor design may be necessary if a melt down is to be avoided.

Hester's basic message is that monetary analysis both inside and outside the Federal Reserve reflects a preoccupation with empiricism that is not well suited to coping with emerging institutional developments and innovations. The resulting failure to monitor and understand these developments, and the lack of appreciation for how the dynamic structure of the financial system and world economy have been changing, may help to explain, in his view, the deterioration in monetary control over the past decade.

The first discussant of Hester's paper, Anthony Santomero, professor of finance at the University of Pennsylvania, believes Hester's concerns about a weakening in monetary control are either unwarranted or unsubstantiated. Santomero analyzes the monetary control issue and the effects of various innovations in a general equilibrim framework, which yields the type of "multiplier model" of the money supply process long associated with the seminal work of Karl Brunner and Allan Meltzer. The control issue then turns on whether the innovations and international developments Hester emphasizes reduce the predictability of the multiplier or alter the meaning (i.e., analytical significance) of the various monetary aggregates.

The final discussant of Hester's paper, Thomas Simpson, a senior adviser to the Board of Governors of the Federal Reserve System, is like Santomero not persuaded on the basis of the evidence presented that the problems Hester identifies are quantitatively significant. Simpson does agree, however, with Hester's argument that various regulations such as those prohibiting payment of explicit interest on demand deposits, limiting interest payments on time and savings deposits, and imposing reserve requirements, have induced innovations and institutional changes. Such changes can be linked, according to Simpson, to the unusual behavior of velocity in recent years--a development that has in all likelihood complicated the formulation and execution of monetary policy. Looking ahead, Simpson suggests that various provisions of the Depository Institutions Deregulation and Monetary Control Act of 1980, will over time reduce some of the distortions and resulting incentive to innovate, thus alleviating to some extent the problems addressed by Hester.

PAPER 9 • *Dale W. Henderson*

The Role of Intervention Policy in Open Economy Financial Policy: A Macroeconomic Perspective

INTRODUCTION

This paper is an analysis of the extent to which alternative financial stabilization policies can be expected to dampen the effects of shocks to macroeconomic equilibrium in open economies. According to the view emphasized here intervention policy is an integral part of open economy financial policy.[1] Intervention operations have effects on macroeconomic variables that can be distinguished from those of monetary operations. Thus the specification of a financial policy regime is not complete until both the intervention and monetary policies of the financial authorities have been described. An alternative view according to which intervention operations have no effects so that the specification of a financial policy regime requires only a description of monetary policy is also discussed briefly.

Intervention operations and monetary operations are defined in the second section. Whether one open economy financial policy regime is better than another usually depends on the source of disturbances to the economy. In the third section this observation is illustrated by a comparison of the effects of different kinds of transitory disturbances to macroeconomic equilibrium in a single open economy under two alternative pure financial policy regimes. Under an "aggregates constant policy" the money supply is kept unchanged and there is no intervention, so the interest rate and the exchange rate vary when disturbances are experienced. Under a "rates constant policy" monetary operations and intervention operations are employed to keep the interest rate and the exchange rate fixed. The tool of analysis is a discrete time stochastic model in which agents have rational expectations. It is shown that for disturbances to the market for the home good, an aggregates constant policy results in less variation in output, and that for disturbances to financial markets, a rates constant policy results in less variation in output. The fourth section is a demonstration that similar results can be obtained when the economy is subject to one kind of permanent disturbance as well as transitory disturbances.

To establish that the nature of the truly optimal financial policy regime depends on the kind of information available to the authorities about the structure of the economy and about the disturbances to which it is subjected is the purpose of the fifth section. There it is argued that under general conditions it is not optimal for the authorities in a single open economy facing transitory disturbances either to rigidly fix the exchange rate or to allow it to fluctuate freely.

In the sixth section attention is turned to the interactions in a two-country world economy that must be considered when choosing financial

policies. It is emphasized that the overall stance of intervention policy is
the result of the intervention policies of both countries. Then it is shown
that with two kinds of transitory disturbances the two countries would agree
on what the overall stance of intervention policy should be while with
another kind of transitory disturbance a policy conflict would arise. The
tool of analysis is an extended version of the model of the third section.
Since intervention policy conflicts can arise, the financial authorities in
different countries have an interest in keeping track of the overall stance
of intervention policy. Some of the practical difficulties encountered by
financial authorities (and private agents) in trying to accomplish this task
are discussed in the seventh section. The eighth section contains some
concluding remarks about the usefulness of the analysis and some suggestions
for extending it.

DEFINITIONS OF MONETARY OPERATIONS AND INTERVENTION OPERATIONS

The stylized balance sheet of the financial authorities in a
hypothetical country, which is called the home country, has the home money
supply as a liability and both home and foreign currency securities as
assets. The home authorities' holdings of foreign currency securities are
their only foreign exchange reserves. At a given exchange rate, changes in
the three balance sheet items must sum to zero, so values for only two of the
three items can be chosen independently. The authorities conduct financial
policy using two kinds of financial market operations: (1) monetary
operations, exchanges of home money for home securities with private agents;
and (2) intervention operations, exchanges of home currency securities for
foreign currency securities with private agents.[2] Monetary operations alter
the mix of money and securities denominated in the same currency available to
the public. Intervention operations alter the supplies of securities
denominated in different currencies available to the public. The
intervention operation just described is often referred to as "sterilized
intervention" because it leaves both the home money supply and the foreign
money supply unchanged. Although the home money supply may change during the
course of the operation, it is returned again to its original value before
the operation is complete. Suppose the authorities sell a foreign currency
security to private agents. They obtain foreign money but sell it back to
private agents for home money, temporarily reducing the home money supply.
However, they then purchase a home currency security from private agents,
thus restoring the home money supply to its original value, in order to
complete the intervention operation.

There is a widely held view that if the authorities sell a foreign
currency security, say, in order to prevent the home currency from
depreciating, they reduce the home money supply either unintentionally or
intentionally. From the description of an intervention operation above it is
easy to see that the home money supply could be lower if the authorities did
not complete the intervention operation by purchasing a home currency
security. Failure to complete the intervention operation would never be
unintentional. That is, if the authorities allow the home money supply to
remain lower, it is because, given the other choices available to them, they
want it to be lower. The view taken in this paper is that if the authorities
sell a foreign currency security and do not purchase a home currency security
with the home money they acquire, their action can most clearly be understood
as being a combination of the intervention operations and monetary operations
defined above. If this view is adopted, only monetary operations change the

home money supply.

It is interesting to define intervention operations in the way suggested above and to study the effects of such operations only if home currency and foreign currency securities are imperfect substitutes in the portfolios of private agents. If these two types of securities were perfect substitutes, an intervention operation as defined above would have no effect on the economy. Financial policy would consist only of monetary operations, and whether the money supply were changed through exchanges for home currency securities or for foreign currency securities would be of no consequence. There is no general agreement among economists that home currency securities and foreign currency securities are imperfect enough substitutes that intervention operations of a reasonable size have any important or lasting effect on the economy. Empirical evidence is accumulating on this issue, but it remains unresolved.[3] The analysis of this paper proceeds under the assumption that home and foreign currency securites are imperfect enough substitutes for one another to warrant inclusion of intervention policy in the study of open economy financial policy.

TRANSITORY DISTURBANCES AND FINANCIAL POLICY RESPONSES IN A SINGLE OPEN ECONOMY

In this section a discrete time stochastic model of a single open economy in which agents have rational expectations is employed to analyze the effects of some transitory disturbances to macroeconomic equilibrium under two pure financial policy regimes, an aggregates constant policy and a rates constant policy.[4] In the first subsection the model is described, and the results are presented and explained.[5] In the second subsection the results are derived more formally.

The Model and the Results

In the real sector of the economy attention is focused on aggregate demand for and aggregate supply of the single home good that is different from the single foreign good. Home output (Y) must be equal to aggregate demand for the home good:

$$Y = y_0 + y_1(Y + \overset{*}{Y}) - y_2 r - y_3 \overset{*}{r} + y_4(e + \overset{*}{p} - p) + y_5 e - y_6 p + \alpha + \beta \qquad (9.1)$$

Here, and in what follows, all coefficients except intercept terms are positive. Aggregate demand depends negatively on the expected real interest rates on home currency securities (r) and on foreign currency securities ($\overset{*}{r}$) and on the (logarithm of the) home currency price of the home good (p). Increases in expected real interest rates raise home and foreign saving. Increases in the price of the home good reduce home and foreign real wealth measured in terms of the home good, and, therefore raise home and foreign saving.[6] Aggregate demand depends positively on home output, on foreign output ($\overset{*}{Y}$), on the (logarithm of the) exchange rate (e) defined as the home currency price of foreign currency, and on the (logarithm of the) relative price of the foreign good ($e + \overset{*}{p} - p$), where $\overset{*}{p}$ is the (logarithm of the) foreign currency price of the foreign good. Increases in home and foreign output raise income at home and abroad and, therefore, spending on the home good.[7] It is assumed that the marginal propensities to consume the home good

(y_1), to consume the foreign good ($\overset{*}{y}_1$), and to save ($s = 1 - y_1 - \overset{*}{y}_1$) are the same in both countries and are all positive.[8] A depreciation of the home currency (rise in e) increases the home currency value of foreign currency assets, thereby raising home and foreign wealth and reducing home and foreign saving. An increase in the relative price of the foreign good shifts home and foreign spending toward the home good and raises foreign income measured in terms of the home good, thereby stimulating foreign spending on the home good. Aggregate demand depends positively on two disturbance terms, α and β. Positive values of α (β) represent increases in the demand for the home good at the expense of saving (demand for the foreign good). These stochastic variables and those introduced below to represent other disturbances are assumed to have zero means and to be mutually and serially uncorrelated.

The expected real interest rate on home currency securities is equal to the nominal interest rate on these securities (i) minus the expected rate of increase in the average home currency price of the consumption bundle of both home country and foreign country residents:

$$r = i - \bar{h}(\bar{p} - p) - (1 - \bar{h})(\bar{e} - e + \bar{\overset{*}{p}} - \overset{*}{p}) \tag{9.2}$$

$\bar{h}$ is the proportion of spending that would be allocated to the home good by residents of both countries if all of the disturbance terms were zero, and $\bar{p}$, $\bar{e}$, and $\bar{\overset{*}{p}}$ are the constant values of p, e, and $\overset{*}{p}$ expected in any period to prevail in the next period. The expected real interest rate on foreign currency securities is equal to the nominal interest rate on these securities ($\overset{*}{i}$) plus the expected rate of depreciation of the home currency minus the expected rate of increase in the average home currency price of the world consumption bundle:

$$\overset{*}{r} = \overset{*}{i} + \bar{e} - e - \bar{h}(\bar{p} - p) - (1 - \bar{h})(\bar{e} - e + \bar{\overset{*}{p}} - \overset{*}{p}) \tag{9.3}$$

Home output must also be equal to aggregate supply, which depends negatively on the (logarithm of the) real wage measured in terms of the domestic good:

$$Y = x_0 - x_1(w - p) \tag{9.4}$$

The (logarithm of the) real wage is equal to the (logarithm of the) nominal wage in the home country (w) minus the (logarithm of the) price of the home good. It is assumed that private agents want to supply each period a given amount of labor which does not change when the real wage changes. If this amount of labor is fully utilized in production, the full employment level of output (Y_f) results. However, since the process of wage negotiation is costly, private agents enter into a labor contract each period before other markets meet. They agree to supply whatever amount of labor firms want at the prevailing real wage. Thus, output can exceed its full employment level if the real wage is low enough. They also agree to set the nominal wage at the constant value ($\bar{w}$), which would insure that employment would equal its full employment level if all disturbances were zero:

$$w = \bar{w} \tag{9.5}$$

In order to calculate $\bar{w}$, private agents must know the parameters of the economic model and the announced values of the financial authorities' policy instruments.

In the financial sector of the model, attention is focused on the markets for two assets, home money and home currency securities. Home (foreign) residents hold home (foreign) money but no foreign (home) money. The supply of home money (M) must equal the demand for home money by home residents:

$$M = m_0 + m_1 p + m_2(e + \overset{*}{p}) + m_3 Y - m_4 i - m_5(\overset{*}{i} + \bar{e} - e) + \gamma + \delta \qquad (9.6)$$

Home money demand depends positively on the price of the home good, the exchange rate, the price of the foreign good, and home output. Increases in all of these variables raise the transactions demand for money balances. Money demand depends negatively on the nominal interest rate on home currency securities and on the expected nominal return on foreign currency securities measured in home currency which is equal to the nominal interest rate on foreign currency securities plus the expected rate of depreciation of the home currency. Money demand depends positively on two disturbance terms, γ and δ. Positive values γ (δ) represent shifts of home residents' asset preferences toward home money and away from home currency securities (foreign currency securities).

The supply of home currency securities (B) must equal the demand for these securities by both home and foreign residents:

$$B = b_0 - b_1 p - b_2 \overset{*}{p} - b_3 Y + b_4 i - b_5(\overset{*}{i} + \bar{e} - e)$$
$$+ b_6(i - \bar{e} + e) - b_7 \overset{*}{i} + b_8 e - b_9 \overset{*}{Y} - \gamma + \varepsilon \qquad (9.7)$$

It is assumed that both home and foreign residents determine the home currency amount that they will hold in securities by subtracting their money demands measured in home currency from the home currency value of their wealth and allocate the same fraction of this amount to home currency securities. The resulting demand for home currency securities depends negatively on the prices of the home and foreign goods, on home and foreign output, on the expected nominal return on foreign currency securities measured in home currency, and on the nominal interest rate on foreign currency securities. Increases in prices and outputs raise the transactions demands for money of both home and foreign residents partly at the expense of their demands for home currency securities. It is assumed that both home and foreign residents regard the three assets they hold as strict gross substitutes. Therefore, the negative effect of an increase in the expected rate of return on foreign securities (the nominal interest rate on foreign securities) on the demand for home securities resulting from the increased relative attractiveness of foreign currency securities dominates the positive effect on this demand resulting from reduced home (foreign) money demand. The demand for home currency securities depends positively on the nominal interest rate on home currency securities, on the expected nominal rate of return on home currency securities measured in foreign currency which is equal to the nominal interest rate on home currency securities minus the expected rate of depreciation of the home currency, and on the exchange rate. Increases in the nominal interest rate on home currency securities (the expected rate of return on home securities) make these securities more attractive relative to foreign securities and reduce home (foreign) money demand. Therefore, $b_4 > m_4$. It is assumed that the positive effect of an increase in the exchange rate on the demand for home currency securities resulting from the increased home currency value of world wealth dominates the negative effect on this demand resulting from increased home currency denominated demand for both home and foreign money for transactions purposes. The demand for home securities depends negatively (positively) on the disturbance term γ (ε). Positive values of γ (ε) represent decreases (increases) in the demand for home currency securities matched by increases (decreases) in the demand for home money (foreign currency securities).

Now the behavior of the home and foreign financial authorities is described. It is assumed that the home authorities do not observe home output and the price of the home good in the current period. They can choose as policy instruments, and set values for, any two of the four financial variables M, B, i, and e. The values of the other two variables are determined by the model. The discussion of the home authorities' balance sheet in the second section implies that if the home authorities seek to change B without changing M, they must also change the supply of foreign currency securities available to the public through intervention operations. It is assumed that the home authorities follow either an aggregates constant policy or a rates constant policy. Under an aggregates constant policy M and B are kept unchanged, while under a rates constant policy M and B are allowed to vary to keep i and e constant. Under each policy regime, the home authorities set and announce the same values for two financial policy instruments before markets meet each period; that is, they either do not observe or elect not to respond to movements in the financial variables for which they do not set values. The announced values of the two financial policy instruments can be chosen arbitrarily because private agents set the nominal wage so that the expected value of Y is equal to Y_f given these announced values. In this and the next two sections it is assumed that the foreign authorities can observe the level of foreign output (Y^*) and the price of the foreign good (p^*) in the current period and that they act to keep these variables as well as the interest rate on foreign currency securities (i^*) fixed at constant values denoted by $\bar{Y}^*$, $\bar{p}^*$, and $\bar{i}^*$.[9] Given the nature of the disturbances and the behavior of the authorities, it is rational for agents to expect in any period that the values of the price of the home good and the exchange rate in the next period will be equal to the constants $\bar{p}$ and $\bar{e}$, respectively, and for home residents to set the nominal wage at the constant $\bar{w}$ each period before other markets meet.[10,11]

Equilibrium schedules for the markets for the home good, home money, and home currency securities are shown in Figure 9.1. In order to construct these schedules it is necessary to eliminate p from these markets with the use of the relationship between p and Y implied by the aggregate supply function when w is set equal to $\bar{w}$. $X_0 X_0$ is an equilibrium schedule for the home good. An increase in i, which lowers demand, must be accompanied by a decline in Y, which raises excess demand. $M_0 M_0$ is an equilibrium schedule for home money. An increase in i, which reduces money demand, must be offset

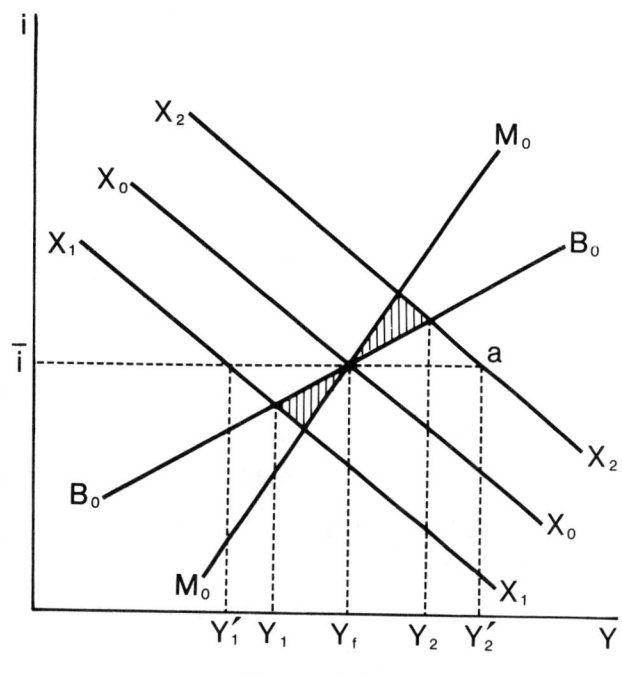

Figure 9.1

by a rise in Y, which raises money demand. B_0B_0 is an equilibrium schedule for home currency securities. An increase in i, which raises demand, must be matched by an increase in Y, which lowers demand. It is assumed that the effect of an increase in Y on the demand for home money is greater than the absolute value of the effect of an increase in Y on the demand for home currency securities.[12] In the next subsection it is demonstrated that this assumption is sufficient to insure that M_0M_0 is steeper than B_0B_0 as shown in Figure 9.1, and the implications of relaxing it are discussed. X_0X_0, M_0M_0, and B_0B_0 are the equilibrium schedules that would result if all disturbances were zero, so they intersect at Y_f. Changes in the exchange rate or the home authorities' holdings of home and foreign securities cause the schedules to shift in a manner described below.

Consider the effects of stochastic shifts in the XX schedule in the range between X_1X_1 and X_2X_2 shown in Figure 9.1. These shifts might result from disturbances affecting home or foreign saving behavior or from disturbances affecting the allocation of spending between home and foreign goods either at home or abroad. If the authorities pursue an aggregates constant policy, levels of output between Y_1 and Y_2 result. For example, suppose an increase in the demand for the home good shifts the XX schedule to

X_2X_2 and gives rise to excess demand for the home good. Output tends to increase, creating an excess demand for home money and an excess supply of home securities. These disequilibria can be removed only by a rise in i and an appreciation of the home currency (fall in e). An appreciation of the home currency raises excess supply in the markets for the home good, home money, and home currency securities. As the home currency appreciates, the X_2X_2, M_0M_0, and B_0B_0 schedules shift toward one another until they intersect at a point in the shaded triangle above X_0X_0.

If instead the authorities pursue a rates constant policy, levels of output between Y_1' and Y_2' result. If the XX schedule shifts to X_2X_2, then the new equilibrium point is at point a. Since there is no change in the exchange rate the XX schedule does not shift back from X_2X_2. The MM and BB schedules are shifted to the right by monetary and intervention operations until they pass through point a. An expansionary monetary operation, a purchase of home securities with home money, shifts both MM and BB to the right. However, BB is shifted farther since increases in income raise the demand for money by more than they reduce the demand for home currency securities. Thus, in order to keep both the exchange rate and interest rate constant, the authorities must undertake an intervention operation, a sale of home securities in exchange for foreign securities, so that the BB schedule does not shift farther to the right than point a. When the only source of shocks to equilibrium is stochastic shifts in the XX schedule, an aggregates constant policy leads to less variation in output than a rates constant policy. Under an aggregates constant policy, disturbances to the home good market induce changes in the interest rate and in the exchange rate that dampen the movement in output.

A different kind of conclusion is reached when shocks to financial markets are considered. For purposes of illustration, attention is focused on a type of shock for which intervention operations are the appropriate remedy. Consider stochastic shifts in the BB schedule between B_1B_1 and B_2B_2, shown in Figure 9.2. These shifts result from changes in preferences between home and foreign securities either at home or abroad. If the authorities pursue an aggregates constant policy, levels of output between Y_1 and Y_2 result. Suppose a shift in asset preferences toward home securities and away from foreign securities causes the BB schedule to move to B_2B_2. The increase in the demand for home securities leads to a decrease in i, which in turn creates excess demand for home money. In order for equilibrium in financial markets to be reestablished, the home currency must appreciate. Appreciation causes the three schedules to shift together as before, so the new equilibrium must lie in the shaded triangle below B_0B_0. Output may fall, rise, or remain the same since the changes in financial variables have opposite effects on demand for the home good.

If instead, the authorities pursue a rates constant policy, output definitely remains unchanged. The BB schedule is shifted back to B_0B_0 by an

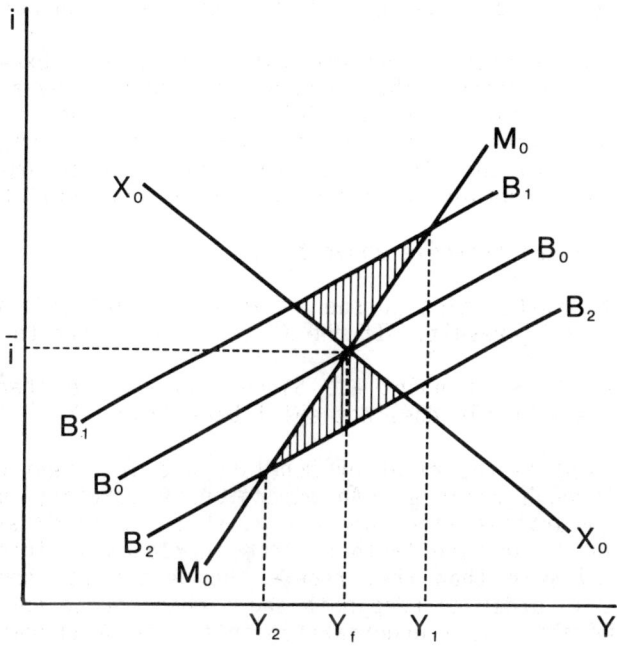

Figure 9.2

intervention operation consisting of a sale of home securities and purchase of foreign securities. When the only source of shocks to equilibrium is stochastic shifts in the BB schedule, a rates constant policy leads to less variation in output than an aggregates constant policy.

Two other possible sources of stochastic shocks to equilibrium are shifts in home residents' preferences between home money and foreign securities which cause movements in the MM schedule and shifts in home residents' preferences between home money and home securities which cause movements in both the MM and BB schedules. In both these cases, a rates constant policy leads to less variation in output than an aggregates constant policy. Under a rates constant policy the transmission of financial market disturbances to the market for the home good through interest rate and exchange rate changes is prevented.

The Derivation of the Results

This subsection contains a formal derivation of the results of the previous subsection. It is convenient to work with the model in a somewhat more compact form. (9.2) and (9.3) are substituted into (9.1), and (9.5) is substituted into (9.4). The modified version of (9.4) is solved for p, and the result is substituted for p wherever it appears in the other equations. Each of these other equations with the disturbances set equal to zero is subtracted from the same equation with the disturbances free to take on any value to obtain

$$0 = -y_Y \hat{Y} - y_2 \hat{i} + y_e \hat{e} + \alpha + \beta \qquad (9.8)$$

$$\hat{M} = m_Y\hat{Y} - m_4\hat{i} + m_e\hat{e} + \gamma + \delta \qquad (9.9)$$

$$\hat{B} = -b_Y\hat{Y} + b_i\hat{i} + b_e\hat{e} - \gamma + \epsilon \qquad (9.10)$$

where

$y_Y = s + \overset{*}{y}_1 + [y_4 + (y_2 + y_3)h + y_5]x_1,$ $\qquad b_Y = b_1/x_1 + b_3$

$y_e = y_4 - y_2(1 - h) + y_3h + y_5,$ $\qquad b_i = b_4 + b_6$

$m_Y = m_1/x_1 + m_3,$ $\qquad b_e = b_5 + b_6 + b_8$

$m_e = m_2 + m_5$

A hat over a variable indicates the deviation of that variable from its constant expected value. It is assumed that relative price and wealth effects outweigh possible "perverse" expected real interest rate effects so that y_e is positive. Foreign variables do not appear in (9.8), (9.9), and (9.10) because they are fixed by the foreign authorities.

The difference between the slopes of the MM and BB schedules of Figure 9.1 is

$$(\hat{i}/\hat{Y})_{MM} - (\hat{i}/\hat{Y})_{BB} = (m_Y b_i - b_Y m_4)/(b_i m_4) \qquad (9.11)$$

It has been assumed that $m_Y > b_Y$. This assumption is sufficient to insure that the MM schedule is steeper than the BB schedule since $b_4 > m_4$ and therefore $b_i > m_4$. The intuitively appealing result that an increase in the demand for the home good ($\alpha > 0$) causes the home currency to appreciate under an aggregates constant policy is obtained if and only if the MM schedule is steeper than the BB schedule.

The variances of home output (σ_Y^2) under a rates constant (RC) and an aggregates constant (AC) financial policy regime are given by

$$\sigma_Y^2|_{RC} = (1/y_Y)^2(\sigma_\alpha^2 + \sigma_\beta^2) \qquad (9.12)$$

$$\sigma_Y^2|_{AC} = (C_1/\Delta_1)^2(\sigma_\alpha^2 + \sigma_\beta^2) + [(C_2 + C_3)/\Delta_1]^2\sigma_\beta^2 + (C_2/\Delta_1)^2\sigma_\delta^2 + (C_3/\Delta_1)^2\sigma_\epsilon^2 \qquad (9.13)$$

$C_1 = m_4 b_e + b_i m_e,$ $\qquad C_3 = y_2 m_e - m_4 y_e$

$C_2 = y_2 b_e + b_i y_e,$ $\qquad \Delta_1 = y_Y C_1 + m_Y C_2 + b_Y C_3$

Since $b_i > m_4$ and it has been assumed that $m_Y > b_Y$, $C_2 + C_3$ and the sum of the second and third terms in Δ_1 are positive. Thus, if $\sigma_Y^2 = \sigma_\delta^2 = \sigma_\epsilon^2$ 0 and either σ_α^2 or $\sigma_\beta^2 > 0$, $\sigma_Y^2|_{AC} < \sigma_Y^2|_{RC}$. This result can still be obtained if $m_Y < b_Y$ but (9.11) is positive or if (9.11) is negative but $y_2(m_Y b_e + b_Y m_e) >$

$|y_e(m_Y b_i - b_Y m_4)|$. If $\sigma_\alpha^2 = \sigma_\beta^2 = 0$ and σ_γ^2 σ_δ^2 or $\sigma_\varepsilon^2 > 0$ then $0 = \sigma_Y^2|_{RC} < s_Y^2|_{AC}$.

PERMANENT DISTURBANCES AND FINANCIAL POLICY RESPONSES IN A SINGLE OPEN ECONOMY

This section contains a brief description of some implications of alternative financial policy responses when a single open economy experiences permanent as well as transitory disturbances. The analysis of the effects of transitory disturbances above proceeds under the assumption that private agents know exactly the structure of the economy that is embodied in the coefficients of an economic model, including the intercept terms of that model. However, they are ignorant of the current values of the transitory disturbance terms when they set the nominal wage given the announced constant values of the financial policy instruments. While the average level of output is its full employment level, there are variations in output about this level. It is into this environment that permanent disturbances are introduced.

As an example of a permanent disturbance consider a once and for all shift up in the demand for the home good. Of course, if private agents know that this disturbance has occurred and take it into account when setting the nominal wage, it has no effect on the average levels of output and employment.

Now suppose that private agents do not realize that this permanent disturbance has occurred. It seems reasonable to assume that the nominal wage would not be changed, at least for a while. During this time the average real wage would be lower and the average level of output would be higher than their full employment values under either an aggregates constant or a rates constant financial policy regime. The results regarding the effects of transitory disturbances under alternative financial policy regimes carry over with minor modifications to cases in which a permanent disturbance is also present. For an unrecognized permanent disturbance in the market for the home good (markets for home money and home currency securities), the deviation of average output from its full employment level is smaller (greater) under an aggregates constant policy than under a rates constant policy. After a while private agents would recognize that levels of output above the full employment value were being observed more frequently than would be suggested by what was known about the joint probability distribution of the transitory disturbances, would conclude that the economic structure had changed, and would change the nominal wage. Important research on how private agents would go about trying to separate permanent from transitory disturbances under various sets of conditions is well under way, but it is not reported on here.[13]

Up to this point only the case of a single permanent disturbance has been considered. Such a disturbance would not call into question the feasibility of a rates constant policy unless it were large enough to require, for example, the sale of most of the authorities' foreign currency securities in intervention operations. However, if there were a series of even moderate-sized permanent disturbances that required the sale of foreign currency securities by the authorities, such as a succession of permanent shifts in asset preferences away from home currency securities and toward foreign currency securities, a rates constant financial policy regime, even though desirable, might not be feasible because the financial authorities might exhaust their holdings of foreign currency securities.

TRANSITORY DISTURBANCES, INFORMATION, AND FINANCIAL POLICIES IN A SINGLE OPEN ECONOMY

The analysis of this section proceeds under the assumption of the third section that the economy experiences only transitory disturbances. In that section conclusions were drawn about which of two alternative financial policy regimes the authorities should choose if all disturbances were in the home good market or if all disturbances were in financial markets. Here it is asked how the financial authorities should proceed when the economy is buffeted by all of the types of transitory disturbances considered above. It is assumed that both the authorities and private agents wish to minimize the the expected squared deviations of output from Y_f. What financial policy is optimal depends on what information the authorities have about the structure of the economy, about the disturbances to which it is subjected, and about the current values of the two financial variables they do not set when implementing their monetary and intervention policies.

Suppose the authorities operate in an environment in which they know, or have unchanging beliefs about, the nonstochastic coefficients of the three linear market equilibrium relations and the joint distribution of the additive disturbance terms. Suppose also that they cannot observe output and the price of the home good, and cannot observe or, at least, do not respond to current movements in the two financial variables they do not set when implementing their monetary and intervention policies. In this environment it makes sense to compare alternative pure financial policies under which values for the two financial variables chosen as policy instruments are set before markets meet each period and are not changed once markets meet. The aggregates constant and rates constant policies considered above are examples of such pure financial policies. Once a policy is found to be superior it is followed period after period unless there are changes in the parameters of the system or the joint distribution of the stochastic disturbances.[14]

The analysis of the third section suggests one kind of conclusion: for example, given the coefficients of the system and all of the other parameters of the joint distribution of the disturbances, there exists a variance of the disturbance term in the market for the home good large enough to insure that an aggregates constant policy leads to lower expected loss than a rates constant policy. Additional conclusions must be based on explicit calculations of expected losses. Suppose that the three equilibrium relations are normalized on income and that the variances of the normalized disturbances are equal.[15] An aggregates constant policy may or may not be better than a rates constant policy whereas under similar assumptions in a closed economy a money supply constant policy dominates an interest rate constant policy.[16] An aggregates constant policy is superior (inferior) to a rates constant policy for large values of the degree of substitutability between home and foreign securities (the responsiveness of home good demand to changes in the exchange rate).

The authorities should proceed differently in a second environment in which the only difference is that they can observe and respond to current movements in the two financial variables not chosen as policy instruments.[17] In this environment one policy instrument can be kept fixed. However, the authorities should choose and announce a linear rule that tells them how to vary the other policy instrument in response to deviations of the remaining two financial variables from their expected values.[18] These remaining two financial variables can be regarded as information variables since deviations in these variables from their expected values provide a basis for making estimates of the current values of the disturbance terms. In general, the coefficients of the decision rule will be functions of both the coefficients of the model and the parameters of the joint distribution of the additive disturbance terms. While the decision rule is the same period after period, the value of the variable policy instrument is changed from period to period since the authorities can learn something about the shocks in the current period from observations on the two information variables. It has been assumed that the authorities change a financial policy instrument in response to current information while the nominal wage remains fixed at a value set before other markets meet. That the authorities rather than private agents should adjust to current information even if it is available to both sets of agents seems reasonable since the costs associated with changing a financial policy instrument are much smaller than the costs associated with renegotiating the nominal wage.[19]

The implication that one financial instrument, for example, the exchange rate, can be kept fixed depends crucially on the assumption that the authorities and private agents are concerned only about expected squared deviations of Y from Y_f.[20] If the authorities and private agents were also concerned, for example, about expected squared deviations in interest-sensitive consumption from some desired level, optimal financial policy would involve variations in both financial policy instruments, so the exchange rate would have to vary no matter whether it was chosen as a policy instrument or was used as an information variable. Thus, in general circumstances it will always be optimal for an individual country to opt for a managed floating exchange rate rather than a fixed or freely floating exchange rate.

TRANSITORY DISTURBANCES AND THE SCOPE FOR AGREEMENT ON FINANCIAL POLICIES IN A TWO-COUNTRY WORLD ECONOMY

Up to this point it has been assumed that the authorities in the foreign country have enough information and a sufficient number of policy instruments to set foreign output and the price of the foreign good in addition to the interest rate on foreign securities. It seems more natural to suppose that the foreign authorities are no better informed than the home authorities and, therefore, cannot fix foreign output and the price of the foreign good so that transitory disturbances such as those considered above affect outputs in both countries of the two-country world economy. Here the model of the third section is extended to incorporate this assumption.[21] For simplicity it is also assumed that the authorities in each country use monetary operations to fix the interest rate on securities denominated in the currency of their country. The overall stance of intervention policy is the net result of the intervention operations of the two sets of authorities. Taken together they can choose as a policy instrument and set a value for either the total supply of home currency securities (and, by implication, the total supply of foreign currency securities) or the exchange rate. In this environment it is interesting to consider whether the authorities in the two countries could agree on a fixed or a freely fluctuating exchange rate. In the first subsection the necessary modifications to the model are described, and the results are presented and explained. In the second subsection the results are derived more formally.

The Modifications to the Model and the Results

The only additional market that must be considered explicitly is the market for the foreign good. Foreign output ($\overset{*}{Y}$) must be equal to aggregate demand for the foreign good:

$$\overset{*}{Y} = \overset{*}{y}_0 + \overset{*}{y}_1(Y + \overset{*}{Y}) - \overset{*}{y}_2 r - \overset{*}{y}_3 \overset{*}{r} - y_4(e + \overset{*}{p} - p) - \overset{*}{y}_5 e - \overset{*}{y}_6 \overset{*}{p} - \beta \qquad (9.14)$$

Aggregate demand depends negatively on expected real interest rates, on the relative price of the foreign good, on the exchange rate, and on the price of the foreign good. Increases in the exchange rate and the price of the foreign good reduce home and foreign real wealth measured in terms of the foreign good and, therefore, raise home and foreign saving. Aggregate demand depends positively on home and foreign output. It is assumed that trade is initially balanced so that the effect of an increase in the relative price of the foreign good on the demand for the foreign good is equal in absolute value to the effect on the demand for the home good.[22] Positive values of β represent decreases in the demand for the foreign good matched by increases in demand for the home good.

Foreign output must also be equal to aggregate supply, which depends negatively on the (logarithm of the) real wage measured in terms of the foreign good:

$$\overset{*}{Y} = \overset{*}{x}_0 - \overset{*}{x}_1(\overset{*}{w} - \overset{*}{p}) \qquad (9.15)$$

The (logarithm of the) real wage is equal to the (logarithm of the) foreign nominal wage ($\overset{*}{w}$) minus the (logarithm of the) price of the foreign good. It is assumed that the nominal wage is set each period before other markets meet at the constant value ($\overset{*}{\bar{w}}$), which would insure that employment would equal its desired level and output would equal its corresponding full employment level ($\overset{*}{Y}_f$) if all disturbances were zero:

$$\overset{*}{w} = \overset{*}{\bar{w}} \qquad (9.16)$$

Equilibrium schedules for the home good, the foreign good, and home currency assets are shown in Figure 9.3. In order to construct these schedules it is necessary to eliminate p and $\overset{*}{p}$ from these markets with the use of the relationships between p and Y and between $\overset{*}{p}$ and $\overset{*}{Y}$ implied by the aggregate supply functions when w and $\overset{*}{w}$ are set equal to $\bar{w}$ and $\overset{*}{\bar{w}}$. $X_0 X_0$ is an equilibrium schedule for the home good. An increase in Y which reduces excess demand must be matched by a rise in $\overset{*}{Y}$ which increases demand. $\overset{*}{X}_0 \overset{*}{X}_0$ is an equilibrium schedule for the foreign good. An increase in Y which raises

Dale W. Henderson

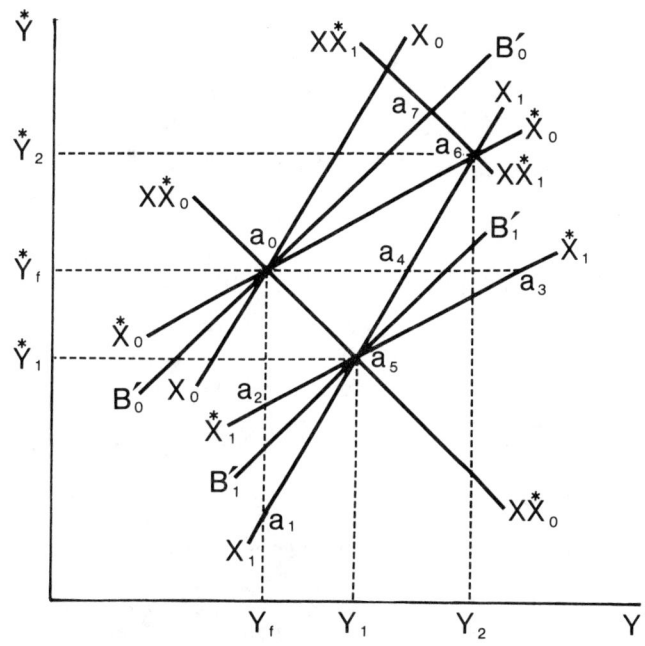

Figure 9.3

demand must be matched by a rise in $\overset{*}{Y}$ which reduces excess demand. The XX schedule is steeper than the $\overset{**}{XX}$ schedule. The absolute value of the reduction in excess demand for the home good caused by a rise in Y which increases home saving as well as home imports exceeds the increase in excess demand for the foreign good caused by a rise in Y which increases not only foreign exports (home imports) but also foreign saving. The increase in excess demand for the home good caused by a rise in $\overset{*}{Y}$ which increases not only home exports (foreign imports) but also home saving is less than the absolute value of the reduction in excess demand for the foreign good caused by a rise in $\overset{*}{Y}$ which increases foreign saving as well as foreign imports. $B_0'B_0'$ is an equilibrium schedule for the combined market for home money and home currency securities. Attention is focused on this combined market for home currency assets because the home authorities alter the supplies of home money and home securities with monetary operations to satisfy any change in the composition of home currency assets desired by private agents at a constant interest rate on home currency securities. An increase in Y which raises the demand for home money plus home currency securities must be offset by a rise in $\overset{*}{Y}$ which raises the demand for foreign money partly at the expense of the demand for home currency securities. The slope of the B'B' schedule may be greater than or less than the slopes of both the XX and $\overset{**}{XX}$

schedules or it may be greater than the slope of the $\overset{**}{XX}$ schedule but less than the slope of the XX schedule as shown in Figure 9.3.[23]

It is useful to consider first the effects of a shift up in the demand for the home good matched by a shift down in the demand for the foreign good which is equal in absolute value. These shifts can be represented by movements in the XX schedule from $X_0 X_0$ to $X_1 X_1$ and in the $\overset{**}{XX}$ schedule from $\overset{*}{X}_0 \overset{*}{X}_0$ to $\overset{*}{X}_1 \overset{*}{X}_1$. At a constant value of Y, XX shifts down farther than $\overset{**}{XX}$ ($a_0 a_1 > a_0 a_2$), since in the market for the home good a fall in $\overset{*}{Y}$ reduces not only home exports (foreign imports) but also home saving, while in the market for the foreign good it raises foreign saving as well as foreign imports. A similar argument can be employed to demonstrate that the demand shift under consideration causes $\overset{**}{XX}$ to shift farther to the right than XX at a constant $\overset{*}{Y}$ ($a_0 a_3 > a_0 a_4$). A series of demand shifts of the type under consideration would trace out the $X\overset{*}{X}_0 X\overset{*}{X}_0$ schedule in Figure 9.3.

Now consider the effect of a depreciation of the home currency. This depreciation raises demand for the home good and lowers demand for the foreign good. If these two demand effects were equal in absolute value, depreciations (and, of course, appreciations) would also trace out the $X\overset{*}{X}_0 X\overset{*}{X}_0$ schedule in Figure 9.3. In many two-country models the two demand effects are necessarily equal in absolute value when depreciations in the neighborhood of balanced trade are considered because the only effect of a depreciation on the markets for the home and foreign goods is to raise the relative price of the foreign good. This increase leads to changes that are equal in absolute value in the markets for the two goods. However, in this model a depreciation affects expected real interest rates and real wealth in addition to the relative price of the foreign good, so the two demand effects of the depreciation are not necessarily equal in absolute value. There is a set of quite stringent assumptions, which, in combination with assumptions already made, is sufficient to insure that the two demand effects are equal in absolute value.[24] In order to simplify the analysis and to make the results readily comparable to those of other models, that set of assumptions is adopted here.[25] Given these assumptions, depreciations (appreciations) of the home currency move the XX and $\overset{**}{XX}$ schedules down (up) so that they continue to intersect on the $X\overset{*}{X}_0 X\overset{*}{X}_0$ schedule.

Now the analysis of the effects of a shift up in the demand for the home good matched by a shift down in the demand for the foreign good that is equal in absolute value can be completed. The shifted XX and $\overset{**}{XX}$ schedules are $X_1 X_1$ and $\overset{*}{X}_1 \overset{*}{X}_1$. Under fixed exchange rates the new equilibrium is at point a_5.

The shift in preferences for goods causes home output to rise and foreign output to fall. Both of these movements tend to raise the demand for home currency assets, so the home currency tends to appreciate. However, the authorities undertake intervention operations, sales of home currency securities in exchange for foreign currency securities which shift the B'B' schedule down. The new B'B' schedule labeled $B_1'B_1'$ passes through a_5. Under flexible exchange rates the home currency appreciates dampening the rise in home output and the fall in foreign output. The B'B' schedule shifts down and the XX and $\overset{**}{XX}$ schedules shift up along $X\overset{*}{X}_0 X\overset{*}{X}_0$ until an equilibrium is reached somewhere on the line segment $a_0 a_5$ above a_5. Thus, for shifts in demands between home and foreign goods there is less variation in both home and foreign output under floating exchange rates, and there is no policy conflict.

Now consider a shift in asset preferences toward home currency assets and away from foreign currency assets. For convenience, suppose that the initial equilibrium is at a_5. The change in asset preferences shifts the B'B' schedule from $B_1'B_1'$ to $B_0'B_0'$. Under fixed exchange rates the new equilibrium is at a_5, which is also the initial equilibrium. The shift in asset preferences puts pressure on the home currency to appreciate. Under fixed exchange rates this pressure is met by intervention operations, sales of home securities in exchange for foreign securities, which shift the B'B' schedule from $B_0'B_0'$ back to $B_1'B_1'$. Under flexible exchange rates the home currency appreciates lowering home output and raising foreign output. B'B' shifts down and XX and $\overset{**}{XX}$ shift up along $X\overset{*}{X}_0 X\overset{*}{X}_0$ until a new equilibrium is reached along the line segment $a_0 a_5$ above a_5. Thus, for shifts in asset preferences between home currency and foreign currency assets there is less variation in both home and foreign output under fixed exchange rates, and there is no policy conflict.

Finally, consider a shift up in home demand for the home good at the expense of home saving. Suppose the initial equilibrium is at a_0. This disturbance initially affects only the XX schedule, which is shifted from $X_0 X_0$ to $X_1 X_1$. Under fixed exchange rates the new equilibrium is at a_6. Home output rises, and as a result of induced home demand for foreign goods, foreign output rises. When the B'B' schedule is steeper than the $\overset{**}{XX}$ schedule, there is pressure on the home currency to appreciate.[26] Under fixed exchange rates this pressure is countered with intervention operations which cause the B'B' schedule to shift down from $B_0'B_0'$. The new B'B' schedule (not shown) passes through a_6. Under flexible exchange rates the home currency appreciates, dampening the rise in home output but exaggerating the rise in foreign output. The B'B' schedule shifts down, and the XX and $\overset{**}{XX}$ schedules shift up along the new $X\overset{*}{X}X\overset{*}{X}$ schedule $X\overset{*}{X}_1 X\overset{*}{X}_1$ until a new equilibrium is reached on the line segment $a_7 a_6$ above a_6. Thus, for shifts in demand for the home good corresponding to shifts in saving there is more variation in home (foreign) output under fixed (floating) exchange rates than under floating (fixed) exchange rates,[27] and there is a policy conflict.[28]

The Derivation of the Results

This subsection contains a formal derivation of the results of the previous subsection. As before it is useful to work with the model in a somewhat more compact form. Equations (9.2) and (9.3) are substituted into (9.1) and (9.14); (9.5) is substituted into (9.4), and (9.16) is substituted into (9.15). The modified versions of (9.4) and (9.15) are solved for p and $\overset{*}{p}$ respectively and the results are substituted for p and $\overset{*}{p}$ wherever they appear in (9.1), (9.6), (9.7), and (9.14). The further modified versions of (9.1) and (9.14) and the sum of the modified versions of (9.6) and (9.7) with the disturbances set equal to zero are subtracted from the same equations with the disturbances free to take on any values, and $\hat{i}$ is set equal to zero to obtain

$$0 = -y_Y \hat{Y} + y_e \hat{e} + y_Y^* \hat{\overset{*}{Y}} + \alpha + \beta \qquad (9.17)$$

$$0 = \overset{*}{y}_Y \hat{Y} - \overset{*}{y}_e \hat{e} - \overset{*}{y}_Y^* \hat{\overset{*}{Y}} - \beta \qquad (9.18)$$

$$\hat{B}' = b'_Y \hat{Y} + b'_e \hat{e} - b'^*_Y \hat{\overset{*}{Y}} + \delta + \epsilon \qquad (9.19)$$

$\hat{B}'$ is the deviation of B from its expected value in addition to the deviation that is equal in magnitude and opposite in sign to the deviation of the money supply from its expected value ($\hat{B} = \hat{B}' - \hat{M}$). y_Y and y_e are defined above, and

$y_Y^* = y_1 + [y_4 - (y_2 + y_3)(1 - \bar{h})]/\overset{*}{x}_1$, $b'_Y = m_Y - b_Y$

$\overset{*}{y}_Y^* = s + y_1 + [y_4 + (\overset{*}{y}_2 + \overset{*}{y}_3)(1 - \bar{h}) + \overset{*}{y}_5]/\overset{*}{x}_1$, $b'_e = m_e + b_e$

$\overset{*}{y}_e = y_4 + \overset{*}{y}_2(1 - \bar{h}) - \overset{*}{y}_3 \bar{h} + \overset{*}{y}_5$, $b'^*_Y = b_2/\overset{*}{x}_1 + b_7$

$\overset{*}{y}_Y = \overset{*}{y}_1 + [y_4 - (\overset{*}{y}_2 + \overset{*}{y}_3) \bar{h}]/x_1$

It is assumed that income, relative price, and wealth effects outweigh possibly "perverse" expected real interest rate effects so that y_Y^*, $\overset{*}{y}_e$, and $\overset{*}{y}_Y$ are all positive. m_Y, b_Y, m_e, and b_e are defined above. It has been assumed above that $m_Y > b_Y$, so b'_Y is positive.

The difference between the slopes of the XX and $\overset{**}{XX}$ schedules of Figure 9.3 is

$$(\hat{Y}/\hat{Y})_{XX} - (\hat{Y}/\hat{Y})^{**}_{XX} = (y_Y \overset{*}{y}^*_Y - \overset{*}{y}_Y y^*_Y)/(y^*_Y \overset{*}{y}^*_Y) \tag{9.20}$$

The XX schedule is steeper than the $\overset{**}{XX}$ schedule since $y_Y > \overset{*}{y}_Y$ and $\overset{*}{y}^*_Y > y^*_Y$. B'B' has a positive slope, but this slope may be greater or less than the slopes of XX and $\overset{**}{XX}$. The difference between the shifts in XX and $\overset{**}{XX}$ schedules at a constant value of Y given a positive β is

$$(\hat{Y}/\beta)_{XX} - (\hat{Y}/\beta)^{**}_{XX} = (y^*_Y - \overset{*}{y}^*_Y)/(y^*_Y \overset{*}{y}^*_Y) \tag{9.21}$$

The XX schedule shifts down farther since $\overset{*}{y}^*_Y > y^*_Y$. It can be shown that the $\overset{**}{XX}$ schedule shifts farther to the right than the XX schedule at a constant value of $\overset{*}{Y}$ given a positive β since $y_Y > \overset{*}{y}_Y$.

Under the assumption that $y_e = \overset{*}{y}_e$ the variances of home output (σ^2_Y) and foreign output (σ^2_*) under fixed (FI) and flexible (FL) exchange rates are given by

$$\sigma^2_Y|_{FI} = (\overset{*}{y}^*_Y/D_1)^2 \sigma^2_\alpha + [(\overset{*}{y}^*_Y - y^*_Y)/D_1]^2 \sigma^2_\beta \tag{9.22}$$

$$\sigma^2_*|_{FI} = (\overset{*}{y}_Y/D_1)^2 \sigma^2_\alpha + [(\overset{*}{y}_Y - y_Y)/D_1]^2 \sigma^2_\beta \tag{9.23}$$

$$\sigma^2_Y|_{FL} = (D_3/\Delta_2)^2 \sigma^2_\alpha + [b'_e(\overset{*}{y}^*_Y - y^*_Y)/\Delta_2]^2 \sigma^2_\beta + [y_e(y^*_Y - \overset{*}{y}^*_Y)/\Delta_2]^2 (\sigma^2_\delta + \sigma^2_\epsilon) \tag{9.24}$$

$$\sigma^2_*|_{FL} = (D_4/\Delta_2)^2 \sigma^2_\alpha + [b'_e(\overset{*}{y}_Y - y_Y)/\Delta_2]^2 \sigma^2_\beta + [y_e(y_Y - \overset{*}{y}_Y)/\Delta_2]^2 (\sigma^2_\delta + \sigma^2_\epsilon) \tag{9.25}$$

$$D_1 = y_Y \overset{*}{y}^*_Y - \overset{*}{y}_Y y^*_Y, \qquad D_3 = y_e b'_* + b'_e \overset{*}{y}^*_Y$$

$$D_2 = [b'_Y(\overset{*}{y}^*_Y - y^*_Y) + b'_*(y_Y - \overset{*}{y}_Y)], \qquad D_4 = y_e b'_Y + b'_e \overset{*}{y}_Y$$

$$\Delta_2 = b'_e D_1 + y_e D_2$$

The values of D_1, D_2, D_3, D_4, and Δ_2 are all positive. Thus, if $\sigma^2_\alpha = \sigma^2_\delta = \sigma^2_\epsilon = 0$ and $\sigma^2_\beta > 0$, then $\sigma^2_Y|_{FL} < \sigma^2_Y|_{FI}$ and $\sigma^2_*|_{FL} < \sigma^2_*|_{FI}$. If $\sigma^2_\alpha = \sigma^2_\beta = 0$ and either σ^2_δ or $\sigma^2_\epsilon > 0$, then $0 = \sigma^2_Y|_{FI} < \sigma^2_Y|_{FL}$ and $0 = \sigma^2_*|_{FI} < \sigma^2_*|_{FL}$. By manipulating the coefficients of σ^2_α in (9.22), (9.23), (9.24), and (9.25), it can be shown that if $\sigma^2_\beta = \sigma^2_\delta = \sigma^2_\epsilon = 0$ and $\sigma^2_\alpha > 0$, then $\sigma^2_Y|_{FL} \lessgtr \sigma^2_Y|_{FI}$ but $\sigma^2_*|_{FL} \gtrless \sigma^2_*|_{FI}$ when $b'_Y \overset{*}{y}^*_Y \gtrless b'_* \overset{*}{y}_Y$. When $b'_Y \overset{*}{y}^*_Y$ is greater (less) than $b'_* \overset{*}{y}_Y$, the B'B' schedule is steeper (flatter) than the $\overset{**}{XX}$ schedule in Figure 9.3 since

$$(\hat{\dot{Y}}/\hat{Y})_{B'B'} - (\hat{\dot{Y}}/\hat{Y})^{**}_{XX} = (b'_Y \dot{y}^*_Y - b'_* \dot{y}^*_Y)/(b'_* \dot{y}^*_Y)$$

KEEPING TRACK OF INTERVENTION POLICY

This section is a description of some of the difficulties encountered by financial authorities and private agents in trying to keep track of the overall stance of intervention policy which is the net result of the intervention policies in many countries.[29] In the last section examples were provided of two types of disturbances for which the authorities in two countries could agree on the overall stance of intervention policy and one type for which they would have different views about the appropriate overall stance of intervention policy. Such examples make it clear that the authorities in a given country need information about other countries' intervention operations in order to negotiate effectively with the authorities in those countries about what actions are required in order to achieve a desirable overall stance for intervention policy. Private agents also need information about intervention policy so that they can base their decisions on reliable forecasts of financial variables, including exchange rates. Up to this point it has been assumed that the authorities in each country hold their international reserves only in the form of stocks of government securities denominated in the currencies of other countries and that changes in these stocks reflect the intervention policies of the authorities. In this section additional forms of international reserve assets are considered. Changes in the stocks of these assets as well as certain other transactions described below can also reflect the intervention policies of the authorities.

Unfortunately keeping track of the intervention policies of the authorities in all the relevant countries is often not an easy task either for the authorities themselves or for private agents. Of course, one source of difficulty is that data on the balance sheet of a country's financial authorities,--the consolidated balance sheet of the treasury, the central bank, and the exchange stabilization fund,--often become available only with a lag, but this is not the most important source. Far more important sources of difficulty are that the balance sheet is often not presented in a way that makes it easy to isolate and determine the net result of intervention policy actions of the financial authorities, which are reflected in different places on the balance sheet, and that not all policy actions properly regarded as intervention policy actions are even recorded on the balance sheet of the financial authorities.

Some of the more obvious pitfalls encountered in attempting to interpret changes in the consolidated balance sheet of the financial authorities are well recognized and can be avoided by an alert observer. A balance sheet must be presented in terms of a single unit of account, for example, home currency units. If the home currency value of the authorities' foreign currency securities or of other reserve assets such as gold, Special Drawing Rights (SDRs), or International Monetary Fund position changes, the home currency value of reserves changes without any intervention policy actions. Such "valuation changes" must be removed to arrive at the relevant changes in reserve totals. New allocations of SDRs lead to changes in reserves when no intervention policy action has occurred, so these must be taken out. Increases or decreases in foreign currency assets matched by increases or decreases in liabilities denominated in the same foreign currency lead to changes in gross reserves but not net reserves. It is changes in net reserves that constitute intervention policy action. The foreign currency denominated Carter bonds issued by the U.S. Treasury are examples of the type of foreign currency borrowing by the financial authorities that must be included in calculations of net reserves. Arriving at a net reserve figure is sometimes tricky because a country's foreign currency borrowing, say, by the Treasury, may be reported at a different point on the consolidated balance sheet from its foreign currency assets held, say, by the exchange stabilization fund.

Less obvious pitfalls remain. Outright forward exchange contracts entered into by the financial authorities are "off balance sheet items" and information about them is not usually available, at least to most private agents. Forward foreign exchange operations are equivalent to intervention policy actions in their impact on financial variables. The net return in terms of home currency to a private agent who sells a home currency security is

$$(\tilde{E}/E)(1 + \overset{*}{r}) - (1 + r) \tag{9.26}$$

where E is the spot price of foreign currency in terms of home currency, and $\tilde{E}$ is the unknown spot price of foreign currency in terms of home currency that will prevail in ninety days. The net return to a private agent who sells $(1 + r)$ units of home currency forward to the authorities in return for forward foreign currency is

$$(\tilde{E}/F)(1 + r) - (1 + r) \tag{9.27}$$

where F is today's home currency price of foreign currency for delivery in ninety days. Covered interest arbitrage ensures that

$$(1 + r) = (F/E)(1 + \overset{*}{r}) \tag{9.28}$$

Substitution of the right-hand side of (9.28) for the first $(1 + r)$ in (9.27) reveals that (9.27) and (9.26) are equal. Private agents regard the security exchange that is implied by an intervention operation and the purchase of the forward contract from the authorities as equivalent transactions because they have the same net return.[30] Thus, these two types of transactions have the same effect on financial variables, and in the absence of knowledge of the authorities' forward foreign exchange operations the intervention policy stance of the authorities cannot be accurately determined.

As part of their intervention policy the financial authorities can persuade private banks or government related institutions to undertake transactions that have the same effect as their own intervention operations would have had. These transactions, which are examples of what some have called the "organization" of capital flows, are reflected on the balance sheets of the private banks or the government related institutions and not on the balance sheet of the financial authorities, so it is difficult if not impossible for other financial authorities and private agents to monitor them. One common example of this type of transaction involves the financial authorities and private banks in a country. The financial authorities buy spot foreign currency from private agents. Instead of using this spot foreign currency to buy foreign currency securities for their own reserves, they sell it to a private bank and agree to buy it back forward, sometimes at a price more favorable than the market price, in a so-called swap transaction. The private bank sells a domestic currency security in order to obtain the spot home currency needed to buy the spot foreign exchange from the authorities. The private bank uses the spot foreign exchange obtained from the authorities to buy a foreign currency security. Thus the effect on the supplies of government securities denominated in home and foreign currencies available to private agents other than home country banks is the same as if the financial authorities had performed a standard intervention operation. The foreign exchange exposure of the home private bank is unchanged because its foreign currency security is matched by a forward contract to receive home currency, and the balance sheet of the financial authorities is unchanged because the forward contract is an off balance sheet item.

Another common example of intervention policy not reflected in the balance sheet of the financial authorities is directed borrowing by government related enterprises. These enterprises issue foreign currency denominated debt instead of domestic currency denominated debt, thereby making the supplies of home currency and foreign currency securities closely related to government securities which are available to private agents different from what they otherwise would have been. Foreign currency borrowing by government related enterprises is usually matched by forward contracts with the financial authorities.

It appears that the organization of capital flows that has occurred from time to time over at least the past decade may now be assuming a more important role in overall intervention policy. Innovations in such hidden intervention that make it more difficult to detect are liable to proliferate. These developments will make the assessment of the overall stance of intervention policy more difficult for both financial authorities and private agents.

SOME CONCLUDING REMARKS

An important advantage of the approach used here is that it yields suggestive qualitative results. For example, it was shown in the sixth section that when disturbances arise from stochastic shifts in asset preferences, the authorities in different countries have a mutual interest in intervening to reduce exchange rate variability. This result helps to explain interest in coordinated official intervention to minimize the exchange rate effects of changes in desired portfolio composition by the oil producing countries and central banks of some other countries.

Most of this paper is devoted to analyzing the effects of serially uncorrelated transitory disturbances under alternative financial policy regimes when current output and price variations are unobservable in at least one country and nominal wages do not deviate from preset paths. The lessons of such analysis seem more relevant when equilibrium in the model is assumed to refer to a "period" of a half year or a year rather than a month or a quarter. The longer the equilibrium period, the more sense it makes to regard disturbances as serially uncorrelated and to presume that alternative financial policy regimes can lead to measurably different outcomes. However, the longer the equilibrium time period, the less plausible it is to assume that current output and price variations are unobservable and to suppose that nominal wages are not adjusted. It is comforting to note that similar results can be obtained in models with serially correlated disturbances for which it seems more natural to take the equilibrium period to be a quarter.

It has been emphasized that in order to decide between alternative pure policy regimes and in order to implement more complicated financial policy regimes that involve rules for changing policy instruments, the authorities need a considerable amount of information. In particular they must know the nonstochastic coefficients of the economic structure and the parameters of the joint distribution of additive disturbances. In studies that attempt to give empirical content to analytical frameworks of the same general type as the one used here, estimates of the relevant coefficients and parameters from existing econometric models have been employed. There is evidence to suggest that this approach can yield useful results.[31] Of course, such a procedure is open to the objection that this type of analytical framework calls for exact knowledge of coefficients and parameters, not estimates. Much progress has been made in modifying the analytical framework to take account of the fact that only estimates of coefficients and parameters will ever be available to the authorities.[32]

In this paper intervention policy has been viewed as part of macroeconomic financial policy in open economies rather than as a tool for stabilizing so called disorderly foreign exchange markets. While the empirical relevance of intervention policy for financial policy has not been firmly established, the interest of the authorities in intervention policy suggests that it is worthwhile to make clear what role it might play. More empirical work attempting to isolate the effects of intervention policy is badly needed. It has been argued that managed floating would be best from the viewpoint of individual countries. Further theoretical work that determines whether this conclusion holds when more attention is paid to the problem of distinguishing between permanent and transitory disturbances would be helpful. It has also been emphasized that the authorities in various countries might find it in their interest to manage the float differently. How conflicts that arise over the proper overall stance of intervention are resolved and how they could be resolved more satisfactorily is another promising area for further research.

APPENDIX

The model of the text is a partly linear and partly log linear approximation to the model sketched out briefly in this Appendix. The symbols used are defined at the end of the Appendix. The approximation is made at the equilibrium that would emerge if all the disturbance terms were zero and trade were balanced. In this equilibrium all of the endogenous variables take on their constant expected values, which are represented by the symbols for these variables with bars over them, and units are defined so that $\bar{E} = \bar{P}^* = \bar{P} = 1$. The coefficients displayed below or beside a given equation are the coefficients of the approximation to that equation.

The aggregate demand equations for the home and foreign goods are given by

$$PY = h(E\overset{*}{P}/P)\{PY + E\overset{**}{PY} - c[a(r, \overset{*}{r})(PY + E\overset{**}{PY}) - (A + \overset{*}{A})]\} \qquad (9.29)$$

$$y_1 = h(1 - ca), \qquad y_4 = h'(Y + \overset{*}{Y}) + h(1 - ca)\overset{*}{Y}$$

$$y_2 = ca_r Y, \qquad y_5 = hc(N + F)$$

$$y_3 = ca_r^* Y, \qquad y_6 = hc(A + \overset{*}{A})$$

$$E\overset{**}{P}Y = [1 - h(E\overset{*}{P}/P)]\{PY + E\overset{**}{P}Y - c[a(r, \overset{*}{r})(PY + E\overset{**}{P}Y) - (A + \overset{*}{A})]\} \quad (9.30)$$

$$\overset{*}{y}_1 = (1 - h)(1 - ca), \qquad \overset{*}{y}_4 = h'(Y + \overset{*}{Y}) + h(1 - ca)\overset{*}{Y}$$

$$\overset{*}{y}_2 = ca_r \overset{*}{Y}, \qquad \overset{*}{y}_5 = (1 - h)c(M + B)$$

$$\overset{*}{y}_3 = ca_r^* \overset{*}{Y}, \qquad \overset{*}{y}_6 = (1 - h)c(A + \overset{*}{A})$$

It is assumed that $0 < h$, $ca < 1$ and that a_r, a_r^*, and $h' > 0$, so all the approximation coefficients are positive, and $0 < y_1$, $\overset{*}{y}_1 < 1$. In deriving y_2, y_3, $\overset{*}{y}_2$, $\overset{*}{y}_3$, and y_4 use is made of the facts that in equilibrium $h(Y + \overset{*}{Y}) = Y$ and $(1 - h)(Y + \overset{*}{Y}) = \overset{*}{Y}$, and that with balanced trade $h\overset{*}{Y} = (1 - h)Y$. The product ca is represented by s in the text. r, $\overset{*}{r}$, and $A + \overset{*}{A}$ are given by

$$r = i - \bar{h}(\bar{P} - P)/P - (1 - \bar{h})[(\bar{E} - E)/E + (\bar{\overset{*}{P}} - \overset{*}{P})/\overset{*}{P}] \quad (9.31)$$

$$\overset{*}{r} = \overset{*}{i} + (\bar{E} - E)/E - \bar{h}(\bar{P} - P)/P - (1 - \bar{h})[(\bar{E} - E)/E + (\bar{\overset{*}{P}} - \overset{*}{P})/\overset{*}{P}] \quad (9.32)$$

$$A + \overset{*}{A} \equiv M + B + E(N + F) \quad (9.33)$$

The aggregate supply equations for the home and foreign goods are given by

$$Y = X(\bar{W}/P), \qquad X_1 = -X' \quad (9.34)$$

$$\overset{*}{Y} = \overset{*}{X}(\bar{\overset{*}{W}}/\overset{*}{P}), \qquad \overset{*}{X}_1 = -\overset{*}{X}' \quad (9.35)$$

It is assumed that X' and $\overset{*}{X}' < 0$, so both the approximation coefficients are positive.

The asset market equilibrium conditions are given by

$$M = QL[(P/Q)Y, i, \overset{*}{i} + (\bar{E} - E)/E] \quad (9.36)$$

$$m_1 = L - m_2, \qquad m_2 = (L - L_1 Y)(1 - \bar{h})$$

$$m_3 = L_1, \qquad m_4 = -L_2, \qquad m_5 = -L_3$$

$$EN = Q\overset{*}{L}[(E\overset{*}{P}/Q)\overset{*}{Y}, i - (\bar{E} - E)/E, \overset{*}{i}] \quad (9.37)$$

$$n_1 = (\overset{*}{L} - \overset{*}{L}_1 \overset{*}{Y})\bar{h}, \qquad n_2 = \overset{*}{L} - n_1$$

$$n_3 = \overset{*}{L}_1, \qquad n_4 = -\overset{*}{L}_2, \qquad n_5 = -\overset{*}{L}_3$$

$$B = k[i - \overset{*}{i} - (\bar{E} - E)/E][A + \overset{*}{A} - QL(\cdot) - Q\overset{*}{L}(\cdot)] \quad (9.38)$$

$$b_1 = k(m_1 + n_1), \qquad b_4 = k'(A - L) + km_4, \qquad b_7 = k'(\overset{*}{A} - \overset{*}{L}) - kn_5$$

$$b_2 = k(m_2 + n_2), \qquad b_5 = k'(A - L) - km_5, \qquad b_8 = k(N + F - m_2 - n_2)$$

$$b_3 = km_3, \qquad b_6 = k'(\overset{*}{A} - \overset{*}{L}) + kn_4, \quad b_9 = kn_3$$

$$EF = \{1 - k[i - \overset{*}{i} - (\bar{E} - E)/E]\}[A + \overset{*}{A} - QL(\cdot) - Q\overset{*}{L}(\cdot)] \qquad (9.39)$$

Q is given by

$$Q = \bar{h}P + (1 - \bar{h})E\overset{*}{P} \qquad (9.40)$$

It is assumed that $0 < k < 1$; that L_1, $\overset{*}{L}_1$, k', $(L - L_1 Y)$, $(\overset{*}{L} - \overset{*}{L}_1 \overset{*}{Y})$, $(A - L)$, and $(\overset{*}{A} - \overset{*}{L}) > 0$; and that L_2, L_3, $\overset{*}{L}_2$, and $\overset{*}{L}_3 < 0$. These assumptions imply that all the asset market approximation coefficients except b_5, b_7, and b_8 are positive. The assumption that wealth holders in both countries regard the three assets they hold as strict gross substitutes implies that b_5 and b_7 are positive, that is, that the positive effect of the increase in the ratio of wealth minus money demand that home (foreign) wealth holders want to hold in home currency securities exceeds the negative effect of the increase in home (foreign) money demand. It is assumed that b_8 is positive, that is, that the positive effect of the increase in wealth on the demand for home currency securities exceeds the negative effect of the increase in money demands. Note that $A = aY$ and $\overset{*}{A} = a\overset{*}{Y}$ in the equilibrium at which the approximation is made. Adding (9.36), (9.37), (9.38), and (9.39) yields the identity (9.33), so only three of the four asset market equilibrium conditions are independent. In this paper the equilibrium condition for foreign currency securities (9.39) is not used.

In the third section it is assumed that

$$m_Y = m_1/x_1 + m_3 > b_Y = k(m_1 + n_1)/x_1 + km_3 \qquad (9.41)$$

which can be rewritten as

$$[(1 - k)/k](m_1 + m_3 x_1) > n_1 \qquad (9.42)$$

This condition is more likely to be satisfied the smaller is k, the proportion of wealth minus money demand allocated by residents of both countries to home currency securities; the larger is m_3, the effect of an increase in home output on home money demand; the larger is x_1, the increase in home output associated with an increase in the price of the home good; and the larger (smaller) is $m_1(n_1)$, the effect of an increase in the price of the home good on home (foreign) money demand.

In the sixth section it is assumed that $y_e = \overset{*}{y}_e$ where

$$y_e = c[-a_r(1 - \bar{h}) + a^*_r \bar{h}]Y + h'(Y + \overset{*}{Y}) + \bar{h}(1 - ca)\overset{*}{Y} + \bar{h}c(N + F)$$

$$\overset{*}{y}_e = c[a_r(1-\bar{h}) - a_r^*\bar{h}]\overset{*}{Y} + h'(Y + \overset{*}{Y}) + \bar{h}(1-ca)\overset{*}{Y} + (1-\bar{h})c(M+B)$$

If in the equilibrium at which the approximation is made home and foreign output are equal when measured in the same units ($Y = \overset{*}{Y}$ so that $\bar{h} = 1 - \bar{h}$), the responsivenesses of the desired ratio of wealth to income to the two expected real interest rates are equal ($a_r = a_r^*$), and the total of home currency assets is equal to the total of foreign currency assets when both totals are measured in the same currency ($M + B = N + F$), then the effects of a depreciation of the home currency on the demands for home and foreign output are equal in absolute value ($y_e = \overset{*}{y}_e$). $Y(M+B)$ can be compared with $\overset{*}{Y}(N+F)$ in the equilibrium at which the approximation is made because $\bar{E} = \overset{*}{\bar{P}} = \bar{P} = 1$.

The symbols are defined as follows:
P = home currency price of home good
$\overset{*}{P}$ = foreign currency price of foreign good
E = home currency price of foreign currency
Y = aggregate demand for and aggregate supply of home good
$\overset{*}{Y}$ = aggregate demand for and aggregate supply of foreign good
A = home residents' wealth measured in home currency
$\overset{*}{A}$ = foreign residents' wealth measured in home currency
h($\cdot$) = proportion of spending allocated by both home and foreign residents to home good
c = constant speed of adjustment of actual to desired wealth by both home and foreign residents
a($\cdot$) = desired ratio of wealth to income for both home and foreign residents
r = expected real interest rate on home currency securities
$\overset{*}{r}$ = expected real interest rate on foreign currency securities
i = nominal interest rate on home currency securities
$\overset{*}{i}$ = nominal interest rate on foreign currency securities
W = home currency money wage of home residents
$\overset{*}{W}$ = foreign currency money wage of foreign residents
X($\cdot$) = aggregate supply function for home good
$\overset{*}{X}(\cdot)$ = aggregate supply function for foreign good
M = supply of home money measured in home currency
B = supply of home currency securities measured in home currency
N = supply of foreign money measured in foreign currency
F = supply of foreign currency securities measured in foreign currency
Q = home currency average price of consumption bundle of both home and foreign residents
L($\cdot$) = demand for real balances of home money measured in terms of consumption bundle of both home and foreign residents

$\overset{*}{L}(\cdot)$ = demand for real balances of foreign money measured in terms of consumption bundle of both home and foreign residents

$k(\cdot)$ = proportion of wealth minus money demand held in home currency securities by both home and foreign residents

NOTES

Discussions with Donald Adams, Matthew Canzoneri, Michael Dooley, Jo Anna Gray, Kenneth Rogoff, and Jeffrey Shafer led to improvements in the paper. The analysis and conclusions of this paper should not be interpreted as representing the views of the Board of Governors of the Federal Reserve System or any other member of its staff.

1. There is no discussion of the use of intervention policy to counter "disorderly markets" or such features of exchange market dynamics as runs or bandwagons. Shafer (1982) addresses these issues among others.

2. Dooley (1979) provides a thorough discussion of intervention operations. Girton and Henderson (1977) compare the effects of intervention operations and monetary operations in a model of financial markets.

3. Frankel's (1979) evidence suggests that home and foreign currency securites are perfect substitutes. Obstfeld (1980), Hansen and Hodrick (1980), and Meese and Singleton (1980) present evidence that is consistent with home and foreign currency securities being imperfect substitutes. When Obstfeld simulates an intervention operation, he finds that the effects are quantitatively significant but relatively short lived.

4. Stein (1963) and Mundell (1968) were pioneers in the analysis of open economy financial policy. Their analysis is extended by Tower and Willett (1976). A recent contribution to this analysis has been made by Kaminow (1979b). Bryant's (1980) analysis of the effects of disturbances under alternative financial policy regimes is similar to the one of this paper. The approach used here is also employed in Henderson (1979, 1980).

5. This model is a partly linear and partly log linear approximation to a nonlinear model sketched out in the Appendix. Explicit expressions for the approximation coefficients are presented in the Appendix.

6. In order to consider a fixed interest rate policy in the model of this section under the assumptions about the behavior of the foreign authorities spelled out below or to consider fixed interest rate policies in the two-country model of the sixth section, it is sufficient but not necessary to assume that real wealth enters the aggregate demand function of at least one country and that tax liabilities corresponding to government securities are not perfectly discounted. For an explanation of why such assumptions are sufficient in the context of a closed economy model, see Canzoneri (1980). For an explanation of why they are not necessary, see Canzoneri, Henderson, and Rogoff (1981).

7. Y and $\overset{*}{Y}$ can be added together because units are chosen so that the relative price of the foreign good is one in the equilibrium about which the approximation is made.

8. Home and foreign residents are assumed to have the same tastes so that shifts of wealth between countries through current account surpluses and deficits will have no effects on the variables of the model. Without this assumption a more complicated, dynamic analysis would be required.

9. The foreign authorities must use monetary operations and two fiscal policy instruments, for example the level of balanced budget government spending and its allocation between the home good and the foreign good, to

achieve these constant values. Strictly speaking, it is foreign disposable income and not foreign output that is kept constant. Turnovsky (1976) and Flood (1979) make different assumptions about the behavior of the foreign authorities.

10. This statement is strictly true only if it is assumed that there are "no speculative bubbles." Sargent (1973) explains the implications of this assumption in the context of a closed economy.

11. Parkin (1978), Flood (1979), and Wallich and Gray (1981) analyze open economy financial policies under the assumption of rational expectations.

12. For an explanation of the exact restriction that this assumption places on the parameters of the underlying model, see the Appendix.

13. Meltzer (1978) has emphasized the importance of the distinction between permanent and transitory disturbances. In Rogoff (1980) private agents must attempt to sort out transitory and "lasting" disturbances and therefore adjust their expectations slowly to new lasting disturbances.

14. This kind of analysis was first employed by Poole (1970) and has been extended by Friedman (1975).

15. That is, suppose equations (9.8), (9.9), and (9.10) are divided by y_Y, m_Y, and b_Y, respectively; that $(\alpha + \beta)/y_Y = \beta'$, $(\gamma + \delta)/m_Y = \delta'$, and $(-\gamma + \varepsilon)/b_Y = \varepsilon'$ are disturbances that may be mutually correlated; and that $\sigma_{b'}^2 = \sigma_{\delta'}^2 = \sigma_{\varepsilon'}^2$.

16. See Poole (1970).

17. It would be interesting to consider optimal behavior for the authorities in yet a third environment in which they cannot observe or elect not to respond to current movements in the financial variables not chosen as policy instruments but in which the coefficients of the economic model are stochastic variables that have a joint distribution with the additive stochastic terms that is known to the authorities, as in Brainard (1967), and to private agents.

18. A rule of this kind was first developed by Poole (1970). Kareken, Muench, and Wallace (1973) and Friedman (1975) significantly generalize and extend Poole's results. Boyer (1978) derives an optimal decision rule in a model in which home and foreign currency securities are perfect substitutes and exchange rate expectations are static. Roper and Turnovsky (1980) show how this rule is affected by the incorporation of a more general hypothesis regarding the formation of exchange rate expectations and an additional type of disturbance. Boyer (1978) considers decision rules for the authorities in a model that is the same as the one used here in all essential respects except that exchange rate expectations are static. Fischer's (1977a) and Frenkel's (1980) optimal rules are derived in models quite different from the one employed here.

19. It could be assumed that the nominal wage was "indexed" to the two financial variables not chosen as policy instruments and that neither financial policy instrument was changed. If such an indexing rule were determined optimally, it would result in the same variation in output as would the authorities' decision rule. It appears that labor contracts involving indexing to financial variables are not negotiated, and conventional indexing is not a perfect substitute for this type of indexing.

20. It also depends on the assumption that the coefficients of the system are known with certainty.

21. Sweeney (1983) analyzes open economy financial policy using a

two-country model.

22. See the Appendix for a demonstration that the assumption of balanced trade has this implication.

23. Whenever a result depends on the relative slope of the B'B' schedule, this fact is mentioned in the footnotes.

24. These assumptions are spelled out in the Appendix.

25. If they were not, the analysis would be somewhat more complicated. If depreciations cause the XX and $\overset{**}{XX}$ schedules to trace out a line with a negative slope, as seems most reasonable, all the results except for those regarding a shift in demand between home and foreign goods are necessarily the same in qualitative terms, but the results for a demand shift may be affected.

26. If B'B' were flatter than $\overset{**}{XX}$, there would be pressure on the home currency to depreciate.

27. If B'B' were flatter than $\overset{**}{XX}$, there would be more variation in home (foreign) output under floating (fixed) exchange rates than under fixed (floating) exchange rates.

28. A game theoretic approach to this and other policy conflicts in open economies has been employed by Niehans (1968), Hamada (1974), and Jones (1979).

29. Black (1980) discusses the issues addressed in this section among others.

30. For a more detailed discussion of this equivalence see Girton and Henderson (1977).

31. This approach is used by Tinsley, Spindt, and Friar (1980).

32. Kalchbrenner and Tinsley (1977) describe a number of refinements.

DISCUSSION • *Herbert G. Grubel*

Dale Henderson's paper is technically competent, deals with an important issue, and makes a significant contribution to the field of study with which it deals. My comments, therefore, are aimed at putting the paper into some historic perspective and raising some questions about its implications for policymakers.

SOME HISTORIC PERSPECTIVES

Henderson's paper uses a model of the open economy that is almost identical to the Keynesian LM-IS-FE model very ably presented by Robert Stern (1973). This Keynesian model had found its most important application in the well-known arguments by Robert Mundell (1968) about the use of monetary and fiscal policies in an optimal mix to assure internal and external balance with fixed exchange rates. However, this model can be and has been used to analyze the effects of exchange rate changes on internal equilibrium operating through the demand for home and foreign goods, the general price level affecting real balances, and the interest rate. Indeed, this model has been used to show that the economic system has a natural tendency to move towards internal and external balance, so that any persistent payment imbalances or exchange rate changes are due to monetary policy (Grubel 1977a). In this work a clear distinction is made between exchange market intervention which is sterilized, that is, not allowed to affect the monetary base (Henderson's "intervention policy"), and intervention which is not sterilized.

Because of the great investment that has been made by many economists in the construction and learning of the LM-IS-FE model, I wish that Henderson had used this analytical framework, rather than his own, to introduce his two main contributions, which in my view are the following.

First, Henderson moves away from the Keynesian preoccupation with the problems of economies that are stuck at underemployment disequilibrium and focuses instead on the problems raised by the existence of random shifts of the three curves due to transitory and permanent disturbances. Henderson's analysis thus brings us back to the pre-Keynesian concerns with economic instability, including presumably classical business cycles, which in my view is the direction research should take in the light of the monetarist-inspired doubts about the liklihood of market economies getting stuck at an underemployment equilibrium. My main criticism of Henderson's paper presented below relates to whether the traditional Keynesian model is suitable for dealing with the newly discovered classical set of problems and deriving conclusions useful for policymakers.

Henderson's second contribution lies in the distinction between "aggregates constant" and "rates constant" policies. The introduction of this distinction at Henderson's level of theoretical analysis sheds light on the controversy over the optimality of monetary (and exchange rate) policies aimed at stabilizing interest rates versus stabilizing money supply growth rates in efforts to minimize fluctuations in output and employment in the presence of random shocks. In my critical comments below I raise doubts about the potential returns from this approach in terms of the insights useful for policymakers. In general, the approach neglects the lack of knowledge about the nature of the disturbances and reactions of the private sector to policies which constitute the monetarist arguments against the interest rates constant policies.

USING THE KEYNESIAN MODEL

This is not the place to review the many shortcomings of the Keynesian model as a tool for deriving policy prescriptions likely to lead to more stable output and employment. Instead, I focus on only one issue, which I feel has not been given the attention it deserves. This issue centers on the question of how to define operationally the full employment level of income, deviations from which are assumed in Henderson's model to call for intervention.

With the rejection of the Phillips curve trade-off as a policy relevant, as contrasted with econometrically verifiable, phenomenon, economists who continue to use the Keynesian analytical framework are faced with the problem of defining full employment operationally, since otherwise it is logically impossible to know whether any observed level of unemployment requires expansionary, contractionary, or neutral demand management policies. There is agreement among monetarists and Keynesians that what may usefully be called the natural rate of unemployment is influenced by demographic factors, labor force participation preferences, welfare and unemployment insurance programs, minimum wages together with unionization, expectations about inflation and therefore real wages, and many other factors.

The critics of Keynesian models argue that all of these influences on the theoretical level of full employment are very pervasive and may be unknowable. They therefore conclude that it makes no sense to aim stabilization policies at an unknown macroeconomic target. The use of capacity utilization rates or deviations from trend in economic growth are subject to the same difficulties as indicators of the direction, magnitude, and nature of disturbances, as is the rate of unemployment.

Yet, as a careful examination of Henderson's paper indicates, all of his conclusions and policy prescriptions are based on knowing operationally the level of full employment around which the economy should be stabilized, and therefore whether any observed deviations of the unemployment, capacity utilization, or growth rates are due to influences that can and should be dealt with through intervention policies.

Perhaps I am excessively pessimistic in my assessment of the probability that economists can or do know full employment and the causes of deviations from it. If I am correct in my pessimism, then Henderson's theorizing, centered on knowing operationally what full employment is, will not lead to useful policy insights. If, on the other hand, economists eventually can get empirical estimates of full employment and deviations from it, then Henderson's work will be very useful.

KNOWING THE NATURE OF DISTURBANCES

In this section I elaborate on the general argument just presented, that good policies require knowledge about the economy that we don't possess, by considering two of Henderson's theoretically most interesting conclusions. These conclusions are that an interest and exchange rates constant policy may be superior to an aggregates constant policy and that a managed exchange rate is likely to be superior to a fixed one. These conclusions make good sense both within the model and intuitively. Thus, if a country suffers a bad harvest it does not seem optimal to attempt stabilizing the economy through an exchange rate change since in the next period an above normal harvest is likely to return the economy to its stable equilibrium path as harvest deficits and surpluses average out. Under these conditions, changes in the exchange rate only induce resource movements in one period that need to be reversed in the next. By analogy, a shift in public preferences toward the holding of foreign securities is best dealt with through the pursuit of an aggregates constant policy and a change in interest rates, as Henderson shows in the text.

All of this is correct and true, but in the real world do, or can, economists ever know the causes of observed disturbances, together with the probability distribution of their being reversed or aggravated or offset by other disturbances? To be sure, guesses on these matters can be made, just as private market participants make them in their pursuit of profits. But in my view there is little evidence that policymakers can do better on average than private market participants, where actions are known to reduce the instabilities associated with random disturbances. It is exactly these reasons, together with the uncertainty over lags, which have led to the monetarist prescription for aggregates constant policies and letting relative prices, the interest and exchange rates, do the adjusting to disturbances.

Again, as in the above analysis of the problem of an operational definition of full employment, I may be too pessimistic in my assessment of the ability of policymakers to know more about trends and cycles, fundamental and temporary disequilibrium, permanent and stochastic shifts in economic variables, than do private entrepreneurs. If I am too pessimistic, then Henderson's model will be more useful for policymaking than if I am not.

SUMMARY AND CONCLUSIONS

The gist of my comments on Henderson's paper is that its usefulness for realizing conclusions relevant for policymakers depends excessively on knowledge about the economy and the disturbances to which it is subject. Thus, while the paper represents an important move away from traditional Keynesian concerns about underemployment equilibrium and toward the classical issue of how to deal with economic instability due to random shocks, I doubt that the Keynesian tools of analysis are likely to be the way to go. I suggest that treating the effects of disturbances as leading to a random walk of exchange rates and using "leaning against the wind" as a guide to policies may be more profitable than the approach chosen by Henderson (see Grubel 1977b).

All of the above criticism, however, should not detract from the heuristic value of Henderson's paper, which shows that disturbances lead to economic instabilities that in principle can be combated by appropriate intervention policies with rates or aggregates constant, depending on the nature of the disturbances. For this achievement, Henderson should be congratulated.

DISCUSSION • *John F. O. Bilson*

In this paper, Dale Henderson makes an extremely useful distinction between "intervention" and "monetary policy." In Henderson's terminology, intervention consists of a change in the currency composition of the central bank's portfolio that specifically does not change the size of the monetary base. In my comments, I shall accept these ground rules by restricting my attention to this type of sterilized intervention. Before doing so, however, I would like to point out how different this concept of intervention is from that of the traditional gold standard model. According to the gold standard "rules of the game," a central bank experiencing an outflow of gold was required to respond to this outflow by selling its domestic credit instruments. Gold standard theorists viewed the positive correlation between reserve flows and open market operations as a necessary method of preserving the country's limited stock of gold or, what amounts to the same thing, maintaining the fixed exchange rate.

The gold standard rules of the game, which served the international monetary system well in Victorian and Edwardian times, contrast with the concept of intervention described in Henderson's paper. Henderson's sterilized intervention requires the central bank to expand its purchases of domestic credit instruments during periods when its stock of international reserves is declining. If the pressure on the exchange rate represents an excess supply of the domestic currency, sterilized intervention will never eliminate the underlying cause of the depreciation because the domestic currency withdrawn from circulation by the sale of foreign securities is immediately replaced by the purchase of domestic debt.

The preceding statement does not mean, however, that sterilized intervention cannot influence the equilibrium value of the exchange rate and indeed the purpose of the Henderson paper is to demonstrate in an explicit and comprehensible manner how this influence is exerted. The conclusions reached by Henderson frankly bother me and, since I am sure that the paper contains no mathematical or logical errors, I must seek the source of my discontent in the "realism" of the paper's assumptions.

The crucial assumption is that wealth holders do not make their portfolio decisions purely on the principle of the maximization of expected

---

NOTE

The views expressed are solely the responsibility of the author and should not be interpreted as representing the views of either the University of Chicago or the National Bureau of Economic Research, Inc.

future wealth. Specifically, wealth holders are risk averse and, since domestic and foreign securities do not have the same risk characteristics, domestic and foreign securities are not perfect substitutes. The importance of this assumption for the efficacy of sterilized intervention may be best seen by tracing through the effects of a central bank operation. Assume that the central bank desires to exchange foreign debt for domestic debt in its portfolio. If the private sector was previously in equilibrium at a given vector of security yields, it will have to be induced to accommodate the central bank by the promise of a higher yield on foreign securities and a lower yield on domestic securities. Alternatively, the intervention will cause the forward exchange rate (dollars per unit of foreign currency) to fall below the anticipated future spot rate. In this scenario, it is the anticipated speculative gain on foreign currency holdings that induces the private sector to increase its demands for foreign securities. It is easy to demonstrate that the two mechanisms are equivalent in their market outcome if the interest rate parity condition holds.

We are not, however, yet at the end of the story since the link between the change in the relative yields on the two securities and the exchange rate has not yet been specified. For the main part of this paper, Henderson assumes that the foreign central bank maintains foreign interest rates and prices at some constant level. This turns out to be a crucial assumption since it implies that the intervention operation described above unambiguously lowers the general level of interest rates in the world and hence increases the demand for both the foreign and the domestic money. However, in the foreign country, the central bank responds to this increase in money demand by increasing the supply in order to maintain their objective of constant prices. It is only in the domestic economy that the effect of the lower interest rates on the demand for money is reflected in the exchange rate. Specifically, the increase in the demand for money creates an excess supply of domestic goods and domestic assets and a reduction in the demand for imported goods and assets. In order to clear this incipient balance of payments surplus, the exchange rate must appreciate.

Although this description does not do justice to the details of the Henderson model, I believe that it is a fair description of the mechanism through which sterilized intervention influences the economy. It also points out an obvious difficulty with the approach: since Henderson's assumptions require the foreign central bank to take action in order to prevent foreign interest rates and prices from reacting to the domestic intervention, it is difficult, if not impossible, to tell if the change in the exchange rate is due to the intervention itself or to the assumed reaction of the foreign central bank. Since the intervention induces an expansionary monetary policy from the foreign central bank, it is likely that the major part of the change in the exchange rate is due to foreign monetary expansion rather than to the domestic intervention. At a later point in the paper, Henderson does consider a full two-country model. However, this analysis is limited by the assumption that both interest rates are fixed by the authorities. It is consequently difficult to analyze the effect of intervention independently of the policies required to maintain the interest rates of their target levels. In conclusion, it is not possible within the structure of Henderson's model to describe the ceteris paribus effect of a change in the portfolio composition of the central bank portfolio.

I would now like to return to the central assumption that domestic and foreign securities are not perfect substitutes. As mentioned above, this assumption is based upon the presumption that wealth holders are risk averse so that their objective is not solely the maximization of expected future wealth. Although this assumption is often found in the international and domestic finance literature, I argue that it is based upon extremely weak theoretical and empirical foundations and that these foundations are certainly not strong enough to form the basis for a socially useful intervention policy.

On theoretical grounds, the major problem with the risk aversity model is that it requires that <u>all</u> market participants be risk averse. While I am perfectly willing to accept the argument that the vast majority of the world's citizens are risk averse, I believe that the probability that the entire population is risk averse is very small and, in addition, I believe that the tendency towards risk aversity declines with wealth as is witnessed, for example, by the recent unfortunate experiences of the Hunt brothers. These propositions are important because they suggest a tendency for asset market prices to be dominated by risk neutral participants. In any large number of trials, the more risk neutral participants will tend to profit more than the risk averse participants since the former are, by definition, closer to the maximization of expected future wealth. Thus eventually the market should be dominated by risk neutral participants and consequently foreign and domestic securities should be perfect substitutes at the margin.

It is also important to remember that the risk from foreign currency speculation is vastly overstated by the variance of the forecast error. The theory of finance is explicit in defining risk in terms of covariation with a market portfolio rather than in terms of the actual variance of the return. Since the unanticipated change in the exchange rate is not strongly correlated with unanticipated changes in the returns on other assets, the risk from foreign currency speculation is likely to be quite small. In addition, the fact that gambles in the foreign exchange market yield returns that are not correlated through time implies that the risk from a large number of gambles is small. The correct analogy here is with the gambler's roulette wheel: although the house may face a large risk on any one spin of the wheel, the return from a large number of spins is practically certain.

From theory we turn to empirical evidence. There are a large number of studies of the speculative efficiency of the foreign exchange market. Although these studies give mixed results with regard to the hypothesis that the forward rate is an unbiased and efficient forecast of the future spot rate, I am aware of no study that has demonstrated that changes in the composition of central bank portfolios have any predictable impact on the forward rate bias. I also find it extremely unlikely that such evidence will ever be found. I base this opinion on two considerations. First, the large variance of forward rate forecast errors makes it extremely difficult to test hypotheses directed at the forward rate bias. Second, intervention by any one central bank constitutes such a small fraction of the total flow through world currency markets that its effect, if any, is likely to be swamped by other transactions. In addition, I also agree with Henderson's point that it is extremely difficult to measure central bank intervention from published sources.

I have spent some time explaining why sterilized intervention is unlikely to work because I believe that the policy implications of this type of analysis are often quite pernicious. The models often imply that the portfolio composition of the central bank portfolio can be used to control the exchange rage so that monetary policy can be directed at the control of interest rates. Henderson's first model of transitory disturbances clearly implies that the most effective means of reducing interest rates is to expand the money supply. This conclusion, which is widely held among central bankers and academic economists, is probably the most costly policy error made by the Federal Reserve before Mr. Volker's redirection of monetary policy towards quantity, rather than rate, management.

The reason why the policy is erroneous is clearly expressed in Henderson's algebraic analysis, although it is more difficult to discern from the text. Henderson assumes that the economy is anticipated to return to a full employment equilibrium in each future period, which implies that the current intervention or monetary policy does not have any effect on future expectations. In a world of rational expectations, this anticipated reaction must occur so that the Henderson model implies that any policy intervention is expected to be reversed in the next period. The policies considered in the paper should consequently be considered to be a combination of both the current policy and its reversal in the next period.

This principle is of particular importance in the analysis of the relationship between monetary policy and interest rates. In Henderson's model, an expansionary monetary policy lowers interest rates predominantly because it causes prices to increase relative to future prices and hence creates an anticipation of a future deflation of domestic prices. In the "real world" an expansion in the money supply if far more likely to lead to an increase in the anticipated rate of inflation and hence to an increase in nominal interest rates. Under certain circumstances, a continued attempt to maintain low interest rates through monetary expansion could lead to a situation in which prices, exchange rates, and interest rates are dynamically unstable. Some would argue that the pre-Volker monetary policy of the Federal Reserve was an example of this instability.

As a last specific comment on the model, I would like to address the motives for intervention described in the Henderson model. In the model, labor is assumed to set the nominal wage for period "t" based upon the information available in period "t-1". This rigidity then implies that unanticipated monetary or real shocks will induce unemployment. Government policies are then required to reduce unemployment or excessive employment (inflation). What is lacking in this analysis is a realistic theory of wage-setting behavior. In its place, Henderson employs a simple distortion in the labor market to justify the introduction of distortions into financial markets. (It is relatively easy to demonstrate that financial income would be maximized if the central bank set the forward rate equal to the future spot rate.) Apart from the classic argument that domestic distortions require domestic policies, the Henderson model does not consider the interaction between the model of wage-setting behavior and the model of central bank intervention behavior. As is well known from the British experience, an anticipated policy of monetary accommodation often results in wage bargaining that is directed against the central bank and the government rather than against the corporation. It is all too possible that a policy of using monetary policy to correct labor market distortions will result in an unstable "vicious circle" of inflation and depreciation.

It is difficult to leave this topic without proposing an alternative. For monetary policy, a stable and predictable monetary growth rate is now being increasingly recognized as the optimal monetary policy for a free market economy. As far as intervention policy is concerned, a good case can be made for the central bank to attempt to maximize its profits from foreign exchange speculation from a publicly announced set of exchange rate forecasts. If these forecasts are accurate, they will have an increasing influence on market expectations and, in combination with a stable underlying monetary policy, will induce greater stability in foreign exchange markets. This type of policy is surely more likely to be successful than the attempt to correct domestic labor market distortions through intervention in the foreign exchange market.

REJOINDER • *Dale W. Henderson*

In my paper open economy financial policymaking is analyzed in terms of what can usefully be referred to as a decision theory approach. According to this approach the appropriate choice of financial policy instruments and optimal variation of those instruments depend on the sources of disturbances to the economy and the type of information available to the authorities. John Bilson and Herbert Grubel raise some important questions regarding the usefulness of this approach. I develop this approach in the context of a particular economic model that implies some specific results. Bilson and Grubel state some objections to this model; Bilson attempts to raise doubt about whether the model possesses a property that is crucial for obtaining my results, and Grubel misstates my main conclusions.

THE USEFULNESS OF A DECISION THEORY APPROACH

A decision theory approach yields principles for generating better macroeconomic outcomes by taking into account the best available information about the structure of the economy and the disturbances to which it is subjected. Grubel questions the usefulness of this approach because he is skeptical about the ability of the authorities to obtain the kind of information needed to improve macroeconomic performance.

Grubel exaggerates somewhat the quality of the information that the authorities must have in order to make constructive use of a decision theory approach. He seems to suggest that policymakers must have better information than private market participants about the economic structure and disturbances. In my paper and many other applications of a decision theory approach, policymakers are no better informed than private agents. The scope for the authorities to improve macroeconomic performance arises because of short-run nominal rigidities in the economy. These rigidities exist because adjustments in at least some nominal variables require time-consuming and costly negotiations. Their importance is widely, but by no means universally, acknowledged. Such a nominal rigidity is present in my model because it is assumed that the nominal wage is set before disturbances are experienced. At a minimum, financial policy instruments must be chosen and values for them must be selected. Given nominal rigidities these decisions matter for the variation in output and employment, so the authorities are well advised to use the best information they have about the sources of disturbances in making them. The possibility that policy rules relating changes in policy instruments to movements in financial information variables may be helpful arises because changes in financial policy instruments can be made more quickly and at lower cost than alterations in some other nominal magnitudes, such as nominal wages. Indeed, policy rules might be helpful even if policymakers were somewhat less well informed than private agents.

Grubel also exaggerates somewhat the extra amount of information required. He argues that a decision theory approach makes necessary an operational knowledge of the level of output that constitutes full employment output. In my paper and many other applications of a decision theory approach such knowledge is not necessary. Throughout most of my paper where the values of policy instruments are held constant during the period, these values are chosen and announced before the nominal wage is set. The nominal wage is then set by private agents at a level that would yield their concept of full employment output given no disturbances. In the part of the paper where instruments are changed during the period, they are varied in response to movements in other financial variables that indicate deviations from this level of output. In a more complex and realistic model with wage contracts that last more than one period, operational knowledge of full employment output would be required because some nominal wages would already have been set when values for policy instruments were chosen. However, in such an environment even a central bank following Grubel's favored monetarist prescription, that it should set a target for the money supply for some period ahead, would need to make an estimate of full employment or potential output in order to avoid causing unwanted unemployment or inflation.

Even though Grubel exaggerates somewhat the quality and quantity of information that the authorities need if a decision theory approach is to make a difference, his skepticism must be taken quite seriously. Often the authorities will have little information about the economic structure and the sources of disturbances. However, there are cases when the source of disturbances is fairly clear. It would have been easy to detect significant changes in the desired currency composition of asset holdings by the authorities in the major oil producing countries in the wake of the Iranian asset freeze had they occurred, and sterilized intervention would probably have been the appropriate response. The Swiss authorities have recognized and accommodated speculative shifts in the demand for their country's money with the concurrence of noted monetarists. Shifts in U.S. and Canadian money demand have been documented and taken into account. In addition, the empirical studies cited in the conclusion to my paper suggest that a decision theory approach can yield useful results. Furthermore, the fact that it is difficult for the authorities to obtain information in which they can place a high degree of confidence cannot be used as a basis for arguing that they should ignore the lessons of a decision theory approach in reacting to the information that they do have. Indeed, sophisticated use of such an approach requires different reactions to pieces of new information depending on their perceived quality.

Bilson calls attention to a significant shortcoming of my exposition of a decision theory approach. It proceeds under the assumption that the financial authorities and private agents have the common objective of minimizing the variation in output and employment. If, instead, labor unions tried to pursue an objective of raising the real wages of their employed members by making high nominal wage demands, a rates constant policy while limiting the induced decline in union employment would result in larger increases in the price level and nonunion employment. A decision theory approach can be used to study the important, game-theoretic problems that arise when there are conflicts between the objectives of the authorities and those of some private agents, but this complicated case is not considered in my paper.

At one point Bilson characterizes the selection of a financial policy regime on the grounds that it minimizes variation in output and employment as an "attempt to correct domestic labor market distortions through intervention in the foreign exchange market." Of course, both my aggregates constant and my rates constant policy regimes imply settings for both monetary policy and intervention policy, so Bilson's view must really be that I employ "a simple distortion in the labor market to justify the introduction of distortions into financial markets." It does not seem useful to classify the real costs of nominal wage renegotiation as a "distortion." Bilson might prefer to subsidize wage renegotiation directly, but such a policy could only shift the incidence of the real costs. Values for financial aggregates or rates, or rules relating these magnitudes, must be chosen. It is indeed important to determine whether any significant real costs are imposed on financial market participants by various financial regimes. In this regard it is interesting to note that my rates constant policy prevents any unanticipated changes in the interest rate and the exchange rate. Even if it is discovered that real costs are imposed on financial market participants, comparisons of alternative financial policy regimes should still take account of their effects on the variation in output and employment that results from disturbances because of the real costs of changing nominal wages.

THE MODEL AND THE RESULTS

Grubel has two objections to my model. Grubel's first objection is that the model is "Keynesian." He acknowledges that my model does not imply that the economy can be "stuck at underemployment disequilibrium" and that I use it to deal with "the pre-Keynesian concerns with economic instability." Indeed the model is closely related to the closed economy model employed by Sargent (1973) to demonstrate why traditional stabilization policies might not be effective. I can see why Grubel might object to what I do with the model, but in my view he does not show that the model possesses any objectionable Keynesian properties. Grubel's second objection is that the model is unfamiliar. He would have preferred that I had used what he calls the IS-LM-FE model. Most versions of that model have well-known shortcomings that are summarized by Stern (1973). The model I use is free of most of those shortcomings and has the additional advantage of focusing attention on the markets for the actual goods and assets that are traded, so the implications of the balance sheet constraint can be exploited quite easily. The balance of payments condition that has been suppressed is a combination of demands and supplies in several markets. A number of the authors cited in Henderson (1977) have used similar models.

Bilson objects to my model because in his view the central assumption that home and foreign securities are imperfect substitutes has "extremely weak theoretical and empirical foundations." This assumption is central because the result that sterilized intervention can affect the exchange rate depends on it. Bilson states correctly that this assumption is based on the presumption that wealth holders are risk averse. His first theoretical objection to models based on risk aversion is that even if there are only a few risk neutral market participants, they will eventually dominate financial markets. It does appear to be true that in a stationary world even a small group of infinitely lived, risk neutral speculators will eventually dominate financial markets. However, to take account of the assumptions underlying this theoretical proposition is to recognize that, by itself, it does not constitute a convincing argument against the use of models based on risk aversion to address current policy problems.

Bilson's second theoretical objection is that risk aversion on the part of participants in exchange markets should not affect desired asset holdings because "the risk from foreign currency speculation is likely to be quite small." His point, that the very large variance of return to speculation almost certainly overstates the risk of foreign exchange speculation because covariation of the return to speculation with the return on a market portfolio rather than actual variance of return is the relevant measure of risk, is indisputable. Much more open to question is Bilson's (empirical) proposition that the "unanticipated change in the exchange rate is not strongly correlated with unanticipated changes in returns to other assets."

Bilson's reading of the empirical evidence that bears on the existence of risk aversion and the effect of intervention policy on the exchange rate is different from mine. Tests of speculative efficiency in the foreign exchange markets can be viewed as tests of the joint hypothesis of risk neutrality and rational expectations. The most recent and most technically sophisticated tests of this joint hypothesis, such as those by Hansen and Hodrick (1980), Meese and Singleton (1980), and Bilson himself (1980), convincingly reject it. While the results of these tests cannot be regarded as a rejection of risk neutrality alone, they certainly cannot be used to cast doubt on the hypothesis that risk aversion is important in foreign exchange markets. Empirical studies of the effect of sterilized intervention have yielded mixed results. Obstfeld (1980) finds a significant, but rather small, effect of sterilized intervention on the spot rate. Frankel (1979) finds no effect of sterilized intervention on the forward rate bias. I agree with Bilson that it will be difficult to obtain precise empirical estimates of the effects of sterilized intervention on the exchange rate because of some of the considerations he mentions. That does not mean we should jump to the conclusion that such intervention is ineffective. As I said in my paper, I believe that whether intervention policy is a significant, independent policy tool is an important and as yet unresolved empirical question.

Bilson attempts to raise doubt about the correctness of the result that sterilized intervention can affect the exchange rate under the assumption that home and foreign currency securities are imperfect substitutes. At the end of his discussion of the effect of an intervention operation in the first version of my model, he asserts that "it is likely that the major part of the change in the exchange rate is due to foreign monetary expansion rather than to the domestic intervention." Later he asserts that "it is not possible within the structure of Henderson's model to describe the ceteris paribus effect of a change in the portfolio composition of the central bank portfolio." Both of these assertions are incorrect.

The effect of sterilized intervention on the exchange rate does not depend on induced changes in the foreign money supply. This proposition can be proved most easily with the use of a two-country, four-asset (home and foreign moneys and home and foreign securities) financial model in which output and the price level in both countries are exogenous, such as the one employed by Girton and Henderson (1977). As an example of a sterilized intervention operation, consider a sale of home currency securities and an accompanying purchase of foreign currency securities by the home authorities.

This operation causes the home interest rate to rise and the foreign interest rate to fall because it creates an excess supply of home securities and an excess demand for foreign securities. These interest rate movements lead to a decrease in the demand for home money and an increase in the demand for foreign money under the reasonable assumption that the demand for each country's money is more sensitive to changes in the interest rate on securities denominated in that country's currency than to changes in the interest rate on securities denominated in the other country's currency. If money supplies remain fixed, there is an excess supply of home money and an excess demand for foreign money, so the home currency depreciates.

It is a little more difficult, but by no means impossible, to describe the ceteris paribus effect of sterilized intervention in the model of my paper. The substitution of the linearized versions of equations (9.31) through (9.35) into the linearized version of equations (9.29), (9.30), (9.36), (9.37), and (9.38) yields five equilibrium conditions in Y, Y^*, i, i^*, and e. The effect on the exchange rate of an unanticipated sale of home securities and purchase of foreign securities by the authorities holding money supplies constant is given by

$$\hat{e}/\hat{B} = (1/\Delta_3)\{(m_4 n_5 - n_4 m_5)(y_Y \overset{*}{y_Y} - \overset{*}{y_Y} y_Y^*)$$
$$+ [n_Y(m_4 - m_5) - m_Y(n_4 - n_5)][y_Y^* \overset{*}{y_2} + \overset{*}{y_Y} y_2]$$
$$+ [n_{Y}^*(m_4 - m_5) - m_{Y}^*(n_4 - n_5)][y_Y \overset{*}{y_2} + \overset{*}{y_Y} y_2]\}$$

The home currency definitely depreciates ($\hat{e}/\hat{B} > 0$) if $m_4 > m_5$, $n_5 > n_4$, and $\Delta_3 > 0$ since $y_Y \overset{*}{y_Y^*} - \overset{*}{y_Y} y_Y^* > 0$. The first two conditions are met under the assumption used above in the analysis of sterilized intervention in a two-country, four-asset financial model; Δ_3 is the determinant of the 5 X 5 matrix of coefficients of the five equilibrium conditions. It is positive under plausible assumptions and must be positive if conventional experiments such as an increase in the home supply through an open market purchase of home securities are to have their usual effects. For convenience, the natural assumptions that $y_2 = y_3$ and that $\overset{*}{y_2} = \overset{*}{y_3}$ have been adopted in the derivation of $\hat{e}/\hat{B}$.

Grubel misstates my main conclusions. These conclusions are that for disturbances to aggregate demand an aggregates constant policy is better because the induced changes in the interest rate and the exchange rate work to offset the disturbances and, therefore, dampen the movements in output and employment, while for disturbances in financial markets a rates constant policy is better because transmission of the disturbances to the market for the home good via interest rate and exchange rate changes is prevented. Models like the one used by Stanley Fischer (1977b), in which the assumptions regarding the structure of the economy, the sources of disturbances, and the objective of the authorities are different from mine, yield conclusions more akin to those stated by Grubel.

GENERAL DISCUSSION

The general discussion revolved around two issues: the conditions necessary to ensure that intervention operations will in fact affect the exchange rate; and the feasibility of operationalizing the type of intervention policy described by Henderson. Discussion of the first issue centered on the degree of substitutability characterizing the relationship between domestic and foreign financial assets. In general, the higher the degree of substitutability, the$_*$ less effect any given intervention operation will have on the exchange rate. The long discussion that ensued, reflecting the divergent empirical evidence, was inconclusive.

The discussion of the second issue focused on the knowledge policymakers have versus the knowledge they don't have. Some wondered whether intervention increased or decreased uncertainty in foreign exchange markets. Put another way, is intervention a correct response to disturbances or is intervention itself a disturbance? Henderson responded that attempts are under way at the Federal Reserve to operationalize the model and to evaluate its potential contribution to stabilization policy.

$*$ Editors' note: Henderson's intervention scheme presumes that foreign assets and domestic assets are imperfect substitutes for one another in investors' portfolios. Accordingly, when the home government sells foreign assets (and buys domestic assets) it changes the relative supply of these assets in the market. The change in relative supply affects interest rates and exchange rates. If, on the other hand, foreign and domestic assets are perfect substitutes for one another, then the effect of the home government's sale of foreign assets on rates is offset by the willingness of private investors to readily substitute the foreign assets for domestic assets in their portfolios. In this case the change of relative supply is irrelevant and has no effect on interest rates and exchange rates.

PAPER 10 • *Donald D. Hester*

The Effects of Eurodollar and Domestic Money Market Innovations on the Interpretation and Control of Monetary Aggregates

INTRODUCTION
 The acid test for a bank or a banking system is its ability to produce good money when under stress. Prior to the emergence of token money a sound bank was expected to be able to pay its depositors in fully valued coin or bullion. Such coin was effectively legal tender although, as Mr. Gresham noted, other coins were often disproportionately used to complete transactions.

Outside Money
 In the United States a watershed was crossed in the 1850s when Congress began to have the Treasury issue token coins and canceled the legal tender standing of foreign coins. Good money thereafter was to be interpreted as domestic legal tender and, with the passage of the National Banking Act, became a quantity that was defined and determined by the Treasury Department throughout the remainder of the nineteenth century. With the establishment of the Federal Reserve System in 1914, the responsibility for defining and and controlling the volume of good money began to shift toward the sometimes autonomous Federal Reserve Board. Today the Federal Reserve alone is responsible for determining the volume of good or "outside" money, the sum of currency outstanding and reserves on deposit at Federal Reserve banks.[1]
 The interpretation of currency as legal tender has not changed appreciably in the last 130 years, and the amount of currency outside banks can be ignored without loss in the present paper. Coin and currency in bank vaults can be used to satisfy reserve requirements and thus serve as substitutes for reserves on deposit at Federal Reserve banks.[2] However, banks view currency and coin as subsidiary assets that are kept on tap to accommodate bank customers. Consequently, paper currency and coin in bank vaults are assumed to be exogenously determined and are ignored without loss in the subsequent discussion.
 The volume of outside money has played a central role in monetary theory. Central banks such as the Federal Reserve are able to vary the volume of outside money when they buy or sell government securities through open market operations. An open market purchase increases the volume of outside money and the ratio of outside money to government debt in the aggregative private sector portfolio. Tobin (1963) has argued that an increase in outside money leads to a reduction in the required rate of return on capital, which in turn is likely to lead to real economic expansion and to the accumulation of physical capital. Tobin and Brainard (1963) have rigorously extended his result to financial regimes that consist of

intermediaries subject to reserve requirements and interest rate ceilings. A similar conclusion about the consequences of an increase in outside money emerges from a monetarist perspective. In this view, an increase in money, inside or outside, leads to increased expenditures that in turn result in rising prices and/or output. Monetarists often postulate the existence of a money supply function that relates the volume of outside money to the volume of inside money--usually deposit liabilities of commercial banks.

Intuitively, the basis for believing that variations in outside money can affect the economy is that it is an ideal medium for executing transactions and maintaining portfolio flexibility, but pays no rate of return at the margin. When the volume of outside money is increased (decreased), individuals and banks are induced to expand (contract) their activity until the increased (decreased) medium is willingly held and the system reaches a state of equilibrium.

Immediately Available Funds

The present paper argues that the role of outside money has changed considerably in the past twenty years because of a series of legal and technological changes and related regulatory agency decisions that served to define "immediately available funds." Immediately available funds are "(1) deposit liabilities of Federal Reserve banks, and (2) certain 'collected' liabilities of commercial banks that may be transferred or withdrawn during a business day on the order of account holders" (Lucas et al. 1977, p. 362). Thus, immediately available funds at commercial banks exceed deposit liabilities of Federal Reserve banks whenever commercial banks are open and able to transfer funds. The two quantities are equal when banks are closed.

During a business day the excess of immediately available funds over deposit liabilities at Reserve banks and those deposit liabilities are very close substitutes. The excess is almost as convenient a medium of exchange as outside money for large organizations and banks. In subsequent sections evidence is reported that this excess has been growing much faster than outside money, both internationally and domestically. One could be very seriously misled by ignoring immediately available funds when monitoring outside money. The ability of the Federal Reserve to control the level of economic activity has been correspondingly weakened, but not destroyed.

The possibility of a difference between immediately available funds and deposit liabilities of Federal Reserve banks exists because of clearing schedules and conventions that the Federal Reserve and other money market institutions have established for settling accounts. For example, a bank selling a security to another bank at the beginning of a business day can act as though it has received funds the moment a security is sold, but the buyer does not have to arrange financing for it before the end of the day. The amount of immediately available funds at a bank fluctuates wildly as funds are transferred by wire and checks are collected. For all banks in the system, the amount of immediately available funds that exists when banks are open is likely to be substantially larger than the overnight level. Banks with offshore branches have especially interesting arrangements that have both diminished their domestic required reserves and expanded their ability to control future levels of immediately available funds. While these schedules and conventions have existed for many years, their quantitative importance for monetary policy has only recently grown large, as a result of innovations and changes that served to considerably reduce transactions costs.

Linkage and the Domestic Demand for Money

With few exceptions (e.g. Minsky 1957; Hester 1972) economists who analyze monetary policy have ignored financial market innovations until very recently. This stance might be rationalized on the grounds that existing empirical relationships linking various official measures of monetary aggregates to national income (money demand functions) were intertemporally stationary (Goldfeld 1973).[3] By 1976 it was obvious to Goldfeld (1976), to Enzler, Johnson, and Paulus (1976), and to most other observers that this alleged robustness of the demand for money was fictitious. Recently Porter, Simpson, and Mauskopf (1979) have stressed the importance of technological progress in money management as a possible explanation for nonstationarity, but their explanation appears to be indistinguishable from one that attributes nonstationarity to a changing regulatory and legal environment.

The recent nonstationarity of the money demand function raises serious questions about the reliability of monetary policy, has led to considerable empirical research, and has caused the Federal Reserve to revise the definitions of monetary aggregates that guide the conduct of monetary policy. One hypothesis that has been studied by Goldfeld (1976) is that there was no major innovation or structural change. According to this hypothesis the original demand for money function was misspecified. He has tentatively rejected this hypothesis by showing that specifications that were able to track money after 1973 were empirically inferior in earlier years. He concluded that a structural change had occurred, but that its nature could not be identified.

Other attempts (e.g. Tinsley, Garrett, and Friar 1978; Garcia and Pak 1979) to patch up the money demand function by adding estimates of net Federal funds purchased to M1 have had some success, but they must be viewed as very tentative since accurate information about net purchased funds is not available for the banking system. Further, some formidable logical conditions must be satisfied before aggregation of dissimilar objects can be justified. Green (1964) has stressed the importance of the principle of functional separability. Empirical studies by Wood (1976), Barnett (1978), and Tinsley, Spindt, and Friar (1980) strongly suggest that summation of components of monetary aggregates is unjustified by this criterion. These studies support arguments of McKean (1949) and will be seen to be relevant for interpreting domestic activities of offshore banks, which are discussed below.

Regulatory Change and Financial Innovation

Institutional changes involving immediately available funds have been occurring since the Federal Reserve came into existence.[4] Changes in regulations are both a response to recent innovations or perceived weaknesses in the financial system and a stimulus leading to future innovations. Table 10.1 summarizes major regulatory changes involving immediately available funds that occurred during the past two decades.

Table 10.1 must be interpreted carefully since it does not purport to represent monetary policy fully, and ignores a number of other innovations that had indirect effects on immediately available funds--e.g. the emergence of certificates of deposit, money market mutual funds, NOW accounts, corporate savings accounts, bank related commercial paper, and bank holding companies. Nevertheless, it will be seen to be a useful point of reference, and it illustrates the extraordinarily complex and wandering path that has been followed by the monetary authorities as they sought to cope with

TABLE 10.1. Selected regulatory changes directly involving immediately available funds

Date	Action
August 1960	Regulatory change permitting some vault cash to be counted against reserve requirements.
November 1960	Regulatory change permitting all vault cash to be counted against reserve requirements.
July 1962	Elimination of central reserve city bank classification, which reduced variation in marginal reserve requirements across member banks.
June 1963	Defined Federal funds transactions to be purchases and sales and therefore exempt from regulations that limited a national bank's transactions with another bank to 10% of the lending bank's equity capital and surplus.
September 1963	Defined Federal funds transactions between two banks belonging to a single holding company to be a <u>loan</u> and <u>not a sale</u>, to prevent evasion of reserve requirements.
February 1964	Opinion that a domestic branch of a foreign bank was equivalent to a nonmember bank for clearing purposes. However, balances due from such branches cannot be deducted from deposits for the purpose of calculating reserve requirements.
August 1964	Opinion that purchases and sales of funds between a nonmember bank and a member bank constituted a Federal funds transaction.
November 1964	Opinion allowing an Edge Act Corporation to trade in Federal funds for "the purpose of adjusting its reserve balance."
October 1966	Authority given to the trading desk to use debt issues of U.S. government agencies when engaging in open market operations.
April 1967	Member banks authorized to make stock investments in foreign subsidiary banks and to make loans to them that are not subject to Section 23A of the Federal Reserve Act.
September 1968	Introduction of lagged reserve accounting.
October 1968	Announcement of contract for Federal Reserve System Central Communications Switch at Culpeper, VA--the first major advance in EFTS at system level in fifteen years.

TABLE 10.1 (continued)

Date	Action
June 1969	Issuance of the "Martin Letter," which asked that activities of Eurobranches be confined to developing new international business and not used as vehicles for shifting deposits away from domestic reserve requirements, etc.
July 1969	Clarification of regulation D to exempt from reserve requirements repurchase agreement transactions that were secured by U.S. government or agency securities--thereby legitimizing repurchase agreement transactions.
August 1969	Imposition of 10% marginal reserve requirement on Eurodollar borrowings and on off-shore branch credit extended to U.S. residents. Also, officers' checks in favor of foreign branches of a bank are ruled to be subject to reserve requirements.
January 1970	For the purpose of interpreting Federal funds borrowing under regulations D and Q, a "bank" was defined to include all (a) member commercial banks, (b) nonmember commercial banks, (c) Edge Act and agreement corporations, (d) branches and agencies of foreign banks, (e) savings banks, (f) building or savings and loan associations, and (g) cooperative banks. In addition purchases and sales by the EXIM Bank, the Minbanc Capital Corporation, federal agencies, and nonbank security dealers were exempt from these regulations.
December 1970	A 20% marginal reserve requirement on Eurodollar borrowings introduced to support the dollar.
August 1971	Announcement that Federal Reserve wire transfer services would be available free of charge if transfers involved $1000 or more.
September 1971	Open market operations involving outright purchases or sales of agency securities authorized.
June 1972	Announced substantial changes in rules concerning speed of crediting and payments in immediately available funds (Regulation J) and realignment of reserve requirements on demand deposits (Regulation D) to achieve a banking system that is "better equipped to participate in a rapidly developing modern payments mechanism."

TABLE 10.1 (continued)

Date	Action
May 1973	Reserve requirements on Eurodollar borrowings cut from 20% to 8%.
January 1974	Opinion barring nonbank participation in the federal funds market.
February 1974	Issuance of routing numbers for checks written against thrift accounts so that they can be cleared through the Federal Reserve.
October 1974	Reclassification of due bills as demand deposits if corresponding securities are not received within three business days.
April 1975	Reduction of reserve requirements on Eurodollar borrowings to 4%.
June 1975	Trading desk authorized to make repurchase agreements with dealer banks.
January 1977	Authorization for long-term borrowing by a member bank through its offshore subsidiary.
November 1977	Reserve requirements on domestic borrowings from Eurobanks reduced from 4% to 1%.
January 1978	Member bank borrowings from member banks whose head office is outside the United States exempted under regulation D.
September 1978	Reduction of reserve requirements on Eurodollar borrowings to 0%.
October 1979	Marginal reserve requirements imposed on member bank purchases of Federal funds from nonmember banks, on member bank purchases of repurchase agreement funds from nonbanking corporations, and on Eurodollar borrowings.
November 1979	Definition of a "bank" under regulation D for the purpose of defining Federal funds extended to include credit unions.
December 1979	Voluntary guidelines provided to banks taking positions in futures markets, standby credits, and forward markets.

Sources: Nichols 1965, Federal Reserve Bulletin

All the above actions except that of June 1963 were taken by the Federal Reserve; the June 1963 decision was taken by the comptroller of the currency. Dates were determined not by effective date but by the issue number of the Federal Reserve Bulletin in which a particular opinion, rule, or definition was announced.

questions involving immediately available funds. To be sure, the Federal Reserve did not take these actions in a vacuum; it may have responded to irresistible pressures from Congress, lobbies, and administrations. The table is not complete enough to support a position about the wisdom of board actions during the last twenty years.

Three financial instruments are frequently mentioned in Table 10.1 and are importantly linked to the growth of immediately available funds. They are Federal funds purchased by commercial banks from other financial institutions and government agencies, net borrowings by commercial banks through repurchase agreements, and net Eurodollar borrowings.[5] The volume of immediately available funds tends to be larger when these liabilities are larger. Sizable fractions of each liability mature at the beginning of a business day and these funds are available to commercial banks and their customers each day as collected funds. To an important extent they are the overnight repositories of the difference between immediately available funds and deposit liabilities of Federal Reserve banks. In the present paper, the "market for immediately available funds" refers to transactions involving these liabilities.

The regulatory changes in Table 10.1 can be collected under four broad categories: (1) technical improvements in the efficiency of the traditional market for immediately available funds; (2) expansion of the scope of the market to include institutions that are not members of the Federal Reserve System, legitimizing repurchase agreement transactions in immediately available funds, and legitimizing inter- and intrabank transactions that involve offshore offices; (3) expansion of the set of securities that is available for open market operations and repurchase agreement transactions to include debt that is issued by U.S. government agencies, and (4) especially after 1968, a series of changes in reserve requirements on Eurodollar borrowings.[6]

Technical improvements in the market permit traders to move funds more rapidly and at lower cost and, therefore, permit a given amount of funds to settle a larger volume of transactions. For large denominations, as is evident with the change of August 1971, funds transfers can be effected at zero cost. These improvements increase the transactions velocity of money, and require that information about the economy and its interpretation improve if a given degree of monetary control is to be maintained (see Hester 1972). Intuitively this is because improved trading techniques permit the amount of immediately available funds to wander further in a business day.

Expansion of the scope of the market has had very complicated consequences, which depend upon how the scope was extended. However, in all cases it is likely that the excess of immediately available funds over deposit liabilities at Federal Reserve banks rose because more participants were involved. Federal Reserve information about the positions of new participants was markedly inferior to information it had about member banks and security dealers.

Expanding the set of securities eligible for open market operations was probably inevitable after Congress decided to create additional off-budget agencies. The initial announcement of the change in trading desk policy had very little effect on the analysis of monetary policy because agency debt was small in relation to outside money and direct obligations of the Treasury. However, the change was to become important after the Federal Reserve's 1969 announcement affirming that agency securities could serve as collateral in repurchase agreement transactions. Agency securities have been growing at a faster rate than other Federal debt in bank portfolios.

Frequent changes in reserve requirements on Eurodollar borrowing are self-explanatory and reflect the rapidly changing state of international banking and the balance of payments. However, as will be seen, they also reflect control problems the Federal Reserve is encountering at the domestic level.

Uneven Regulation of Immediately Available Funds

Several years elapsed between the 1963 and 1964 regulatory changes concerning Federal funds and the perception by the financial community at large that regulation of immediately available funds was flabby. However, high interest rates and disintermediation caused by regulation Q ceilings in 1966 and particularly in 1968 and 1969 led some bankers to experiment with Eurodollars, and with repurchase agreements involving all sorts of collateral. By 1969 the board and Congress recognized that financial control was disintegrating; reforms adopted included reserve requirements on bank related commercial paper and Eurodollar borrowings, the June 1969 "Martin letter," the July 1969 restrictions on eligible collateral for repurchase agreements, and the January 1970 determination of who could deal in the Federal funds market. These reforms were ex post facto responses to apparent aneurysms in the financial circulatory system rather than the result of any deep analysis of the role of the market for immediately available funds in the United States.

With the Penn Central crisis of June 1970, attention was shifted from immediately available funds. The Eurodollar reserve requirement increase in December 1970 was designed to cope with a balance of payments crisis by keeping Eurodollar balances abroad. Apart from technical reforms in January and October 1974, the board did little to deter rapid growth in the amount of immediately available funds until its actions of October 6, 1979, when substantial marginal reserve requirements were imposed on several liabilities that were overnight repositories for immediately available funds. By June 1980 at least two further adjustments to these marginal reserve requirements had been made.

The Congress was more persistent and, after several sets of hearings and investigations, passed the International Banking Act, the Electronic Funds Transfer Act, the Financial Institution Regulatory Act, and the Depository Institutions Deregulation and Monetary Control Act. These acts place additional supervisory and regulatory burdens on the Federal Reserve, and significantly modify the environment in which financial institutions operate. No doubt a new round of financial innovations and regulatory responses will ensue!

The reasons for the hiatus in the board's attention to immediately available funds are not obvious, but I suspect it occurred because the board failed until very recently to recognize its own responsibility for controlling the volume of immediately available funds. Instead the board focused on conventionally measured monetary aggregates. It also reflected a preoccupation with empiricism that was not well suited to coping with the emerging instruments, since essential data about immediately available funds were not being collected. In addition, the time span of observation of several important repositories of immediately available funds was too short to permit useful statistical inferences.

Synopsis

To summarize this unavoidably intricate discussion, it may help to consider what has been said by examining a few hypothetical diagrams that refer to all banks that are members of the Federal Reserve System. Figure 10.1A shows the expected value of the time path of immediately available funds over a typical business day before any of the changes mentioned in Table 10.1. The path rises above the overnight level as securities are shifted about but then settles back to its overnight level at the end of the day. (It is assumed that there is no leakage from the system of member banks and that float and discount window borrowing do not change). Figure 10.1B shows the expected value of the same time path in 1979. The step increase at 9:00 AM when the system opens and the step decrease at 5:00 PM when the system closes refer to the destruction and re-creation of all overnight and some term Federal funds, repurchase agreements, and Eurodollar transactions. In addition to the step changes, the path arches up more during a day because of improvements in the funds transfer mechanism.

The solid line in Figure 10.1C shows a hypothetical time series of the ratio of the sum of net funds acquired through repurchase agreements, net Federal funds purchases, and net Eurodollar borrowings to member bank reserves. The dotted line in the same figure shows the ratio of the average intraday level of immediately available funds to member bank reserves.

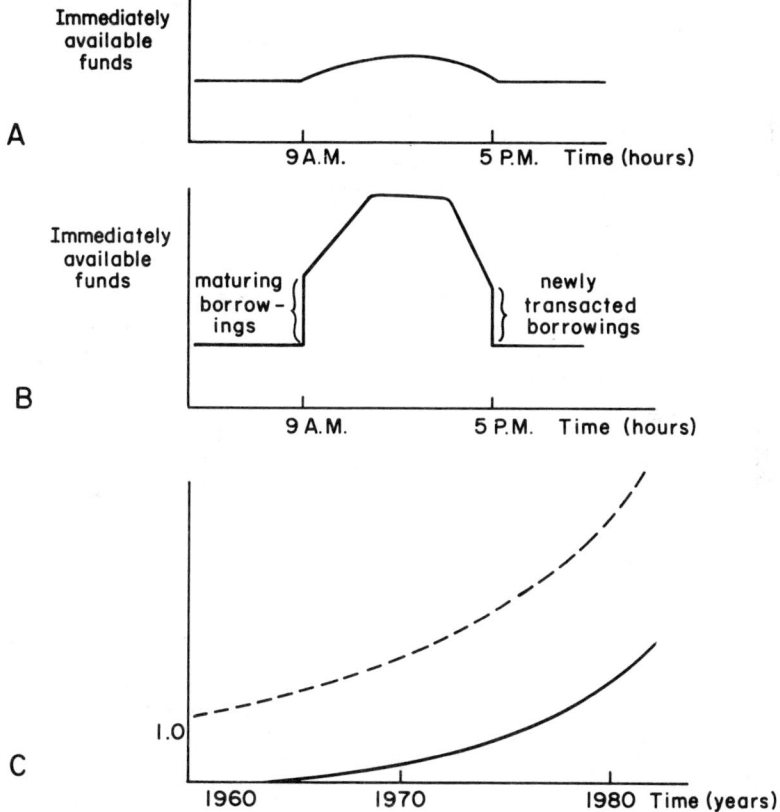

Figure 10.1. Hypothetical profiles for all member banks.
(A) Typical business-day time profile, circa 1959. (B) Typical business-day time profile, circa 1979. (C) Ratios of end-of-day, short-term borrowed liabilities (———) and average intraday levels of immediately available funds (------) to member bank reserves.

The solid line indicates the hypothetical cumulative percentage error since 1959 that might be made by focusing on published reserve bank credit rather than the more appropriate volume of intraday immediately available funds.

Figure 10.1C is likely to understate the effects of the surging volume of immediately available funds on nonfinancial sectors of the economy. Improvements in the technology of funds transfer will permit the expanding volume of immediately available funds shown in the figure to finance an even more rapidly expanding volume of transactions in goods markets as time passes. More importantly, because the Federal Reserve does not appear to monitor the intraday volume of immediately available funds, the probability confidence intervals about paths in the Figures have almost surely widened with the passage of time. Control must necessarily be looser and stabilization actions appear more erratic when uncertainty is greater.

The next section examines evidence about the surging Eurodollar market and interprets its consequences for domestic monetary policy. The third section focuses on how the rapidly growing volumes of net Federal funds purchased and repurchase agreement transactions have affected domestic monetary policy. The final section reports fragmentary evidence that domestic monetary control is weakening, and concludes with several proposals that are designed to strengthen monetary policy.

EURODOLLARS, MULTINATIONAL ENTERPRISE, AND DOMESTIC MONETARY POLICY

Eurodollars are dollar deposits at foreign banks outside the United States and at offshore branches of American banks. In the middle of 1979 there were about $900 billion of such deposits, of which perhaps $150-$200 billion were bank liabilities to individuals other than banks and central banks. While Eurodollar deposits are predominantly time deposits, Frydl (1980) reports that about one-third of nonbank Eurodollar deposits have a maturity of less than eight days. The volume of Eurodollars has been growing at a rate of about 25 percent per year in the past decade. By one reckoning (Resler 1979) the volume of U.S. domestic bank liabilities to "Eurobanks," foreign banks and offshore U.S. branches, rose by $26 billion in the first eight months of 1979.

This section examines three aspects of Eurodollar growth. First, what accounts for the rapid growth of Eurodollars in the past fifteen years? Second, what is the connection between Eurodollars and immediately available funds? Finally, what consequences does the existence of a large Eurodollar market have for the implementation of domestic monetary policy and for the international coordination of monetary policy?

Sources of Eurodollar Growth

The emergence of the Eurodollar market can be traced to the cold war and to exchange controls and impedences to capital flows that variously were imposed on both sides of the Atlantic. One large American bank chose to establish a large international banking system during the post-World War II period, but as recently as 1965 the scale of overseas banking by American banks was quite limited. It could plausibly be interpreted as a legitimate response to the postwar recovery and expansion that followed the restoration of currency convertibility in 1958. With the Vietnam escalation of 1966 and attendant restrictive credit policy, the nature of American overseas banking changed greatly. Thereafter, overseas banks were at least partly a pressure valve whereby large American banks could replenish their reserves and partially escape the restrictive consequences of binding regulation Q ceilings, rising domestic interest rates, and oppressive reserve requirements.

Evidence supporting this interpretation is reported in Table 10.2.

TABLE 10.2. Selected statistics on multinational and Eurodollar activity by American firms

Year End	(1) Total assets of Overseas Branches of Member Banks ($ billion)	(2) Number of Overseas Branches of Member Banks	(3) Total Domestic Assets of Member Banks ($ billion)	(4) Gross Domestic Fixed Non-residential Investment ($ billion)	(5) Gross[a] Foreign Capital Expenditures by U.S. Affiliates ($ billion)	(6) Sum of U.S. Imports and Exports, NIA ($ billion)
1965	NA	211	313.4	NA	NA	71.5
1966	12.4	244	335.5	81.4	8.7	80.5
1967	15.7	295	374.6	82.1	9.7	86.2
1968	23.0	375	413.5	89.3	10.0	97.6
1969	41.0	459	433.1	98.9	11.6	107.6
1970	52.6	536	466.2	100.5	14.1	121.0
1971	67.1	577	511.8	104.1	16.3	129.6
1972	77.4	627	585.5	116.8	16.7	148.6
1973	118.0	694	656.3	136.0	20.6	196.0
1974	140.5	732	715.9	150.6	25.3	269.8
1975	162.7	762	733.8	150.2	26.8	274.2
1976	193.9	731	772.9	164.9	24.7	318.7
1977	227.9	730	861.8	189.4	27.5	361.7
1978	257.6	761	957.3	221.1	30.7	424.7
1979	312.9	789	1048.8	253.9	37.4[b]	518.3

Sources: Federal Reserve Bulletin, Survey of Current Business, various issues.
[a] Majority owned foreign affiliates of U.S. corporations.
[b] Latest plans.

Between 1966 and 1978, assets of overseas branches of member banks increased twentyfold and the number of overseas branches tripled. During this same period the nominal value of the sum of American imports and exports in the national income accounts rose from $80.5 billion to $424.7 billion. Offshore deposits of member banks grew at annual rates of about 50% or more during 1968, 1969, and 1973--all years in which domestic interest rates rose rapidly or established twentieth century highs. Between 1966 and 1969 the sum of exports and imports rose about 10% per annum. It seems very unlikely that the growth in offshore American bank deposits can be explained by trade growth, expected or realized.

Another possible explanation is associated with growing production of subsidiaries of American companies in foreign countries. No reliable data exist about America's stake abroad, but information about annual gross capital expenditures by majority owned, foreign subsidiaries are regularly collected by the Commerce Department. Columns 4 and 5 of Table 10.2 indicate that foreign subsidiaries received a growing share of gross investment between 1965 and 1972, and that since 1972 foreign affiliates absorbed a constant 15 percent of gross domestic fixed nonresidential investment. Again, there is no apparent economic reason for the disproportionate growth of deposits at offshore branches relative to domestic banking assets, except avoidance of restrictive domestic monetary policy.[7]

The number of banks with offshore branches rose from 8 in 1960 (Little 1975, p. 83) to more than 150 in 1975. In 1965 foreign offices were quite evenly spread across economically active regions of the globe.[8] However, new entrants to the Eurodollar market often had only one or two offshore offices, frequently in London and/or the Grand Cayman Islands. Recently large banks have been opening additional offices in Bahrain, Singapore, and financial centers in other time zones. Such concentrations strongly suggest regulatory avoidance rather than the presence of nonpecuniary locational rents.

As American deposits fled the United States, an imbalance developed. Foreign banks could borrow Eurodollars as cheaply as American branches and, until the International Banking Act, they were largely unregulated in the United States. As a result the number of foreign bank branches in the United States rose from 110 in 1972 to 282 in June 1978. In New York and California, commercial and industrial loans made by branches of foreign banks were 40 percent of commercial and industrial loans at all weekly reporting banks in those states in 1978 (Federal Reserve Bank of Chicago, International Letter, number 377). The assets of branches of foreign banks grew 38 percent in 1978, 30 percent in 1979, and sixfold between 1972 and 1979. In December 1979 only 25 percent of $168 billion in assets was financed by domestic demand, time, or savings deposits. Given this reverse flow from Europe, it is hardly surprising that the dollar began to strengthen and that the Federal Reserve was increasingly able to reduce reserve requirements on Eurodollar borrowings after 1973. The foreign banks have extended a considerable amount of domestic credit that was not matched by growth in domestic deposits or in conventionally measured monetary aggregates such as M1. Surely the meaning of the conventionally measured aggregates should have changed! (See McKean 1949).

Eurodollars and Immediately Available Funds

The relation between Eurodollars and immediately available funds in the United States is determined by conventions that domestic banks establish with their nonbank customers, by rules that define the relation between (New York) clearinghouse funds and immediately available funds, and by clearing arrangements that exist among Eurobanks. Outside the United States collected or good funds denominated in dollars are not formally defined by the Federal Reserve. Until recently domestic branches of foreign banks have not had their own accounts with the Fed. The amount of immediately available funds in Eurobanks is, therefore, an amorphous quantity that is determined by what these banks view collected funds to be at any moment.[9] Since large multinational banks are operating in many time zones, there need be no moment of time in which all of a bank's branches are closed. There is nothing that corresponds to the end-of-day position of a domestic bank, when a bank's immediately available funds are equal to its Federal Reserve bank deposits. Good money can include uncollected drafts on a bank's own branches or other banks in different countries, which are reported as interbank deposits.

The system permits Eurobanks to alter the volume of what amounts to immediately available funds outside the United States by altering the volume of interbank deposits. These funds can be used to clear international dollar transactions, including those of domestic nonbanking firms, that may shift funds from domestic banks to Eurobanks in response to interest rate differentials. The system also permits Eurobanks to lend Eurodollars to American domestic banks without hindering their dollar transactions at offshore locations. Technically these loans are executed by large American banks that deposit checks drawn on their offshore branches in favor of their own account at the New York clearinghouse. After one day clearinghouse funds are accepted by the Federal Reserve as being collected and become immediately available funds for domestic banks. The amount that can be transferred from Eurobanks to domestic American banks is limited only by the amount of funds that Eurobanks are willing to lend.

Effects of Eurodollar Flows on Domestic Policy

Eurodollar borrowings are analogous to bank float in the domestic banking system since they are an addition to the volume of Federal Reserve sanctioned outside money that occurs because of differences in the times when items are defined to be collected officially (one day) and when they are actually collected (possibly a very long time). As in the case of domestic bank float, the Federal Reserve can sterilize changes in Eurodollar borrowings by open market transactions.[10] Changes in the volume of Eurodollar borrowings are likely to dwarf changes in domestic bank float, and become increasingly disruptive as the volume of Eurodollars continues to expand. Open market transactions required to sterilize these changes can be expected to grow in volume over time and result in growing volatility of domestic interest rates. Evidence that this loss of control by the Federal Reserve is in fact occurring is reported in the fourth section. The large number of changes in reserve requirements on Eurodollar borrowings reported in Table 10.1 also suggests that the Fed is having difficulty with Eurodollars.

The dollars that return to the United States through the Eurodollar market are partly dollars that leaked out earlier through balance of payments deficits and partly dollars that have been created abroad. During the 1960s foreign central banks often acquired dollars in order to prevent their own currency from appreciating in the fixed exchange rate system. Little (1975, pp. 96-97) reports that central banks occasionally placed the dollars acquired in these support operations in the Eurodollar market in order to earn high Eurodollar interest rates. No doubt some of these funds flowed back to the United States and forced the Fed to undertake additional sterilization operations. Domestic monetary policy in the United States would have been facilitated if the European central banks had simply retained the Eurodollars, but that would have entailed a loss of interest income for them. Monetary policy tends to be weak in fixed exchange rate systems with or without a Eurodollar market, so the incidents were not of great import.

With the shift toward a floating exchange rate system in 1973, the existence of the Eurodollar market has become a much more serious problem in the conduct of monetary policy. As OPEC prices rose and the American balance of payments deficit continued, a large quantity of new Eurodollars came into existence. European central banks could protect their economies from rising OPEC prices by allowing the dollar to plummet and perhaps by selling some of their own dollar holdings. In these circumstances and in the face of weak domestic monetary growth, the Federal Reserve responded by driving domestic interest rates to historically high levels in 1974 and again in 1979 and 1980. These actions succeeded in making Eurodollars even more attractive and invited sharp interest rate adjustments by European central banks in 1979 and 1980 as the appreciating dollar began to aggravate severely the effects of OPEC price increases. In the fourth section it is proposed that international agreements are needed that serve to limit multinational banks' ability to create a close substitute for a country's own outside money, especially the American dollar.

REPURCHASE AGREEMENTS AND FEDERAL FUNDS MARKET INNOVATIONS

In this section attention is restricted to events occurring within the United States in order to interpret further the changing nature of immediately available funds. Between 1963 and 1979 the number of participants in the Federal funds market increased greatly to include government agencies and many financial institutions that were not commercial banks or members of the Federal Reserve System.[11] Technical improvements in equipment that moved funds and the elimination of fees on funds transfers reduced transactions costs, expanded the variety of transfers, and led to exotic concepts like remote disbursing facilities that exploited weaknesses of the check clearing system. Repurchase agreements grew like topsy until 1969 when the Federal Reserve defined what assets member banks could use to collateralize such transactions. Table 10.1 provides a rough chronology of these changes.

Evidence of Technical Progress in Funds Transfers

Table 10.3 reports an attempt to measure changes in immediately available funds over the past twenty years from very fragmentary data. The first four columns describe numbers of items and volumes of funds that have been transferred through the facilities of the Chicago Federal Reserve Bank.[12] The number of checks cleared quadrupled between 1961 and 1979, and the amount of funds cleared through checks almost quintupled. By way of contrast the number of wire transfers expanded more than tenfold and the amount of funds transferred via wire grew more than thirtyfold during the same period. The percentage of funds cleared with checks declined from about 40 percent to about 10 percent. Since wire transfers are effected within a business day (often within a few minutes) and checks clear within a few days, it is obvious that the excess of immediately available funds over deposit liabilities at Federal Reserve banks could be considerably larger on average in 1979 than in 1961, as suggested in Figure 10.1.

The final two columns of Table 10.3 clearly indicate the effects of improved technical efficiency in the transfer mechanism. The volume of debits to demand deposit accounts, exclusive of debits to interbank and U.S. government accounts, rose eighteenfold in eighteen years. The annual rate of turnover of demand deposits, net of interbank and U.S. accounts, rose fivefold, if allowance is made for a revision in the reporting base. Thus, immediately available funds surely did finance a vastly larger volume of transactions, although one cannot be sure of the extent to which they were merely moving paper as opposed to goods and services.

It remains to attempt to apportion the increasing volume of transactions between an increasing velocity of a fixed volume of immediately available funds and an increasing volume of such funds moving at a constant velocity.[13] This apportionment is very crude because the Federal Reserve never reports immediately available funds except at the end of a day when tautologically they are equal to deposit liabilities at Federal Reserve banks. In the present discussion the excess of intraday immediately available funds over deposit liabilities of Federal Reserve banks is estimated by "net purchased funds," the sum of net Federal funds purchases and net funds acquired through repurchase agreements. Funds acquired through repurchase agreements are related to bank debits and turnover, because demand deposit accounts of sellers of funds are debited when the transaction is completed.

The two columns concerning net purchased funds strongly suggest that rising demand deposit turnover is related to growing volumes of immediately available funds, in addition to rising velocity.[14] Net purchased funds by weekly reporting banks grew 700 percent in a decade. As a percentage of outside money, net purchased funds grew from about 13 percent to about 45 percent in this period. Comparable data for all commercial banks from call

TABLE 10.3. Wire transfers, net purchased funds, debits, and annual demand deposit turnover

	Chicago Federal Reserve District				Weekly Reporting Banks[a]	All Commercial[a] Banks		Debits to Demand Deposits ($ trillions)	Demand Deposit Turnover
	Number of items		Amounts ($ trillions)		Net purchased funds ($ billions)	Net purchased funds ($ billions)	Outside[b] money ($ billions)		
Year	Checks collected (billions)	Wire transfers (millions)	Checks	Wire transfers					
1961	0.56	0.46	0.192	0.334	NA	NA	50.5	3.1	38.2
1965	0.75	0.67	0.263	0.686	NA	0.3	60.2	5.2	48.1
1966	0.81	0.75	0.309	0.890	NA	0.3	63.3	5.9	52.6
1967	0.86	0.82	0.310	1.078	NA	1.5	66.9	6.7	56.5
1968	0.93	0.91	0.331	1.311	NA	1.8	71.5	8.0	62.0
1969	1.00	1.03	0.390	1.701	9.5	6.1	75.6	9.2	68.0
1970	1.06	1.17	0.442	2.035	10.8	3.2	79.8	10.9	77.0
1971	1.14	1.29	0.512	2.392	15.5	6.9	84.9	12.4	83.7
1972	1.23	1.53	0.557	2.931	20.0	9.5	89.3	14.8	90.7
1973	1.40	1.90	0.642	3.783	29.5	19.1	97.8	18.6	110.2
1974	1.50	2.40	0.703	4.729	41.8[c]	18.5	105.9	22.2	128.0
1975	1.60	2.80	0.714	4.949	37.8[c]	19.7	109.9	23.6	131.0
1976	1.80	3.40	0.799	6.008	51.2	32.6	117.1	28.9	153.5
1977	2.00	3.70	0.906	7.100	52.4	41.9	126.5	34.3[e]	129.2[e]
1978	2.00	4.20	0.992	7.900	61.5[d]	NA	139.2	41.8[e]	139.3[e]
1979	2.10	5.00	1.114	9.500	68.7[d]	NA	152.1	54.0[e]	172.6[e]

Sources: Annual Reports, Federal Reserve Bank of Chicago, Federal Reserve Bulletin, various issues.
[a] The sum of Federal funds purchased and funds acquired through repurchase agreements, less Federal funds sold to banks (end of year figures).
[b] Data are the sum of December total reserves at member banks and currency component of the money stock, not seasonally adjusted and not adjusted for lagged reserve accounting basis.
[c] These numbers refer to end of November, since conspicuous window dressing was evident in published data for end of December.
[d] Weekly reporting bank sample was reduced; reported number refers only to banks with more than $750 million in domestic assets at the end of 1977.
[e] Reporting basis changed in June 1977; data are not strictly comparable to earlier numbers.

reports show a higher rate of growth; as a percentage of outside money, their net purchased funds rose from 8 percent in 1969 to 33 percent in 1977. Large increases in net purchased funds by weekly reporting banks coincide with large increases in bank debits and demand deposit turnover.

Consequences for the Implementation of Monetary Policy

Technical improvements in funds transfers and rapid growth in net purchased funds have created five major problems for the implementation of monetary policy. The most basic problem is that the restrictive effect of open market sales of securities has been seriously weakened. Before repurchase agreements were widely used, an open market sale by the Fed removed immediately available funds from the economy and replaced them with Treasury securities, which were awkward to use as a transactions medium. Today, an open market sale of securities replaces one transactions medium with another that is identical so long as the newly sold securities are used as collateral against overnight repurchase agreements.[15] The $12.00 (or less) fee for processing large-denomination repurchase agreement transactions is not sufficient to deter the use of securities as a medium of exchange. In effect, one can wire securities as easily as one can wire money! Possible interest rate risks from using intermediate or long maturity securities as a transactions medium are easily and cheaply hedged in the rapidly growing futures markets for Treasury securities. It is hardly surprising that one of the recent Federal Reserve chairmen discovered that the old medicine wasn't working anymore; the outstanding volume of immediately available funds was out of his reach!

Relatively strong indirect evidence of this slippage in the effectiveness of monetary policy exists in the movements of short-term interest rates. Suppose monetary policy is loose and relatively accommodating. One should expect interest rates on Treasury bills to be similar to yields on prime commercial paper and Federal funds, for which they are close substitutes. On the other hand, if restrictive policy is in effect, short-term government securities are attractive to banks and others for an additional reason--they are eligible collateral for repurchase agreements. Therefore, one should expect to observe a gap open up between the Treasury bill rate and the Federal funds rate when monetary policy is binding. Inspection of end-of-quarter monthly averages of the Federal funds rate and the market yield on 91-day Treasury bills between 1965:I and 1980:I indicates that the Federal funds rate exceeded the bill rate by 100 basis points or more during 1969:II-1970:I, 1973:I-1974:IV, and 1979:I-1980:I. In no other quarter did the two rates differ by as much as 100 basis points.[16] Repurchase agreements generated a strong demand for bills precisely when the Fed was attempting to drive up interest rates through open market sales.

The second problem concerns required reserves. With improved funds transfer technology, the banking system can collectively lower its required reserves for a given volume of deposits by moving deposits to nonmember banks or to member banks with low marginal reserve requirements and then sending funds back to large banks through the Federal funds market. With improvements in data processing and high speed funds transfers, banks and their corporate clients can profit considerably by making use of remote disbursing offices. By using these mechanisms in combination with offshore branches, a number of exotic procedures have been developed that substantially reduce required reserves for the banking system, without inconveniencing banks or their clients. A second major tool of monetary policy is slowly but steadily being weakened, even when announced reserve requirements are unchanging.

Third, as new financial instruments emerged and the rate of mutation increased, the usefulness of the Federal Reserve's reporting system for controlling immediately available funds deteriorated. In part this was unavoidable; change creates uncertainty and the Federal Reserve's ability to impose reporting requirements on institutions other than member banks was limited. In part, however, the Fed has been slow in comprehending the import of innovations. Until very recently, except for call reports, there has been no systemwide reporting of repurchase agreements or gross funds purchases by type of seller, and there has been a reduction in reporting requirements for small banks. It is very difficult to control things that are not observed.

Fourth, while there has been much discussion within the Federal Reserve system about how much the Fed should charge for different services provided to banks, there has been little public discussion of the linkage between service charges and the efficacy of monetary policy. Many years ago William Baumol (1952) applied a simple inventory theoretic model to cash management; if there are no transactions costs, his model implies that no money should be held for transactions purposes. The Federal Reserve's decision to impose no charges for transfers of $1,000 or more over the Fed wire obviously has led to a reduction in money balances demanded throughout the economy relative to the volume of transactions occurring. Technical progress does not invalidate the distinction between private and social costs; when it comes to monetary policy the distinction probably ought to be more sharply drawn.

Fifth, the Federal Reserve's decision to assess no charges against transfers above a certain size smacks of unfairness and raises a very disturbing question about the distribution of the burden of monetary policy. In a different context, this question has been raised by Governor Wallich (1979) when testifying before Congress about the access of banks and firms of different sizes to the Eurodollar market. It is at least as important on the domestic front. Only large enterprises can wire funds around the country frequently and take advantage of sophisticated funds concentration schemes. Small savers may benefit from trickle down flows, but evidence about the magnitude of such flows is wanting.

EVIDENCE OF LOOSENING CONTROL AND SOME POLICY SUGGESTIONS

The preceding sections have suggested that innovations and regulatory changes are likely to have weakened the Federal Reserve's ability to control monetary aggregates and economic activity. Evidence about this suggestion is necessarily indirect. The problem is rather like watching generally reliable dials in the control room of a nuclear power plant; one cannot legally or physically observe the reactor directly. Nevertheless, available evidence strongly suggests that vibrations within the monetary reactor are becoming more severe; more control rods and a different reactor design may be necessary if a melt down is to be avoided.

Weakening Control

Table 10.4 records three distinct signals that Federal Reserve control is weakening. First, despite substantial improvements in check clearing procedures, Federal Reserve float is growing faster than system demand deposits and reserves, especially since 1965. Float is a direct measure of the accuracy with which the Fed is able to match its actual collections with its own administratively established schedules. The Fed has an obligation to keep float small since it amounts to an indefensible interest free transfer

TABLE 10.4. Control and variability in the money market

Years	(1) Total Reserves[a] ($ billion)	(2) Float[a] ($ billion)	(3) Reserve bank[a] credit ($ billion)	(4) Monthly[b] Transactions ($ billion/month)	(5) Large T-Bill[c] Rate Changes (absolute)	(6) Positive[c] T-Bill Rate Changes	(7) Negative[c] T-Bill Rate Changes	(8) Mean[d] Absolute T-Bill Rate Change
1952-54	19.9	0.88	25.6	NA	0	0	0	0.19
1955-59	18.9	1.13	26.3	NA	3	1	2	0.40
1960-64	19.7	1.65	32.1	0.39[e]	1	0	1	0.18
1965-69	24.5	2.09	50.0	0.50	2	1	1	0.38
1970-74	32.1	2.88	76.3	1.06	13	5	8	0.67
1975-79	36.7	4.10	113.4	3.35	6	5	1	0.61
1975	34.9	2.20	95.2	2.38	2	1	1	0.90
1976	34.2	2.83	104.5	2.86	2	0	0	0.36
1977	35.1	3.78	111.6	4.47	0	0	0	0.38
1978	38.2	5.55	123.5	3.21	2	2	0	0.53
1979	41.4	6.15	132.2	3.83	2	2	0	0.90

Sources: Federal Reserve Bulletin, Banking and Monetary Statistics, Annual Statistical Digest.

[a] Daily averages for last month in a quarter (mean over indicated years).
[b] Mean absolute value of monthly net change in System Open Market Account.
[c] The number of quarters in the indicated time interval that the three-month Treasury bill rate averaged daily over a quarter, changed by more than 75 basis points.
[d] Mean absolute value of quarterly changes in the three-month Treasury bill rate, averaged daily over a quarter (expressed as percent/annum).
[e] This entry is based on data for the years 1961-1964; the underlying series was not reported in 1960.

to some individuals at the expense of others and because it results in a loss of revenue to the Treasury (Wolkowitz and Lloyd-Davies 1979).

Second, the absolute values of monthly net changes in the system's open market portfolio are rising much faster than either bank reserves or total reserve bank credit. Between the early 1960s and the late 1970s, the average absolute net portfolio change grew tenfold while Federal Reserve bank credit grew only about fourfold. Obviously the trading desk was becoming much more active in its attempts to control. Mere activity does not, of course, imply lack of control, but it is apparent that the Fed was increasingly finding it necessary to make purchases and sales that had to be reversed within a few months.

Third, since 1952 money market interest rates, such as the Treasury bill rate, have been rising faster than if they were simple exponential functions of time--surely an indication of a critical reactor. The volatility of interest rate changes has also been rising over time. In large part, interest rate volatility reflects active discretionary policy by the Fed. The origin of shocks to the economy, however, is not necessarily the Federal Reserve, and large interest rate fluctuations do not necessarily reflect deteriorating stability in the money market alone. With this caveat in mind, it is nonetheless remarkable how volatile interest rates have become. It would seem that the Federal Reserve has had to push interest rates harder, upward and downward, to get the economy to respond. Table 10.4 indicates that 76 percent of large positive and negative quarterly changes in the Treasury bill rate over the last twenty-eight years have occurred during the most recent decade. The average quarterly change during the 1970s was twice as large as the change during the preceding two decades.

One obvious interpretation is that growing amounts of dollars in money and capital markets are immunized from discretionary policy shocks. Both interest rate movements and the volume of Federal Reserve transactions must be <u>relatively</u> larger than previously to have the same domestic effects.

Policy Suggestions

In the remaining space four proposals for improving monetary control are briefly described. The proposals are pragmatic extensions of theoretical arguments reported by Phillips (1957) and Brito and Hester (1974). They are made at a time when the consequences of implementing the International Banking Act and other legislation that extends reserve requirements to nonmember banks are not fully evident. No analyses of the difficult problems of coordinating monetary policies in different countries or of the very complex negotiations and related political factors which would be encountered are presented.

The most important proposal in an international setting is to establish a rigorous formula that defines immediately available funds for each currency in an international system and to convince different central banks that all financial institutions dealing in these currencies should be constrained not to lend or pay out more of each currency than they have collected. The definition of collected funds should include the feature that at least 24 hours must elapse between the time funds are received by an office of a bank and the time they are defined to be collected, in order to avoid time zone games. If reserve requirements are imposed by a country on deposits denominated in its own currency in its own domestic institutions, then symmetry suggests that cooperating central banks ought to require that their banks and branches are similarly constrained in handling deposits denominated in that currency. This would serve to discourage funds flows that are designed to avoid the requirements. Central banks and countries that refuse to join the system should be isolated, and funds transfers in all currencies from banks in such countries should be subject to temporary embargoes, as described next.

Second, in the event that the foregoing proposal is not adopted, a markedly inferior method for deterring unwanted Eurodollar flows to the American economy is to raise the cost of such transfers. This could be accomplished by requiring that any Eurodollar flows to the United States be embargoed in a zero-interest-bearing transit account at the Federal Reserve for, say, ten days before they are defined to be collected. The Federal Reserve might require that the acquiring domestic bank hold reserves against such transit deposits. This procedure would reduce Eurodollar borrowings and allow the Federal Reserve to undertake sterilization operations with less disruption to domestic capital markets.

Third, at the domestic level there seems to be no justification for the Fed to move funds about the country costlessly, when such transfers are disrupting monetary control and likely to be contributing to inflation. It would be relatively easy for the Federal Reserve to put a meter at its switch at Culpeper, Virginia, and in Federal Reserve banks. A fee could substantially reduce the attractiveness to large corporations and government units of moving funds into overnight repurchase agreement hoards. The effect of a transfer fee would be both to reduce the vertical segments and the arching that exist in Figure 10.1b; it would reduce immediately available funds relative to deposit liabilities of Federal Reserve banks. A simple fixed fee per transfer, unrelated to the volume of a flow, would impose a heavy burden on movers of small amounts and should be avoided. On the other hand, a fee that is only proportional to the amounts transferred would appear to be inefficient because it would encourage large numbers of small denomination tranfers. No doubt a formula could be derived that takes into account the capacity of the Federal Reserve System to move funds and the contributions of different individual transfer amounts to the control problem. The formula itself could be varied over time, as if it were a policy instrument. Technical improvements in funds transfers and the design of policy must be coordinated!

Finally, the Federal Reserve should have the capacity to monitor funds and securities transfers through the Culpeper switch and different reserve banks. A time series of such transfers should prove very helpful in predicting changes in velocity and the volume of immediately available funds. There is no published evidence that such monitoring occurs. One can do little in ignorance. Perhaps this final suggestion, that close monitoring of the wire and other mechanisms should be initiated, ought to be at the top of the agenda.

NOTES

I am grateful to Thomas Mayer and Thomas Simpson and to the editors of this volume for helpful comments on an earlier version of this paper. Research support from National Science Foundation grant no. SES-7920283 is gratefully acknowledged.

1. Gurley and Shaw (1960) emphasized the distinction between outside money that is issued by the government and inside money that is created by financial intermediaries; they argued that this distinction is essential for interpreting monetary policy.

2. The interpretation of currency and coin as substitutes for deposits

at reserve banks in the satisfaction of reserve requirements was badly muddled by the Federal Reserve's 1968 decision to introduce lagged reserve accounting at member banks. This institutional inelegancy will be ignored in the subsequent discussion.

3. In fairness to Goldfeld it should be noted that at about the same time Goldfeld and Blinder (1972) were forcefully arguing that one could not infer from reduced form models that monetary policy instruments were either potent or being appropriately applied.

4. The institutions that move immediately available funds had their origins in the 1920s when the Federal funds market and the Fed wire came into existence. These institutions hibernated during the depression, World War II, and the immediate postwar years. They began to revive during the 1950s as interest rates started their postwar ascent, but little is lost by starting the narrative in 1960.

5. An overnight repurchase agreement between a bank and a firm is a transaction in which a bank transfers government securities to a firm at the end of a business day in exchange for Federal funds, and reverses this transfer the next morning. The firm earns interest on the funds lent and the bank is not required to hold reserves against its overnight borrowings. Federal funds purchases are typically overnight transactions as well; they differ from repurchase agreements because they usually involve no collateral, can only be arranged among certain financial institutions and government agencies, and bear a slightly higher interest rate. Eurodollar borrowings are described in the second section of this paper.

6. Excellent technical descriptions of the markets for Federal funds and repurchase agreements appear in Willis (1964), Lucas et al. (1977), and Simpson (1979). The markets for Eurodollars are well described by Little (1975), Stigum (1978), and Frydl(1980).

7. It is possible that foreign affiliates of American nonbanking firms borrow abroad and then recycle these borrowings to their American owners through intracompany transfers. This could account for slow loan growth in the mid-1970s. It is not possible to examine this topic further in the present paper, although such recycling does constitute a serious potential weakness of domestic monetary policy.

8. However, the distribution among banks was quite uneven. Citicorp's predecessor, the First National City Bank of New York, alone had 177 overseas offices at the end of 1965, when the Federal Reserve reported that all member banks had 211 overseas branches.

9. Frydl (1980, p. 12) reports: "For example, in the Caribbean offshore Eurodollar market, it is customary for branches of United States banks to transfer overnight Eurodollar deposits into immediately available funds without penalty."

10. If changes in float or Eurodollar borrowings are not offset, they are incorporated in outside money and immediately available funds. If new Eurodollar borrowings are not sterilized as they occur, the volume of intraday immediately available funds is affected.

11. Even in the case of member banks, participation in the Federal funds market soared after 1968 (see Gambs and Kimball 1979, p. 6).

12. This bank was chosen because information about its transactions was conveniently available and because it is roughly representative of the system. In 1975 the total amounts of checks handled and wire transfers by the Federal Reserve System were $4.3 and $31.4 trillion, respectively; the numbers of items, respectively, were 11.4 billion and 17 million. The Chicago district had a little less than one-sixth of all member bank assets

in 1965 and in 1975.

13. For obvious reasons the text ignores second order terms in the expression, $\Delta T = F\Delta V + V\Delta F + \Delta F\Delta V$, where T, V, and F respectively are transactions, velocity, and funds.

14. Net purchased funds by weekly reporting banks are larger than those of all commercial banks because the larger weekly reporting banks are net purchasers from smaller commercial banks and because data from weekly reporting banks are less subject to window dressing than are call report data.

15. In this discussion I am ignoring marginal reserve requirements that were imposed on repurchase agreements funds on October 6, 1979.

16. A comparison of end of quarter monthly averages of the Federal funds rate and the rate on prime commercial paper reveals no such cyclical pattern. The differential between the rates on prime commercial paper and Treasury bills shows almost the same pattern as described in the text.

DISCUSSION • *Thomas D. Simpson*

During the 1970s the Federal Reserve came to rely more heavily on the monetary aggregates as intermediate targets of monetary policy. Indeed, since 1975 the Federal Reserve has publicly announced its targets for the primary monetary aggregates and bank credit. The efficacy of such a monetary aggregates targeting procedure depends importantly on the existence of a stable and predictable demand for money by the public. Expressed alternatively, monetary aggregates targeting relies on a stable and predictable velocity, which algebraically equals the reciprocal of the public's holdings of money relative to GNP.

The stability and predictability of velocity, however, has been questioned as the past 5 or 6 years have witnessed episodes in which the public's money holdings relative to GNP have dropped sharply compared to what was expected in light of historical experience. Such aberrant behavior has been most evident in the narrow, transactions-type aggregates. For example, the velocity of old M1 (basically the same measure as M1A) was about 16 percent higher in late 1979 than would have been expected on the basis of a standard econometric specification of money demand behavior that described actual behavior quite well before mid-1974. Most of the weakness in the M1 measures can be traced to the demand deposits of nonfinancial corporations, depositors that have become very highly sophisticated in the art of managing cash positions. Shifts have also been evident in some of the broader aggregates, although the most pronounced departures have been registered at the M1 level.

As an explanation for these departures of velocity, some have argued that new financial instruments have emerged--such as repurchase agreements, money market mutual funds, and NOW accounts--that provide the same transactions services as demands deposits, and thus the problem can be resolved by including such instruments in the M1 measure.[1] Others, though, have emphasized that the public has been able to make its transactions with smaller amounts of transactions balances because of a variety of financial innovations. The implications of this interpretation for the resolution of the M1 velocity problem are not as simple. They suggest that unless the process of such innovations is better understood and perhaps slowed or stopped, policy objectives may be thwarted by the emergence of further shifts that are unpredictable both in terms of their timing and intensity. Of the two interpretations, Hester's views are most closely aligned with the latter. He attributes policy difficulties largely to regulatory actions that have encouraged a greater reliance of the financial system on immediately available funds. Moreover, he has several recommendations that are aimed at standardizing the treatment of immediately available funds internationally and discouraging the use of transfers in immediately available funds both in domestic and international transactions.

The term "immediately available funds" has been used in the emerging literature on this subject in at least three ways and it is helpful to briefly discuss each. First, the term immediately available funds is most often used to denote a specific kind of payment. It means good or collected funds (also "Federal funds") that can be used on the day of the transaction. A bank receiving immediately available funds can use them that day to make a loan, to acquire a security for its investment portfolio or trading account, or to satisfy its reserve requirements. Many domestic money market instruments that are actively used by corporations in the management of cash positions--such as RPs, certificates of deposit, and commercial paper--call for payment in immediately available funds.[2] Some others--most notably Treasury securities--typically involve payment in collected balances the next business day, as did the bulk of Eurodollar deposits prior to the adoption of same-day settlement in October 1981. A second use of the term is to denote certain very short-term financial instruments that are typically arranged in immediately available funds. Usually, the term refers to the amount of Federal funds and RP liabilities of banks.[3] The third use of the term is to denote the deposit liabilities of the Federal Reserve System which are reserve balances that banks maintain with the Federal Reserve. These balances--assets of banks--can be used to readily transfer funds from the account of one party to the account of another. The Fed's wire transfer network plays an important role in this transfer process. This third use of the term is also related to the theoretical construct of "outside money"--which equals reserve balances plus currency--a variable that takes on a prominent role in a variety of models dealing with the impact of monetary policy on the domestic economy and exchange rates.

Hester defines immediately available funds in a way that encompasses both the second and third uses of the term. Immediately available funds are defined to consist of reserve balances at the Federal Reserve plus "certain 'collected' liabilities of commercial banks that may be transferred or withdrawn during a business day on the order of account holders."[4] The latter are generally regarded by the author to involve Federal funds borrowed by commercial banks from nonbank parties, RPs issued by commercial banks, and net Eurodollar borrowing of commercial banks. Thus, the term is used to apply to both assets and liabilities of commercial banks and to both inside and outside balances. Unfortunately, though, Hester does not satisfactorily explain why this definition of the term is meaningful theoretically as a variable that is closely related to spending and economic activity or the public's demand for the money stock.

According to Hester, regulatory changes--to a large extent those of the Federal Reserve Board, especially ones involving the Fed wire--have enabled the financial system to finance a larger volume of transactions in the economy with a given amount of immediately available funds. It is implied that these developments contributed to slippage between the stock of money and aggregate spending or GNP. It is further suggested that the Federal Reserve has been losing its control over the stock of immediately available funds, particularly the intraday amount. During the course of the day, it is argued, the supply of immediately available funds expands considerably above opening-of-business levels--in part, because of certain security transactions involving intraday extensions of credit--and then contracts at the end of the day toward the amount outstanding at the beginning of the day; thus, it is maintained, the end-of-day amount of immediately available funds--which equals only reserve balances at the Fed--is not representative of the effective amount that is associated with RPs and Eurodollars. Moreover, it is maintained that the more relevant effective amount of immediately available funds has grown relative to the end-of-day amount in the past twenty years. In addition, Hester argues that the Federal Reserve has been losing control over the amount of immediately available funds, as banks have been able to augment the supply of immediately available funds with Eurodollar borrowing, which it is argued is analogous to float; and regulatory decisions that broadened participation in the Federal funds market to include nonmember banks and thrift institutions have added to slippages in monetary control by enabling a given stock of measured reserve balances to support a larger stock of money. Furthermore, it is maintained that monetary policy has been weakened because open market operations involve the trading of one kind of money for another--the Treasury and agency securities involved give rise to money when used as RP collateral--and because member banks and the public have jointly sought to develop transactions that escape the application of reserve requirements, thereby eroding the effectiveness of reserve requirements as a tool on monetary policy.

Before proceeding to an alternative interpretation of financial innovation--one directed more toward the abnormal behavior of M1 velocity in recent years--some comments on these points seem warranted. First, it is not clear how the intraday pattern of immediately available funds--rising early in the business day and then dropping toward opening-of-business levels by the end of the day--affects behavior in the way suggested by Hester. Indeed, there appears to be virtually no such intradaily patterns to reserve balances at the Federal Reserve. While some factors affecting aggregate reserve positions--such as Federal Reserve float and Treasury balances--do fluctuate, they do not produce a systematic tendency for reserve balances to rise temporarily during the day; even in the event that a funds transfer were to result in the paying bank's reserve account being overdrawn, aggregate reserve balances would be unchanged, as the additional balances in the receiving bank's account would be just matched by a deficiency in the paying bank's account. Moreover, borrowing in the Eurodollar market does not serve to augment the aggregate amount of balances within the banking system, on an intraday or interday basis, as it merely transfers funds from the reserve account of one bank to the account of another; also, until late 1981 borrowing in this market typically was not in immediately available funds but rather in next day funds.[5] Demand deposit balances appear more likely to have the arched intraday pattern that is emphasized by Hester, but this tendency does not appear to have important behavioral implications. Customers placing funds with banks in overnight RPs typically arrange these transactions by late morning and they authorize the transfer of funds from their demand accounts afterward; since banks may return funds to the demand deposit accounts of the previous day's overnight RP customers before they receive funds from the accounts of the current day's customers, there may be a tendency for demand balances to rise in the meantime. But there is no compelling reason to believe that those customers experiencing this temporary buildup in their demand balances behave much differently than they would if the repayment and receipt of RP funds were perfectly synchronized; indeed, many customers may not even be aware that their demand balances have temporarily risen, as they appear to be concerned mostly about finding outlets for collected balances available from investments maturing on that day, regardless of when such balances are actually delivered to their account.

Second, even though an open market operation may result in a change in demand deposits and an equal but offsetting change in RPs, this does not mean that the operation leaves the amount of money unchanged. For example, an open market sale by the Fed's trading desk initially causes aggregate reserve balances and deposits (if arranged with a nonbank dealer) to decline and securities in the hands of the dealer to increase by the same amount; should the dealer in turn issue an RP of this amount using these securities as collateral, the volume of RPs would expand by an amount equal to the reduction in reserve balances and demand deposits. Although the public in the first round has given up one liquid asset (demand deposits) in return for another (RPs), reserve balances of banks have declined and the amount of deposits in the system must contract by some multiple, leaving a net contraction. Moreover, of course, there is disagreement about whether RPs--those issued by bank and by nonbank dealers--are transactions balances like demand deposits.[6]

Finally, the evidence of the past decade or even longer is consistent with the point, made by Hester, that the monetary system has evolved in such a way as to lower the reserve burden of noninterest-earning reserve requirements. Reserve requirements can be likened to a tax--one that varies directly with market interest rates--and the rapid growth of nonmember bank deposits, Eurodollar deposits, and RPs over this period of high interest rates suggests that financial institutions and the public have discovered ways of lowering this tax. This presents a highly vexing dilemma from the standpoint of monetary control, since on the one hand, reserve requirements serve as an important element linking the supply of reserves to the stock of money, while, on the other hand, the imposition of reserve requirements establishes an incentive to develop and utilize substitutes for those monetary liabilities subject to reserve requirements.

Returning to the matter of the abnormal behavior of M1 velocity, it is useful to view the reduction in money demand relative to GNP, at least in part, as a market response to the prohibition on the payment of interest on demand deposits, high reserve requirements on demand deposits of member banks, and certain developments that have effectively lowered the cost of monitoring deposit balances and of converting demand balances into short-term interest-earning assets. The existence of immediately available funds and wire transfers has been a part of this process.

With high market rates of interest and the prohibition on the payment of interest on demand deposits, the public has had an incentive to actively find ways to conduct its transactions using smaller amounts of money so that more funds can be invested in assets with market related yields. Many of the techniques that have been developed, mainly by larger corporations and state and local governments, act to lower uncertainty about end-of-day cash positions so that a smaller cushion in demand balances is needed for unexpected withdrawals prior to the close of business each day. Wire transfers of reserve balances have played a part in this development inasmuch as controlled disbursement and cash concentration accounts have been used to lower uncertainty. With controlled disbursement, a corporation makes payments using a bank that is presented with checks only once per day, normally early in the morning, so the corporate treasurer knows early in the day what the amount of clearings are against the firm's account and can then wire in funds to cover them. With a cash concentration account, a corporation having accounts with many banks around the country is able to lower its overall cushion of demand deposit balances by pooling the variability of its many accounts into a single concentration account with its lead bank; the corporation maintains relatively steady balances in these many accounts by transferring amounts in excess of targeted levels to its concentration account--often by wire--and by covering deficiencies in individual accounts by transferring funds from its concentration account. In addition, a single investment of projected excess demand balances can be made from its concentration account, instead of many from its other accounts; in this way, transactions costs are lowered and the firm can avail itself of better terms of large-block transactions.

On the other side of the market, there has been considerable incentive for financial institutions to attract transactions related funds from the public by offering highly liquid assets with market related yields (and with low or no reserve requirements) having characteristics similar to demand deposits. Included among these are RPs (at both commercial banks and nonbank dealers), money market mutual fund shares, certain kinds of Eurodollars, and commercial paper. As noted above, transactions in these instruments typically call for settlement in immediately available funds and often involve balances being moved over the Fed wire.

Thus, the interaction of efforts by the public to pare holdings of relatively unattractive demand balances and of financial institutions to provide the public with more attractive transactions related instruments apparently has contributed to the unusual velocity behavior of recent years. Clearly, the existence of immediately available funds and wire transfers have played a role in this development. However, it is likely that downward shifts would have occurred in the public's money holdings relative to GNP in any event. Indeed, it appears likely that the private sector could have replicated many of the balance-transfer services that the Federal Reserve has provided, regardless of whether the final settlement asset would have been balances at the Federal Reserve or at large private banks. The capability likely would have been there, although the cost per transfer to the public may have been a little higher. It should be noted that the Monetary Control Act of 1980 requires that the Federal Reserve price the Fed wire and other services provided to depository institutions on the basis of direct and indirect costs and the Federal Reserve Board has begun implementing this provision. Thus, the cost per transfer to the public likely will increase, which may act to damp somewhat the use of wire transfers.

If the financial innovations that have contributed to a reduction in the public's money holdings relative to GNP have been a market response to the prohibition on the payment of interest on demand deposits, high reserve requirements on member bank deposits, and technological factors lowering transactions costs, then a set of solutions emerges that differs somewhat from those of Hester. He proposes that wire transfers of balances be discouraged through the use of transfer fees, a development that is already scheduled to occur in early 1981. In the international area, he suggests that there be international cooperation regarding the definition and treatment of immediately available funds (a one-day lag be imposed between the receipt and collection of funds), that reserve requirements be imposed on external (Eurocurrency) deposits denominated in a country's currency that are similar to those on its domestic deposits, and that the Eurodollar flows to the United States be discouraged by introducing a substantial delay between the time when Eurodollar funds are received in the United States and when they are defined to be collected. With the exception of Eurocurrency reserve requirements, it is not clear that these proposals get to the heart of the problem. Instead, it could be argued that a more effective approach would be to permit the payment of explicit interest on transactions accounts; the authorization of nationwide NOW accounts under the Monetary Control Act of 1980 is a step in this direction. Also, the application of the same structure of reserve requirements to all monetary instruments--regardless of issuer--and the payment of interest on required reserve balances would limit the scope and reduce the incentive for the development of new unregulated instruments with characteristics like those of established monetary assets; the Monetary Control Act of 1980 imposes the same schedule of reserve requirements on the transactions and nonpersonal time deposits of all domestic depository institutions, although it does not authorize the payment[7] of interest on reserve balances that satisfy regular reserve requirements. Since some of the innovations that have altered the public's demand for money have involved deposits booked offshore, this principle would suggest that the same reserve requirement structure should be imposed on Eurodollar deposits as is imposed on domestic deposits, a recommendation made by Hester.[8]

NOTES
  The views expressed in these comments are those of the author and do not necessarily reflect the views of the Board of Governors of the Federal Reserve System or other members of its staff.
   1. The Federal Reserve Board redefined the monetary aggregates in early 1980 to include NOW accounts (along with ATS and credit union share draft accounts) at the M1 level, in M1B. Money market mutual fund shares and overnight RPs of commercial banks were also considered as components of M1, but the evidence did not strongly support their inclusion at that level. Money market mutual funds shares and overnight RPs, however, are included in the redefined M2.
   2. A major reason why such cash management instruments involve immediately available funds is uncertainty. Given that firms are uncertain about the amount of checks that are likely to be presented against their accounts each day and the timing of collections, they are generally better able to commit good funds for overnight (or longer) investments on that day rather than the next day. Thus, if they discover that their demand deposit balance has dropped below expectations, good funds from the maturing investment will be available sooner to replenish the demand account; similarly, a large unexpected buildup of demand balances during a day can be gainfully invested that day instead of remaining in a demand account until the next day.

3. This is the way that the term "immediately available funds" is used in Tinsley, Garrett, and Friar (1978).

4. The definition of this term is that of Lucas, Jones, and Thurston (1977).

5. On a related matter, greater participation in the interbank Federal funds market may have strengthened the Federal Reserve's control over the monetary aggregates using a reserves operating target. To the extent that participation in the Federal funds market enables banks to hold minimal amounts of excess reserves, fluctuations in excess reserves are damped and the predictability of the relationship between reserves and the money stock is improved.

6. The same conclusions apply to an open market sale of securities to a bank dealer, even though demand balances are unaffected in the initial round. However, demand deposits are lowered in the second round as the bank issues an RP using its newly acquired securities as collateral.

7. The act, though, does authorize compensation on balances satisfying the supplemental reserve requirement on transactions accounts (of up to 4 percent) that can be imposed by the Federal Reserve Board when it is deemed essential for the conduct of monetary policy.

8. As Dale Henderson has noted, to be most effective, interest would be paid on required reserves against Eurodollars. Otherwise, there would be an incentive for Eurobanks to book deposits in some other currency and provide depositors with matching forward contracts that get them back into dollars at the times their deposits mature. When the same schedule of reserve requirements is imposed on all Eurocurrency deposits, banks would be encouraged to book deposits in the currency having the lowest level of nominal interest rates--that is, the lowest opportunity cost of required reserve balances--and to provide matching forward contracts that return depositors to their preferred currencies when their deposits mature.

DISCUSSION • *Anthony W. Santomero*

Financial Innovation: The Macroeconomic Issue

The paper by Donald Hester has, at its core, two aims. First, it catalogues the financial innovation of the last two decades in both the domestic and Eurodollar money markets. It treats us to a vivid review of the contrast between the old and the new by listing the changes (Table 10.1) that have occurred and by describing the potential for extensive manipulation of funds in the new regime. The exactness of this scenario and its detailed presentation will not be questioned here, as I trust that Professor Hester has carefully researched the issue. Further, the other discussant, Thomas Simpson, is infinitely more knowledgeable than I on these matters. I, accordingly, defer to him.

The second goal of the paper is essentially a macroeconomic one. It "argues that the role of outside money has changed considerably in the past twenty years because of a series of legal and technological changes. . . . The ability of the Federal Reserve to control the level of economic activity has been correspondingly weakened. . ." It is to this part of the paper that I will address my comments. I argue that much of Hester's concern is either unwarranted or unsubstantiated. It rests upon a view of the financial markets and the multiplier that is essentially too simplistic for the current environment. Monetary control is possible and may be as efficient as in the preinnovation period with a more exact, albeit more complicated multiplier. The benefits of this additional complexity will be better control than Hester implies is currently available and less concern over the continuing wave of financial innovation.

At the outset it should be clear that neither Professor Hester nor I argue that the innovation has made control, even with a simplistic view of the financial markets, impossible. His view, stated quite explicitly in the published version of his paper is that "Federal Reserve . . . control . . . has been correspondingly weakened, but not destroyed." His solution to the reduction in control is to offer a series of fairly onerous, complex, and arbitrary additional regulations on financial markets, both domestic and international. I, on the other hand, believe that it would seem more direct and socially useful for the Federal Reserve to price and regulate only where it is socially costly and use a paradigm that conforms more closely to reality. In the next section I sketch such a paradigm, while its implications, which differ from Hester's recommendations, are outlined in the third section.

MONETARY CONTROL IN A GENERAL EQUILIBRIUM FRAMEWORK

Before turning to the analysis, a few words are in order to explain the origins of the approach in this paper. Surely, I am not first to consider a broader range of financial assets and their effect on monetary control. In fact, the approach taken here can be traced directly to two distinct but complementary analytical frameworks. The first of these, in rather arbitrary order, is the work of Brainard and Tobin: Tobin and Brainard (1963), Brainard (1964), and Tobin (1969). The development of a general equilibrium financial framework and its popularization are clearly the result of these seminal papers. The second branch of research, which for the present purposes is quite complementary to the first, is the approach employed by Brunner and Meltzer (1963, 1964a, 1964b, 1968). Using a rather small, general equilibrium model, these authors were quite careful in demonstrating the true nature of the multiplier. They specified its functional dependencies, and offered the use of the multiplier framework as a first approximation. The present analysis is part of an ongoing set of research conducted with my colleague, J. J. Siegel, in which these two lines of work are synthesized and extended (Santomero and Siegel 1981, 1982).

In order to move directly into the analysis of monetary control, let us begin by developing a consistent view of the financial environment. Assume a financial environment in which there are high-powered, or outside money, $n - 1$ types of intermediary deposits, a bond market, and an equity market. There are, therefore, $n + 2$ markets, numbered as follows:

The high-powered or outside money market is market 0.

Depository markets are markets $1 \ldots n - 1$. (Assume, for example, demand deposits are market 1, time deposits at commercial banks are market 2, etc.)

The bond market is market n.

The equity market is market $n + 1$.

The household is assumed to have typical general equilibrium gross substitute demand functions for all assets, subject to the aggregate budget constraint for the sector. The depository institutions may hold high-powered money, other depository institutions' deposits, and bonds (loans). Firms issue equity to support capital ownership, and because of the Modigliani-Miller theorem their bond issuances (if any) are suppressed. The sole net supplier of bonds is the government, and in the present analysis these assets are assumed to be viewed as net wealth.[1]

The set of equations that is implied by this view of the financial sector can easily be written as a set of equilibrium conditions. To lend substance to and to simplify the subsequent analysis, more specific characteristics of the financial institution sector are in order. Specifically, assumptions about the determination of deposit rates must be made. In considering the nature of financial institutions' deposit liabilities, two distinct types emerge. First, there are those deposits that have their rates set primarily by regulation at some fixed level, e.g., demand deposits and passbook savings account. Second, there are those deposits that have yields that move closely with open market rates. This latter dependence may be due to regulatory constraints on such liabilities, (e.g., nonmember Fed funds, the money market certificate) or it may be due to the production and pricing pattern of the industry. For example, an institution facing a constant cost schedule may pay the depositor the return on the portfolio less some fee independent of the size of the deposits. Money market mutual funds fall into this category.

The result of these two assumptions on the pricing of depository liabilities is to make the supply of these assets dependent upon the demand for these deposits at either the fixed rate of return dictated by regulation or the net yield obtained from the portfolio of assets. The size of these depository markets, therefore, is demand-side determined. The number of equations in the system is reduced from n + 2 to 3, namely, the equilibrium conditions for high-powered money, bonds, and equity.

By Walras's Law only two of the three equations are independent so we can write the system as the equilibrium conditions for high-powered money and bonds, with equity determined by the system's budget constraint. If we assume the price level is exogenous, then the system contains the endogenous variables r_b (the return on bonds), r_E (the return on equities), and Y (real income). Hence the system can be solved as a generalized "LM" locus in (r_E, Y) space. Alternatively, the model can be solved for r_b and Y for a given r_E.

The two equilibrium conditions have more intuitive appeal if they are written as the excess demand for high-powered money, equation (10.1), and the excess demand for all liquid assets defined as all assets less equity, equation (10.2).

$$\sum_{i=0}^{n} k_i A_{ih}^d = H^s \qquad (10.1)$$

$$\sum_{i=0}^{n} A_{ih}^d = H^s + B_g \qquad (10.2)$$

where k_i is the required reserve ratio on asset i, A_{ih}^d is the demand for asset i by the household, H^s is the supply of outside money, and B_g is the supply of government bonds outstanding. Equilibrium in the economy exists when the total demand for liquid assets equals the exogenous supply (high-powered money plus government bonds) and the reserve-weighted demand for liquid assets equals the supply of high-powered money.

To use this supply to derive multipliers some additional notation is required. Define a_i as the percentage of total wealth allocated to the ith asset, namely

$$a_0 \equiv H_h^d/W, \quad a_i \equiv A_i^d/W, \quad a_n \equiv A_n^d/W, \quad a_{n+1} \equiv A_{n+1}^d/W$$

Note that these are simply scaled demand functions. Following Tobin (1969), it is assumed that the a_i is homogeneous of degree zero in aggregate wealth. Accordingly, the two-equation system may be written as

$$\sum_{i=0}^{n} k_i(r_b) a_i(r_b, Y) W = H^s \qquad (10.3)$$

$$\sum_{i=0}^{n} a_i(r_b, Y) W = H^s + B_g^s \qquad (10.4)$$

where the k_i and the a_i are shown to be a function of the bond rate and income.

Equation (10.3) is central to the monetary control issue as it is the centerpiece of multiplier analysis. It can be used to derive the money multipliers traditionally seen in monetary analysis. To demonstrate this, first derive an aggregate wealth multiplier conditional upon the equilibrium in all financial markets, as

$$W = H^S / \left(\sum_{i=0}^{n} k_i a_i \right) \equiv m_W H^S \qquad (10.5)$$

The equilibrium quantity of any monetary aggregate, j, which consists of the sum of the first j assets, can be written as

$$M_j = \frac{\sum_{i=0}^{j} a_i}{\sum_{i=0}^{n-1} k_i a_i} H^S \equiv n_j m_W H_W^W = m_j H_j^S \qquad (10.6)$$

For example, if currency is asset 0, and the commercial banks' demand deposit asset is asset 1, then the equilibrium value of M1 - A is immediately

$$M1 - A = \frac{\sum_{i=0}^{1} a_i}{\sum_{i=0}^{n-1} k_i a_i} H^S \equiv (a_0 + a_1) m_W H^S = m_1 H^S \qquad (10.7)$$

M1B, M2, and all other multipliers are similarly derived.

The multiplier, therefore, is a function of all reserve and asset ratios. Hence the jth monetary aggregate is critically dependent on both the level and the comparative static properties of $\sum_{i=0}^{j} a_i(r_b, Y)$ and $\sum_{i=0}^{n} k_i(r_b) a_i(r_b, Y)$. Specifically, for any arbitrary exogenous shift, x_0, the multiplier would shift by

$$\frac{dm_j}{dx_0} = \frac{\partial m_j}{\partial x_0} + \frac{\partial m_j}{\partial r_b} \frac{dr_b}{dx_0} + \frac{\partial m_j}{\partial Y} \frac{dY}{dx_0} \qquad (10.8)$$

where dr_b/dx_0 and dY/dx_0 are calculated directly from the comparative statics of the general equilibrium system equations (10.3) and (10.4). The first term on the right of equation (10.8) is the partial effect of any exogenous change, such as a change in a reserve ratio, k_i, or a shift in asset preference, a_j, which would be derived from the mechanical application of money multiplier analysis. The second term represents the <u>induced</u> general equilibrium effect on the a_i's and k_i's of the subsequent shift in income and interest rates which can be exactly determined from the solution to equations (10.3) and (10.4).

Likewise, and perhaps more importantly to a discussion of Hester's proposition, a change in the financial environment that creates a new asset, such as money market funds, overnight repos, etc., will affect the relationship between the usual monetary aggregates and the quantity of outside money. Specifically, a new financial asset's entry into the market may be captured by a shift in a_i from zero to some positive value. Its effect on the multiplier is

$$\frac{dm_j}{da_i} = \frac{\partial m_j}{\partial_i} + \frac{\partial m_j}{\partial r_b}\frac{dr_b}{da_i} + \frac{\partial m_j}{\partial Y}\frac{dY}{da_i} \tag{10.9}$$

In general we should expect equation (10.9) to be nonzero, and for the types of innovation to which Hester refers its value will be positive. Innovations which shift funds into lower reserve requirement assets will increase the volume of credit and financial assets supported by a given quantity of outside or high-powered money.

CONTROL AND THESE FINANCIAL INNOVATIONS

The previous sections developed the general methodology necessary to analyze the financial sector. It argued that, using a general equilibrium model, multipliers will spring from the equilibrium in the market for high-powered money. The multiplier itself is, however, a rather complicated function of all financial asset reserve ratios and asset ratios, which in turn are functions of the endogenous variables in the system. Hence any change in either the exogenous variables over time or the financial environment that leads to a change in the set of assets available will have both direct and indirect effects on the relationship between the sum of relevant financial assets and outside money, i.e., the multiplier. This has two distinct implications for the issue of control.

First, a mechanical multiplier analysis that looks at the ratio of some set of financial assets to outside money need not, indeed probably will not, be terribly stable. If one views the issue of monetary control as dependent upon such a fixed, rigid form one could not accurately forecast the relationship between monetary aggregates, outside money, and economic activity unless all reserve ratios and asset preferences are fairly smooth and little innovational or structural shifts occur. Hester appears to presume that such a consistent relationship should be expected. However this view appears too simplistic. In a complex financial environment such as the one described by Hester one can only hope for a well-defined functional relationship between some monetary aggregate, be it immediately available funds or what have you, and outside money. Hester presented nothing to suggest that such a relationship does not exist; hence, one can conclude little as to the impact of the catalogued innovations on monetary control. If it could be shown that these innovations rendered the macroeconomy inherently less stable even within a more complex framework, then one would have concern over the ability of the monetary authority to control. Unfortunately the bulk of Hester's time is spent documenting the change in the generalized multiplier rather than its predictive stability. Observations about the time series properties of float and/or open market portfolio changes don't really address stochastic issues, and his reference to nominal, rather than real, rates is rather beside the point. The effect of these innovations on the ability of the Federal Reserve to control the economy by standard monetary policy is still an open question requiring more analysis and data.

Second, we would do well to obtain estimates of all the asset demands so as to more accurately predict the current multiplier. I think Hester and I agree on this point. Rather than bewailing the loss of control that appears to occur whenever a new liquid asset attracts funds, a direct application of the shifts in a_i on the multiplier can be applied. One would not have to depend upon time series data on the historical ratios of the two assets that have been impacted so greatly by financial innovation, i.e., demand deposits and time deposits. Rather one could estimate the k_i from time series and use current data values for the a_i in the multiplier.[1] This would yield more accurate values for the multiplier, negate the apparent need for the additional regulation Hester recommends, and more closely correspond to the reality of the financial environment. This, of course, is a far cry from what Hester suggests. He seems to feel that additional regulation can somehow be used to force reality back to a simpler time. Perhaps, but innovation would not stop. Soon we would need new regulations for new innovation, and regulation itself would complicate our understanding of the economic condition. This seems less than preferred.

But Hester's concerns are not without merit. In his attempt to forestall innovation he raises a very important point. To understand and predict the behavior of financial markets, the data must be available. As he mentions, the necessary data on important parts of the market have not been kept, nor are we sure today that we have all the data that could be available. He states: "One can do little in ignorance. Perhaps this final suggestion, that close monitoring of the wire and other mechanisms be initiated, ought to be at the top of the agenda." I agree.

NOTE

1. If government bonds are not considered net wealth, the analysis proceeds with open market operations equivalent to high-powered money issuance, and government deficits having no effect.

Donald D. Hester

REJOINDER • *Donald D. Hester*

Anthony Santomero asserts that my concern about controllability is misplaced and "rests upon a view of the financial markets and the multiplier that is essentially too simplistic for the current environment." The word "multiplier" does not appear in my paper, nor should it. Multipliers, impact or the comparative static variety that Santomero apparently prefers, may be useful for understanding how to manipulate instruments in order to reach targets, but they are not sufficient to assess monetary control. Phillips (1957) and Brito and Hester (1974), referenced in my paper, have shown that control unavoidably involves speeds of adjustment, feedback, and information lags. These features of model specification are notably absent from Santomero's equations. At the very end of his comment he states: "Hester appears to presume that . . . one could not accurately forecast the relationship between monetary aggregates, outside money, and economic activity unless all reserve ratios are fairly smooth and little innovational or structural shifts occur." I do not make or require these assumptions.

It is easy to write down a dynamic model in which lags and innovations lead to instability, but that was not my assignment. Such models may have well-defined impact or long-run equilibrium multipliers. Nothing in my paper precludes such multipliers from being elaborate, accurate, or time varying. Instead, in the spirit of the foregoing references, my paper argued that the Federal Reserve was not monitoring innovations in a timely fashion, not recording essential information, and not appreciating how the dynamic structure was changing. Changes that I proposed were designed to enhance the Fed's monitoring and to make the financial structure more controllable. Finally, as Thomas Simpson notes, imposing fees on wire transfers introduces no new regulatory burdens. My proposal only concerns the formula for determining the fees.

Tom Simpson observes that immediately available funds may be defined in different ways and comments that I do "not satisfactorily explain why [my] definition of the term is meaningful theoretically as a variable that is closely related to spending and economic activity or the public's demand for the money stock." I confess that my explanation is incomplete in these respects; space was limited and the New York Federal Reserve Bank staff's definition was convenient for my diagrams. I believe, nevertheless, that immediately available funds as defined are analogous to currency; they are both capable of buying goods and services. Does it really matter that currency goes to sleep on a dresser and immediately available funds in a repo? The difference between immediately available funds during a day and at the end of a day consists of funds created through clever timings of wire transfers, including "daylight overdrafts," which the Federal Reserve has recently sought to curb. Daylight overdrafts and other creations <u>are</u> spendable. Simpson's report that these creations and aggregative reserve balances are uncorrelated in no way diminishes their spendability; it only demonstrates once again that something is often lost when one looks at net rather than gross quantities in aggregative balance sheets.

GENERAL DISCUSSION

A number of participants noted that the phenomena Hester highlighted represent classic and predictable response to government regulations. This being the case many wondered why some policymakers appeared to believe that <u>more</u> regulations and or international cooperation and surveillance will reduce the distortions and resulting incentives to innovate. In this context, it was pointed out that since policymakers often fail to recognize that imposing and removing financial regulations do not have symmetrical effects on the domestic and international monetary systems, they frequently underestimate the deadweight losses to society sometimes associated with expanding regulations. Some suggested that the continuing expansion of regulation around the world in the face of such losses and various redistributive effects represents a fertile area for research by both political scientists and economists.

The remainder of the discussion focused on the extent to which structural relationships (such as the demand for money and the money supply process), and therefore policy, were affected by developments such as those examined by Hester. Were policymakers in the dark or was policy deftly adjusted in response to emerging developments? More specifically, were any of the economic outcomes of the past decade the result of policy "errors" generated by the failure of policymakers to monitor, understand, and react accordingly to ongoing shifts in the structure of financial relationships? The ensuing discussion, reflecting in part the lack of hard evidence on what policymakers knew or thought they knew at a particular point in time, produced little in the way of a consensus. It did, however, demonstrate the pressing need for scholars to partition the causes of purported policy errors into constituent elements.

BIBLIOGRAPHY

Acheson, Keith, and John F. Chant. 1973. Bureaucratic theory and the choice of central bank goals. Journal of Money, Credit and Banking (May): 637-55.
Adelman, Morris. 1972-1973. Is the oil shortage real? Foreign Policy 9 (winter):69-107.
Akerlof, G. A. 1979. Irving Fisher on his head: The consequences of constant threshold-target monitoring of money holdings. Quarterly Journal of Economics 93(2):169-87.
Alt, James E. 1979. The Politics of Economic Decline. Cambridge, England: Cambridge University Press.
Amacher, Ryan C., Robert Tollison, and Thomas D. Willett. 1975. Budget size in a democracy: A review of the arguments. Public Finance Quarterly (April): 99-122.
Amacher, Ryan C., Robert Tollison, and Thomas D. Willett, eds. 1976. The Economic Approach to Public Policy. Ithaca, N.Y.: Cornell University Press.
Amacher, Ryan C., Robert Tollison, and Thomas D. Willett. 1976. Risk avoidance and political advertising: Neglected issues in the literature on budget size in a democracy. In Ryan Amacher, Robert Tollison, and Thomas D. Willet, eds. The Economic Approach to Public Policy. Ithaca, N.Y.: Cornell University Press. pp. 405-33.
Amacher, Ryan C., Robert Tollison, and Thomas D. Willett. 1979. The divergence between (trade) theory and practice. In Walter Adams et al., eds. Tariffs, Quotas and Trade: The Politics of Protectionism. San Francisco: Institute for Contemporary Studies, pp. 55-66.
Arak, Marcelle, and Christopher J. McCurdy. 1979-80. Interest rate futures. Federal Reserve Bank of New York Quarterly Review 4(4):33-46.
Argy, Victor, and Joanne Salop. 1979. Price and output effects of monetary and fiscal policy under flexible exchange rates. I.M.F. Staff Papers 26(June): 224-56.
Aronson, Jonathan. 1979. Money and Power: Banks and the World Monetary System. Beverly Hills and London: Sage Publications.
Artus, Jacques, and Andrew D. Crockett. 1978. Floating Exchange Rates and the Need for Surveillance. Princeton Essays in International Finance, no. 127 (May).
Aubrey, Henry. 1969. Behind the Veil of International Money. Princeton Essays in International Finance, no. 71 (January).
Baldwin, David. 1978. Power and social exchange. American Political Science Review 72(December):1229-42.
———. 1979. Power analysis and world politics: New trends versus old tendencies. World Politics 31-32(January):161-94.
Barnett, William A. 1978. A Fully Nested System of Monetary Quantity and Dual User-Cost Price Aggregates. Washington, D.C.: Board of Governors, Federal Reserve System.
Barro, Robert J. 1977. Long-term contracting, sticky prices, and monetary policy. Journal of Monetary Economics 3(July):305-16.
Baumol, William J. 1952. Transactions demand for cash: An inventory theoretic approach. Quarterly Journal of Economics 64(4):545-56.
Becker, Gary. 1974. A theory of social interactions. Journal of Political Economy 82(November/December):1063-96.

Bergsten, Fred C. 1975. *The Dilemmas of the Dollar: The Economics and Politics of U.S. International Monetary Policies.* New York: New York University Press.
Bilson, John F. O. 1979. The vicious circle hypothesis. *I.M.F. Staff Papers* 26(March):1-37.
———. 1980. The "speculative efficiency" hypothesis. National Bureau of Economic Research, Working Paper no. 474 (April).
Black, Stanley W. 1973. *International Money Markets and Flexible Exchange Rates.* Princeton Studies in International Finance, no. 32.
———. 1977. *Floating Exchange Rates and National Economic Policy.* New Haven: Yale University Press.
———. 1978. Policy responses to major disturbances of the 1970's and their transmission through international goods and capital markets. *Weltwirtschaftliches Archiv* 114 (4):614-41.
———. 1979. The political assignment problem and the design of stabilization policies in open economies. In Assar Lindbeck, eds. *Inflation and Employment in Open Economies.* Amsterdam: North Holland, Chapter 10.
———. 1980. Central bank intervention and the stability of exchange rates. In Richard M. Levich and Clas G. Wihlborg, eds. *Exchange Risk and Exposure.* Lexington: Lexington Books, pp.137-47.
Block, Fred. 1977. *The Origins of International Economic Disorder.* Berkeley: University of California Press.
Board of Governors of Federal Reserve System. 1974. *The Federal Reserve System: Purposes and Functions.* 6th ed. Washington, D.C.: Board of Governors, Federal Reserve System.
Borins, Sanford. 1972. The political economy of "the Fed". *Public Policy* 20:175-98.
Boxer, C. R. 1965. *The Dutch Seaborne Empire.* New York: Knopf.
———. 1969. *The Portuguese Seaborne Empire.* New York: Knopf.
Boyer, Russell S. 1978. Optimal foreign exchange market intervention. *Journal of Political Economy* 86(December):1045-55.
———. 1980. Interest rate and exchange rate stabilization regimes: An analysis of recent Canadian policy. In David Bigman and Teizo Taya, eds. *The Functioning of Floating Exchange Rates: Theory, Evidence, and Policy Implications.* Cambridge, Mass.: Ballinger.
Brainard, William C. 1964. Financial intermediaries and the theory of monetary control. *Yale Economic Essays*, pp. 431-25.
———. 1967. Uncertainty and the effectiveness of policy. *American Economic Review* 57(May):411-25.
Brandon, Henry. 1972. *The Retreat of American Power.* New York: Dell.
Branson, William M. 1979. Exchange rate dynamics and monetary policy. In Assar Lindbeck, ed. *Inflation and Employment in Open Economies.* Amsterdam: North Holland, Chapter 8.
Braun, Anne Romanis. 1976. Indexation of wages and salaries in developed economies. *I.M.F. Staff Papers* 23(March):226-71.
Brito, D. L., and D. D. Hester. 1974. Stability and control of the money supply. *Quarterly Journal of Economics* 88(2):278-303.
Brito, D. L., and J. David Richardson. 1975. Some disequilibrium dynamics of exchange-rate changes. *Journal of International Economics* 5(1):1-13.
Brunner, Karl. 1978. Introduction to symposiac examination of books by Coombs and Solomon. *Journal of Monetary Economics* 4:389-95.
Brunner, K., and A. H. Meltzer. 1963. Predicting velocity: Implications

Bibliography

for theory and policy. *Journal of Finance* (May):319-54.
———. 1964a. Some supply functions for money. *Journal of Finance* (May):240-83.
———. 1964b. The Federal Reserve's attachment to the free reserve concept. U.S. House of Representatives, Committee on Banking and Currency, Subcommittee on Domestic Finance, May 7. Washington, D.C.: Government Printing Office.
———. 1968. Liquidity traps for money, bank credit and interest rates. *Journal of Political Economy* (February):1-37.
Bryant, Ralph C. 1980. *Money and Monetary Policy in Interdependent Nations*. Washington, D.C.: The Brookings Institution.
Buchanan, James M., and Gordon Tullock. 1962. *The Calculus of Consent*. Ann Arbor: University of Michigan Press.
Buchanan, James M., and Richard Wagner. 1977. *Democracy in Deficit*. New York: Academic Press.
Burns, Arthur F. 1978. *Reflections of an Economic Policy Maker: Speeches and Congressional Statements, 1969-1978*. Washington, D.C.: American Enterprise Institute.
———. 1979a. Two views on the budget balancing amendment. *The A.E.I. Economist* (April):1-4.
———. 1979b. The anguish of central banking. Per Jacobsson Lecture, Belgrade, Yugoslavia.
Cagan, Phillip. 1978. The reduction of inflation by slack demand. In *Contemporary Economic Problems 1978*. Washington, D.C.: American Enterprise Institute.
Cameron, David. 1978. The expansion of the public economy: A comparative analysis. *American Political Science Review* 72-74 (December):1243-61.
Camps, M. 1980. The new Bretton Woods. *International Journal* (Spring):240-62.
Canzoneri, Matthew B. 1980. Wealth effects in the new neoclassical models. *International Finance Discussion Papers*, Board of Governors, Federal Reserve System, no. 158 (April).
Canzoneri, Matthew B., Dale W. Henderson, and Kenneth S. Rogoff. 1981. The information content of the interest rate and optimal monetary policy. *International Finance Discussion Papers*, Board of Governors, Federal Reserve System, no. 192 (November).
Casas, F. R. 1978. The short run efficiency of monetary policy under floating exchange rates reconsidered. *Journal of International Economics* 8(1):55-63.
Chace, James, and Earl Ravenal, eds. 1976. *Atlantis Lost*. New York: New York University Press.
Chalmers, E. 1972. *The International Interest Rate War*. New York: St. Martin's Press.
Clarke, Stephen V. O. 1967. *Central Bank Cooperation: 1924-31*. New York: Federal Reserve Bank of New York.
Clausewitz, Karl von. 1976. *On War*. Translated by M. Howard, and P. Paret. Princeton: Princeton University Press.
Clifford, Jerome A. 1965. *The Independence of the Federal Reserve System*. Philadelphia: University of Pennsylvania Press.
Cohen, Benjamin J. 1977. *Organizing the World's Money*. New York: Basic Books.
Coombs, Charles A. 1976. *The Arena of International Finance*. New York: Wiley.
Cooper, Richard N. 1971. *Currency Devaluation in Developing Countries*.

Princeton Essays in International Finance, No. 86.
———. 1975. Commentary. In David Meiselman and Arthur Laffer, eds. The Phenomenon of Worldwide Inflation: Proceedings. Washington, D.C.: American Enterprise Institute.
———. 1976. Monetary theory and policy in an open economy. Scandinavian Journal of Economics 2:146-63.
Corden, W. N. 1977. Inflation, Exchange Rates and the World Economy: Lectures on International Monetary Economics. Chicago: University of Chicago Press.
Cottrell, Alvin, and Thomas Moorer. 1977. U.S. Overseas Bases: Problems of Projecting American Military Power Abroad. Washington Papers, no. 47. Washington, D.C.: Georgetown Center for Strategic and International Studies.
Darby, Michael R. 1980a. The monetary approach to the balance of payments: Two specious assumptions. Economic Inquiry 18 (April):321-26.
———. 1980b. The international economy as a source of and restraint on United States inflation. In William A. Gale, ed. Inflation: Passion, Economics, and Statistics. Forthcoming.
Darby, Michael R., and Alan C. Stockman. 1980. The Mark III International Transmission Model. National Bureau of Economic Research, Working Paper no. 462 (March).
Darmstadter, Joel, and Han H. Landsberg. 1976. The economic background. In Raymond Vernon, ed. The Oil Crisis: In Perspective. New York: W. W. Norton, pp. 15-37.
Davis, L. J. 1980. Bankers' casino. Harpers (February):43-57.
Deardoff, Alan, and Robert Stern. 1978. The terms of trade effect on expenditure: Some evidence from econometric models. Journal of International Economics, pp. 409-14.
Destler, I. M. 1980. Making Foreign Economic Policy. Washington, D.C.: The Brookings Institution.
deVries, Margaret Garritsen. 1976. The International Monetary Fund 1966-1971. Washington, D.C.: International Monetary Fund.
Dewald, William. 1972. The national monetary commission: A look back. Journal of Money, Credit and Banking (November):930-56.
Dooley, Michael P. 1979. Foreign exchange market intervention. In Michael P. Dooley, Herbert M. Kaufman, and Raymond E. Lombra, eds. The Political Economy of Policy-Making. Beverly Hills: Sage, pp. 221-31.
Dornbusch, Rudiger. 1976a. Exchange rate expectations and monetary policy. Journal of International Economics 6(3):231-44.
———. 1976b. Expectations and exchange rate dynamics. Journal of Political Economy 84(6):1161-76.
Dornbusch, Rudiger, and P. Krugman. 1976. Flexible exchange rates in the short run. Brookings Papers on Economic Activity, no. 3, pp. 537-75.
Downs, Anthony. 1957. An Economic Theory of Democracy. New York: Harper and Row.
The Economist. 1971. August 21.
Edgren, G., K. Faxen, and C. Odhner. 1973. Wage Formation and the Economy. London: Macmillan.
Elster, J. 1976. Some conceptual problems in political theory. In B. Barry, ed. Power and Political Theory: Some European Perspectives. London: Wiley, pp. 245-70.
Emminger, O. 1977. The D-Mark in the Conflict Between Internal and External Stability. Princeton Essays in International Finance, no. 122.

———. 1980. The International Monetary System under Stress. American Enterprise Institute Reprint, no. 112 (May).
Enzler, Jared, Lewis Johnson, and John Paulus. 1976. Some problems of money demand. Brookings Papers on Economic Activity, no. 1, pp. 261-79.
Ethier, Wilfred, and Arthur I. Bloomfield. 1975. Managing the Managed Float. Princeton Essays in International Finance, no. 112.
Fabra, Paul. 1979. 'Les flus monétaires dans un monde ecartelé entre l'inflation'et la déflation. In P. Fabra, P. M. Henry, F. Herrera and R. Tamames, eds. Le Nouvel Ordre Economique/Nuevo Orden Economico Internacional. Madrid: jointly by Instituto de Cooperacion Intercontinental, Madrid and Fondation Europeenne de la Culture, Amsterdam, 1978.
Federal Reserve Bank of Chicago. Various years. Annual Report.
———. Various years. International Letter.
Fellner, William. 1949. Competition among the Few. New York: Knopf.
———. 1979. The credibility effect and rational expectations. Brookings Papers on Economic Activity, no. 1, pp. 167-89.
Fischer, Stanley. 1977a. Long term contracts, rational expectations, and the optimal policy rule. Journal of Political Economy 85:191-206.
———. 1977b. Stability and exchange rate systems in a monetarist model of the balance of payments. In Robert Z. Aliber, ed. The Political Economy of Monetary Reform. London: Macmillan.
———. 1980. On activist monetary policy with rational expectations. In S. Fischer, ed. Rational Expectations and Economic Policy. Chicago: University of Chicago Press, pp. 211-47.
Fischer, Stanley, and Franco Modigliani. 1978. Toward an understanding of the real effects and costs of inflation. Weltwirtschaftliches Archiv 114(4):810-33.
Flood, Robert P. 1979. Capital mobility and the choice of exchange rate system. International Economic Review 20(June):405-16.
Forsyth, J. 1980. The Problem of Sterling. London: Royal Institute of International Affairs.
Frankel, Jeffrey A. 1979. A test of existence of the risk premium in the foreign exchange market vs. the hypothesis of perfect substitutability. International Finance Discussion Papers, Board of Governors, Federal Reserve System, no. 149 (August).
Frenkel, Jacob. 1980. International reserves under alternative exchange rate regimes and aspects of the economics of managed float. In Helmut Frisch and Gerhard Schwödiauer, eds. The Economics of Flexible Exchange Rates, supplements to Kredit and Kapital, vol. 6.
Frenkel, Jacob, and Michael Mussa. 1981. Monetary and fiscal policy in an open economy. American Economic Review, Papers and Proceedings, (May):253-58.
Freund, William. 1980. Productivity and inflation. U.S. Congress, Joint Economic Committee. Washington, D.C.: Government Printing Office.
Frey, Burro S. 1978. Political-economic models and cycles. Journal of Public Economics 9(2):203-20.
Friedman, Benjamin M. 1975. Targets, instruments, and indicators of monetary policy. Journal of Monetary Economics 1(October):443-73.
Friedman, David. 1980. Many, few, one: Social harmony and the shrunken choice set. American Economic Review 70 (March):225-32.
Friedman, Milton. 1953. The case for flexible exchange rates. In Milton Friedman, Essays in Positive Economics. Chicago: University of Chicago

Press, pp. 157-203.

———. 1970. <u>The counter-revolution in monetary theory</u>. London: IEA Occasional Paper, no. 33.

Friedman, Milton, and Rose Friedman. 1980. <u>Free to Choose</u>. New York: Harcourt, Brace, Jovanovich.

Frydl, E. J. 1980. The debate over regulating the Eurocurrency markets. <u>Federal Reserve Bank of New York Quarterly Review</u> 4(4):11-20.

Gall, Norman. 1980. How much can the system take? <u>Forbes</u> (June 23):91-98.

Gambs, Carl M., and Donald V. Kimball. 1979. Small banks and the Federal funds market. <u>Federal Reserve Bank of Kansas City Economic Review</u> 64(9):3-12.

Garcia, Gillian, and Simon Pak. 1979. Some clues in the case of the missing money. <u>American Economic Review</u>, Papers and Proceedings, 69(2):330-34.

Gardner, Richard N. 1980. <u>Sterling-Dollar Diplomacy in Current Perspective</u>. New York: Columbia University Press.

Gershman, Carl. 1980. The rise and fall of the new foreign policy establishment. <u>Commentary</u> (July):13-34.

Gilpin, Robert. 1975. <u>U.S. Power and the Multinational Corporation</u>. New York: Basic Books.

Girton, Lance, and Dale W. Henderson. 1977. Central bank operations in foreign and domestic assets under fixed and flexible exchange rates. In Peter B. Clark, Dennis E. Logue, and Richard J. Sweeney, eds. <u>The Effects of Exchange Rate Adjustments</u>. Washington, D.C.: Government Printing Office.

Goldfeld, Stephen M. 1973. The demand for money revisited. <u>Brookings Papers on Economic Activity</u>, no. 3, pp. 577-638.

———. 1976. The case of the missing money. <u>Brookings Papers on Economic Activity</u>, no. 3, pp. 683-730.

Goldfeld, Stephen M., and Alan S. Blinder. 1972. Some implications of endogenous stabilization policy. <u>Brookings Papers on Economic Activity</u>, no. 3, pp. 585-640.

Goldstein, Henry. 1966. Moderated exchange rate variability: A comment. <u>The National Banking Review</u> (September):97-100.

Goldstein, Morris. 1980. <u>Have Flexible Exchange Rates Made Macroeconomic Policy More Difficult? A Survey of Issues and Evidence</u>. Paper presented at Conference on Macroeconomics under Flexible Exchange Rates, Madrid, Spain, (September 1979). Princeton Special Papers in International Finance, no. 14.

Goldthorpe, John. 1978. The current inflation: Towards a sociological account. In F. Hirsch and J. Goldthorpe, eds. <u>The Political Economy of Inflation</u>. Cambridge: Harvard University Press, pp. 186-214.

Gordon, Robert J. 1975. The demand and supply of inflation. <u>The Journal of Law and Economics</u> (December):807-36.

———. 1976. Recent developments in the theory of inflation and unemployment. <u>Journal of Monetary Economics</u> 2(April):185-219.

———. 1977. World inflation and monetary accommodation in eight countries. <u>Brookings Papers on Economic Activity</u>, no. 2, pp. 409-68.

Gray, Colin. 1977. <u>The Geopolitics of the Nuclear Era</u>. New York: Crane, Russak.

Green, H. A. John. 1964. <u>Aggregation in Economic Analysis: An Introductory Survey</u>. Princeton: Princeton University Press.

Grubel, H. G. 1977a. <u>International Economics</u>. Homewood: Richard D. Irwin.

———. 1977b. How important is control over international reserves? In R. A. Mundell and J. I. Pollak, eds. <u>The New International Monetary</u>

System. New York: Columbia University Press, pp. 133-61.
Gurley, John G., and Edward S. Shaw. 1960. *Money in a Theory of Finance*. Washington, D.C.: The Brookings Institution.
Haas, E. 1964. *Beyond the Nation State*. Stanford: Stanford University Press.
———. 1980. Why collaborate? Issue linkage and international regimes. *World Politics* 32(3):357-405.
Haberler, Gottfried. 1964. Integration and growth in the world economy in historical perspective. *American Economic Review* 54(March):1-22.
———. 1980. Notes on rational and irrational expectations. In Emil Kung, ed. *Wandlungen in Wirtschaft und Gesellschaft: Die Wirtschafts-und die Sozialwissenschaften vol neuen Cufgaben*. Lubingen. Washington, D.C.: American Enterprise Institute. Reprint no. 111.
Haberler, Gottfried, and Thomas Willett. 1971. *A Strategy of U.S. Balance of Payments Policy*. Washington: American Enterprise Institute.
Hafer, R. W., and Scott E. Hein. 1979. Evidence of the temporal stability of the demand for money relationship in the U.S. *Federal Reserve Bank of St. Louis Review* 61(12):3-14.
Hagerty, Herbert. 1977. Forward Deployment in the 1970s and 1980s. National Security Affairs Monograph 77-2. Washington, D.C.: National Defense University.
Hamada, Koichi. 1974. Alternative exchange rate systems and the interdependence of monetary policies. In Robert Z. Aliber, ed. *National Monetary Policies and the International Monetary System*. Chicago: University of Chicago Press, pp. 13-33.
Hansen, Lars P., and Robert J. Hodrick. 1980. Forward exchange rates as optimal predictors of future spot rates: An econometric analysis. *Journal of Political Economy* 88(October):829-53.
Harsanyi, John. 1971. The dimension and measurement of social power. In K. W. Rothschild, ed. *Power in Economics*. Baltimore: Penguin Books, pp. 77-96.
Havrilesky, Thomas. 1979. A theory of monetary instability. In M. Dooley, H. Kaufman, and R. Lombra, eds. *The Political Economy of Policy-making*. Beverly Hills: Sage, pp. 59-88.
Hayek, Friedrich A. 1948. Individualism: True and false. In *Individualism and Economic Order*. Chicago: University of Chicago Press, pp. 1-32.
———. 1967. Degrees of explanation. In *Studies in Philosophy, Politics and Economics*. Chicago: University of Chicago Press, pp. 3-21.
———. 1975. Nobel Lecture.
———. 1976. *Law, Legislation, and Liberty*. Vols. 1 and 2. Chicago: University of Chicago Press.
Henderson, Dale. 1977. Modeling the interdependence of national money and capital markets. *American Economic Review* 67(February):190-99.
———. 1979. Financial policies in open economies. *American Economic Review* 69(May):232-39.
———. 1980. Analyzing arrangements for reducing exchange rate variability: A comment. In Karl Brunner and Allan H. Meltzer, eds. *Monetary Institutions and the Policy Process*. Carnegie-Rochester Conference Series on Public Policy, vol. 13, pp. 223-37.
Hester, Donald D. 1972. Monetary policy in the "checkless" economy. *The Journal of Finance* 27(2):279-93.
Hibbs, Douglas. 1977. Political parties and macroeconomic policy. *American Political Science Review* 71(4):1467-87.
———. 1978. Mass political support and macroeconomic policy.

Department of Government, Harvard University, unpublished paper.
———. 1980a. Public concern about inflation and unemployment in the United States: Trends, correlates, and political implications. Nontechnical essay, National Bureau of Economic Research (May).
———. 1980b. Economics and politics in France: Economic performance and mass political support for Presidents Pompidou and Giscard d'Estaing. Department of Government, Harvard University.
———. 1980c. On the demand for economic outcomes: Macroeconomic performance and mass political support in the United States, Great Britain, and Germany. Department of Government, Harvard University.
Hibbs, Douglas, and Heino Fassbinder, eds. 1981. Contemporary Political Economy. Amsterdam: North Holland.
Hickman, Bert G. 1977. Comment on Salant, 1977. In Lawrence Krause and Walter Salant, eds. Worldwide Inflation. Washington, D.C.: The Brookings Institution, pp. 227-32.
Hicks, Sir John. 1975. What is wrong with monetarism? Lloyd's Bank Review (October):1-13.
Hirsch, Fred. 1978. The ideological underlay of inflation. In Fred Hirsch and John Goldthorpe, eds. The Political Economy of Inflation. London: Martin Robertson, pp. 263-84.
Hirsch, Fred, and Michael W. Doyle. 1977. Politicization in the world economy: Necessary conditions for an international economic order. In F. Hirsch, M. Doyle, and Edward L. Morse, eds. Alternatives to Monetary Disorder. New York: McGraw-Hill, pp. 11-64.
Hirsch, Fred, and John H. Goldthorpe, eds. 1978. The Political Economy of Inflation. Cambridge: Harvard University Press.
Hirschman, A. 1945. National Power and the Structure of Foreign Trade. Berkeley: University of California Press.
Hobbs, T. 1951. Leviathan. M. Oakeshott, ed., Oxford.
Hoffman, Stanley. 1975. Notes on the elusiveness of power. International Journal 30(Spring): 183-206.
Hooper, Peter, and Barbara Lowrey. 1979. Impact of the dollar depreciation on the U.S. price level. International Finance Discussion Papers, Board of Governors, Federal Reserve System, no. 128 (January).
Houthakker, Hendrik S. 1978. The breakdown of Bretton Woods. In Werner Sichel, ed. Economic Advice and Executive Policy: Recommendations from Past Members of the Council of Economic Advisors. New York: Praeger, pp. 45-64.
International Monetary Fund. IMF Survey World Economic Outlook, Washington, D.C.: International Monetary Fund. Various issues.
Imlah, A. 1958. Economic Elements in the Pax Britannica: Studies in British Trade in the Nineteenth Century. Cambridge, Mass.: Harvard University Press.
Isard, Peter, and Michael Porter. 1977. A note on the monetarist analysis of devaluation. Journal of International Economics (November):407-9.
Johannes, J. M., and R. H. Rasche. 1979. Predicting the money multiplier. Journal of Monetary Economics 5(3):301-25.
Johnson, Harry G. 1970. The case for flexible exchange rates, 1969. In C. Fred Bergsten et al. eds. Approaches to Greater Flexibility of Exchange Rates: The Burgenstock Papers. Princeton: Princeton University Press, pp. 91-111.
Johnson, Paul. 1979. Washington and Bonn: Dimensions of change in bilateral relations. International Organization 33(Autumn):451-80.
Jones, C. Michael. 1979. Policymaking efficiency and the international

monetary system. Ph.D. diss., Yale University.
Kalchbrenner, John H., and Peter A. Tinsley, with James Berry and Bonnie Garrett. 1977. On filtering auxiliary information in short-run monetary policy. In K. Brunner and A. Meltzer, eds. Optimal Policies, Control Theory, and Technology Exports, Carnegie-Rochester Series on Public Policy, vol. 7, pp. 39-84.
Kaminow, Ira P. 1979a. Fed policy under resolution 133 (1975-1978): Is what they said what they did? Government Research Corporation, Working Paper.
———. 1979b. Economic stability under fixed and flexible exchange rates. Journal of International Economics 9(May):277-85.
Kane, Edward J. 1973. The central bank as big brother. Journal of Money, Credit and Banking 5(November):979-81.
———. 1974a. The re-politicization of the Fed. Journal of Financial and Quantitative Analysis 9(November):743-52.
———. 1974b. All for the best: The Federal Reserve Board's 60th annual report. American Economic Review 64(December):835-50.
———. 1975. New congressional restraints and Federal Reserve independence. Challenge 18(November-December):37-44.
———. 1978. EFT and monetary policy. Journal of Contemporary Business 7(Spring):29-50.
———. 1979a. Statement. In U.S. Senate, Committee on Banking, Housing and Urban Affairs, Hearings, Federal Reserve's First Monetary Policy Report for 1979, February 20 and 23, 1979, pp. 154-60.
———. 1979b. The three faces of commercial-bank liability management. In M. P. Dooley, H. M. Kaufman, and R. E. Lombra, eds. The Political Economy of Policy Making. Beverly Hills: Sage, pp. 149-74.
———. 1980a. Politics and Fed policymaking: The more things change, the more they remain the same. Journal of Monetary Economics 6(April): 199-211.
———. 1980b. Accelerating inflation and the distribution of savings incentives. Mimeographed. Columbus: Ohio State University.
Kareken, John, Thomas Muench, and Neil Wallace. 1973. Optimal open market strategy: The use of information variables. American Economic Review 63(March):156-72.
Katzenstein, Peter. 1976a. International relations and domestic structures: Foreign economic policies of advanced industrial states. International Organization 30(1):1-46.
———. 1976b. West Germany's place in American foreign policy: Pivot, anchor, or broker? In R. Rosencrance, ed. America as an Ordinary Country. Ithaca, N.Y.: Cornell University Press, pp. 110-35.
Kemp, Geoffrey. 1977. The new strategic map. Survival (March/April):50-59.
Kenen, Peter B. 1978. New views of exchange rates and old views of policy. American Economic Review 68(2):163-67.
Keohane, Robert. 1978. Economics, inflation and the role of the state: Political implications of the McCracken report. World Politics (October):108-28.
———. 1979. United States foreign economic policy toward other advanced capitalist states: The struggle to make others adjust. In Kenneth Oye et al., eds. Eagle Entangled: U.S. Foreign Policy in a Complex World. New York: Longman, pp. 91-122.
———. 1980a. The theory of hegemonic stability and changes in international economic regimes, 1967-1977. In Ole Holsti, Randolph Siverson, and Alexander L. George, eds. Change in the International System.

Boulder, Colo.: Westview Press.

———. 1982. Hegemonic leadership and U.S. foreign economic policy: Lessons for the 1980s from the "long decade" of the 1950s. In William Avery and David Rapkin, eds. *America in a Changing World Political Economy*. New York: Longman's.

Keohane, Robert, and Joseph Nye. 1970. *Transnational Relations and World Politics*. Cambridge, Mass.: Harvard University Press.

———. 1975. International interdependence and integretion. In Fred Greenstein and Nelson Polsby, eds. *Handbook of Political Science*. Vol. 8. Reading: Addison Wesley, pp. 363-414.

———. 1977. *Power and Interdependence: World Politics in Transition*. Boston: Little, Brown.

Kindleberger, Charles P. 1973. *The World in Depression 1929-1939*. Berkeley: University of California Press.

———. 1978. *Economic Response: Comparative Studies in Trade, Finance, and Growth*. Cambridge: Harvard University Press.

Kissinger, Henry A. 1979. *White House Years*. Boston: Little, Brown.

Knorr, Klaus. 1975. *The Power of Nations*. New York: Basic Books.

Komiya, Ryutaro. 1975. Recent U.S. foreign economic policy from a Japanese point of view. In C. Fred Bergsten, ed. *Toward a New World Trade Policy: The Maidenhead Papers*. Lexington, Mass.: Lexington Books, pp. 359-63.

Kraft, Joseph. 1980. The rattle in the background. *Washington Post*, February 19.

Krasner, Stephen D. 1976. State power and the structure of international trade. *World Politics* (April):317-47.

———. 1978a. *Defending the National Interest*. Princeton, N.J.: Princeton University Press.

———. 1978b. United States commercial and monetary policy: Unravelling the paradox of external strength and internal weakness. In P. Katzenstein, ed. *Between Power and Plenty*. Madison: University of Wisconsin Press, pp. 51-87.

Krause, Lawrence B., and Sueo Sekiguchi. 1976. Japan and the world economy. In Hugh Patrick and Henry Rosovsky, eds. *Asia's New Giant*. Washington, D.C.: The Brookings Institution, pp. 383-458.

Krugman, Paul, and Lance Taylor. 1978. Contractionary effects of devaluation. *Journal of International Economics* 3(August):445-56.

Laidler, D. E. W. 1975. *Essays on Money and Inflation*. Chicago: University of Chicago Press.

———. 1977. *The Demand for Money: Theories and Evidence*. New York: Harper and Row.

Landes, Elisabeth. 1980. The effect of state maximum-house laws on the employment of women in 1920. *Journal of Political Economy* 88(June): 476-94.

Laney, Leroy, and Thomas Willett. 1980a. The political business cycle and monetary policy in the U.S. Claremont Working Papers.

———. 1980b. The international liquidity explosion and global monetary expansion: 1970-72. Claremont Working Papers.

———. 1982. *The Political Economy of Global Inflation: The Causes of Monetary Expansion in the Major Industrial Countries*. Washington, D.C.: American Enterprise Institute.

Laqueur, Walter. 1980. Euro-neutralism. *Commentary* 69(June):21-27.

Lindbeck, Assar. 1976. Stabilization policy in open economies with endogenous politicians. *American Economic Review*, Papers and

Proceedings, 66(May):1-19.
Little, Jane Sneddon. 1975. Eurodollars: The Money Market Gypsies. New York: Harper and Row.
———. 1979. Liquidity creation by Eurobanks: 1973-1978. New England Economic Review (January/February):62-72.
Lombra, Raymond E. 1979. Policy advice and policy-making: Economic, political and social issues. In Michael Dooley et al., eds. The Political Economy of Policy-Making. Beverly Hills: Sage, pp. 13-34.
Lombra, Raymond E., and Michael Moran. 1980. Policy advice and policy-making at the Federal Reserve. In K. Brunner and A. Meltzer, eds. Monetary Institutions and the Policy Process. Carnegie-Rochester Conference Series on Public Policy, vol. 13, pp. 9-68.
Lombra, Raymond E., and Frederick Struble. 1979. Monetary aggregate targets and the volatility of interest rates: A taxonomic discussion. Journal of Money, Credit and Banking (August):284-300.
Lucas, Robert E. 1976. Econometric policy evaluation: a critique. Journal of Monetary Economics, Supplement, (January):19-46.
Lucas, Charles M., Marcos T. Jones, and Thom B. Thurston. 1977. Federal funds and repurchase agreements. Federal Reserve Bank of New York Quarterly Review 2:33-48.
Luce, R. Duncan, and Howard Raiffa. 1957. Games and Decision. New York: J. Wiley and Sons, Chapter 5.
McCallum, Bennett T. 1978. The political business cycle: An empirical test. Southern Economic Journal (January):504-15.
McKean, Roland N. 1949. Liquidity and a national balance sheet. Journal of Political Economy 57(6):506-22.
McKinnon, R. I. 1978. Review of "Floating exchange rates and international monetary reform," by T. Willett, and "Floating exchange rates and national economic policy," by Stanley Black. Journal of Economic Literature (December):1469-71.
McPherson, C. P. 1972. Tariff Structures and Political Exchange." Ph.D. diss. University of Chicago.
MacRae, C. Duncan. 1977. A political model of the business cycle. Journal of Political Economy 57(6):506-22.
Maier, Charles. 1978. The politics of inflation in the twentieth century. In F. Hirsch and J. Goldthorpe, eds. The Political Economy of Inflation. Cambridge, Mass.: Harvard University Press, pp. 37-72.
Maisel, Sherman J. 1973. Managing the Dollar. New York: W. W. Norton.
March, James G. 1966. The power of power. In David Easton, ed. Varieties of Political Theory. New York: Prentice-Hall, pp. 39-70.
Marris, Stephen N. 1970. Comment. In C. Fred Bergsten, ed. Approaches to Greater Flexibility of Exchange Rates: The Burgenstock Papers. Princeton: Princeton University Press, pp. 392-99.
Mason, Will E. 1963. Clarification of the Monetary Standard: The Concept and Its Relation to Monetary Policies and Objectives. University Park: The Pennsylvania State University Press.
Mayer, Martin. 1980. The Fate of the Dollar. New York: Times Books.
Meese, Richard A., and Kenneth J. Singleton. 1980. Rational expectations, risk premia, and the market for spot and forward exchange. International Finance Discussion Papers, Board of Governors, Federal Reserve System, no. 165 (July).
Meiselman, David, and Arthur Laffer, eds. 1975. The Phenomenon of Worldwide Inflation: Proceedings. Washington, D.C.: American Enterprise Institute.

Meltzer, Allan H. 1978. The conduct of monetary policy under current monetary arrangements. Journal of Monetary Economics 4(April):371-88.
Meltzer, Allan H., and Scott F. Richard. 1981. A rational theory of the size of government. Journal of Political Economy (October):914-27.
Mendelsohn, S. 1979. Money on the Move. New York: McGraw-Hill.
Miller, Preston, and Arthur Rolnick. 1980. The CBO's policy analysis: An unquestionable misuse of a questionable theory. Journal of Monetary Economics (April):171-98.
Minsky, H. P. 1957. Central banking and money market changes. Quarterly Journal of Economics 71(2):171-87.
Modelski, George. 1978. The long cycle of global politics and the nation-state. Comparative Studies in Society and History 20(April):214-35.
———. 1980. The theory of long cycles and U.S. strategic policy. In R. Harkavy and E. Kolodziej, eds. American Security Policy and Policy-Making. Lexington, Mass.: D. C. Heath, pp. 3-19.
Modigliani, Franco, and Tommaso Padoa-Schioppa. 1978. The Management of an Open Economy with "100% Plus" Wage Indexation. Princeton Essays in International Finance, no. 130 (December).
Modigliani, Franco, and Lucas Papademos. 1978. Optimal demand policies against stagflation. Weltwirtschaftliches Archiv 114:736-81.
Moore, Basil. 1979. The endogenous money stock. Journal of Post-Keynesian Economics (Fall):49-70.
Morgenthau, Hans. 1968. Power among Nations. 5th ed. New York: Knopf.
Mork, Knut Anton, and Robert E. Hall. 1979. Energy prices, inflation, and recession, 1974-75. National Bureau of Economic Research, Working Paper no. 369 (July).
Morley, Samuel A. 1979. Inflation and Unemployment. Hinsdale: Dryden Press, Chapter 4.
Morse, Edward. 1976. The Atlantic economy in crisis. In J. Chace and E. Ravenal, eds. Atlantis Lost. New York: New York University Press, pp. 149-82.
Mueller, Dennis C. 1979. Public Choice. Cambridge, Mass.: Cambridge University Press.
Mueller, Robert, Robert D. Tollison, and Thomas D. Willett. 1972. Representative democracy via random selection. Public Choice (Spring):57-68.
———. 1976. Solving the intensity problem in representative democracy. In Ryan Amacher, Robert Tollison, and Thomas Willett, eds. Economics and Public Policy. Ithaca, N.Y.: Cornell University Press, pp. 444-73.
Mundell, R. A. 1962. The appropriate use of monetary and fiscal policy under fixed exchange rates. I.M.F. Staff Papers 9(March):70-79.
———. 1968. International Economics. New York: Macmillan.
Mussa, Michael. 1979. Macroeconomic interdependence and the exchange rate regime. In Rudiger Dornbusch and Jacob Frenkel, eds. International Economic Policy. Baltimore: The Johns Hopkins University Press, pp. 160-204.
New York Times. 1980. August 20, p. A5.
Nichols, Dorothy M. 1965. Trading in Federal Funds: Findings of a Three-Year Survey. Washington, D.C.: Board of Governors, Federal Reserve System.
Niehans, Jürg. 1968. Monetary and fiscal policies in open economies under fixed and flexible exchange rates: An optimizing approach. Journal of Political Economy 76(July/August):893-920.
———. 1975. Some doubts about the efficacy of monetary policy under

flexible rates. *Journal of International Economics* (August):275-81.
Niskanen, William A. 1971. *Bureaucracy and Representative Government*. Chicago: Aldine-Atherton.
Nixon, Richard M. 1978. *RN: The Memoirs of Richard Nixon*. New York: Grosset and Dunlap.
Nordhaus, William D. 1975. The political business cycle. *Review of Economic Studies* 42(April):169-90.
Nye, J. S. 1971. *Peace in Parts: Integration and Conflict in Regional Organization*. Boston: Little, Brown.
———. 1976. Independence and interdependence. *Foreign Policy* 22 (Spring):130-61.
Obstfeld, Maurice. 1980. Portfolio balance, monetary policy, and the dollar-Deutsche mark exchange rate. Mimeographed. New York: Columbia University.
Odell, John. 1979. The United States and the emergence of flexible exchange rates: An analysis of foreign policy change. *International Organization* 33-1(Winter):57-81.
OECD (Organization for Economic Cooperation and Development). 1973. *OECD Economic Outlook*, no. 14, December.
———. 1975. *OECD Economic Outlook*, no. 18, December.
———. 1976. *OECD Economic Outlook*, no. 19, July.
———. 1977a. *OEDC Economic Outlook*, no. 22, December.
———. 1977b. *Towards Full Employment and Price Stability*, (the McCracken Report). OECD: Paris.
———. 1979a. *OECD Economic Outlook*, no. 26, December.
———. 1979b. *Monetary Targets and Inflation Control*. OECD: Paris.
Olson, Mancur, Jr. 1965. *The Logic of Collective Action: Public Goods and the Theory of Groups*. Cambridge: Harvard University Press.
Olson, Mancur, Jr. and R. Zeckhauser. 1966. An economic theory of alliances. *Review of Economics and Statistics* (August):266-79.
Organski, Kenneth. 1968. *World Politics*. 2nd. ed. New York: Knopf.
Papademos, Lucas. 1979. Rational Expectations and the Inflation-Unemployment Trade-Off. Discussion Paper Series, no. 45. Department of Economics, Columbia University.
Parkin, Michael. 1975. Where is Britain's inflation going? *Lloyd's Bank Review* (October):1-13.
———. 1978. A comparison of alternative techniques of monetary control under rational expectations. *The Manchester School of Economics and Social Studies* 46(September):252-87.
Penrose, Edith. 1976. The development of crisis. In Raymond Vernon, ed. *The Oil Crisis: In Perspective*. New York: W. W. Norton, pp. 39-57.
Phillips, A. W. 1957. Stabilization policy and the time-forms of lagged Responses. *The Economic Journal* 67(266):265-77.
Pierce, James. 1979. The political economy of Arthur Burns. *Journal of Finance* 34(June):485-96.
Pigott, Charles, and Richard James Sweeney. 1980. Purchasing power parity and exchange rate dynamics. Mimeographed. Claremont, Calif.: Claremont Graduate School.
Pigott, Charles, John Rutledge, and Thomas D. Willett. 1980. Some evidence on the instability of estimates of the inflationary effects of exchange rate changes. Mimeographed. Claremont: Claremont Graduate College.
Pincus, Jonathan J. 1977. *Pressure Groups and Politics in Antebellum Tariffs*. New York: Columbia University Press.

Polanyi, Karl. 1944. The Great Transformation. New York: Rinehart; 1957, Boston: Beacon Press.
Poole, William. 1970. Optimal choice of monetary policy instruments in a simple stochastic macro model. Quarterly Journal of Economics 84 (May):197-216.
———. 1976. Interpreting the Fed's monetary targets. Brookings Papers on Economic Activity, no. 1, pp. 247-59.
Porter, Richard D., Thomas D. Simpson, and Eileen Mauskopf. 1979. Financial Innovation and the Monetary Aggregates. Brookings Papers on Economic Activity, no. 1, pp. 213-37.
Resler, David H. 1979. Does Eurodollar borrowing improve the dollar's exchange value? Federal Reserve Bank of St. Louis Review, no. 8, pp. 10-16.
Revzin, Philip. 1980. Sir Geoffrey stays the course. Wall Street Journal, May 27, p. 24.
Robbins, Lionel. 1954. The Economist in the Twentieth Century. London: Macmillan.
Roberts, Steven M. 1978. Congressional oversight of monetary policy. Journal of Monetary Economics 4(August):543-56.
Rogoff, Kenneth. 1980. A reformulation of the identification problem between slowly adjusting markets and slowly adjusting expectations. Mimeographed. Board of Governors, Federal Reserve System.
Roosa, Robert. 1967. The Dollar and World Liquidity. New York: Random House.
Roper, Don E., and Stephen J. Turnovsky. 1980. Optimal exchange market intervention in a simple stochastic macro model. Canadian Journal of Economics 13(May):296-309.
Rosencrance, Richard, ed. 1976. America as an Ordinary Country. Ithaca, N.Y.: Cornell University Press.
Rosen, Steven. 1979. The proliferation of new land-based technologies. In S. Neuman and R. Harkavy, eds. Arms Transfers in The Modern World. New York: Praeger, pp. 109-30.
Rothschild, K. 1971. Power and Economics. Baltimore: Penguin.
Rousseau, J. J. 1917. A Lasting Peace. Translated by C. E. Vaughan. London: Constable and Co. Ltd.
Russett, B., ed. 1965. Economic Theories of International Politics. Chicago: Markham.
Sachs, Jeffrey. 1979a. Wage indexation, flexible exchange rates, and macroeconomic policy. International Finance Discussion Papers. Board of Governors, Federal Reserve System.
———. 1979b. Wages, profits, and macroeconomic adjustment: A comparative study. Brookings Papers on Economic Activity, no. 2, pp. 269-320.
Safire, William. 1975. Before the Fall. Garden City, N.Y.: Doubleday.
Salant, Walter. 1977. International transmission of inflation. In Lawrence Krause and Walter Salant, eds. Worldwide Inflation. Washington, D.C.: The Brookings Institution, pp. 163-227.
Salter, W. E. G. 1959. Internal and external balance: The role of price and expenditure effects. Economic Record 35(August):226-38.
Samuelson, Paul A. 1979. Two views on the budget balancing amendment. The A.E.I. Economist (April):4-6.
Santomero, A. M. 1980. Stochastic control in a general equilibrium framework. University of Pennsylvania, unpublished manuscript.
Santomero, A. M., and John J. Seater. 1978. The inflation-unemployment tradeoff: A critique of the literature. Journal of Economic

Literature 16(2):499-544.
Santomero, A. M., and J. J. Siegel. 1981. Bank regulation and macroeconomic stability. American Economic Review (March):39-53.
Santomero, A. M. and J. J. Seigel. 1982. A General Equilibrium Money and Banking Paradigm. Journal of Finance (May).
Sargent, Thomas J. 1973. Rational expectations, the real rate of interest, and the natural rate of unemployment. Brookings Papers on Economic Activity, no. 2, pp. 429-72.
Saxonhouse, Gary R. 1972. A review of recent U.S.-Japan economic relations. Asian Survey (September):726-52.
Schmiegelow, Henrik, and Michele Schmiegelow. 1975. The new mercantilism in international relations: The case of France's external monetary policy. International Organization (Spring):376-92.
Schuler, G. Henry M. 1976. The international oil negotiations. In I. William Zartman, ed. The 50% Solution. New York: Doubleday Anchor Books, pp. 124-207.
Schultz, Frederick. 1980. The Position of the Dollar. Speech in Bermuda, May 23. Washington, D.C.: Board of Governors, Federal Reserve System.
Scitovsky, Tibor. 1978. Market power and inflation. Economica (August): 221-33.
Servan-Schreiber, J. J. 1968. The American Challenge. New York: Atheneum.
Shafer, Jeffrey R. 1982. Discussion of exchange rate volatility and intervention policy. In Jacob S. Dreyer, Gottfried Haberler, and Thomas Willett, eds. The International Monetary System under Stress. Washington, D.C.: American Enterprise Institute.
Shapiro, Harold T. 1977. Inflation in the United States. In Lawrence Krause and Walter Salant, eds. Worldwide Inflation. Washington, D.C.: The Brookings Institution, pp. 267-94.
Shubik, Martin. 1970. A curmudgeon's guide to microeconomics. Journal of Economic Literature 8:405-34.
Silk, Leonard. 1976. America in the world economy. In R. Rosencrance, ed. America as an Ordinary Country. Ithaca, N.Y.: Cornell University Press, pp. 158-73.
Simon, Herbert. 1976. From substantive to procedural rationality. In Spiro J. Latsis, ed. Method and Appraisal in Economics. Cambridge: Cambridge University Press.
Simpson, Thomas D. 1979. The Market for Federal Funds and Repurchase Agreements. Staff Study, no. 106. Board of Governors, Federal Reserve System.
Solomon, Robert. 1977. The International Monetary System 1946-1976: An Insider's View. New York: Harper and Row.
―――. 1980. Exchange Rates and Inflation. Mimeographed. Washington, D.C.: The Brookings Institution.
Stein, Herbert. 1975. The politics of inflation. In David Meiselman and Arthur Laffer, The Phenomenon of Worldwide Inflation: Proceedings. Washington, D.C.: American Enterprise.
Stein, Jerome L. 1963. The optimum foreign exchange market. American Economic Review 53(June):384-402.
Stern, R. 1973. The Balance of Payments: Theory and Economic Policy. Chicago: Aldine.
Stigum, Marcia. 1978. The Money Market. Homewood: Dow Jones-Irwin.
Stobaugh, Robert, and Daniel Yergin. 1979. Energy: An emergency telescoped. Foreign Affairs, America and the World, pp. 563-95.
Strange, Susan. 1970. Sterling and British Policy: A Political Study of

an *International Currency in Decline*. Fair Lawn, N.J.: Oxford University Press.
———. 1975. What is economic power and who has it? *International Journal* 30-2(Spring):207-23.
Strotz, Robert H. 1956. Myopia and inconsistency in dynamic utility maximization. *Review of Economic Studies* 23(3):165-80.
Sweeney, Richard J. 1982. Automatic stabilization policy and exchange rate regimes: A general equilibrium approach. In Richard J. Sweeney and Thomas D. Willett, eds. *Studies on Exchange-Rate Flexibility*. Washington, D.C.: American Enterprise Institute, forthcoming.
Sweeney, Richard J., and Thomas D. Willett. 1976a. The inflationary impact of exchange rate changes: Some theoretical considerations. In Peter B. Clark, Dennis E. Logue, and Richard James Sweeney, eds. *The Effects of Rate Adjustments*. Washington, D.C.: Government Printing Office, pp. 45-61.
Sweeney, Richard J., and Thomas D. Willett. 1976b. The international transmission of inflation. In Michele Fratianni and Karel Tavevnier, eds. *Bank Credit, Money, and Inflation in Open Economies*, supplements to Kredit und Kapital 3:441-517.
———. 1982. *Studies on Exchange Rate Flexibility*. Washington, D.C.: American Enterprise Institute, forthcoming.
Swoboda, Alexander K. 1977. Monetary approaches to worldwide inflation. In L. Krause and W. Salant, eds. *Worldwide Inflation*. Washington, D.C.: The Brookings Institution, pp. 9-51.
Taylor, John B. 1980a. Recent developments in the theory of stabilization policy. In *Stabilization Policies: Lessons from the '70s and Implications for the 80s*, Proceedings of a conference sponsored by the Center for the Study of American Business and the Federal Reserve Bank of St. Louis,
———. 1980b. Aggregate dynamics and staggered contracts. *Journal of Political Economy* 88(1):1-23.
Thompson, Earl A. 1979. An economic basis for the "national defense argument" for aiding certain industries. *Journal of Political Economy* 87(February):1-36.
Thompson, Scott, ed. 1980, *From Weakness to Strength*. San Francisco: Institute for Contemporary Studies.
Tideman, Nicholas, and Donald P. Tucker. 1976. The tax treatment of business profits under inflationary conditions. In Henry J. Aaron, ed. *Inflation and the Income Tax*. Washington, D.C.: The Brookings Institution, pp. 33-74.
Tinsley, Peter A., Bonnie Garrett, and Monica E. Friar. 1978. The measurement of money demand. *Special Studies Paper*, no. 133. Board of Governors, Federal Reserve System.
Tinsley, Peter A., Paul A. Spindt, and Monica E. Friar. 1980. Indicator and filter attributes of monetary aggregates: A nit-picking case for disaggregation. *Journal of Econometrics* 14(September):61-91.
Tobin, James. 1963. An essay on the principles of debt management. *Fiscal and Debt Management Policies* (prepared for the Commission on Money and Credit). Englewood Cliffs: Prentice Hall, pp. 143-218.
———. 1969. A general equilibrium approach to monetary analysis. *Journal of Money Credit and Banking* (February):15-29.
———. 1972. Inflation and unemployment. *American Economic Review* (March):1-18.
Tobin, James, and W. C. Brainard. 1963. Financial intermediaries and the

effectiveness of monetary controls. *American Economic Review* 53(2):383-400.
Tower, Edward. 1975. Money demand and the terms of trade. *Weltwirtschaftliches Archiv* 111(4):623-33.
Tower, Edward, and Thomas D. Willett. 1976. *The Theory of Optimum Currency Areas and Exchange-Rate Flexibility.* Princeton University. Special Papers in International Economics, no. 11 (May).
Triffin, R. 1978-79. The international role and fate of the dollar. *Foreign Affairs* 57(2):269-86.
Tsiang, S. C. 1966. "Walras'" Law, Say's Law and Liquidity Preference in General Equilibrium Analysis. *International Economic Review* (September):329-45.
Tufte, Edward. 1978. *Political Control of the Economy.* Princeton: Princeton University Press.
Turner, Louis. 1978. *Oil Companies in the International System.* London: George Allen and Unwin.
Turnovsky, Stephen J. 1976. The relative stability of alternative exchange rate systems in the presence of random disturbances. *Journal of Money, Credit and Banking* 8(February):29-50.
U.S. News and World Report. 1980. Can alliance survive? June 9, pp. 21-23.
U.S. Senate. 1974. Committee on Foreign Relations, Subcommittee on Multinational Corporations, *Multinational Corporations and United States Foreign Policy*, 93rd Cong., 2d Sess., part 5.
U.S. Senate. 1979. Committee on Foreign Relations, *United States Foreign Policy Objectives and Overseas Military Installations.* Congressional Research Service, Library of Congress. Washington, D.C.: Government Printing Office.
Viner, Jacob. 1948. Power versus plenty as objectives of foreign policy in the seventeenth and eighteenth centuries. *World Politics* 1(October):1-29.
———. 1951. *International Economics.* Glencoe, Ill.: Free Press.
———. 1956. Some international aspects of economic stabilization. In Leonard P. White, ed. *The State of the Social Sciences.* Chicago: University of Chicago Press, pp. 283-98.
Wallerstein, Immanuel. 1974. *The Modern World-System.* New York: Academic Press.
Wallich, Henry C. 1979. Statement before House of Representatives Subcommittee on Domestic Monetary Policy. *Federal Reserve Bulletin* 65(8):611-17.
Wallich, Henry C., and Jo Anna Gray. 1981. Stabilization policy and vicious and virtuous circles. In John S. Chipman and Charles P. Kindleberger, eds. *Flexible Exchange Rates and the Balance of Payments: Essays in Honor of Egon Sohmen.* Amsterdam: North Holland.
Walters, Robert. 1974. *The Nuclear Trap.* Baltimore: Penguin.
Waltz, Kenneth N. 1979. *Theory of International Politics.* Reading, MA: Addison-Wesley.
Weintraub, Robert E. 1978. Congressional supervision of monetary policy. *Journal of Monetary Economics* 4(August):341-62.
Whalen, Richard. 1980. Negotiable instruments. *Harpers* (March):24-27.
Wight, Martin. 1979. *Power Politics.* New York: Penguin.
Willett, Thomas D. 1976. The Eurocurrency market, exchange rate systems, and national financial policies. In Carl H. Stem, John H. Makin, and Dennis Logue, eds. *Eurocurrencies and the International Monetary System.* Washington, D.C.: American Enterprise Institute, pp. 193-221.

———. 1977. *Floating Exchange Rates and International Monetary Reform*. Washington, D.C.: American Enterprise Institute.
———. 1978a. It's too simple to blame the surplus countries. *Euromoney* (February):89-96.
———. 1978b. Alternative approaches to international surveillance of exchange-rate policies. In *Managed Exchange-Rate Flexibility*. Proceedings of a conference sponsored by the Federal Reserve Bank of Boston, October, pp. 148-72.
———. 1979a. It's too easy to blame the speculators. *Euromoney* (May): 111-20.
———. 1979b. Review of international monetary relations, by Susan Strange. *Journal of Money, Credit and Banking*, 11(3):375-80.
———. 1980a. The causes and effects of exchange rate volatility. Claremont Working Papers. Presented at the A.E.I. Conference on the International Monetary System under Stress, February, forthcoming in conference volume.
———. 1980b. *International Liquidity Issues*. Washington, D.C.: American Enterprise Institute.
Willett, Thomas D., and Leroy Laney. 1978. Monetarism, budget deficits, and wage push inflation: The cases of Italy and the United Kingdom. Banca Nazionale del Lavora, *Quarterly Review* (December):315-31.
Willett, Thomas D., and John Mullen. 1982. The discipline debate and inflationary biases under alternative exchange-rate systems. In Richard Sweeney and Thomas Willett, eds. *Studies on Exchange Rate Flexibility*. Washington, D.C.: American Enterprise Institute.
Williamson, John. 1977. *The Failure of World Monetary Reform 1971-74*. New York: New York University Press.
Willis, Parker B. 1964. *The Federal Funds Market*. Boston: Federal Reserve Bank of Boston.
Wilson, T. 1976. Effective devaluation and inflation. *Oxford Economic Papers* 28(1):1-24.
Witte, Willard E. 1979. Dynamic adjustment in an open economy with flexible exchange rates. *Southern Economic Journal* 45(1):1072-90.
Wolfers, A. 1962. *Discord and Collaboration*. Baltimore: Johns Hopkins Press.
Wolkowitz, Benjamin, and P. R. Lloyd-Davies. 1979. Reducing federal reserve float. *Federal Reserve Bulletin* 65(12):945-50.
Wood, Cynthia W. 1976. Nonbank financial intermediation and the effectiveness of monetary policy. Ph.D. diss., University of Wisconsin-Madison.
Woolley, John T. 1980. Congress and the conduct of monetary policy in the 1970s. Political Science Paper, no. 52, April. St. Louis: Washington University.
Yeager, Leland B., ed. 1962. *In Search of a Monetary Constitution*. Cambridge: Harvard University Press.
———. 1968. Discipline, inflation and the balance of payments. In Nicholas Beadles and L. Aubrey Drewery, Jr., eds. *Money, the Market and the State*. Athens: University of Georgia Press, pp. 1-34.
———. 1976. *International Monetary Relations: Theory, History and Policy*. New York: Harper and Row.

CONTRIBUTORS

Robert Z. Aliber received his Ph.D. from Yale University in 1962. He currently teaches international finance at the University of Chicago. Professor Aliber has consulted for various governmental agencies, research institutes, and private firms. He has written extensively about exchange rates, gold, and international financial relations.

John F. O. Bilson holds a Ph.D. from the University of Chicago, and he is presently an associate professor of international economics there. He is also a research associate of the National Bureau of Economic Research and a national fellow of the Hoover Institution at Stanford University.

Stanley W. Black received his Ph.D. from Yale University in 1965. At present, he is professor of economics at Vanderbilt University. Professor Black has previously been associated with Princeton University, the University of Stockholm, and Yale University. He also served as special assistant to the undersecretary, U.S. Department of State. He is the author of Floating Exchange Rates and Economic Policy, as well as numerous articles in various journals.

Michael R. Darby holds a Ph.D. from the University of Chicago. He is professor of economics at the University of California, Los Angeles, and also a senior research associate of the National Bureau of Economic Research. Professor Darby has authored many articles and several books on macroeconomics.

William G. Dewald received his Ph.D. from the University of Minnesota. Currently he is professor of economics at the Ohio State University in Columbus and editor of the Journal of Money, Credit and Banking. Professor Dewald previously taught at the University of Chicago, and he has published articles in a number of professional journals in the United States and Europe.

Michael W. Doyle received his Ph.D. from Harvard in 1977. At present he is assistant professor of public and international affairs at the Woodrow Wilson School, Princeton University. Professor Doyle is coauthor (with Fred Hirsch and Edward Morse) of Alternatives to Monetary Disorder.

Henry N. Goldstein received his Ph.D. from Johns Hopkins University in 1967. Currently he is professor of economics at the University of Oregon.

He has previously been associated with Washington State University and served as a staff economist at the Federal Reserve Board.

Herbert G. Grubel received his Ph.D. from Yale University in 1962. He is now professor of economics at Simon Fraser University, Burnaby, British Columbia. In the past he has been associated with the University of Pennsylvania and the University of Chicago. He is the author of numerous books and articles on international economics.

Robert E. Harkavy holds a Ph.D. from Yale University and is associate professor of political science at The Pennsylvania State University. He has served with the U.S. Atomic Energy Commission and the U.S. Arms Control and Disarmament Agency. Professor Harkavy is the author of The Arms Trade and International Systems, as well as other books and articles.

Dale W. Henderson received his Ph.D. from Yale University. He was on the faculty of the University of Pennsylvania and since 1971 has been on the staff of the Division of International Finance at the Board of Governors of the Federal Reserve System. Mr. Henderson's articles and comments dealing with the macroeconomics of closed and open economies and with the gold market have appeared in numerous professional journals.

Donald D. Hester received his Ph.D. from Yale University in 1961. At the present time, he is professor of economics at the University of Wisconsin. He has also been on the faculty at Yale University and was a visiting senior economist at the Federal Reserve Board of Governors. He serves as associate editor of the Journal of Money, Credit and Banking and is chairman of the Social Systems Research Institute at the University of Wisconsin. Professor Hester has published widely in professional journals.

Ira P. Kaminow received his Ph.D. from the University of Rochester in 1961. He is currently the Director of Economic Studies at the Government Research Corporation. He has previously taught at Ohio University and served as visiting lecturer at the Wharton School, University of Pennsylvania. Dr. Kaminow is coeditor and contributor to Studies in Selective Credit Policies, and the author of articles in several major journals.

Edward J. Kane received his Ph.D. from the Massachusetts Institute of Technology in 1960. He occupies the Everett D. Reese Chair of Banking and Monetary Economics at Ohio State University. Previously, he taught at Boston College, Princeton University, and Iowa State University. Professor Kane is past president of the American Finance Association and currently serves on the editorial boards of several professional journals.

Peter J. Katzenstein received his Ph.D. from Harvard University in 1973. He is currently professor of government at Cornell University and editor of International Organization. Professor Katzenstein has published in numerous professional journals and is the author of Between Power and Plenty: Foreign Economic Policies of Advanced Industrial States.

Robert O. Keohane received his Ph.D. from Harvard University in 1966. He is currently Professor of Politics at Brandeis University. Professor Keohane has previously been associated with Stanford University and Swarthmore College. He has published in several professional journals and is

Contributors

the coauthor (with Joseph S. Nye, Jr.) of <u>Power and Interdependence: World Politics in Transition</u>. His contribution to this volume is part of a larger research project that will be published in a forthcoming volume tentatively entitled <u>The International Political Economy in an Age of Hegemonic Decline</u>.

Leroy O. Laney received a Ph.D. from the University of Colorado. He currently is senior economist in the Research Department of the Federal Reserve Bank of Dallas. Mr. Laney has written widely in the area of international monetary economics.

Raymond E. Lombra received his Ph.D. at The Pennsylvania State University and served as a senior staff economist at the Federal Reserve Board until 1977. Currently, he is professor of economics at The Pennsylvania State University. His publications include numerous articles on monetary policy.

Will E. Mason received his Ph.D. from Princeton University in 1952. He currently holds the position of professor emeritus of economics at The Pennsylvania State University. Professor Mason has published in numerous economics journals and is the author of <u>Clarification of the Monetary Standard: The Concept and Its Relation to Monetary Policies and Objectives</u>.

Thomas Mayer received his Ph.D. from Columbia University in 1953. He currently is professor of economics at the University of California, Davis. In the past he has been associated with the Treasury Department, the University of Notre Dame, and the University of California, Berkeley. He is the author of numerous articles in professional journals and several books, including <u>The Structure of Monetarism</u>.

Allan H. Meltzer is Maurice Falk Professor of Economics and Social Science at Carnegie-Mellon University. He coedits the Carnegie-Rochester Conference Series on Public Policy and is a founding member of the Shadow Open Market Committee. He has published extensively in the area of monetary theory and policy.

John Mullen is a graduate student in economics at Claremont Graduate School.

John S. Odell received his Ph.D. from the University of Wisconsin in 1976. Since that time he has been assistant professor of government at Harvard and research fellow of the Center for International Affairs. Professor Odell's articles have appeared in various professional journals and edited volumes.

Lucas Papademos received his Ph.D. from the Massachusetts Institute of Technology. He is currently assistant professor of economics at Columbia University and has served as a visiting economist at the Federal Reserve Bank of Boston. His articles have appeared in several professional journals.

J. David Richardson received his Ph.D. from the University of Michigan in 1970. Currently he is professor of economics at the University of Wisconsin, Madison, and research associate with the National Bureau of Economic Research. He has had articles in numerous professional journals and is the author of <u>Understanding International Economics</u>.

Anthony M. Santomero holds a Ph.D. from Brown University and currently is professor of finance at the Wharton School of the University of Pennsylvania. He is also an associate editor of the Journal of Finance, the Journal of Money, Credit and Banking, and the Journal of Banking and Finance.

Thomas D. Simpson received his Ph.D. from the University of Chicago. He is currently on the staff of the Board of Governors of the Federal Reserve System and was previously on the faculty of Macalester College. He has authored a leading money and banking textbook and several articles on monetary economics.

Robert Solomon holds a Ph.D. from Harvard University and presently serves as guest scholar at the Brookings Institution. From 1965 to 1976 he served as advisor to the Board of Governors of the Federal Reserve System. He has published articles in various financial journals and is the author of The International Monetary System 1965-1976.

Susan Strange is Montague Burton Professor of International Economics at the London School of Economics and Political Science. She has written on international political economy for numerous professional journals and is the author of Sterling and British Policy and International Monetary Relations in the 1960s.

Alan C. Stockman received his Ph.D. from the University of Chicago in 1978. Currently he serves as assistant professor of economics at the University of Rochester and is a research fellow with the National Bureau of Economic Research. His papers have appeared in major professional journals and in several books.

Henry C. Wallich has been a member of the Board of Governors of the Federal Reserve System since 1974. Governor Wallich received a Ph.D. from Harvard University and from 1951 to 1974 was on the faculty of Yale University. He served as a member of the President's Council of Economic Advisors from 1958 to 1961.

Thomas D. Willett holds a Ph.D. from the University of Virginia and presently is Horton Professor of Economics at Claremont Graduate School and Claremont Men's College. He has previously taught at Harvard and Cornell Universities, served as senior staff economist at the President's Council of Economic Advisors, and as deputy assistant secretary for international research and planning and director of the Office of International Monetary Research at the U.S. Treasury. He has written widely in the areas of international monetary economics and public choice analysis. His latest book is International Liquidity Issues.

Willard E. Witte received his Ph.D. from the University of Wisconsin. He is currently assistant professor of economics at Indiana University and was previously on the faculty of The Pennsylvania State University. He has published articles in several professional journals.

John T. Woolley received his Ph.D. from the University of Wisconsin. He formerly was a research fellow at the Brookings Institution and currently is assistant professor of political science at Washington University in St. Louis.

Political Economy *of* International and Domestic Monetary Relations

emphasizes the complexity of the U.S. monetary policy process by presenting current research which views the process from a variety of perspectives: that of the monetary economists, both opened and closed economies; that of the political scientist, from both the U.S. and European viewpoints; that of the policy advisor; and that of the policymaker.

THE IOWA STATE UNIVERSITY PRESS • AMES, IOWA

ISBN: 0-8138-1372-7